New Directions in
Human Resources
A Handbook

New Directions in Human Resources
A Handbook

Mary F. Cook

Mary Cook & Associates
2700 Youngfield Street
Suite 206
Lakewood, CO 80215

Prentice-Hall, Inc.
Englewood Cliffs, New Jersey

Prentice-Hall International, Inc., *London*
Prentice-Hall of Australia, Pty. Ltd., *Sydney*
Prentice-Hall Canada, Inc., *Toronto*
Prentice-Hall of India Private Ltd., *New Delhi*
Prentice-Hall of Japan, Inc., *Tokyo*
Prentice-Hall of Southeast Asia Pte. Ltd., *Singapore*
Editora Prentice-Hall do Brasil Ltda., *Rio de Janeiro*
Prentice-Hall Hispanoamericana, S.A., *Mexico*

© 1987 *by*

PRENTICE-HALL, INC.

Englewood Cliffs, N.J.

Library of Congress Cataloging-in-Publication Data

Cook, Mary F., 1937-
    New directions in human resources.

    Includes index.
    1. Personnel management.   I. Title.
HF5549.C7244   1987   658.3   87-1286

ISBN 0-13-612433-X

PRENTICE HALL
BUSINESS & PROFESSIONAL DIVISION
A division of Simon & Schuster
Englewood Cliffs, New Jersey 07632

OTHER PRENTICE-HALL BOOKS BY THE AUTHOR

The Human Resource Director's Handbook
The Personnel Manager's Portfolio of Model Letters
The Human Resource Manager's Daily Planner

ABOUT THE AUTHOR

MARY F. COOK is President of Mary Cook & Associates, a Denver-based human resources management consulting firm. Ms. Cook has over 15 years experience as a corporate human resources generalist. For seven years prior to starting her company, she was Director of Employee Relations for the mining subsidiary of the Union Pacific Corporation. She is actively sought as a lecturer and has written numerous articles for business and trade journals. She is the author of three books published by Prentice-Hall, Inc., *The Human Resource Director's Handbook*, *The Personnel Manager's Portfolio of Model Letters*, and *The Human Resource Manager's Daily Planner*. Ms. Cook also publishes a human resources trend report called *The Cook Report*.

Ms. Cook is a recipient of the top national research award from The American Society for Personnel Administration, and The Personnel Administrator of the Year Award from the Colorado Society for Personnel Administration. She is a member of the Board of Trustees of Mile High United Way.

ACKNOWLEDGMENTS

Katherine Armstrong
Bank of America
San Francisco, CA.

Virginia M. Berg
Consultant
Athens, GA.

Gregory J. Brandes, Attorney
Cotter & Company
Chicago, IL.

Mary A. Brauer, Managing Partner
Reinhart, Boerner, Van Deuren,
    Norris & Rieselbach
Denver, CO.

Stanley E. Degler
Vice President & Executive Editor
Bureau of National Affairs
Rockville, MD.

Dale R. Detlefs, Manager
Social Security Division
Mercer-Meidinger, Inc.
Louisville, KY.

Hoyt Doyel, Consulting Principal
A.S. Hansen, Inc.
Denver, CO.

Kenneth J. Fisher, ACSW
Psychotherapist
Denver, CO.

James Frohne
A.S. Hanson, Inc.
Denver, CO.

Glen Head
ICOM Communications
Boulder, CO.

John J. Heilman
Personnel Relations Manager
Tektronix, Inc.
Beaverton, OR.

Robert G. Heiserman, Attorney
Denver, CO.

Carl E. Johnson, Attorney
Seyfarth, Shaw, Fairweather &
    Geraldson
Chicago, IL.

George Kauss, Director, National
    Sales
La Quinta Motor Inns
San Antonio, TX.

Kwasha Lipton, Inc.
Fort Lee, NJ.

Bob Moss
Pannell Kerr Forster
Denver, CO.

James A. Moss
Vice President
Classified Ads
Knight-Kidder Newspapers

Charles W. Newcom, Partner
Sherman & Howard, Attorneys at
    Law
Denver, CO.

Marcia Pear
Adia Personnel Services
Menlo Park, CA.

Dennis Rezendes
Vice President
National Alliance of Business
Washington, DC.

Eve Sandoval, Partner
New Visions
Denver, CO.

Christine Seltz
Hewitt Associates
Lincolnshire, IL.

Lynn Smelkinson
Chamber of Commerce of the U.S.
Washington, DC.

Charles D. Spencer & Associates,
   Inc.
Chicago, IL.

Warren L. Tomlinson, Attorney
Holland & Hart
Denver, CO.

Linda L. Trice, Office Manager
Corporate Communications
Hay Management Consultants
Philadelphia, PA.

Dennis Unkovic, Attorney at Law
Meyer, Unkovic, and Scott
Pittsburgh, PA.

Honora Zimmerman
Seminar Leader
CBS, Inc.
New York, NY.

WHAT THIS BOOK WILL DO FOR YOU

New Directions in Human Resources: A Handbook provides innovative, workable ideas, procedures, and actual program examples for successfully managing an effective human resources function in today's fast-changing climate.

It's full of practical and effective guidance written in plain language with a simple format for easy reference. This book emphasizes *new directions* in human resources management and new types of benefits, compensation, training, and employee relations programs. It points out the need for new approaches to employee communications and an entirely different approach to attracting, retaining, and managing the diverse workforce that we will encounter in the 1990s.

Here are just a few of the situations for which this book offers practical ideas, helpful solutions, and examples of what other organizations are doing in the human resources area:

- How corporations are using the organizational development skills of HR professionals and consultants to revitalize and pull together their companies. Examples of matrix management programs and of management succession planning programs.

- Examples of how to protect your company from costly litigation when terminating employees, review of the termination-at-will doctrine as it applies to today's organizations.

- Why corporations are moving to multiple compensation strategies and how they are working. A look at two-tier wage plans, companies that are going to salaried plants, and how the lump sum pay increase is helping some companies.

- A review of current employee rights issues. Balancing corporate needs with employee demands, and how some companies address workplace privacy.

- How to manage new worker issues that are arising in most large corporations today—the issues of the dual career couple, managing romance and marriage on the job, and managing the homosexual worker and how to handle homophobia.

- A review of some of the new benefits that workers are insisting on— benefits like child care assistance, flexible working hours, flexible benefit programs, and so forth. Ideas on benefits cost containment and a review of some other new benefits being offered like legal advice, car insurance, and the rest.

- Where we are today with affirmative action plans, a review of some new EEO legislation in the cable industry, and justice department opinions that impact all companies. Dealing with minority boycotts and how one company settled a long-standing boycott.

- A sample employee assistance program, how to start a program or find an outside consultant. Testing for drugs and privacy issues.

- An analysis of employee compensation and benefit provisions in the Tax Reform Act of 1986.

- A legislative update that includes a review of the challenges employers face under the new Immigration Reform and Control Act of 1986.

- Sample letters and information companies need for use under the Consolidated Omnibus Budget Reconciliation Act (COBRA) that became law on April 7, 1986.

- How one employer developed an AIDS policy and a sample of the policy. A legal overview of AIDS in the workplace.

- A legal overview of employee drug testing.

- Addressing the need in multinational organizations for cross-cultural and bilingual training programs. How to pick the person that is most likely to succeed in an overseas assignment, and a sample expatriate personnel policy.

- A look at some of the new ideas in training. Using business games in training, how assessment center methods are working, and training programs to defuse sexual harrassment problems on the job. There is also a model provided for training cost analysis.

- An update on the HRIS, new uses for the HRIS including organizational analysis, forecasting the salary program, and tracking personnel in a merger.

- Sample computer literacy programs, how to install them and how to "sell" them to managers. A look at robots versus people, facts on the number of robots planned to replace people in the next ten years and the implications of a mechanical workforce.

- An update on pension and retirement benefits. A review of the new Comprehensive Omnibus Budget Reconciliation Act (COBRA) that became law in 1986, and a list of the changes in pension fund financial accounting standards.

- How to recruit the 1990s workforce, advertising for husband and wife teams, employing older workers, and how to "screen in" handicapped workers. Using alternative work hours to recruit, renting math whizzes, leasing employees, and using temporary help.

- Sample personnel policies on smoking, dealing with AIDS, discipline and discharge, employee complaint procedures, managing expatriates, and so forth.

- New ideas that work in the area of employee communications. Insights from a revealing survey by a national consulting firm on what employees expect from a job today.

- The growing concern about terrorism and what human resource directors need to know to be ready for any event. Ways to deal with employee protection, who is liable when an employee is kidnapped, and helping employees cope with violence.

- Review of a new issue HR directors are concerned with, the theft of trade secrets, starting a program to stop theft, including a sample employee secrecy agreement. A look at honesty tests and the end of polygraph exams.

This handbook not only tells you what the human resources trends are but also shows you how you can implement them. *New Directions in Human Resources: A Handbook* provides you with all the step-by-step checklists, charts, models, sample personnel policies, and "how-to-do-it" programs to help meet your organization's human resources needs.

HOW TODAY'S SUCCESSFUL HUMAN RESOURCE
DIRECTORS ARE DEALING WITH THE NEW CORPORATION
AND THE NEW WORKER

A new type of corporation is emerging in our work lives. This new corporation may have different organizational styles; flexible working hours and benefits; multiple compensation strategies, including two-tier pay plans and salaried plants; futuristic training and telecommunications programs; more reasonable personnel policies; a variety of working styles; and a new organizational culture that is more open and flexible in dealing with employees. It may be leaner and meaner if airlines and telephone companies are an example. This new corporation may be the result of a merger of one or more organizations, trying to mesh a variety of organizational cultures and management styles.

This new type of corporation is not coming into our lives quietly, without stress and some kicking and screaming along the way on the part of human resource professionals. Many HR people lean toward straight-line thinking, assuming that the way things are today is the way they will also be tomorrow and the next day (with minor glitches along the way). Recent events, however, have left us rather shaken as crisis after crisis hits the headlines.

"Postal Employee Murders Fellow Workers"

"American Businessman in Beirut Kidnapped"

"Mitsubishi Employee Convicted of Stealing IBM Trade Secrets"

"Employee of the Navy Department Passes Top Secret Information to Russian Agents"

"Employee with AIDS Terminated—Sues the Company"

"No Smoking Policies Anger Employees"

"Trans World Attendants Lose Round in Strike Fight"

"Two-Tier Labor Contract Angers Pilots"

"IBM Tries to Sidestep Layoffs"

"Federal Government Going to Mandatory Drug Tests in Sensitive Jobs"

"Polygraph Tests Outlawed in 27 States"

"Employees Have a Right to Know About Work Hazards and OSHA Violations"

"Workers on Drugs"

These headlines overshadow the human resource function and they tip us off to the major issues rocketing towards us in the future. Another area of major change is in the area of organizational structure. Either because of obsolescense, downsizing, or merger, organizations are changing their structures in an attempt to improve productivity and profits. For example, there is a company in New Jersey that has no titles, no bosses, and no organization chart. They have two objectives: to make money and to have fun. It works! Sales have grown forty percent a year over the past five years.

Another example of a successful structural change is Scandinavian Airlines. In a single year SA turned around from losing eighteen million dollars to earning three times that. They turned the organization chart upside-down. Those people who are dealing with customers run the company; everyone else reports to them. This is a unique approach, but many organizations today are being forced to try new ideas in order to retain good people and make a profit.

In the next five years, companies will be competing for the best people in a shrinking labor pool; and we will be seeing more unusual, even radical, changes in the way organizations are run. Organization development programs will play an important part in corporate strategic planning. And, we are finding that management succession planning is becoming more critical in order to ensure the right people are groomed and available when needed.

Human resource directors can't just try to prepare for innovative organizational changes—we must be an integral part of the design and implementation of them. This book provides some ideas for managing effectively in a matrix management mode. Matrix management has become more popular in organizations that have "downsized" and don't want to gear back up to previous staff levels.

Today, the human resources function is so different in scope and responsibility from the old personnel administrative function that it challenges old assumptions and old ways of thinking about the personnel department. In today's new business age, the human resources function is at the top of the pyramid, a place of prestige and importance, responsible for coming to grips with the technological, sociological, and ideological revolutions that have fundamentally and irrevocably altered the workplace.

A powerful tide is sweeping across all organizations today—a tide that is bringing tremendous change in structure, in employees, in the way we work, in productivity, human rights, and employee motivations and values. This same tide is gradually eating away at the old traditional ways organizations do things . . . how they handle people and their policies and procedures. Who would have thought five years ago that we would be concerned with the issues of terrorism, homophobia, or a disease like AIDS?

What we don't seem to understand, however, is that all of these changes are interrelated. They are not isolated situations. Our problem in the past has been that we treated changes as occasional isolated occurrences, and we designed programs or wrote policies and procedures to handle these isolated situations. We seemed not to understand their interrelation and the larger implications.

America is experiencing a clash of old versus new values, a revolution in technology, new geopolitical relationships, new lifestyles, new politics, new ethics, modes of communication, living, working, and so on. Ten years ago we were concerned when we asked an employee to relocate . . . and he said he would if we would also pay to move his live-in "significant other." Today it's a common occurrence. In fact, today we have a new benefit called "transplacement," help for a relocating spouse in finding a job in the new location.

We are just beginning to understand the pressures between men and women on the job with the huge influx of women into the workforce. We are beginning to give credence to the problems of the dual-career couple and the single mother who is the sole support of children and needs day-care assistance. Five years ago we would not have considered letting an employee work at home—today it's a fairly common practice. We are finally facing up to the challenges of putting handicapped people to work and putting women into top management positions (not in huge numbers yet, but in a few significant jobs).

According to one national publication, less than ten percent of the senior executives of most corporations today understand and endorse office automation; but they will all soon have to. Some organizations use a sophisticated combination of electronic and voice mail, word processing, video-conferencing, and high-speed communications that permit top executives to cut levels of management in half. Chicago-based FMC Corporation installed a voice mail system in one of its groups that allows salesmen and their regional and district sales managers to exchange messages at any time via telephone "mailboxes." This change allowed the corporation to cut out an entire level of management.

Cutting levels of management sounds wonderful to corporate executives, but the resultant dislocation and trauma of middle managers who are out of work today is a growing national problem—a problem that must be solved by retraining programs and serious concern on the part of business. Both business and government view this problem with concern, and the National Alliance of Business in Washington, DC, has instituted programs to help industry deal with this issue. And today we are having to deal with more frightening situations in the workplace. Terrorism, kidnapping, the theft of trade secrets, drugs, and murder, are all issues human resources managers have to deal with in both the public and private sectors. We are having to learn how to handle situations like the postal department murders and the aftermath of such an emotional crisis. We are finding help through the use of Employee Assistance Programs and crisis counseling . . . elements of contemporary organizations that were not needed in slower, less traumatic times.

If we can't learn to deal with controversial issues, we will be left behind to tend our policy manuals and guard the status quo in organizations that aren't keeping up with the times. Ultimately, we and our organizations will be lost in the race for profits and huge economic rewards that will come to people and organizations who *are* keeping up.

I caution all of another trend I see from time to time in HR management. There is a sort of naïve (but thought-to-be-chic) approach by many of those new to the industry that HR management can be applied by rote to all organizations like a technological game with applied software and computer modeling. We can't apply a paint-by-number approach to HR management. It doesn't work—people are different and they respond in different ways. Organizations grow and shrink, ebb and flow. They become more sophisticated and successful at times and at times fall back to primitive actions and disappointing performance. We have to learn to respond quickly and effectively to all these situations.

Being the eternal optimist, I know we will find a happy medium between theory and practice, between too much unorthodox behavior and new values and too little response to needed change. The extremes seem never to work well in HR management. As effective HR managers we have learned to be "issues managers," to identify the new issues speeding toward us so we can positively influence not only their impact but also their final outcome.

In this book, I have attempted to capture the leading edge of the new wave of change in the HR function—to identify some of the new directions in which we are moving, to search for effective solutions to both the old and new problems in the workplace, and to look on them as opportunities for the successful advancement of the HR profession.

MARY F. COOK

CONTENTS

1 ORGANIZATIONAL DEVELOPMENT: WHY IT IS THE KEY TO YOUR FIRM'S FUTURE SUCCESS 1

WHY UNDERSTANDING THE ORGANIZATIONAL DEVELOPMENT PROCESS IS CRITICAL FOR YOU AND YOUR COMPANY   3

What is Organizational Development 3 ● Using "Change Agents"— from Both Inside and Outside the Company 4 ● Seven Key Objectives to Include in Your Organizational Development 6 ● A Four-Step Process for New OD Programs 8 ● Effective Organizational Development Interventions Used by Organizations 8 ● How Corporate Culture Influences Organizational Development 9 ● Eleven Factors Found in Corporate Culture 10 ● The Human Resource Manager's Role in Organizational Development 11

MATRIX MANAGEMENT: A POPULAR CHOICE OF CONTEMPORARY ORGANIZATIONS   12

Elements of Matrix Management Systems 12 ● Guidelines for Implementing a Matrix Program 13

MANAGEMENT SUCCESSION PLANNING: THE KEY TO ORGANIZATIONAL EXCELLENCE   15

WHO NEEDS MANAGEMENT SUCCESSION PLANNING?   15

How to Prepare a Succession Plan Backup Summary Form 16 ● Individual Development Plans 17

USING DUAL-CAREER LADDERS IN SUCCESSION PLANNING   17

A Case Example: ARCO 20 ● What to Ask Before Implementing Dual-Career Ladders 20 ● How Computers Help Keep Tabs on Corporate "Fast Trackers" for the Succession Plan 21 ● Case Example: Southland Corporation 21 ● Suggested Resources for Management Succession Planning 22

MERGER MANIA—A HEADACHE FOR THE HUMAN RESOURCE DEPARTMENT   22

Five Key Elements of a Successful Merger 23 ● Human Resource Problems in Merger/Acquisitions 23 ● The Need to Communicate with Employees During a Merger/Acquisition 24 ● Being in Touch with the Big Picture 24

2 INNOVATIVE APPROACHES TO MULTIPLE COMPENSATION STRATEGIES, PR PROGRAMS, AND PERKS 27

ELEVEN WAYS IN WHICH COMPENSATION PROGRAMS ARE CHANGING   29

WHY MULTIPLE COMPENSATION PROGRAMS ARE POPULAR   31

Four Key Elements to Consider When Developing Pay
Strategies 31 ● Rethinking the Single Pay
Structure 32 ● Answers to Questions on Contemporary
Compensation Issues 33

THE LUMP SUM SALARY INCREASE: A FAST WAY TO IMPROVE
MORALE AT LITTLE ADDED COST   35
How the Lump Sum Salary Increase Works 35 ● How to Implement
a Lump Sum Plan 36

EXECUTIVE COMPENSATION AND PAY-FOR-PERFORMANCE
PROGRAMS   37
How Four Companies Successfully Implemented Pay-for-Performance
Programs 37

EXECUTIVE COMPENSATION TRENDS   40
How Executive Compensation Works 40 ● How U.S. West
Telephone Company Ties Key Executives' Pay to
Performance 41 ● Executive Incentive Arrangements 42 ● Cash
Incentive Programs 44 ● Stock-Based Incentive Programs 45

DEFERRED COMPENSATION: HOW EXECUTIVES MIGHT DELAY
TAXATION   49
Who Should Consider Income Deferral 49 ● Supplemental
Executive Retirement Plans 50 ● Basic Features of a Rabbi
Trust 51 ● Reasons for Increased Interest in Rabbi
Trusts 52 ● Practical Considerations in Designing a Rabbi Trust 53

HOW TO EVALUATE YOUR COMPENSATION PROGRAM   56
Six Elements to Consider When Evaluating Your Company's
Program 56 ● Compensation Program Evaluation
Checklist 57 ● Company Policy 57 ● Job
Description 58 ● Job Evaluation 58 ● Salary
Structure 59 ● Policies 59 ● Performance
Appraisal 60 ● Administrative Procedures 61 ● Three Areas to
Push for Better Cost Control 61 ● How to Identify and Measure
Human Resources Costs 62 ● Three Case Examples of Cost
Analysis 62

HOW TO PROVIDE ADEQUATE COMPENSATION FOR
MULTINATIONAL EMPLOYEES   64
Determining Method of Payment 65 ● Ten Ways to Cut Expatriate
Staff Costs 66

NEW TYPES OF INCENTIVES SOME COMPANIES OFFER
EMPLOYEES   67
Financial Incentives Offered to Help Employees Purchase Personal
Computers 67 ● Large Cash Prizes and New Cars Offered by an
Insurance Company 67 ● A Home Away from

Home 67 ● Incentives to Get Employees to Take Assignments
Overseas 68

**3 BALANCING CORPORATE NEEDS WITH EMPLOYEE RIGHTS
ISSUES AND WORKERS' ATTITUDES** 69

Labor and Management—Mutual Interest
Bargaining 71 ● Employment Relationships Are Changing 72

MEETING THE DEMANDS OF THE NEW WORKER   72

CREATIVE IDEAS FOR MANAGING THE NEW WORKFORCE   74

The Most Effective Way to Deal with the New Worker 74 ● Ten
Examples of Corporate Communications Programs 74

EMPLOYEE RIGHTS: HOW DOES YOUR COMPANY SIZE UP
LEGALLY?   77

Key Federal and State Laws That Protect or Impact
Employees 77 ● Landmark Cases in Human Rights at Work 78

TERMINATION-AT-WILL: CAN YOU STILL FIRE AN EMPLOYEE ANY
TIME YOU FEEL LIKE IT?   80

When Is Firing Unjust? 81 ● How to Protect Your Company from
Litigation: Eleven Recommendations 81

BIG BROTHER IN THE WORKPLACE? THE GROWING DEMAND FOR
PERSONAL PRIVACY   83

How Private Are Personnel Records? 83 ● The Trend Toward
Respecting Employee Privacy 84 ● The Privacy Act of
1974 84 ● General Recommendations on Maintaining Employee
Privacy 85

COMPANY-REQUIRED MEDICAL EXAMS   86

Case Example: Williams Pipe Line Company versus Oil, Chemical, and
Atomic Workers 86 ● When Use Turns to Abuse: Medical Records
and Their Effect on Promotions 87

MORE BIG BROTHER IN THE WORKPLACE: COMPUTER
MONITORING OF EMPLOYEES   89

MANAGING HOMOSEXUALITY IN THE WORKPLACE: A GROWING
ISSUE   89

Wrongful Discharge in a Sexual Preference Case: Three Points to
Consider 90 ● Extending Benefits to Same-Sex Partners: Still an
Open Issue 91 ● Homosexuals and Social
Attitudes 91 ● Homophobia: Facing the Fear of Homosexuality at
Work 92

THE DUAL-CAREER COUPLE: HOW TO HANDLE THEIR SPECIAL
NEEDS   92

Managing the Dual-Career Couple 93 ● Transplacement for Dual-

Career Couples 93

MINORITY DISCRIMINATION: BOYCOTTS ARE GAINING
GROUND   94

Case Example: The Adolph Coors Company 94

SEX AND SALARY: THE SHIFT TOWARD COMPARABLE
WORTH   96

COMBATING THE SEX-BASED WAGE DISCRIMINATION
CLAIM   96

How to Know if You Have a Comparable Worth Problem 98 • Hay
Management Consultants' Advice to Clients on Comparable Worth 99

EQUAL EMPLOYMENT OPPORTUNITY ISN'T DEAD—COURT CASES,
NEW LEGISLATION, AND JUSTICE DEPARTMENT OPINIONS KEEP
IT ALIVE   100

The Justice Department Takes Action 101 • New Legislation in the
Cable Industry 101 • Supreme Court Guarantees Job in Maternity
Leave 102

CORPORATE SOCIAL RESPONSIBILITY AND ORGANIZATIONAL
CHANGE   102

FIFTEEN OTHER ISSUES AND THEIR POTENTIAL IMPACT ON
HUMAN RESOURCES   103

An Up-Beat Philosophy of Human Resources Management 106

4 BENEFIT PROGRAMS: HOW TO MAKE THEM WORK AND
ACHIEVE MAXIMUM ADVANTAGES FOR YOUR COMPANY 107

INTRODUCTION   109

Retirement Counseling 111 • Employee Stock Ownership
Plans 112

TWELVE SIGNIFICANT FORCES RESHAPING BENEFITS PROGRAMS
IN AMERICA   112

Nine Trends and How They Are Affecting Benefits 114 • New
Benefits Offered by Some Companys 115

A An Analysis of Employee Benefit Provisions in the Tax Reform Act of
1986   7

ANALYSIS OF EMPLOYEE BENEFIT PROVISIONS IN THE TAX
REFORM ACT OF 1986   117

QUALIFIED RETIREMENT PLANS   119

Coverage Requirements 119 • New 50 Employee/40%
Test 120 • Integration Rules 120 • Top-Heavy Accrual
Rule 120 • Sec. 415 Limits 121 • Vesting
Requirements 122 • Profit-Sharing Carryover 122 • Two-Plan
Deduction Limit 122

SEC. 401(k) PLANS 123

DISTRIBUTIONS, LOANS, WITHDRAWALS 124

Commencement of Benefits 125 • Contributory
Plans 125 • Limit on Annual Distribution 125 • Rule for Nongrandfathered Distributions 126 • Loans Tightened 126 • Sec.
401(k) Hardship Withdrawals 127

IRAs, MISCELLANEOUS PROVISIONS 127

Asset Reversions 127 • Money Purchase Plan
Reallocation 128 • Cashing Out Accrued Benefit 128 • Penalty
for Overfunding 128 • Employee Leasing 129 • Technical
Amendments to REA 130 • Survivor Benefit
Requirements 130 • Qualified Domestic Relations
Orders 130 • Other Provisions 131

ESOPs 131

1984 ESOP Incentives Retained 132 • Technical Corrections Clear
Up 1984 Ambiguities 133

WELFARE BENEFIT PROVISIONS 134

Inclusion in Tax 134 • Discrimination Tests 135 • Eligibility
Tests 135 • Benefits Test 136 • Alternative to Benefits,
Eligibility Tests 136 • Special Rules for Health
Plans 137 • Valuing Benefits 137 • Highly Compensated
Employees 138 • Excludable Employees 138 • Line of Business
Rule 138 • Effective Dates 139 • Other Provisions 139

CAFETERIA PLANS 139

Definition Modified 140 • Other Definitions 140

**B What You Should Know About COBRA, The Consolidated Omnibus
Budget Reconciliation Act of 1985 141**

What You Should Know About COBRA 141 • Sample COBRA
Letter to Employees 142

HOW THE LAW WILL APPLY 143

THE FULL 18 OR 36 MONTH EXTENSION WILL NOT
APPLY IF 143

How to Obtain This Continuation Coverage 143

YOUR COST FOR CONTINUATION COVERAGE 144

THIS DOES NOT AFFECT YOUR NORMAL CONVERSION
PRIVILEGE 144

C A Look at Innovative New Benefits Some Companies Are Offering 146

CHILD CARE: MEETING THE NEEDS OF WORKING PARENTS 146

The Results of a National Survey on Child Care and the Clerical
Workforce 146 • Potential Child Care Costs 147 • How One

Company Offset a High Employee Turnover Rate with Day
Care 148 ● Seven Ways to Introduce Child-Care Services in Your
Company 150 ● Child Care Task Force
Assignments 155 ● Nanny Care—A New Trend 157

ADOPTION BENEFITS: AN INEXPENSIVE PLUS FOR
EMPLOYEES   157

PARENTAL LEAVE   157

PREPAID LEGAL SERVICES: A LOW-COST BENEFIT   158

How Do The Plans Work? 158 ● How Is the Plan
Administered 158 ● Do Employees Like and Use the
Plans? 159 ● What Do the Plans Cost a Company? 159

CHARGING HEALTH CARE SERVICES: A GROWING TREND   159

BIRTHING CENTERS: A COST EFFECTIVE ALTERNATIVE TO
HOSPITALS   160

FOUR KEY AREAS OF HOME HEALTH CARE   160

SEVEN BENEFITS OF EMPLOYEE PHYSICAL FITNESS PROGRAMS
(PFPs)   161

ENCOURAGING MENTAL FITNESS WITH PAID
SABBATICALS   163

SUBSTANCE ABUSE: WHEN TO BEGIN AN EMPLOYEE ASSISTANCE
PROGRAM   163

Ten Key Ingredients of a Successful EAP 164 ● Two Main Types of
EAP Structures 165

D   Flexible Benefits   **167**

WHY FLEXIBLE BENEFITS MAY BE THE BEST CHOICE FOR YOUR
ORGANIZATION   167

How to Operate a Flexible Benefits Program: Three Main
Phases 167 ● How Flexible Benefits Work at American Can
Company 170

E   Pension and Retirement Benefits   **172**

TWO POPULAR EMPLOYEE BENEFITS   172

401k Pension Plans 172 ● How Does the 401k Plan Work? How
Exxon Launched Its 401k Plan 173 ● Employee Stock Ownership
Plan (ESOP) 173 ● How One ESOP Leveraged Buy-Out May Have
Actually Hurt Employees 174

WHAT YOU SHOULD KNOW ABOUT PENSION AND RETIREMENT
BENEFITS   175

Pension Welfare Obligations 175 ● Department of Labor
Publications on ERISA 178

CHANGES IN PENSION FUND FINANCIAL ACCOUNTING
STANDARDS   179

KEY ASPECTS OF THE TWO MAJOR QUALIFIED RETIREMENT
PROGRAMS   179

1. Defined Contributions Plans 180 • Five Types of Defined
Contribution Plans and What They Offer 181 • 2. Defined Benefit
Retirement Plans 182 • How the Four Main Types of Defined
Benefit Retirement Plans Work 183 • 3. Supplemental Retirement
Programs (SERPs) 184

INCOME REPLACEMENT: HOW TO DETERMINE WHAT EMPLOYEES
NEED FOR A COMFORTABLE RETIREMENT   185

POTENTIAL DRAWBACKS TO PRIVATE PENSIONS   188

Pension Security and the "Defined Benefit" Plan 188 • Pension
Asset Reversion: Legal and Ethical Implications 188 • The
Traditional Pension May Be a Thing of the Past 189

HOW TO HANDLE PRERETIREMENT COUNSELING   189

Why Is Preretirement Education Important 191 • Where to Look
for More Information on Preretirement Programs 192

F **Medical Cost Containment**   **194**

THE RISING COST OF EMPLOYEE BENEFITS   194

FIFTEEN WAYS TO CONTAIN MEDICAL COSTS   194

FOUR COST-CONTAINMENT PROGRAMS AND HOW THEY
WORK   195

G **Calculating the Cost of Benefits**   **200**

WORKSHEET FOR USE IN CALCULATING THE COST OF
BENEFITS   200

H **Employee Benefit Communications**   **204**

EMPLOYEE BENEFIT COMMUNICATION   204

Communicating the Value of Employee Benefits 204 • Five Items to
Include in Your Benefits Letter or Statement 204 • Five New Ways
to Communicate Employee Benefits 205

5 **NEW TRAINING TECHNIQUES IN HUMAN RESOURCE
DEVELOPMENT** **209**

TWENTY-FOUR FORCES RESHAPING THE HRD FUNCTION   212

HOW TO IDENTIFY KEY HRD NEEDS IN YOUR COMPANY   213

Training Needs Checklist 214

A TOP-DOWN APPROACH TO GAINING SUPPORT AT ALL
ORGANIZATIONAL LEVELS   215

Sample Objectives for HRD Programs 215

RETRAINING VERSUS DISPLACING THE WORKFORCE—HOW
CALIFORNIA IS TAKING POSITIVE ACTION 217

Four Major Reasons Why Retraining Rather than Replacing Workers is
Good Business 218

NEW WAYS TO TEACH WORKERS WHAT'S NEW: A VIDEODISC
UPDATE 218

The Corporate Look in Music Video 220 ● Customizing Sales
Training with Videotapes 221 ● Tips on How to Write a Video
Script and a Sample Page Layout 221

ELEVEN STEPS FOR ESTABLISHING A COMPUTER LITERACY
PROGRAM FOR MANAGERS 224

TELECOMMUNICATIONS—TRAINING BY TELEPHONE 225

Who Uses Teleconferencing? 225 ● Case Example: How Bennet &
Sloane, Inc. Set Up Their Teletraining Program 226 ● Planning
Guidelines for Teletraining 226

CROSS-CULTURAL AND BILINGUAL TRAINING: HOW TO
INTERNATIONALIZE EMPLOYEES 228

Companies that Have Cross-Cultural and Bilingual Programs 231

USING BUSINESS GAMES IN TRAINING 231

Some Corporations that Include Business Games in HRD 231 ● Case
Example: Hewlett-Packard's Business Game 232

PROS AND CONS OF TRAINING GAMES 233

Six Benefits of Using Games in Training Seminars 234

A TRAINING TREND: "QUICKIE" SKILL-BUILDING SEMINARS USING
ASSESSMENT CENTER METHODS IN SELECTION OF MANAGEMENT
EMPLOYEES 236

6 INFORMATION RESOURCE MANAGEMENT: HR'S NEW
RESPONSIBILITY IN THIS IMPORTANT MANAGEMENT
FUNCTION 237

KEY ISSUES OF INFORMATION RESOURCE MANAGEMENT 239

How Workers and Executives Are Meeting the Challenge of Office
Automation 240 ● How Office Automation Has Changed Four
Major United States Companies 240 ● Resistance to Change—The
Biggest Obstacle 241

HUMAN RESOURCE INFORMATION SYSTEMS: A LOOK AT WHAT
THEY ARE AND HOW THEY WORK 242

Ten Common Mistakes Made When Installing an HRIS 242 ● Six
Stages in HRIS Planning 243 ● To Change or Not to Change—
Performing the Needs Analysis 244 ● Guidelines for Purchasing

HRIS Software 245 ● Vendors of Micro Human Resource
Information Systems 245 ● Mini and Mainframe Human Resource
Management Systems 247 ● Other Vendors 249 ● The HRIS
and the Merger 250

SOME INNOVATIVE WAYS COMPANIES USE HRIS   250

Case Example: Polaroid Profiles Personnel Trends 250

COMPUTER MONITORING OF EMPLOYEE PERFORMANCE   251

Organizational Analysis by Computer 251

USING THE COMPUTER TO FORECAST SALARY PROGRAM
COSTS   251

Simulation of Wage/Salary Costs 252

THE TELECOMMUTING REVOLUTION: WHAT IT MEANS TO
HUMAN RESOURCE MANAGEMENT   253

Case Example: Fair International, Ltd. 254

ROBOTS VERSUS PEOPLE: THE IMPLICATIONS OF A MECHANICAL
WORKFORCE   254

COMPUTER LITERACY—WHAT YOU DON'T KNOW COULD HURT
YOU   256

Computer Training Programs for Executives 257

PERSONAL PRIVACY VERSUS THE COMPUTER AND THE
HRIS   259

Three Steps to Avoid Invasion 260 ● Protecting the Privacy of
Computerized Personnel Records 261

7 RECRUITING THE 1990s WORKFORCE......................... 263

RECRUITING THE NEW WORKER   265

A PROFILE OF THE 1990s WORKER   266

FOURTEEN ADAPTABLE IDEAS FOR RECRUITING CAPABLE
PEOPLE   268

HOW TO USE ADVERTISING AND PUBLICITY TO ATTRACT THE
NEW WORKER   271

ADVERTISING FOR HUSBAND AND WIFE TO WORK TOGETHER:
A NEW APPROACH TO AN OLD TABOO   271

How One Company Uses Publicity for Recruiting and Public
Relations 271 ● How Other Companies Uses Publicity to Aid
Recruiting 274

CREATIVE IDEAS FOR RECRUITING FOR THOSE HARD-TO-FILL
JOBS: ADAPT ONE OF THESE APPROACHES TO
YOUR COMPANY   274

Why Hiring the Disabled Is Good Business 275 ● How Disabled

Employees Are Cracking the Managerial
Barriers 275 • Handicapped Litigation 276 • Screening in
Handicapped Workers 276 • Do's and Don'ts for Interviewing the
Handicapped Applicant 276 • A Test for Executives—Do Your Job
Requirements "Screen Out" the Handicapped 277 • Eight Reasons
for Employing Older Workers 277 • Case Example: Retirees Fill
Temporary Positions at Travelers Insurance 282 • Case Example:
Retiree Fills a New Management Position 282 • Business-Oriented
Organizations that Address Older Worker Issues 282 • National
Alliance of Business Clearinghouse Database 283 • Recruiting and/
or Relocating the Dual-Career Couple 283 • Five Areas in Which
You Can Prevent Potential Conflict in Recruiting Dual-Career
Couples 284 • Transplacement: A New Employee
Benefit 284 • Economic Considerations in Dual-Career
Relocations 284 • How to Handle the Employment of Related
Persons 285 • Sample Hiring Policy for Related
Persons 285 • Job Sharing: Making the Most of Two for the Price of
One 286 • Advantages and Disadvantages of Job
Sharing 286 • Outside Temporary Agencies 287 • Employee
Leasing: Wave of the Future 288 • Companies that Use Employee
Leasing 290 • Pros and Cons of Employee
Leasing 291 • Renting Math Whizzes: A New Idea 292

SUCCESSFUL INTERVIEWING TECHNIQUES   292

Interview Checklist: Twenty-one Pointers for Developing Your Own
Style 292 • Questioning Techniques for Getting Useful
Answers 296 • Sample Interview Questions 297 • Inappropriate
Questions to Ask Applications 298 • Inappropriate Questions to Ask
Candidates for Promotion 299 • Errors Commonly Made by the
Interviewer 299 • Checklist for Use in Evaluating Interview
Data 300

PRE-EMPLOYMENT SCREENING AND TESTING OF
APPLICANTS   302

Checking an Applicant's References 303 • Reference Checking:
Some Horror Stories 304 • Reference Checking Guidelines: Making
It Easier 305 • Polygraph Tests 305 • Screening Applicants
Who Are Potential Thieves 306 • Why Honesty Tests Are Becoming
More Popular 307 • Examples of Employee Theft Highlight the
Need for Improved Hiring Procedures 307 • Where to Get
Tests 308 • Testing for Alcohol and Drugs 308 • Genetic
Testing: A Question of Privacy 316 • Six EEOC Testing Guidelines
to Help Establish Objective Standards 317 • The Laws on Selection
Procedures 317

MAKING THE RIGHT EMPLOYMENT DECISION: FIVE QUESTIONS
TO CONSIDER 318

8 PERSONNEL POLICIES AND EMPLOYEE COMMUNICATIONS:
HANDLING NEW ISSUES IN TODAY'S WORK ENVIRONMENT ... 319

AN OUNCE OF PREVENTION—WHY PERSONNEL POLICIES ARE A
MUST 321

Guidelines for Writing a Personnel Manual 322 • Tips for Making
Your Personnel Policies Easy to Read 323 • Checklist of Personnel
Policies 323

SAMPLES OF THREE KEY PERSONNEL POLICIES 325

SAMPLE POLICY 1: EMPLOYEE COMPLAINT PROCEDURE 325

I. Policy 325 • II. Procedure 325 • III. Documentation and
Procedure Control 326

SAMPLE POLICY 2: DISCIPLINARY ACTION AND WARNING
NOTICES 326

I. Policy 326 • II. Procedure 326 • III. Repeat
Offenses 327 • IV. Retention of Records 327

SAMPLE POLICY 3: TERMINATIONS 328

I. Policy 328 • II. General Rules 328 • III. Termination
Procedures 328 • IV. Timing 328

NO-SMOKING POLICIES—A SMOLDERING ISSUE 329

Guidelines for Smoking Policies 330 • No-Smoking Policies 330

SAMPLE POLICY 4: NO-SMOKING POLICY 331

Policy 331

SAMPLE POLICY 5: NO-SMOKING POLICY 331

Policy 331

POLICIES ON LIFE-THREATENING ILLNESSES SUCH AS AIDS 332

MANAGING ROMANCE AT WORK 334

Denver-Based Law Firm Morrison and Foerster 334 • Love Between
Managers: Conflict of Interest? 335 • Look for the Real Issues
Behind Office Romances 336 • Planning Checklist for Handling
Romance on the Job 337 • Procedures for Handling Work
Romances 338 • Romance Awareness Training
Workshop 339 • Case Example: Romance on the Job 339

SEXUAL HARASSMENT: TRAINING IS THE KEY TO ELIMINATING
IT AT WORK 340

What Organizations Are Doing to Stop Sexual Harassment 342

TRAINING MANAGERS TO OVERCOME THEIR HOMOPHOBIA—
THE FEAR OF HOMOSEXUALS 343

How to Deal with AIDS in the Workplace   343   ●   Supreme Court
Extends Handicap Law to AIDS Victims   344   ●   Guidelines for
Managing Employees with AIDS   350   ●   Where to Find Reference
and Educational Materials on AIDS   351

A LOOK AT WHAT'S NEW IN EMPLOYEE COMMUNICATIONS 352

Installing an Employee Hotline   352   ●   The Company
Newsletter   352   ●   Hottest Tool in Employee Communications—The
Corporate Video Newscast   353   ●   Employee Communications
Programs Can Take Many Forms   353   ●   Case Example: Offbeat
Lectures Stimulate Employee Communication at Bell
Labs   354   ●   Case Example: U.S. Home's Unusual Communication
Program   354   ●   Typing Employee Communications to the Corporate
Culture   354

WHAT EMPLOYEES EXPECT FROM THEIR JOBS: INSIGHTS FROM A
REVEALING SURVEY   354

9   SPECIAL CONCERNS FACING HR MANAGERS: TERRORISM,
THEFT OF TRADE SECRETS, ALCOHOLISM, AND DRUG ABUSE   357

HUMAN RESOURCE DIRECTORS ARE UNPREPARED FOR
TERRORISM   359

Four Ways to Deal with Employee Protection   359

HELPING CORPORATE EXECUTIVES AVOID THE TERRORIST
THREAT WHEN TRAVELING ABROAD   360

WHO IS LIABLE WHEN AN EMPLOYEE IS KIDNAPPED?   362

Case Example: Industries Gran Colombia, S.A.   362

HELPING EMPLOYEES COPE WITH VIOLENCE   363

THEFT OF TRADE SECRETS: CORPORATE SECURITY GOES
UNDERCOVER   363

Some Actual Examples of Employee Trade Secret
Theft   364   ●   Soviet Spies—FBI Director Says Your Firm Could Be
the Next Target   365   ●   Case Example: Lockheed Corp.   365

EMPLOYEE LOOSE TALK SPILLS TRADE SECRETS   366

Employees Are the Greatest Threat to Trade Secrets   367

CORPORATE TECHNIQUES FOR GAINING INFORMATION ABOUT
COMPETITORS   368

Monitoring Competitive Information in Help Wanted
Ads   368   ●   Executive Search Firms Can Be Sources of Competitor
Information   368   ●   How One Personnel Director Tracked Down a
Corporate Scam   369

TIPS ON PROTECTING COMPUTER SECURITY   369

Guidelines for Implementing a Basic Security

Program   370   •   Security Staffing   371

COMPANY ACTIONS IN CASES OF EMPLOYEE THEFT   371

WHERE THE SECURITY FUNCTION REPORTS IN MOST
ORGANIZATIONS   371

FIGHTING ALCOHOLISM AND DRUG ABUSE IN BUSINESSES   374

Who Abuses Drugs?   374   •   How to Stop Drug Abuse in Your
Company   375   •   What to Do with Suspected Pushers on the
Payroll   376   •   Clues to Suspected Drug Use or Sale   376   •
A Hot Issue—The Right to Search for Drugs at Work   377   •   Testing
Applicants or Employees for Drugs   377

GENETIC SCREENING OF APPLICANTS   378

HOW TO START AN EMPLOYEE ASSISTANCE PROGRAM FOR DRUG
AND ALCOHOL ABUSE   378

How Drug and Alcohol EAPs Work   378   •   Employee Assistance
Program Policy No. 1   381   •   Sample EAP Announcement
Letter   384   •   Employee Assistance Program Policy No. 2
385   •   Success Rates of EAPs   387

**10 HOW THE INTERNATIONALIZATION OF BUSINESS IMPACTS
HRM** **389**

KEY ISSUES FACING MULTINATIONAL OPERATIONS   391

Internationalization: The Trend Toward Hiring Foreign
Managers   391   •   Globalization: Increasing Market Share by
Standardizating Products Worldwide   392   •   What Globalization
Means for Businesses   393

HOW TO CHOOSE THE RIGHT EMPLOYEES FOR OVERSEAS
ASSIGNMENTS   394

What to Look for When Selecting Job Qualifications   394   •   Key
Reasons Why Some Expatriates Fail   395

HOW TO PREPARE A SELECTION MODEL FOR RATING APPLICANTS
FOR MULTINATIONAL ASSIGNMENTS   396

Four Task Related Areas to Consider   397   •   Other Important
Factors   400   •   Sample Expatriate Policy for Overseas
Employees   400

COMPENSATING OVERSEAS EMPLOYEES: THIRTEEN MAJOR ITEMS
TO CONSIDER   408

TIPS ON CONTROLLING EXPATRIATE COSTS   410

Expatriate Cost Checklist   410

CULTURE SHOCK AND HOW TO OVERCOME IT   411

Case Example: PHI International's Success Has Been Built on Cross-
Cultural Savvy   411   •   Tips for Maintaining Cultural

Sensitivity   412   ● Case Example: Getty Oil Company's Three-Day
Cross-Cultural Orientation   413   ● Companies that Have Cross-
Cultural Training and Orientation Programs   413

EMPLOYERS FACE NEW CHALLENGES UNDER THE IMMIGRATION
REFORM AND CONTROL ACT OF 1986   413

11 LABOR RELATIONS: A NEW ERA 423

WHERE LABOR RELATIONS ARE HEADING IN THE 1990s   425

Wage Increase Patterns   425   ● Two-Tier Labor Contracts and How
They Work   426   ● Case Example: American Airlines Likes Multiple
Tiers   426   ● Case Example: Two-Tier Wage Plan in
Supermarkets   426   ● Why Salaried Plants Are Becoming
Popular   427   ● Setting Compensation Levels: Three Variables to
Consider   428   ● Case Example: Why MADTEX Manufacturing, Inc.
Moved to a Salaried Plant   428   ● Labor's Biggest Push—A Job for
Life   430   ● Case Example: The General Motors Contract   430

DOES EVERY COMPANY NEED A UNION?   430

Fourteen Common Issues in the Grievance Arbitration
Process   431   ● Labor Overview   432

MANAGER'S GUIDE TO EMPLOYEE RELATIONS—A LABOR
RELATIONS HANDBOOK   436

INTRODUCTION   436

Employee Relations Problems—Common Causes   436   ● Recognizing
Problems   437   ● Handling Problems   438   ● Policy on Third Party
Representation   441   ● Conclusion   444

PREVENTIVE LABOR RELATIONS: A CASE STUDY   446

TEK POLICY   448

UNIONS AND OTHER OUTSIDE INVOLVEMENT   448

CRITICAL ISSUES FACING LABOR IN THE 1990s   450

MANAGEMENT'S CRITICAL ISSUES FOR THE 1990s   453

OTHER IMPORTANT LABOR RELATIONS ISSUES AND TRENDS FOR
OF THE FUTURE   454

The Quest for Equal Opportunity for Women in the
Workforce   454   ● Increased Use of Industrial Robots   455   ● The
Rise of Part-time Workers   455   ● An Improvement in the Image of
Unions   456   ● Management Will Continue to Fight to Keep Unions
Out   456

SAFETY—A RENEWED CONCERN FOR BOTH GOVERNMENT AND
INDUSTRY   457

Health and Safety—Growing Issues with American Workers   457

NEW DIRECTIONS IN EMPLOYEE RIGHTS   458

INDEX 459

Organizational Development: Why It Is the Key to Your Firm's Future Success

CHAPTER 1

WHY UNDERSTANDING THE ORGANIZATIONAL DEVELOPMENT PROCESS IS CRITICAL FOR YOU AND YOUR COMPANY

When Organizational Development is done right, it creates a highly adaptive organization . . . the type of organization that will be most successful in the 1990s and into the twenty-first century. Every human resource manager seems to have an idea of just what Organizational Development (OD) really is. There are as many definitions of organizational development as there are writers of books and articles about it . . . and to some extent all of them are accurate. OD, when it is effective, encompasses all the critical elements of an organization. It is a planning process, a culture identification process, an educational process, and the means by which organizations increase effectiveness and assimilate organizational change. Organizations are changing today faster than ever before. Mergers, acquisitions, and cutbacks are all occurring in short spans of twelve to eighteen months. It's critical for human resource managers to understand the OD process in order to help their organizations successfully assimilate change.

What is Organizational Development?

Organizational development covers a wide variety of issues depending on the company, but most successful organizational development plans include the following elements.

- a comprehensive process of assessing an organization, in order to plan needed changes

- a collection of ideas, strategies, and techniques that help an organization deal with change

- a specific planning process, including manuals, forms, and communications programs

- an educational process for middle management and employees in understanding the assessments made, and the strategies to be used to effect change

- a method for implementing change and strategies for dealing with critical issues

3

- a way of identifying the corporate culture and business style, and communicating the culture and values of the organization to employees so they can readily identify with them
- a process for improving the effectiveness of the organization by training the people and changing the technology as needed
- a technique that can be used to assess the organization on a stage-by-stage basis, spotlighting those parts of each function that need improvement and implementing changes in a logical, effective way as the organization evolves
- a company-wide communication program
- a formal program for building trust and team spirit among individuals and groups at all levels

As you can see from the preceding checklist, OD is a pretty straightforward process of actualizing organizational change in an effective, logical, and pragmatic fashion. The overall process may take months, depending on the size of the organization and the level of the programs planned. However, with top management support and some advance training of managers and key executives, the OD plan can be systematically implemented.

Using "Change Agents"—from Both Inside and Outside the Company

Because so few human resource professionals have a comprehensive background in organizational development, some companies look outside for an OD consultant to assist their human resource people; however, more human resource managers today are taking advanced training in the critical skills needed to implement comprehensive OD programs.

The role of an outside consultant or outside "change agent" has both advantages and disadvantages. The *advantages* are being independent, having an outsider's perspective, and possibly having more credibility as an expert.

The *disadvantages* are the lack of an insider's understanding of organizational problems and opportunities, lack of intimate knowledge of the players, and the lack of understanding of the corporate culture and business style. The human resource manager enjoys the advantage of having all the expertise the outside consultant lacks. But as inside change agents, HR managers must take risks that could jeopardize their function. That is why so many companies use both HR executives and outside consultants in OD. If your firm is planning to implement an OD program you might start by completing the following checklist to find out where you are now in the OD process. Completing the checklist will also indicate to you whether or not you are knowledgeable enough to carry out the project internally, and just how much risk you may need to take to effect desired change in your organization.

Checklist for Initiating Organizational Development Processes

	Can Do	Need Help

Can you:
- Identify the organization's cultural and business style? Do you thoroughly understand the organization? _____ _____
- Identify the business systems . . . . where the power is, who the leaders are, the fast-trackers and strategic power points? _____ _____
- Communicate the value systems of both the company and the employees and work comfortably to marry these value systems? _____ _____
- Communicate the organization's norms, beliefs, attitudes, and behaviors? _____ _____
- Analyze overall corporate situations from an objective point of view? _____ _____
- Energize the interrelationships and promote a team effort that is needed to build trust among individuals and groups at all levels? _____ _____
- Initiate and carry out the educational processes that are needed to implement an OD function? _____ _____
- Persist and sustain an ongoing OD effort in order to make the inroads necessary to implement planned change? _____ _____
- Sustain the credibility of the executives in your organization that is needed to carry out OD programs like succession planning and team processes over a period of time? _____ _____
- Sense the best timing in implementing the various aspects of OD so that people at all levels will be open and susceptible? _____ _____
- Guarantee the resources, both inside and outside, of the organization to implement an OD function? _____ _____
- Personally handle, or have someone on your staff to handle, individual interventions? Have you some expertise in one-on-one counseling of employees at all levels of an organization? _____ _____
- Effectively handle confrontation and are you successful when leveling with employees as well as managers? _____ _____
- Be a good problem-solver? Do you quickly come up with creative solutions to organizational problems?

- Help management plan effective organizational strategies?
- Develop a network of experts, either consultants or people in other companies in charge of OD, to call on for advice and support in an intricate OD intervention?

Most human resource people will be able to answer about half of these questions in the "Can Do" category and will answer the other half in the "Need Help" category. Before undertaking a major organizational development effort, you should assess your own expertise in each of these areas. You might then plan strategies that combine individual expertise with the expertise of outside consultants on an "as needed" basis.

Seven Key Objectives to Include in Your Organizational Development

Most organizations start an organizational development effort by establishing objectives for the function. There can be many objectives, depending on the size of the company, the industry, location, competitive position, and so forth. Here are seven objectives many companies include in their organizational development function.

1. Identify the organization's philosophy and business style, and communicate it effectively to all employees on an on-going basis.

2. Improve the organization's ability to adapt to its environment, including the ability of managers to understand organizational problems and consistently reach effective solutions.

3. Create an environment in which it is possible to find exciting and challenging work. Provide opportunities for employees to develop their full potential. Utilize a participative management style.

4. Improve internal behavior patterns, including such things as interpersonal and intergroup effectiveness . . . improve the level of trust and support, the openness of communications, and the participation in the planning of organization strategy and human resource development.

5. Improve organizational performance and measure performance by tracking profitability, turnover, and innovation.

6. Increase the sense of "ownership" of organizational goals and objectives by linking employee performance and attitudes to corporate growth and profitability.

7. Build trust and a team spirit among individuals and departments throughout the company.

One of the most understandable books on OD is *Organizational Development*, a total systems approach to positive change in any business organization, by Dr. Karl Albrecht, Prentice-Hall, Inc., 1983. Dr. Albrecht's main concerns in his book are with people, processes, power, politics, and technology and how all of these complex parts can work effectively together to produce a successful and highly motivated organization. He approaches organizational development from a systems perspective.

A systems perspective utilizes a logical approach to complex problems. It concentrates on the analysis and design of the *whole* as distinct from the components or the *parts*. It looks at a problem in its entirety, taking into account all the variables, and relates the social to the technological aspects. As solutions are considered, they are expressed in the form of a system, combining people and machines, assigning functions to each, specifying the use of materials and the pattern of information flow, so that finally the whole system represents an optimum program for achieving the organizations stated goals. Most OD consultants try to keep systems modest, and easy to install and operate effectively over time.

Dr. Albrecht utilizes four systems fairly comprehensively.

The Technical System—facilities, machinery, work processes, and methods

The Social System—the people including executives, managers, and employees at all levels

The Administrative System—policies, procedures, reports, and information flow required to operate

The Strategic System—the management family, supervisors, the chain-of-command, reporting relationships, power values, the planning processes, the moving forces of the organization

The key to the success of a systems approach to OD is in the expertise of the individual installing the program. Success also lies in the person's ability to effectively communicate the program at all levels of the organization.

Dr. Albrecht says: "There comes a time in the history of almost every organization, no matter what kind it is, when it becomes more or less out of tune. A small out-of-kilter condition eventually becomes a large out-of-kilter condition because things change."

Later he states: "This out-of-tune condition does not necessarily result from weak or ineffective management, although it certainly can. More often than not, it results from the fundamental inertia that exists in virtually all human organizations . . . the tendency of the people who work there to adopt a workable 'status quo' mode of operating and to refine it, cherish it, and eventually defend it against all outside forces and invite them to change it." Organizational development should help an organization change the "status quo" if it isn't working.

A Four-Step Process for New OD Programs

Human resource managers that have worked in the OD function know that there is a four-step process that is initiated at the beginning of a full-blown organizational review.

1. Assessment—The first stage, in which the CEO and top executives, working together with the human resource manager and/or organizational development consultants, use various methods and instruments to assess the total organization.

2. Problem Solving—Based on the results of the organizational assessment the same group that participated in the assessment of the organization will make decisions on what changes need to take place, when they should occur, and at what cost.

3. Implementation—Actual carrying out of the changes agreed on, the strategies for implementation, and the timing, assignment of projects and check points for monitoring implementation.

4. Follow-through and Evaluation—Progress is monitored and the whole project is evaluated. Successes are reviewed, failures are assessed, plans are established for needed changes or revisions.

Effective Organizational Development Interventions Used by Organizations

Organizational development is normally a long-range effort to introduce planned change that involves the entire organization and requires constant updating and follow through. It is not a one-time, one-shot program. This ongoing process naturally requires some intervention. Here are some examples.

- Team Building—The basic building blocks of organizations are groups of people; therefore, the basic changes must address groups, not just individuals. Groups have to learn to be more collaborative, cooperative, and innovative, and to eliminate the "we" and "they" games people play.
  Groups can become more effective by learning different decision-making procedures, and by improving communication skills. They usually need to practice more openness, acceptance, trust, and respect.

- Goal Setting and Planning—Manager and subordinate teams throughout the organization learn to carry on performance improvement programs, sometimes using the Management by Objective (MBO) approach, usually with improved long-term results.

- Third Party Interventions—Using a skilled consultant to help diagnose problems and opportunities for improvement. Many times an outside consultant can handle difficult one-on-one situations in a more productive manner than in-house personnel. Interventions sometimes work better in an arms-length relationship.

- Confrontation Meetings—When there are particularly difficult, widespread problems, it is good to use an action-research format, bringing an entire management group together to discuss problems that are affecting all of them. The meeting can be facilitated either by the human resource manager, the organizational development manager, an outside consultant, or a combination of all three.

An effective organizational development effort brings together people at all levels to achieve mutual goals . . . people should begin to see themselves as a resource to others, as team players with other people throughout the organization. In contrast to pure management development, which is oriented toward the individual, organizational development focuses on groups and improving relations between people and departments. Organizational development should increase an organization's capacity to understand and manage conflict and change.

How Corporate Culture Influences Organizational Development

Any organizational development effort will be strongly influenced by the culture of the organization. A good book on corporate culture is Terrance Deal and Allen Kennedy's book, *Corporate Cultures, the Rites and Rituals of Corporate Life*, Addison-Wesley Publishing Company, 1982. Their premise is that corporate culture has a great deal to do with the success of the business. The culture is established by the leader of the organization, the CEO, and carried out through the ranks by managers.

A very important part of the culture are the values; the values are the organization's foundation . . . they are the essence of a company's philosophy. Values, say Deal and Kennedy, "provide a sense of common direction for all employees and guidelines for their day-to-day behavior. Since organizational values can powerfully influence what people actually do, we think that values ought to be a matter of great concern to managers."

As you prepare to implement an organizational development program, it will become apparent that the corporate culture and employee attitudes must be linked together in order to achieve growth and profitability for the company.

In the Hay Management Report entitled "Linking Employee Attitudes and Corporate Culture to Corporate Growth and Profitability, 1984,"* George G. Gordon, a partner at Hay, reports on how corporate culture relates to an organization's success.

For over 15 years, Hay has conducted hundreds of Management Climate studies, in which we have systematically collected the perceptions of individuals in the top four or five levels of management about their company's "ground rules." Thus, we have been building a data base of corporate cultures as seen through management's eyes.

We chose to study Corporate Culture through this upper level group because we believe that the cultural values held by management are reflected throughout an organization. Further, if a company wishes to modify its culture, the thrust must come from the top. Although numerous authors have written about the resistance of culture to change, our own work proves that cultures *can* change, but only through the perseverance of its leadership.

Our surveys provide a wealth of data on some very important elements of culture, going back as far as 1974, with responses from over 50,000 managers and professionals. Usually we took a census of the top four or five levels of management from the CEO down, rather than examining a sample of people at all levels. By focusing on the top of the pyramid, we obtain a clear picture of some of the major values driving a company. For example, if the company is to act humanistically toward its employees, such a philosophy must be held at the top, or at least, be accepted by those who lead the company. Or if a company is to act in an entrepreneurial manner, the people at the top must believe they are encouraged to be opportunistic; otherwise, it will not happen at the bottom.

Our report reviews some of the trends we found in our studies. In particular, it examines the relationships between culture and types of industry and between culture and corporate performance, and it addresses a central question: Can we change a company's culture if we want to? The conclusion drawn in this report is that indeed a company's culture can be changed, but that the key to changing a culture resides in the leader or leaders.

Eleven Factors Found in Corporate Culture

After a rigorous analysis of a large number of questions asked in hundreds of companies, Hay refined a set of eleven factors or elements in corporate culture. The resulting framework holds up over a wide variety of organizations.

---

* "Linking Employee Attitudes and Corporate Culture to Corporate Growth and Profitability," Hay Group, Inc. Reprinted with permission.

1. *Clarity of Direction* is the extent to which the company emphasizes creating clear objectives and plans to meet them.
2. *Company Stretch* is the extent to which the company sets venturesome goals and approaches its business innovatively.
3. *Integration* is the extent to which units are encouraged to operate in a coordinated manner.
4. *Top Management Contact* is the extent to which people get clear communication and support from upper management.
5. *Encouragement of Individual Initiative* describes an emphasis on a high degree of delegation.
6. *Overt Conflict Resolution* is the extent to which people are encouraged to air conflicts and criticisms openly.
7. *Performance Clarity* is the extent to which the company makes performance expectations clear to individuals.
8. *Performance Emphasis* is the extent to which the company demands high levels of performance from individuals and holds them personally accountable for results.
9. *Action Orientation* refers to the timeliness with which decisions are made, a sense of urgency to get things done and a responsiveness to changes in the marketplace.
10. *Compensation* is the extent to which people perceive the company as paying competitively and fairly, as well as relating that pay to performance.
11. *Human Resource Development* is the extent to which companies provide opportunities for individuals to grow and develop within the company.

For a copy of the entire report, contact Hay Management Consultants, 229 South 18th Street, Rittenhouse Square, Philadelphia, PA 19103.

The Human Resource Manager's Role in Organizational Development

The human resource manager and/or the OD manager should act as a catalyst for change. A catalyst helps overcome the tendency on the part of organizations to sweep problems under the rug . . . hoping they will disappear. A catalyst's function is to make problems and employee dissatisfaction known, to upset the status quo when it needs to be upset and to put energy into the problem-solving process. For example, if employees are not being given the training they need to perform their jobs effectively, it is the catalyst's responsibility to inform management and to suggest resources be allocated and programs defined.

Another role for the human resource manager is the role of process person; showing the organization how to get involved in processes that will bring about planned change—how to recognize and define organizational needs, how to diagnose problems correctly, and how to set viable objectives to address the problems; how to identify the needed resources and how to bring them into the organization; then, how to carry out the solutions that have been proposed and to evaluate them after they have been applied over a period of time. In other words, how to actuate the four-step process described on page 8.

Human resource managers can be agents for change in their organizations. The overall task is to establish credibility and build relationships in order to be able to orchestrate change, to work collaboratively in the problem-solving processes and to help the CEO and other top management people in support of change throughout the organization.

MATRIX MANAGEMENT: A POPULAR CHOICE OF CONTEMPORARY ORGANIZATIONS

In the 1970s matrix management was widely used in the aerospace industry, but not many other types of organizations tried it . . . or they tried it and were not able to make it work. Matrix management is a form of project management, however.

Today matrix management has grown far beyond the project management context. In multinational corporations, product, functional, and geographic managers work in the sharing mode of matrix management. Matrix management is a kaleidoscope of organizational systems. It is a departure from the classic model of management to a multidimensional system of sharing decisions, results, resources, and rewards in an organizational culture characterized by many authority-responsibility-accountability relationships.

Each organization that moves to a matrix management system designs its own criteria for implementation and on-going management of the program. There are, however, always some combination of the following systems present.

Elements of Matrix Management Systems

- Organizational problems/opportunities are handled by using temporary task forces or project teams that are formed for specific short-term assignments.
- Support functions like human resources, accounting, marketing, and so forth are made available to support the project team, but no specific individuals in any of these functions reports directly to a

project manager. Therefore, employees assigned as project managers must have the interpersonal skills and ability to negotiate for their services.

- Team culture dominates management style. Managers must come to grips with the fact that they have to be more collaborative and honest in their interactions at all levels of the organization.
- Consensus decision making is more widely practiced throughout the organization.
- Superiors share performance evaluations with lateral managers and peer groups.
- Participative management is a way of life.

When companies move to a matrix management mode there is frequently a period when the managers fight the new system . . . they may not have the interpersonal skills that are needed to be successful, or they are not used to working in a teamwork environment. There is usually an initial period when the whole concept is rejected by managers who don't understand it. This is the time that you can be most helpful in providing training programs to help managers acquire the skills they need to be more successful and it is the time to provide counseling and support. Skills like crediting, clarifying, confirming, building, constructive criticism, leveling, and positively managing differences are critical to a manager's success.

Matrix management seems to work best in a young organization. People may not be as set in their ways as managers in older, more bureaucratic companies. The matrix system is difficult to launch and challenging to operate on an on-going basis. Many organizations instituted matrix management when downsizing an organization was a necessity and important projects couldn't be launched any other way.

The success of a matrix management organization depends on a company's ability to meet the tough daily challenges.

Guidelines for Implementing a Matrix Program

- Develop a scheme for organizational objectives, goals, and strategies that will provide the framework for an emerging matrix management culture.
- Promote by word and example an open and flexible attitude in the organization. Encourage the notion that change is inevitable, and that a free exchange of ideas is necessary to make matrix management work.
- Patience is absolutely necessary. It takes time to change the system and to orient managers who must make a matrix system work.

- Accept the idea that some people may never be able to adjust to the unstructured, democratic ambience. If you want to retain those people, let them work in the more structured departments, probably staff rather than line functions.
- Be mindful of the importance that team commitment plays in managing the project.
- Provide a forum whereby conflict can be resolved before it deteriorates into interpersonal strife. The human resource manager can serve as the release valve for pressures by being the catalyst that brings them out in the open and assists in conflict resolution.
- Realize that project management is not a panacea for all organizational problems. On the contrary, implementation of a matrix management system will bring to light many organizational problems that have remained hidden in the conventional line and staff organization.
- The route an organization follows to get to the matrix design evolves out of the existing culture. The culture may have to change and this takes time, considerable effort, and effective communication programs.
- Recognize that senior management support and commitment are essential to success. Without it a matrix management program cannot succeed.
- Work for participative up-and-down communication programs within the company. Information requirements for project management require definition. Managers who have a "need to know" require access to information to do their job. Those in key positions have to understand and use project-generated information systems. All of this requires specific training.
- Be aware that shifting to a matrix form of organization is easier for the younger organization. Large, well-established companies with a rigid bureaucracy will find the change difficult.
- Institute a strong educational effort to acquaint executives, key managers, and professionals with the theory and practice of matrix management. Do this at the start of the change to project management.

Many corporations are using project/matrix management as one of their tools to develop fast-track managers. They only assign high performance managers to projects, with the idea that the matrix experience will groom them for larger assignments and promotions down the road. They establish projects in the minds of everyone in the organization as special development opportunities with top level visibility in which only high performance people have the opportunity to participate. Matrix management is therefore a part of the company's succession planning program.

MANAGEMENT SUCCESSION PLANNING: THE KEY TO ORGANIZATIONAL EXCELLENCE

Succession planning is basically a procedure for identifying people who can replace key executives and professionals, and after identifying them, deciding what development programs are needed to prepare them for moving into higher positions. There are basically three key elements of an effective succession plan.

1. *The succession planning statement.* This is basically a mission statement that sets out the objectives and top level commitment of the organization to succession planning.
2. *The succession planning back-up summary.* This summary lists the key positions and the back-up personnel are identified.
3. *Individual development plans.* After successors have been identified, individual development plans must be made and carried out.

Succession planning is an important part of organizational development and should be done for at least four levels of the organization—president, vice-president, director, and manager. It should be done eventually for all levels, but the significant dislocation that can be suffered within the organization if someone leaves would be at the higher levels, and it is best to start with these positions. It is also at these levels that development frequently takes place in preparation for promotion. Development here can take a great deal of time, so advance planning is necessary.

WHO NEEDS MANAGEMENT SUCCESSION PLANNING?

No matter what size a company is, it should do some management succession planning. Succession planning forces senior executives to think more carefully about what they need to do to develop their staff. Even smaller companies make a mistake by not developing their employees to move up. Small companies that have only six to twelve million dollars in revenues and thirty to fifty employees have a senior management and support staff, but no middle management. If something happens to one or more of the senior executives, there can be a real problem . . . a lack of continuity, no succession candidates, and, perhaps, a loss of profitability for a short period while new people are recruited.

No two companies do succession planning in the same way. Some emphasize identification of successors only, others put their emphasis on development of younger or middle managers and programs to prepare them to move up. Companies often use some sort of code assessments of candidates for promotion.

For example: A manager's evaluation might read "S, 12 + C," meaning the employee's performance is Superior (S); the employee will be ready in twelve to eighteen months (12); and the employee's potential is considerable (+C).

How to Prepare a Succession Plan Backup Summary Form

It is important for top management to prepare a key position backup summary for the succession plan. When the key positions have been listed and their backup personnel identified, the individual development plans can be formalized on each of the backup personnel.

These forms are merely suggested formats. To be successful, the succession plan should be simple and flexible enough to meet the requirements of the organization. You can design forms that better fit your specific needs.

SUCCESSION PLAN BACKUP SUMMARY

Key Position	Dept.	Yrs. in Co.	Yrs. in Position	Performance Level	Current Salary	Salary Range Min. Mid. Max.	Technical or Managerial Career Ladder?	Comments
Name	Location							

BACKUPS

Key Position	Dept.	Yrs. in Co.	Yrs. in Position	Performance Level	Current Salary	Salary Range Min. Mid. Max.	Technical or Managerial Career Ladder?	Comments
Name	Location							

Individual Development Plans

The human resource planning process is integrated with individual development, through performance appraisals, establishing career paths, and training and development. Appraisals of potential also may determine the possibility of an individual taking on more responsibility. The plan should be integrated with a program to move people through the organization as they gain skills and experience.

The following individual development form may be used in structuring your individual development plans. Indicate the individual's name in the space for "Employee," your name as "Manager," and the current date. Under "Present Job," indicate the position the employee now holds. Under "Potential Job," there are three alternatives—an existing specific job you think is most likely to be the employee's next assignment, a hypothetical job that could be created and that is likely to be his assignment, or a statement of the kinds of additional responsibilities the individual is likely to assume. You make the choice and fill in the line under "Potential Market."

The sections entitled "Knowledge" and "Skills" are intended to be triggers to your thought process in identifying development needs. Blank spaces are indicated under both for other items that may occur to you. Put an X after those items where the employee is fully adequate, and XX by those items where development is needed. If development is indicated in the present job, the development needs should be listed specifically and communicated to the employee as soon as possible.

If development for a potential job is indicated, it should be listed and communicated to the employee. In addition, employees should be asked to identify needs they feel they have in specific areas.

The lower half of the form is intended to be the basis for an individual development plan. Checked items from above will be converted into a specific training and experience need. For example, you may check "Technical" under "Knowledge for the Present Job." If the present job is Manager of XYZ Department, the specific training need might be indicated as a better understanding of interpersonal communication. The second half of the form is titled "How to Accomplish." You might check "School," filling in the appropriate course and university. You also might check "Assignment Shadowing." "Shadowing" means to assign an executive with potential to "shadow" a higher level executive with specific expertise so the novice executive can learn that expertise firsthand.

USING DUAL-CAREER LADDERS IN SUCCESSION PLANNING

Most organizations that employ both business and technical managers have installed dual-career ladders in order to provide promotional opportunities

INDIVIDUAL DEVELOPMENT PLAN

_____   Date _____

Employee

_____

Manager

Present Job:

1. _____

Potential Job:

2. _____

Knowledge	1	2	Skills	1	2
Technical Business	___	___	Managerial	___	___
General Business	___	___	Technical	___	___
Knowledge of the			Leadership	___	___
Organization	___	___	Problem Solving	___	___
Company Policy	___	___	Decision Making	___	___
Company Procedures	___	___	Administrative	___	___
_____	___	___	Communication		
_____	___	___	Oral	___	___
_____	___	___	Written	___	___
			Organization	___	___
			Planning	___	___
			Precision	___	___
X = fully adequate			Motivation	___	___
XX = needs development			Handling Stress	___	___
			Sensitivity to People	___	___
			Interpersonal Skills	___	___
			_____	___	___
			_____	___	___

Training or Experience Need	√	How to Accomplish	Date to Be Accomplished
	___	School _____	_____
	___	Seminar _____	_____
_____	___	Assignment Shadowing ___	_____
	___	Months Experience in _____	
		_____ Position	_____
_____	___	Temporary Assignment as ___	
		_____	_____
	___	Special Emphasis on _____	
		_____	_____
_____	___	_____	_____

for both career professionals. One of the most successful organizations with the dual-career ladder concept is Exxon. A respected manager can rise to the position of senior vice-president in the management career ladder, while an equally valued scientist with as much seniority and good performance can become a senior scientist in the technical or scientific career ladder. The two jobs carry equal salaries and prestige.

SAMPLE DUAL CAREER LADDERS

v

MANAGERIAL LADDER		TECHNICAL/SCIENTIFIC LADDER	
Title	Salary	Title	Salary
Vice-President Marketing	$90,000	Research Fellow	$90,000
Director, Marketing	$70,000	Senior Research Scientist	$70,000
Manager, Marketing	$50,000	Research Scientist	$50,000
Senior Market Analyst	$35,000	Research Analyst	$35,000
Market Analyst	$25,000	Laboratory Tech.	$25,000

It has been said that technical/scientific people do not necessarily make good managers. They are not always effective in dealing with people in a managerial role on a daily basis. In the past, when companies have promoted these employees up through the managerial ranks, they failed at managing large groups of people. They were still effective in their technical or scientific calling, but, when they failed in management, the organization had no other alternative but to demote them back into their jobs as "individual contributors," or to fire them.

Many companies, therefore, adopted the dual-career ladder approach, so that technical/scientific people had opportunities for promotion where they could remain successful as they moved up. Companies had to find ways to promote them in order to keep them. Dual-career ladders have not always been successful, but many companies like Exxon have put the time and effort into making the dual ladders successful in order to retain good people.

The key to the success of a dual-career ladder is in the close attention paid to both management and technical performance in succession planning, and in the ability of management to communicate opportunities to both managerial and technical people. One way to ensure success is to include job opportunities in both career ladders through an up-to-date computer database. It is important that hiring managers in a far-flung operation consult the database when they are looking for people to fill jobs at higher levels of the organization.

A Case Example: ARCO

The Atlantic Richfield Company (ARCO) has installed a technical career program that provides career path opportunities for scientists and other technical people who want to stay in research rather than move up in a managerial career ladder for which they may not be suited. The senior technical manager in each of ARCO's operating companies administers the program for that company. Employees may qualify at four levels: Advisor, Senior Advisor, Executive Advisor, and Distinguished Advisor. Individuals are nominated by their managers, based on technical achievements, innovation, and creativity. The review process is conducted by members of an operating company committee, the majority of whom are technical people. Nominations to the higher levels must be approved by the New Technology Council, a group composed of senior research people in each operating company, and the Corporate Technology department. Eight of ARCO's nine operating companies have implemented the technical career program and over fifty employees have been accepted into the program as advisors. Like many organizations, Atlantic Richfield is trying to cope with the need to improve its position in the area of technology development and the need to develop outstanding people.

What to Ask Before Implementing Dual-Career Ladders

Before implementing dual-career ladders there are many questions to be answered in the area of program design, implementation, and administration.

- Exactly what are the needs of our organization?
- Is there a significant enough problem to warrant establishment of dual-career ladders?
- What are the issues of employees in both of the managerial and technical areas?
- What are the advantages and disadvantages of dual-career ladders?
- Will they be properly used if implemented? Can we ensure top management will follow through and support the concept?
- What would be the level of acceptance of dual-career ladders on the part of top management?
- How should the structure be designed? How will we define the jobs of people in the technical career program?

- How should such a system be communicated to be rest of the organization?

- How should people be selected for both career ladders?

- How will power be balanced between those employees in management and those in technical high-level positions?

- Will status, salary, and responsibility be equal in both career ladders?

- How should the program be administered and controlled? Where should responsibility for the program be assigned?

- What will the program cost—short term? long term?

It's a good idea to appoint a task force of people who will be involved in the program to study its adaptability and costs for your organization before establishing dual-career ladders. There is no doubt that dual-career ladders increase payroll costs. You need to weigh the costs of dual-career ladders against the costs of losing good (normally hard to find) technical/scientific people.

How Computers Help Keep Tabs on Corporate "Fast Trackers" for the Succession Plan

The career paths of managers and professionals are now being charted on corporate computers. Software is available that monitors professional and executive talent, does succession planning, and keys availability of specific people into the succession plan, the affirmative action program, and the company's strategic human resource planning programs.

Case Example: Southland Corporation

Southland Corporation, the Dallas-based parent of 7-Eleven stores, has computerized its search process for fast-trackers.

Twice a year, Southland executives file reports on the computer regarding the promotability of their subordinates. Personnel people then consolidate the reports on the computer and a final printout provides a list of people with specific expertise and abilities who can move up . . . it also spotlights the areas where there are no people ready to move up.

A separate report helps produce career development plans, highlighting weaknesses and suggesting actions like university courses, in-house training and mentoring possibilities, special assignments, and so forth.

In the past, many companies did succession planning through the "old boy network." Charlie knows someone in marketing who has a protégé who might be good for a job in Sales. Talent was uncovered mostly by word-of-mouth. Now a computerized database in most organizations has expanded the human resource internal search capabilities tremendously.

Within minutes you can pinpoint all the people in the company with five years of marketing experience who have supervised more than twenty-five people, speak Japanese, and are willing to relocate.

The computer can also fill the gaps in personnel. When you make a promotion the computer makes you consider who will fill the vacancy that will be created by the promotion. It can also point out potential hitches. If the candidate you choose to fill a specific position is the only one that has the expertise to fill a vacancy that is expected in another department six months from now, it can point that out before it is too late.

Succession planning today is becoming more sophisticated. Some companies that use computers to manage careers and do succession planning are: Security Pacific National Bank; CTE Corp.; Avon Products; Northern Telecom, Inc.; Aetna Life & Casualty; Gulf + Western Industries, Inc.; and even the United States Army is considering a system to track generals' careers.

Suggested Resources for Management Succession Planning

- The American Society for Personnel Administration offers seminars on management continuity planning and management reviews. These advanced-level seminars are open to all. Contact the American Society of Personnel Administration, 606 North Washington Street, Alexandria VA 22314; 703-548-3440.

- The Human Resource Planning Society offers workshops on management-succession planning and publishes a book that contains a section on the subject, *The Challenge of Human Resource Planning*, edited by James W. Walker. To find out more about the seminars or to order a copy of the book, contact the Human Resource Planning Society, P.O., Box 25553, Grand Central Station, New York, NY 10163; 212-837-0630. Mary Cook & Associates, 2700 Youngfield, Suite 206, Lakewood CO, 80215, also publishes a book on Succession Planning and conducts management reviews and seminars.

MERGER MANIA—A HEADACHE FOR THE HUMAN RESOURCE DEPARTMENT

Human Resource consultants who specialize in organizational development and management succession planning say that one of their biggest headaches today is working with organizations after a merger has taken place. The discontinuity, organizational politics, the problem of two people in the same job, and overall dislocation create serious problems in organizational effectiveness and negatively affect the "bottom line" results of the surviving organization for years. The headaches of corporate mergers have been felt in nearly every American industry including major airlines, oil companies, banks, and communication networks; both retail and wholesale chains have been bought and sold on a whirlwind scale. But, do the takeovers work? Not very often, according to some experts. The acquiring companies usually take on huge debts and when times get tough they have to default. The meshing of personnel, especially top management personnel, usually doesn't work and the corporate culture of the new organization is fragmented.

Five Key Elements of a Successful Merger

In the past four years, there have been over 9,000 mergers or acquisitions of corporations. Some of the mergers made good sense and were successful; however, many were disastrous. There are normally five key elements in place in mergers and acquisitions that are successful.

1. The companies are in closely related businesses.
2. The merger is often financed by stock swaps or cash in the bank, rather than by borrowing more money.
3. The price doesn't include a high premium.
4. The management of the acquired company stays on to run the business.
5. The new management communicates effectively with all employees.

The corporations that have been most successful in mergers are the ones that have spent a great deal of advance time in planning, including human resource planning and organizational development. One of the elements of a very successful corporation is the ability of the top management team to lead the company to sustain that success. When there is a merger, management turnover is a chronic problem that plagues the surviving organization. In fact, fifty-two percent of top management typically jumps ship within three years after the takeover. It is a common practice for executive search firms to contact top management executives in companies targeted for takeover when recruiting, as a source of people to fill open slots in other organizations.

Human Resource Problems in Merger/Acquisitions

One of the biggest problems merger/acquisition organizations face is the low morale of the employees in general and the turnover of the best management employees in the acquired company. I have talked to people in half a dozen companies that were acquired and the one theme that comes across most often is that neither company in the merger did an adequate job of communicating with their employees either before or after the merger.

Part of the planning for a merger should include a comprehensive employee communications program to be implemented by the human resource executives of both organizations.

The Need to Communicate with Employees During a Merger/Acquisition

At the very least employees should be told the following information before, during or after a merger/acquisition.

- As soon as the critical time for making an announcement of a merger/acquisition has passed, employees of both companies should be told that a merger/acquisition is in the offing.

- If you plan to lay some people off, it is best to make a general statement that there is a possibility of a layoff, and discuss the timing of a layoff. If you tell employees there will be no changes in personnel and no layoffs when you do expect them, you are lying; and when you lie to employees, they will find out and your credibility will drop to zero. Tell the truth in as much detail as you can without hurting negotiations.

- Provide employees with a timetable of events and ask for their assistance in making the transition a pleasant, productive one. If you plan to lay off certain people but need them through a specific date, provide a monetary incentive to motivate them to stay.

- Provide a special weekly newsletter as things "heat up" and the merger/acquisition grows near.

- Provide counseling and stress management workshops for employees on an as-needed basis.

- Provide outplacement services to employees who will be part of a layoff.

If it is important to your continuity and profitability to retain key management or technical personnel in a merger or acquisition, you should implement special retention strategies and communications programs for those groups.

Being in Touch with the Big Picture

Very few people in an organization see the "big picture." They are too busy keeping the place going. They all need, however, a sense of continuity, and of structure and permanence. Today many organizations are losing that feeling of structure and permanence, and human resource managers are the ones that people turn to for continuity. In many organizations the human resource managers define the environment and communicate the culture and style.

We are the ones that hold the nucleus together during a merger, or a change to matrix management, or any other major organizational upheaval. We are the ones that have to know how organizational development should work and we are the ones that help our organizations deal with the life passages through which they all go.

Innovative Approaches to Multiple Compensation Strategies, Programs, and Perks

Compensation programs are taking on a new look. In fact, the entire compensation area is undergoing major change. Pay-for-performance is "in" and many American companies are moving away from single policy lines and one compensation objective across the board to multiple-compensation programs. This major shift to multiple-compensation strategies and programs on the part of most organizations makes it more important than ever before for human resource executives to understand the variety of options available to them in designing new programs.

The major reasons for multiple programs and a variety of pay strategies are: (1) one compensation method, program or system will not meet the needs of today's multinational, multiproduct organizations, (2) neither will one program meet the needs of today's more vocal employee who seeks money, more paid time off, flexible benefits and working hours, and a larger variety of perks (employees today will give up certain monetary considerations to gain others), and (3) organizations cannot afford the constant acceleration of pay and benefits without corresponding gains in productivity.

ELEVEN WAYS IN WHICH COMPENSATION PROGRAMS ARE CHANGING

Here are eleven items to consider when developing your pay strategies for new salary programs.

1. Consider developing and implementing plans that marry compensation systems to company goals. Find more tangible ways of linking employee productivity goals to corporate profits and thereby actualizing pay-for-performance objectives.

2. The move to multiple-compensation objectives allows a company to save in some areas . . . putting that money into programs that will provide a better return on investment. For example: an organization might announce its intention to move to a third quartile pay level in hard-to-fill technical jobs but remain at first quartile pay levels in staff jobs where the first quartile is externally competitive.

3. Many companies have already moved to multiple policy lines in salary programs. For example, there may be one policy line for

hourly non-exempt employees, another for salaried exempt professionals, and still a third for executives.

4. There is a trend to salaried manufacturing plants. Some companies feel productivity increases at salaried plants. Dow Chemical, TRW, Rockwell International, and Dana Corp. have all tried this concept. Companies still pay overtime to workers, but have eliminated time clocks and treat all levels of employees as salaried, attempting to increase self-worth and self-esteem.

5. Many organizations are developing innovative pay-for-performance programs and taking them seriously. More union contracts are linking scheduled pay increases to specific measurable productivity improvements. Even the teaching profession has experienced new incentive programs. One school board links pay to performance by paying salary incentives of up to $7,000 based on measurable performance improvements.

6. Deferred compensation is becoming more popular. Management employees and professionals who have the option more and more prefer to defer taking pay increases until retirement.

7. There is a continuing push to institute a lower minimum wage youth differential in order to employ more young people. Paying less than the current minimum wage to youths who swell the ranks of the unemployed could conceivably alleviate a chronic unemployment problem.

8. Comparable worth claims are escalating as more women enter the workforce. This emotional issue will continue to plague companies that employ large groups of low-paid female workers. Be sure new programs are designed with this in mind.

9. The high tech industry is more innovative in terms of pay, benefits, and perks and these differences will begin to run over into other industries, like the information and service industries, as more high tech people cross over to work for service and information companies.

10. More companies are considering implementing lump sum pay increases that don't increase base pay. The auto, aerospace, and insurance industries already have plans in effect. One-time lump sum pay increases may or may not increase base pay, which has been accelerating at an incredible rate in some industries.

11. There is a move by many organizations to two-tier pay in labor contracts. American Airlines claims it has saved over $100 million per year with its two-tier contract. Labor unions and employees do

not approve of two-tier contracts that penalize new workers by paying them much less than long-term employees doing the same job, but companies that have two-tier pay programs say they have gone to them out of necessity to remain in business.

What is most obvious is that compensation programs have become a collage of changing, innovative thought. The same old salary solutions don't work in today's environment.

WHY MULTIPLE COMPENSATION PROGRAMS ARE POPULAR

Three trends have contributed substantially to the need for a multiple approach to salary administration.

1. Companies today are more diverse, typically operating in several businesses with different labor pools, on a more global basis.

2. Mergers and layoffs occur more frequently.

3. Supply and demand shift constantly and pay markets have become more fragmented.

Four Key Elements to Consider When Developing Pay Strategies

There are four key elements to consider when developing pay strategies. Should we pay by industry, function, geography, job size, or some element of each? In addition, companies have a difficult time trying to accurately identify their job marketplace and market pricing. There are consultants that perform this function for a company and most of these consultants have computerized programs that allow quick access to current data. One such company is The Hay Group, 229 South 18th Street, Rittenhouse Square, Philadelphia, PA, 19103. They have what they call the HAY ACCESS system that provides the capability for collecting and analyzing detailed compensation data. Here are some examples from the Hay data base:*

> **Pay Level by Industry.** At level A the average scientific salary in manufacturing companies is $36,000, whereas the same jobs are paid at an average of $50,000 in petroleum companies that have not recently experienced significant layoffs.

> **Pay Level by Function.** In industrial companies the average quality assurance job is paid $40,800 at Level A, while the average accounting job is paid $37,400.

---

* "Linking Employee Attitudes and Corporate Culture to Corporate Growth and Profitability," by Hay Group, Inc. Reprinted with permission.

Pay Level by Geography. Average EDP salaries are $44,000 in California versus $36,000 in Minnesota at Level A.

Pay Level by Job Size. In industrial sales forces, incentive consistently averages 13 percent of salary, except at the senior sales representative level, where it averages 21 percent.

The primary reason for so much diversity is that there is generally no such thing as a national labor market. Compensation levels are determined by supply and demand in a large number of industry, functional and geographic submarkets.

Several years ago, for example, there was a shortage of EDP people and the price of EDP jobs rose. As the supply of EDP professionals increased, prices have come back in line. On the demand side, relative compensation levels are changing, based on industry profitability. This situation is also dynamic. On the surface, high technology pay appears below average for most functions. However, the industry maintains a high pay practice, which is masked by a rapid degree of upward promotion.

Rethinking the Single Pay Structure

Rethinking the traditional concept of a single pay structure should result in many solutions, rather than a single consensus solution. In fact, while some organizations manage two to five salary policies, others now manage hundreds. There are several broad-based questions to ask.

	YES	NO	POSSIBLY
• Can we restructure our organization for optimal cost control?	—	—	———
• Can we identify changing job market characteristics and benefit by changing our pay strategy?	—	—	———
• Can we improve our human resource utilization?	—	—	———
• Can we ensure that people costs directly relate to our business objectives?	—	—	———
• Would multiple pay policies work in our organization?	—	—	———
• Do we operate in multiple industries? If so, have we considered this in our pay structure?	—	—	———
• What are the sources of recruitment for each job? Are we able to readily fill jobs at all levels and in all classifications through normal recruiting methods?	—	—	———
• Are certain functions more critical to the success of the business than others? Are we able to keep jobs in those functions filled?	—	—	———
• Is any function or department more vocal about competitive compensation than others?			

- Should we consider paying higher salaries in certain departments and not others?   ___ __ _____
- Does the current salary policy overpay geographically or underpay geographically?   ___ __ _____
- Does the current salary policy overpay or underpay by function?   ___ __ _____
- Is it difficult to attract and retain key contributors in any area of the organization?   ___ __ _____
- Is turnover excessive? Where?   ___ __ _____
- Is it increasingly difficult to prepare credible communications about internal equity or external competitiveness?   ___ __ _____

The underlying question in this whole inquiry must be: Does our compensation plan support our organization's business and human resource plans? By considering your answer to each question independently, you can develop an informative list of pay practices and possible problem areas for attention. This list can also form a preliminary database for your next annual salary program.

Answers to Questions on Contemporary Compensation Issues

Q. I know that companies are trying to reduce the impact of wage hikes on total compensation. How are they doing it?

A. Many auto and aerospace workers received their 1985 and 1986 raises in lump-sum payments that were not figured into the wage base. Some thirty percent of workers who bargained in 1984 got lump-sum payments. It appears that lump-sum increases may stay popular through the end of the 1980s. The lump-sum pay increase that does not increase base pay and benefits is catching on in several industries.

Q. Please explain the so-called two-tier labor contracts we hear about more frequently today.

A. Two major labor agreements, one with the Teamsters Union and one with Pan American World Airways flight attendants are called two-tier agreements. Basically under a two-tier structure, newly hired workers get paid less than employees already on the payroll and often substantially less than provided in a prior contract. Two-tier pay systems have been accepted by some unions in lieu of wage cuts for the already employed in situations where employers needed economic relief.

At Giant Food stores in Baltimore, a food clerk is hired in at $5.00 an hour and after two years progresses to the top rate of $8.95, compared with $11.14 an hour for someone on the top tier.

In another type of system, at Packard Electric, a division of General Motors, newly hired workers are being added to the payroll at fifty- five percent of the wage received by long-time employees on the production line.

At Lockheed all employees hired after October 1, 1983 in all but the most skilled unionized jobs need over two to four years to achieve the minimum starting rate paid workers hired before the cutoff date.

Q.   I have heard that some companies are shifting hourly workers to a salary basis. What does this mean and what companies are doing it?

A.   Management and workers are trying to cooperate and all pull in the same direction. Salaried plants are part of this new trend. Companies like TRW, Dow Chemical, Dana Corporation, Eaton Corporation, and Rockwell International today regard the concept as a human resources alternative to traditional management and compensation methods.

Some companies wait until they plan a move to start the salaried plans, others go to them gradually over the years, like Dow Chemical has done. Over the past eighteen years, Dow has gradually shifted to salary plans for both new plants and existing facilities with long histories of union representation.

In TRW's Lawrence, Kansas, plant, the 115 salaried production workers fill out time cards each week, but only to keep track of vacations and overtime. There aren't any time clocks.

There are a lot of pros and cons with salaried plants . . . unions are against them, calling them a "transparent" attempt by management to impress workers with a false sense of self-worth and self-esteem.

The jury is still out on whether or not they are the best way to go. Talk to a company who is trying the salaried approach before making a switch.

Q.   What is the so-called "subminimum wage"?

A.   It has been proposed to move to a $2.50 subminimum wage for sixteen- to nineteen-year-olds during the summer months, paying below the current minimum wage in order to employ more young people. If Congress approves this proposal, the minimum wage would be superseded by the new lower rate for working teens. So far, however, there hasn't been much acceptance of the idea.

Many companies we have talked to do not intend to lower their minimum wage even if a subminimum wage is approved by Congress. They say that kids cannot make enough as it is and they want to attract and retain good workers, even teenagers.

The Labor Department says that 400,000 new jobs would be created by this new subminimum wage. Unions do not think the bill would translate to more jobs for teenagers, and the Oil, Chemical, and Atomic Workers International Union says it is very much opposed to the bill.

Q. I keep hearing about teachers bonuses. What is happening in this regard?

A. Teachers are profiting from innovative new incentive plans to boost their pay. In Tennessee, teachers move up a five-step career ladder paying annual salary incentives up to $7,000 based on performance as judged by the school board.

Some New Jersey teachers will get a $5,000 raise as "master" teachers who counsel new ones or do extra work in a pilot program. Some Florida teachers can receive a $3,000 bonus if approved by their principals.

THE LUMP SUM SALARY INCREASE: A FAST WAY TO IMPROVE MORALE AT LITTLE ADDED COST

Companies that have tried the lump sum pay increase say that it has enabled them to improve worker motivation and morale at no added cost to the organization.

A lump sum increase is simply a method of paying an annual salary increase all at once rather than dividing it into twelve, twenty-six, or fifty-two installments in the regular paycheck. This defers the increase in base salary for one year. The objective is to offer employees the option to choose the method of receiving a pay increase that best suits their needs.

How the Lump Sum Salary Increase Works

Lump sum salary increase programs are designed to give participating employees their salary increase in the form of a lump sum. The single payment is made in advance and is equivalent to the total increase that normally would have been received over twelve months. The increase is treated as a cash advance, and all taxes and deductions are withheld at the same rate as if no lump sum had been taken.

The concept originated in the insurance industry to provide many of the same benefits as a bonus. Most major insurance companies now have lump sum programs and the idea has spread to a number of non-insurance companies.

Advantages

1. Employees can immediately accumulate a fairly substantial sum of money for major purchases, paying debts, vacation, or investment.

2. A lump sum program helps overcome the negligible effects of a small increase on take-home pay. For example, an employee can receive a $600 lump sum rather than $50 per month.

3. For nonbonus companies, it offers some of the advantages of bonuses without any serious disadvantages.

4. It conveys the impression that the company is doing something different and perhaps better than other companies.

5. It offsets potential disappointment with a relatively small previous year's program.

6. Employees receive two morale boosts from one increase—the first when the lump payment is made and the second when it goes into their base salary a year later.

Some companies give one-time lump-sum increases that never increase base pay. This type of increase or one time "bonus" is not as well accepted by employees.

Disadvantages

1. The effect diminishes with time. The employee forgets about the lump sum received and spent, and feels there is no more money than last year.

2. A lump sum program generates additional administrative work.

3. If the lump sum is not discounted, it represents an added cost to the company. When a company gives an employee a normal raise strung out over a year, it actually has the money to invest at interest for a period of months. When it pays in a lump sum at the beginning of the year, it has to "discover" the total amount because it is losing interest by paying the employee "up front."

4. There is the possibility of loss through termination of an employee after he or she receives an increase. (However, the experience of most companies has shown this risk to be minimum, even if repayment is not required.)

How to Implement a Lump Sum Plan

-   Establish a committee composed of representatives from the Payroll, Tax, Legal, Data Processing, and Human Resource Departments to work out the details of a program.

- Review the concept with the committee and obtain its input. Each function will have specific problems to be overcome.
- Design a plan and timing for implementation.
- Obtain necessary approvals.
- Communicate the program to employees. This is one of the most important items of any new program. If employees do not understand it, there will be serious problems in implementation.

Three companies that have implemented lump sum plans are B. F. Goodrich Company, Minnesota Mutual Insurance, and Equitable Life Assurance Society. The Equitable Life Assurance Society is willing to share information and experiences. For more information, write to the Society at 1285 Avenue of the Americas, New York, NY, 10019.

EXECUTIVE COMPENSATION AND PAY-FOR-PERFORMANCE PROGRAMS

Thanks to a healthy economy and the merger and acquisition of many corporations, there are bigger profits and most organizations are sharing the wealth with their leaders. Of the largest industry leaders, over 163 have received significantly higher salaries and bonuses. (Middle managers in those organizations did not fare as well.)

T. Boone Pickens led the pack in the mid-1980s. Mesa Petroleum rewarded Pickens for his raid on Gulf Oil Corporation by boosting his salary and bonus 789 percent to $4.2 million in one year! Chrysler Corporation and Cummins Engine Company were happy with their CEOs. Chrysler Corporation gave Lee A. Iacocca a 152-percent pay increase and Cummins gave Henry B. Schacht a 144-percent increase in pay in one year.

Also within one year General Dynamics hiked Chairman David S. Lewis' annual pay by 109 percent to $1 million. The average CEO's total compensation salary, bonus, and long-term income rose by 22 percent to $1.1 million. Besides salary and bonuses, most executives of these large companies have as many as six different types of long-term or deferred compensation that can multiply their earnings in years to come.

How Four Companies Successfully Implemented Pay-for-Performance Programs

More and more frequently human resource professionals are called on to design and administer executive pay programs. The key phrase today is "pay-for-performance." Every president says that his company has a pay-for-performance program that ties pay to accomplishment. It is not easy to pinpoint actual programs, but here are four companies that have implemented programs.

1. Honeywell: A Decentralized Pay System

The Honeywell Corporation went to a decentralized pay system of making pay decisions at local plant levels because company management decided they needed different pay plans for various parts of their business. Because nearly fifty percent of Honeywell's revenues are paid out in salaries, management feels it must tie pay to performance. Two departments at Honeywell handle special pay situations in unique ways.

1. A department in Phoenix gives a one-time or lump sum cash bonus that doesn't increase base pay. Instead of raises for outstanding work, a bonus for a job well done for, say two or three months, is less expensive over the long run than a larger increase paid over thirty years.

2. In Connecticut, one Honeywell unit makes valves under a gain-sharing program. Employees are given the previous labor costs for making a specific number of valves. Management then agrees that any labor savings or gain will be shared with the workers.

2. General Motors: No More Cost-of-Living Increases

General Motors has eliminated a cost-of-living adjustment for its huge salaried staff, about 110,000 workers. The Cost-of-Living-Adjustment (COLA) had been given to that group since 1948. It was costing GM $6,000 per employee.

In the past, because of the large COLA that went to everyone, there wasn't enough money left to give the top performers a "pat on the back." By eliminating the COLA, GM has changed pay practices and cut payroll costs in order to tie pay to performance and increase productivity.

3. Bank of America Corporation: Performance Bonuses for Those Who Produce

Bank of America Corporation's business services division pays performance bonuses to increase productivity. Some people have received several thousand dollars in bonuses—others, who were considered less productive, received nothing.

Pay-for-performance obviously gets mixed reviews, depending on the perception of employees. Even though pay-for-performance is a negative for some, for others it is one of the hottest management tools around. It works best in jobs where productivity standards are easily set; for example, so many widgets produced per hour or so many widgets sold per month, year, etc. In a bank, the productivity standards might be the number of new accounts opened or customers serviced in a given time frame.

4. VALTECH, Inc.: How Pay Is Tied to Performance

VALTECH, Inc., a mid-sized high technology organization on the West Coast, has instituted a pay-for-performance program that has increased productivity and cut turnover. The basics of their programs stress:

- a compensation system that rewards productivity and customer service, two issues the company feels are most important
- internal equities that stress equal pay
- pay competitive with local high tech organizations to allow VALTECH to attract and retain the best people
- organized salary administration that utilizes a computerized human resource information system
- open discussions by the supervisors and managers with their employees about VALTECH's compensation and benefits programs. How they work and how the issues of external competitiveness and internal equity are addressed.

VALTECH installed a hotline that employees could use when the new compensation program was instituted so that employees who felt their questions were not answered could call the personnel department and be provided with answers specific to their individual cases.

VALTECH started their pay-for-performance system by identifying performance criteria. At the beginning of the year every manager sits down with each employee and discusses the productivity measure that is to be established for that particular job. That way every employee knows in advance what is expected.

In addition, the following basic compensation practices are in place.

- Job descriptions accurately reflect the duties performed and skills required.
- A workable job evaluation system has been established.
- Local salary surveys and competitive pay practices have been reviewed.
- A determination has been made with regard to methods of measuring employee performance.
- Managers and supervisors are trained to carry out the performance appraisal program.
- Managers pay is tied to performance through VALTECH's Management by Objective (MBO) program.
- Executive pay and bonuses are tied to the company's increase in sales and revenues.

The program has worked well for the last three years, probably because VALTECH pays a great deal of attention to the overall communications process at all levels of the organization.

EXECUTIVE COMPENSATION TRENDS

Compensation for chief executives of American companies is increasing at a rapid rate in spite of the fact that it is slowing for middle managers and lower level professionals. Why is executive compensation rising? There are several reasons, but two seem to stand out as being most significant. First, even though most organizations have compensation committees, it is still the chief executive who has the most input and control over what pay and benefits are provided. Second, there is an abuse of salary surveys in most United States companies. Salary surveys provide a coherent statistical analysis for what could be a rather subjective exercise, but surveys provide a group of averages that most organizations want to exceed. After all, no one wants to be just "average." So, as companies move to get their chief executives at or above average, they are in a race to accelerate executive pay.

How Executive Compensation Works

There has been a great deal of media attention paid to executive compensation in the last few years, much of it critical. Some experts think consultants are largely responsible for the large increases. Consultants provide the surveys and get their client companies' executive compensation on a rapid upward trend, and most compensation consultants are hired at the direction of the CEO. There is a fairly standard operating procedure in most companies for handling executive compensation.

- The process begins with the corporate personnel executive assembling the surveys available from the top consultants in the field. The surveys reflect what other companies in various industries are paying their top executives.

- The personnel executive then reviews the company's performance for that year.

- The personnel executive obtains executive compensation surveys from a variety of compensation consultants; and, after reviewing the surveys and organizations performance, the personnel executive makes a recommendation to the compensation committee or the board of directors. There is usually some input from the CEO.

The obvious issue here, however, is the fact that the personnel executive reports to the chief executive, and this relationship is bound to weigh heavily on the personnel executive's decision. The compensation committee may seek added expertise from an outside consultant, but the consultant is also normally hired by the chief executive, and is indebted to him for business. Directors also have a stake in the decision because they frequently owe their position on the board to the CEO. So there is rarely a totally independent decision on executive compensation.

How U.S. West Telephone Company Ties Key Executives' Pay to Performance

At least one chief executive has decided to "bite the bullet" and hold directors responsible for shareholders' interests in setting executive compensation.

Jack MacAllister, President of U.S. West Telephone Company after the AT&T breakup, was formerly chief of the Northwestern Bell. When the new U.S. West Telephone Company was formed, they needed an entirely new compensation program. MacAllister decided to place the whole compensation issue in the hands of the board of directors.

He did set some guidelines by letting the compensation committee know approximately where he felt the company should be salary-wise in relation to organizations he felt were his competitors for an effective workforce. MacAllister also wanted an incentive plan that would tie bonuses and stock grants to how well the shareholders did with company stock. This is a new slant on pay for performance. Many executives have said they should be reviewed against such performance criteria but few have implemented such a program.

What the compensation committee at U.S. West ended up with is a performance plan that ties compensation directly to stockholders' interests. To be paid a bonus, Mr. MacAllister and sixty-seven other top executives at U.S. West and its subsidiaries must meet a combination of targets for net income, growth in earnings per share, and return on stockholders' equity. U.S. West's long-term incentive plan calls for comparing, over three years, the company's total return to stockholders with the return of companies in two different groups. The first is a group of other regional telephone companies; the second is a collection of corporate giants such as GE, IBM, and 3M.

If more organizations start relating executive pay to stockholders' gain, there will undoubtedly be less criticism in the media about executive pay versus performance being only a "buzz word" with little substance behind it. Corporate executives who pay lip service to the issue of pay for performance have been embarrassed in the past when proxy statements and annual reports reflected poor corporate performance and executives received large pay increases.

The whole issue of executive compensation is a very difficult one to understand. There are so many other elements, like benefits and perks, and so forth, with which to be concerned.

Executive Incentive Arrangements

The average human resource manager or vice president is not an expert in executive compensation or incentive pay and, therefore, relies heavily on consultants to assist with compensation programs. Executive compensation is changing almost as rapidly as the variety of compensation programs being designed to meet the needs of the huge number of organizations doing business in the United States, and internationally. I thought it was important to include more than a passing reference to executive compensation in this book where we discuss new directions in human resource management, so I asked one of the major consulting firms in the compensation field, A. S. Hansen, Inc., to provide a comprehensive review of the more common types of executive compensation programs being used today. I am grateful to Hoyt Doyel, Consulting Principal, with Mercer-Meidinger-Hansen* in Denver, for providing the following indepth report on the subject of executive incentive pay.

A majority of U.S. firms provide incentives for their executives. In fact most firms have several incentive arrangements including a short-term bonus plan and several stock arrangements. There are key decisions that have to be made in the design of an incentive plan. Following is a list of primary design considerations:

Primary Design Considerations

1. *Purpose*—The starting point in designing an incentive plan is to determine why an incentive arrangement might be appropriate. Purposes range from a basic need to allow payroll to expand or contract based on the company's varying ability to pay . . . to trying to motivate certain specific behaviors (such as employee retention or improving sales). The more clearly the organization understands the plan's purpose, the more carefully the plan can be tailored. It is important to realize however, that while a plan can be designed to meet a specific purpose, you don't want to accidentally motivate other behaviors (for instance, a plan to stimulate profit may accidentally discourage maintenance).

2. *Eligibility*—In defining the group of participants, selection should be made considering the role each plays within the organization. If the plan has a narrow purpose, affecting only one department or division, participation should also be limited. You may need plans for different participant groups. In general, only managers who can have a substantial impact on productivity or profits are included, but competitive pressures or team building considerations may warrant a broader group.

---

* Report provided by A. S. Hansen, Inc., Denver, CO.

3. *Performance Measure*—Typically, the "pool" of money available for payment to participants will be determined based on specific measures of performance. Plans frequently consider such items as net profits, return on stockholder equity market share, attainment of budget, and so forth. These measures usually are tied to a formula that determines (1) whether a pool will exist and (2) the size of the total pool available for payments. For stock based plans, the most frequent measure is the fair market value of the stock, although many variations do exist that consider other measures as well.

4. *Time Frame*—Should the plan relate to performance for a quarter, one year, three years, five years or more? Shorter time frames are generally more popular for cash plans as they are frequently planning sensitive. Stock plans tend to cover ten-year periods.

5. *Incentive Opportunity*—The incentive amounts should be large enough to focus the attention of participants on the achievement of the plan's objectives, but not so large that payment exceeds reasonable compensation levels. Most cash-based executive incentive plans are "capped," providing a ceiling of forty to eighty percent of pay for top executives, while most stock-based plans provide unlimited upside potential. Competitive practices and stockholder safeguards are the primary benchmarks for determining minimum, target, and maximum incentive payments. You should be careful to consider "ripple" effects of plans . . . where incentive payments might affect other benefits such as retirement or insurance.

   You should also consider the ability of various participants to handle variations in their pay level. A large bonus is easy to handle, however the lack of a bonus after having had payments for several years in a row may create financial problems for an executive. For this reason, incentive awards are generally limited for employees with salaries less than $40,000 to $50,000 a year and are scaled upwards as a percent of pay for higher paid employees.

6. *Individual Award Determination*—One of the toughest design issues is how to treat individual participants. Typically the size of the incentive award is scaled to the pay or salary level of each participant. Significant leverage can be attained, however, if the plan can consider individual performance in the determination of the awards. Many companies provide for a fixed percentage (for example, fifty percent) of the pool to be awarded based on participant organization rank or salary with the remainder allocated based on personal achievement of objectives. This allows both team membership and individual contributions to be recognized.

7. *Administration and Communication*—The plan must be clear and straightforward enough to allow participants to understand it if it is to succeed. Similarly it should not create an administrative nightmare. Obviously, all legal and accounting issues must comply with the appropriate rules and regulations.

Cash Incentive Programs

Experience indicates that it is easiest to understand the variations in cash incentive arrangements when you consider the creation of the incentive pool and the distribution of the pool as separate steps. The following diagram illustrates the primary plan types and their major features.

Representative Incentive Levels		
Employee	Base Salary Level	Normal Incentive Range
A	$ 25,000	5–20%
B	50,000	10–40%
C	75,000	15–45%
D	100,000	15–50%
E	150,000	20–60%
F	200,000	25–70%
G	300,000	30–75%

1. *Creating the Pool Judgmental Arrangements.* Most companies desire a formula that will delete the annual "day of reckoning" when the board or top management must determine the pool size. However, the most common approach in United States firms is the discretionary incentive as it provides maximum flexibility in considering compensation and individual performance in light of all external factors.

   A relatively rare variation of the discretionary plan allows either fixed formulas or objectives-based methods to be used, but the board selects among three payout scales based on its views of the environment during the year. For instance, an "A" rating would indicate that the results occurred in a much tougher market than normal, while a "C" rating would indicate that the market was more favorable than normal. Incentive payments would be scaled accordingly with the same performance resulting in (for example) a fifty percent higher bonus in an "A" year than in a "C" year.

   Fixed Formulas. A variety of fixed formula approaches are used by companies. Frequently, formulas indicate a threshold below which no incentive pool is created (for example, net profit must equal at least five percent of assets). Beyond the threshold, the formula may indicate the size of the pool either as a function of the measure (for example, one percent of pretax profits is reserved for bonuses) or as a factor in determining incentive levels (for example, minimum bonus levels are established at a five percent R.O.I. with maximum bonus levels established at fifteen percent R.O.I., where bonus levels equal a predetermined percent of participant salaries).

Formulas may relate to either absolute performance levels, performance as measured against prior periods, or performance as measured against a peer group of competitors where published data is available on a regular basis.

Fixed formulas work well in established industries with known standards of performance, where the key statistical measures of success can be reduced to one or two numbers. The peer comparison technique allows it to be extended to industries that are subject to broad cyclical variations.

Objective Based. In organizations with established planning processes and credible methods of assessing the reasonableness of the target budgets, many firms use their operating or financial budgets as a basis for determining pool size. This approach is especially valuable in determining pool size for units such as maintenance or production that represent only part of the organization.

2. *Distributing the Pool* Timing dictates the two primary choices in distributing the pool. *At the beginning* of the time period, the pool can be allocated by (1) indicating that the pool will be distributed based on each participant's grade level, salary, or service relative to the entire group, or (2) allocating "units" to each participant that will each equal a final percent of the fixed pool.

   At the end of the time period, the pool may be allocated considering events that occurred during the time period, such as the relative performance of divisions or participants. Discretionary arrangements typically attempt to consider performance during the year, but allocate bonuses without the use of a formula.

3. *Normal Incentive Levels* While significant variations exist based on industry category and the philosophy of individual firms, the following table represents the normal range of incentive targets, assuming that company unit and individual peformance are high enough to warrant paying incentives.

Stock-Based Incentive Programs

Executive Stock Programs are incentive arrangements that are designed to align the interest of the executive with stockholders by creating a situation in

PRIMARY METHODS OF CREATING AND DISTRIBUTING
THE MANAGEMENT INCENTIVE POOL

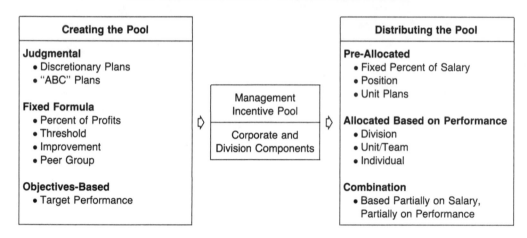

Creating the Pool		Distributing the Pool
Judgmental • Discretionary Plans • "ABC" Plans **Fixed Formula** • Percent of Profits • Threshold • Improvement • Peer Group **Objectives-Based** • Target Performance	Management Incentive Pool Corporate and Division Components	**Pre-Allocated** • Fixed Percent of Salary • Position • Unit Plans **Allocated Based on Performance** • Division • Unit/Team • Individual **Combination** • Based Partially on Salary, Partially on Performance

which the executive either acquires stock or receives an incentive based on growth in the value of the stock.

Because stock programs normally involve a formal security and have traditionally involved the favored tax status of long-term capital gains, they are typically subject to more regulations and limitations imposed by the SEC, the IRS, public stock exchanges, and numerous state and industry regulations. Stock programs typically require legal document approval by the stockholders that specify the number of shares for the plan's operation as well as the details of the plan's provisions. Professionally managed firms also normally adopt a procedure outlining grant frequency and levels for various types of participants.

For these reasons, the following section focuses on the general features of the primary types of stock programs. Professional consulting and legal and accounting assistance should be obtained in designing a stock program. You should also remember that while the 1986 Tax Law has changed the capital gains tax rates so that they will equal ordinary income tax rates, "capital gains" will continue to exist for determining alternate minimum taxes as well as for distinguishing income for corporate deduction purposes. You should also be alert to the fact that at the time this is being written, the Financial Accounting Standards Board (FASB) is considering accounting changes that may result in a charge to earnings for stock option plans.

1. *Nonqualified Stock Options*
   As the "work horse" of executive stock programs, the non qualified option provides the maximum flexibility. The basic features are:

- Company grants executive or board members stock at present market price with specified date by which stock must be acquired.
- At the time the option is exercised, the executive pays the option cost to the company and ordinary income tax to the IRS and the company receives a compensation deduction for the amount of ordinary income recognized by the executive, but has no charge to earnings.
- When executives sell the stock, they may qualify for long-term capital gains depending on the length of time since exercise.

2. *Incentive Stock Options (ISOs)*
   While much more restrictive, the ISO allows the executive to postpone taxes. Much of the ISO's advantage was eliminated by the 1986 Tax Law which removed the discount for capital gains taxes. (In fact, due to the alternate minimum taxes, the ISO may result in taxes greater than the normal ordinary tax rates which apply to nonqualified options.)
   The features are:

   - company grants executive stock options at the current market price for a period of time not to exceed ten years of which only $100,000 may become exercisable in any one year.
   - at the time the executive sells the stock (not earlier than one year after exercise or two years after grant) the executive receives long-term capital gains for any appreciation since the grant date

3. *Discounted Nonqualified Options*
   In this plan, the executive receives a nonqualified option at a price less than the current market value of the stock. The tax treatment is identical to the Nonqualified Option except that the company incurs a charge to earnings for the amount of the discount spread over the period of the option. This form of option provides some value to the option holder (and holding power for the company) even when the stock value is slightly depressed.

4. *Restricted Stock Grants*
   Restricted grants are virtually identical to Discounted Nonqualified Options where the grant price equals zero. Normally, however, the executive is given ownership of the shares at the time of the grant with a margin restriction indicating that if the conditions of the grant (normally three to five years of service) are not met, the stock reverts

to company ownership. The executive may pay taxes either at the time of grant (nonrecoverable if the stock is forfeited) or at the time the restrictions lapse. This timing option is referred to as the 83(b) election and is established by IRS Code Section 83(b) and is also available for other property transfer tax situations.

The restricted stock grant is particularly valuable to the company in recruiting new executives who forfeit value in plans at their prior firm, as it has value even when the stock declines and is perceived as a low risk compensation form to both the company and the executive. It also is tax effective to the company as the tax deduction exceeds the charge to earnings if the only restrictions relate to length of service.

5. *Performance Share/Unit Plans*
   Performance Share Plans are long-term bonuses where the employee receives a bonus equal to the market value of a specified number of shares at the end of a time period (typically three to five years). Normally the number of shares will vest based on either corporate or division performance during the time period (for example, if all objectives are met, the 100 percent of shares vest, if only 70 percent of objectives are met then 0 percent of shares vest with amounts prorated between these levels). The accounting for this type plan is the same as for any long-term bonus plan, with a charge to earnings anticipated each year during the program.

6. *Stock Appreciation Rights (SAR)*
   An SAR is a bonus program where the executive is given a right to demand a bonus equal to the appreciation of the stock for a specified number of shares from the date of grant for a specified time frame. Frequently, an SAR is coupled with a stock option (in which case it is called a tandem option right) and the executive is provided a choice of exercising either the stock option or the SAR.

   Although the SAR is treated like a long-term bonus for tax and accounting purposes, SARs have proven to be highly valued by executives as they require no financial outlay. They have also proven to be very expensive to companies who must charge earning for significant amounts of appreciation, yet who do not receive a corresponding deduction until the SAR is exercised.

7. *Umbrella Plans*
   A growing number of companies are developing the strategy of adopting several types of stock arrangements within one plan. Frequently combinations include:

- Incentive Stock Options to provide maximum tax deferred gains to executives,

- Nonqualified Options to overcome $100,000 annual ISO limitations and provide options that are more cost efficient for the company,

- Restricted Stock Grants to provide an enticement in recruiting new high level executives or to provide stock value even in a declining stock market, and

- Stock Appreciation Rights to provide incentives to top executives with limited cash raising ability due to insider trading restrictions.

- The very existence of umbrella plans serves to highlight the need to efficiently design stock programs to meet certain objectives.

DEFERRED COMPENSATION: HOW EXECUTIVES MIGHT DELAY TAXATION

Probably the hottest item in executive compensation circles is deferred compensation. Because human resource managers tend not to be the experts in this field, I asked Hoyt Doyel of A. S. Hansen to once again provide us with some current thinking on deferred compensation.

> The deferral of compensation by an executive on a nonqualified basis (i.e., outside of a tax qualified plan) is virtually always for the purpose of delaying taxation. Deferral is most likely to occur when the executive is in a high tax bracket currently and anticipates being in a lower tax bracket when the deferred income is eventually received, (perhaps at retirement).

The 1986 Tax Law results in a situation in which many executives will not be in a lower tax bracket at retirement. Accordingly, the power of deferral for many executives will depend on the leverage of receiving interest or earnings on pretax amounts over the deferral period.

Who Should Consider Income Deferral

Only a few categories of executives should consider income deferral. The primary group where income deferral may be appropriate includes executives within eight to twelve years of retirement who can be reasonably sure of receiving favorable earnings rates over the deferral period.

The next group of executives might include those in a high tax bracket that anticipate tax law changes that will significantly reduce the top rates in a year or two. While this is a riskier assumption, some executives may feel that the probability is great enough to warrant the manuever. However, most executives believe that the low tax rates created by the 1986 Tax Law will probably be raised rather than lowered. Deferring income from 1987 to 1988 may still be beneficial for many executives. In either case, the executive should:

1. seek to assure that the risk of forfeiture is low but still present. (You may want to investigate "Rabbi Trusts" discussed later in this chapter.)

2. try to obtain some form of interest during the deferral period (for example, the deferral is equivalent to a loan to the company)

3. be sure the deferral is absolute for tax purposes (if the IRS determines that the income was deferred after the executive had constructive receipt then it may tax the amount even though the executive does not have current access to the funds—definitely an undesirable event)

4. schedule the future payments so that they yield maximum future after-tax value (for instance, a lump sum paid at a November retirement may not yield lower tax rates, while a lump sum paid the following January 1 or in five annual payments may provide tax savings)

5. be sure that foregone benefits from other company benefit plans or social security don't exceed the value of the tax savings

Supplemental Executive Retirement Plans

The other situation in which nonqualified income deferrals may be appropriate is when the company is willing to provide a deferred pay arrangement to fund a deficiency in the executive's retirement program. Such deficiencies are frequently due to either:

1. the executive's pay and qualified retirement plan exceeding the maximum legal limit stipulated by ERISA for qualified plans and therefore being limited below the replacement rates provided for their employees, or

2. the executive's being hired by the company so late in his career that the qualified retirement plan will fail to generate a significant retirement amount.

In either of these cases, many firms provide company paid income deferral arrangements to provide supplemental retirement benefits to the executives. These supplemental arrangements are typically subject to the reporting and disclosure requirements imposed by ERISA. As with other nonqualified income deferral arrangements, the deferred amount should be charged to earnings over the years in which it is earned, although the tax deduction is not available to the company until the amount is paid to the executive.

When human resources managers discuss deferred compensation with executives today, it is important for them to know the basic tax consequences of deferred compensation agreements including the so-called "rabbi trust." The Denver Managing Partner of Reinhart, Boerner, Van Deuren, Norris and Rieselback, Mary A. Brauer, provides the following overview of the rabbi trust.

Basic Features of a Rabbi Trust

The term "rabbi trust" is used broadly to describe the use of a trust to hold assets intended for future payments to eligible employees of the employer who establishes the trust. The payments held in a rabbi trust are typically compensation that the employee has earned but chosen to defer to a later year. The rabbi trust is also often used for supplemental retirement benefits that the employer wants to pay to executive employees, and, in some cases, it is used for "parachute" payments to an executive upon change in the employer's corporate ownership. In each case, the use of a trust is intended to provide the employee stronger assurances that the promised future payments will be made.

The rabbi trust is considered a "nonqualified" deferred compensation arrangement because the trust does not qualify for tax exempt status under Internal Revenue Code sections 401 and 501. To avoid current taxation of the trust corpus and income to the individual to whom the rabbi trust will make future payments, the rabbi trust must satisfy two tests formulated by the IRS and the courts: the "constructive receipt" and "economic benefit" doctrines.

IRS and court rulings on constructive receipt of deferred compensation indicate that, as a general rule, deferred compensation is not currently taxable if: (i) the taxpayer agrees to the deferral before the start of the tax year in which the compensation will be earned (or after the start of the year but before the amount of the deferral is known, in limited cases such as an undetermined year-end bonus); and (ii) the deferred amount is not set apart so that the taxpayer may draw upon it at any time or so that the taxpayer may draw upon it during the tax year after notice of intent to withdraw. Income is not constructively received if the taxpayer's control of its receipt is subject to substantial limitations or restrictions. The second test, the "economic benefit" doctrine, provides for immediate taxation of a deferred amount if the amount is irrevocably placed with a third party or otherwise set aside, thus creating a "fund," and if the taxpayer's interest in the fund is nonforfeitable. Under this rule, a specified amount that is irrevocably set aside for future receipt is taxable as a current economic benefit unless it is subject to a significant risk of loss.

The constructive receipt and economic benefit rules create a dilemma for the taxpayer who wants to defer income but needs certainty that the deferred amounts will be paid on a future date. These rules require that the taxpayer clearly give up any current right to collect the deferred amounts and leave the taxpayer without absolute assurance of future payment. The rabbi's response to this dilemma was to establish a trust in an attempt to better assure that the promised amounts would be paid to him. The trust held assets that the congregation agreed to pay the rabbi's upon his death, disability, retirement or termination of service. The trust paid the rabbi quarterly installments of income earned on the trust corpus, but did not allow the rabbi to assign, alienate or encumber the trust assets. The IRS ruled (PLR 8113107, December 31, 1980) that the rabbi's interest in the trust was not taxable to him until he actually received payment. The IRS reasoned that the trust did not create taxable income for the rabbi because the assets of the trust were subject to the claims of the creditors of the congregation and the rabbi's access to the funds was sufficiently restricted until he actually received trust payments.

The IRS provided a detailed statement of the rationale for its rabbi trust rulings in GCM 39230 (January 20, 1984), emphasizing that the assets in the rabbi trust must be subject to claims of the employer's creditors. The importance of creditors' access to rabbi trust assets was also confirmed in a recent case, *Minor v. U.S.*, 772 F.2d 1472 (9th Cir. 1985). The court acknowledged that its decision "severely stretches the limits of a non-qualified deferred compensation plan" because the rabbi trust assets were so closely controlled by the employees to whom they would be paid. (The employees were also trustees of the rabbi trust and the likelihood of diversion of the trust assets to creditors appeared to be minimal.) Nonetheless, the court concluded that the accessibility of the trust assets to creditors of the employer precluded the IRS from taxing the employees on the value of the trust assets.

Reasons for Increased Interest in Rabbi Trusts

The rabbi trust has attracted considerable attention as the popularity of nonqualified deferred compensation has grown, because the rabbi trust is, in the employee's view, often an improvement over deferred compensation arrangements that do not use a trust. The growing popularity of nonqualified deferred compensation is chiefly due to three advantages of nonqualified over tax qualified retirement plans: the nonqualified arrangement may discriminate in favor of officers, shareholders and highly compensated employees; it may provide for contributions and benefits in excess of those permitted for a qualified plan; and it is less costly to maintain than a qualified plan because of the minimal requirements for ongoing compliance with federal law. Beginning with the passage of ERISA in 1974, changes in tax laws have steadily increased the significance of these differences between qualified and nonqualified plans. The nonqualified plan is often the only way to target extra retirement benefits to executives. Nonqualified plans are also especially useful in times when key executives frequently change jobs, as during the recent spate of corporate mergers and acquisitions. A nonqualified agreement may supplement a transferred executive's pension to the extent necessary to provide the pension benefit the executive would have received if all of his past service were with his new employer. In addition, nonqualified retirement or termination benefits often are a part of a "parachute" compensation package, designed to protect executives in unfriendly corporate take-overs.

The attractions of nonqualified plans must be weighed against their disadvantages, which are: (a) less favorable tax treatment, particularly the current taxation of rabbi trust income to the employer and the delay of an employer deduction until benefits are taxable to the employee; and (b) less assurance to the employee that promised benefits will be paid when due. A nonqualified plan does not carry all of the protections that the IRS, Department of Labor and Pension Benefit Guaranty Corporation offer to qualified plan participants. The rabbi trust is a small, but often psychologically important, step toward assuring the employee that the promised benefits have not merely been noted in the company's books but have, in fact, been set aside in a trust that is physically separate from the employer's general assets.

Practical Considerations in Designing a Rabbi Trust

In those situations where an employer and employee agree that a rabbi trust is appropriate, a number of decisions must be made in drafting the rabbi trust agreement. The following paragraphs list some of the relevant issues (many of which are also important to the design of a nonqualified deferred compensation agreement that does not use a rabbi trust).

1. *Eligibility.* The rabbi trust should be designed to avoid application of most ERISA requirements. To achieve this goal, the rabbi trust must generally limit eligibility to "a select group of management or highly compensated employees." These terms have not been clearly defined in cases or regulations, so care must be taken to limit participation to employees who undoubtedly fall into a "management" or "highly compensated" category.

2. *Timing of Deferral Election.* If the rabbi trust is part of a deferred compensation plan that allows the employee to elect, from year to year, how much compensation to defer, care must be taken to assure that the deferral election will pass IRS standards for avoiding constructive receipt of the deferred amount. The IRS requires that an election to defer income be made before the start of the period of service for which the compensation is earned and, with limited exceptions, must be irrevocable during

that period. The election may, in some cases, be made after the employee begins to earn the compensation, but then only if the amount being deferred is unknown when the election occurs.

3. *Events Triggering Distribution.* The rabbi trust must not allow employees access to deferred amounts at their whim. The trust may provide that employees receive payments at specified times such as retirement or termination of employment. To avoid constructive receipt, payment in other circumstances should be severely limited, e.g., to clear cases of extreme financial hardship.

4. *Contribution Limits.* Although the nonqualified trust will not be subject to Internal Revenue Code limitations on contributions, the employer may want to limit the amount or percentage of compensation that an employee may defer. Because the deferrals may grow to potentially significant future liabilities for the employer, they should not be unlimited.

5. *Interest Assumption.* The trust should specify an interest rate, or a method to calculate an interest rate, that will apply to the deferred amounts until pay-out. The rate should be high enough to assure the employee that the deferral is worthwhile, but should not create inordinate costs for the employer.

6. *Nonalienation Clause.* An important requirement of the rabbi trust rulings is that the trust not be subject to assignment, alienation, pledge, attachment or claims of the creditors of the employee or his beneficiaries. These prohibitions should appear in the trust agreement.

7. *Social Security Taxes.* An employee's benefits under a nonqualified deferred compensation agreement will be subject to Social Security (FICA and FUTA) taxes at the later of the time the employee performs the services for which the compensation is payable or when "there is no substantial risk of forfeiture" of the employee's right to the deferred amount. (Internal Revenue Code sections 3121(v) (2) and 3306(r) (2).) If carefully designed and administered, a rabbi trust may pay benefits that are not subject to FICA or FUTA taxes. This may be accomplished by making sure that the employee completes all necessary services and earns a vested right to the benefits in a year for which the employee's compensation will already exceed the Social Security wage base. By subjecting the rabbi trust to FICA and FUTA taxes in such a year, no FICA or FUTA tax will be owed on the rabbi trust assets when paid to the employee.

8. *Availability of Trust Assets to Creditor's Claims.* The IRS rulings on rabbi trusts consistently require that the rabbi trust assets be subject to the claims of the employer's creditors. Two IRS

rulings liberalize that requirement slightly by approving rabbi trusts subject to claims of "judgment creditors", thus apparently exempting the trusts from creditors' claims for which there is no court judgment. (PLR 8325100, March 23, 1983 and PLR 8439012, June 22, 1984.) The temptation to limit creditors' access to rabbi trust assets will inevitably come up in the preparation of a rabbi trust agreement. The more restrictions placed on creditors' rights, the more real security the trust provides to the employee. Yet this is a dangerous area in which to experiment, because efforts to protect the employee's benefits from the employer's creditors may only destroy the employee's protection from immediate taxation. Further, protections from creditors may destroy the rabbi trust's exemption from many complex and administratively burdensome ERISA requirements. In order to qualify for exemption from ERISA participation, vesting, funding and fiduciary requirements, the rabbi trust must be "unfunded." On December 13, 1985 the Department of Labor (the agency responsible for interpreting these ERISA rules) sent the IRS a letter indicating that it will determine whether a rabbi trust is "funded" according to the same standards the IRS applies to determine if the rabbi trust assets are taxable to the employee. (Letter written by E. Daniel, DOL Assistant Administrator for Regulations and Interpretations.) The need for accessibility to the rabbi trust assets by the employer's creditors is, therefore, important for both tax and ERISA purposes.

9. *Alternative Approaches to Securing Deferred Compensation.* The rabbi trust is not the only method by which an employer may differentiate assets held for future payments of nonqualified deferred compensation from the employer's general assets. The IRS has also approved the use of life insurance (PLR 8607031, November 15, 1985), bank escrow accounts (PLR 8418105, January 31, 1984) and surety bonds (PLR 8406012, November 3, 1983) to secure payment of nonqualified deferred compensation. To avoid current taxation to the employee, these rulings also require that the life insurance and escrow accounts be accessible to the employer's creditors. In addition, the IRS ruling on use of a surety bond requires that the employer not pay for or reimburse the bond costs.

10. *ERISA Reporting Requirements.* ERISA requires a one-time filing with the Department of Labor by an employer who maintains an "unfunded or insured pension plan for a select group of management or highly compensated employees." (29 C.F.R. section 2520.104-23.) An employer who establishes a rabbi trust for deferred compensation or supplemental retirement pay-

ments should file the required statement with the Department of Labor. Compliance with this filing requirement may help substantiate the employer's position that the rabbi trust is "unfunded" for tax and ERISA purposes.

Conclusion

The rabbi trust is an important financial planning alternative to consider for management and highly compensated employees who seek advice on arrangements to defer compensation, to supplement retirement benefits or to provide "parachute" payments upon change in corporate ownership.

HOW TO EVALUATE YOUR COMPENSATION PROGRAM

Every human resource director wants a compensation program that is as effective overall as it can be. But, until you determine what your program objectives are and what they should be to make your organization successful, you don't even know if you are on target. The best way to find out if your program is effective is to take stock of where you are now. A compensation audit is the best way to do this.

Six Elements to Consider When Evaluating Your Company's Program

1. Review changing conditions outside your company. Look at competitors and what they are paying and review overall compensation and benefit programs of other organizations. Do employees feel they are being paid competitively in relation to other companies?

2. Look at internal equity in all job classifications. If employees in similar jobs are being paid at vastly different rates, you could have a problem.

3. Review turnover. If you are having a high turnover in certain job classifications, you may need to look at pay for those positions. If it also takes longer today than it did a year ago to fill positions, pay could be the reason.

4. Is your compensation plan adequately communicated to all employees? Do you have a communication program in place for doing that?

5. Are employees happy and productive? You can measure productivity of most workers and this is just one way to ascertain whether or not employees are happy with their work and are as productive as they can be.

6. Have you established career ladders to allow you to move people up in the organization as they mature and gain experience? If you don't know about career ladders, review my book *The Human Resource*

Directors Handbook, Prentice-Hall, Inc., 1984 for a good explanation and ways to implement career ladders.

Most human resource managers and executives have some experience auditing compensation, but every company has a different set of guidelines to follow. It is important to understand how people and compensation needs change and to review your programs frequently to ensure they are still doing the job they were designed to do.

In addition, pay systems should not be set in concrete. If they are not doing the job for you, quickly identify the problems and change the system. Frequently monitor and test the waters regarding established policies. Take a fresh look at value systems and what employees find meaningful.

Many so-called merit systems reward poor and mediocre performers better than the best workers. Good performers wind up with smaller raises because the system puts them at the top of their range. Don't get caught in this trap. An effective compensation program pays employees for their contributions to company goals, not just for the activities of their jobs; and pay ranges must be reviewed and changed yearly.

Compensation Program Evaluation Checklist

If you have not performed a thorough audit of compensation before, here is a fairly standard procedure to use and some additional tips on completing the project so that the information obtained will be most relevant to your actual compensation picture.

Company Policy

Answer the following questions.

- Who are your competitors and what will your competitive posture be? What is your current position?

- What is your company's preferred mix of pay? How does base salary compare with bonuses, benefits, and other components? If your salaries appear to be "low," it may be because your fringe benefits package is so expensive. In many companies, benefits are costing thirty-seven percent to forty percent of payroll and management cannot afford to increase base pay and still provide benefits.

- How could you better relate salary to individual effort and good performance? Can you set performance standards in most jobs, and then relate pay incentives to productivity gains?

- What emphasis should you give to performance rather than seniority or COLA? Most companies are putting far more emphasis on productivity and in many cases have eliminated COLAs altogether.

- Do you pay attention to practices of your industry? Should the same policies apply to all locations? If your company has been involved in mergers and acquisitions, your overall policies probably need a critical review. Check with human resource directors in similar organizations and with your industry associations to ensure your practices are competitive but not overly generous.

- Do you need a change in the policy itself, or do you just need to modify the mechanics to update a policy that is basically sound? By reviewing your policies on a regular basis, you may find policies that cost you money could be eliminated as times change.

- Review your relocation and transfer practices. Consider the real necessity of assignments to high cost living either in the United States or overseas if you have international operations.

- Overseas employees policies need review. Some companies are now changing policies that were set up for United States expatriates, in favor of using local nationals whenever possible to eliminate the high cost of relocation of American employees.

Job Description

- Are there current job descriptions for every job? Job descriptions should be revised as jobs change.

- Do descriptions support job evaluations, provide guides for selection and recruiting, meet EEO and other legal requirements? Do they stress job content?

- Who writes your job descriptions? Is the person trained? Do you know what the job really entails?

- Are descriptions reviewed by higher management?

- Do you have a regular updating schedule so that if the job is split or downsized the job descriptions and job evaluations are revised?

Job Evaluation

- Are the JE factors appropriate to the tests to which your program is likely to be subjected?

- Are factors defined sufficiently and have you looked at relationships?

- Are evaluaters trained and knowledgeable? Watch out for a "down bias" in ratings of jobs that are held by minorities and women.

- Do employees have an appeal mechanism if they don't agree with the evaluation? Most employee handbooks provide an employee complaint procedure. Be sure you have one.

- What does it cost to administer? Some plans are so complex that there are unreasonable costs to administer the plans. If your costs are too complex, review and simplify them to cut costs of administration. If you don't have time to do it, hire a consultant to assist you with the project.

- Is your plan market-oriented or job/content-oriented? Can you defend a market-based approach? Job evaluation plans that are market-oriented have been ruled in some courts to be discriminatory against women. It is best to use a specific job-content-oriented evaluation program to avoid charges of sex or pay discrimination.

Salary Structure

- Check compa-ratios: Where are the majority of your jobs placed within your salary ranges? Are compa-ratios very low or very high? Extremes can be a danger signal. Compute compa-ratio by dividing employees current salary by the salary midpoint. A compa-ratio of 80% places employees at minimum of the salary range, 100% at midpoint, and 120% at maximum of range.

- Check internal relationships. Watch for signs of compression. Particularly watch where this problem is arising—in hourly operations or in professional categories?

- Has the plan been kept up to date with the minimum wage and wage hour regulations?

- Do you review geographic and industry differentials regularly to ensure the plan is competitive?

- Do you pay shift differentials? Are they competitive in your industry?

- Are survey sources still relevant? Periodically review and evaluate sources. If you feel survey data are weak, consider starting a new survey group to compare relevant data.

- Check communications: How much do you tell employees about the plan, and how good a job do you do? Do you get feedback from employees on your plan?

Policies

- Check written policies on hiring, promotion, transfers. Do the same rules apply to individuals in all departments?

- How good are merit guide rules? Have they flattened out so that, in effect, most people are getting "average" raises, thus turning your "merit" program into a longevity system?

- What basis are you using for making these individual determinations: Merit? Performance? Cost of living? A combination? What proportion of the raise is allocable to each factor?

- Measure whether your program is in fact doing what your policy says: Do this by going back to increases that were given and see how they check out against the employees' performance. Can you defend your choices?

- If your system is truly performance-related, do you follow through to check performance ratings?

- What is your timing for giving raises: Annual, Semiannual? Is this policy working well?

- When individuals are promoted, are promotional raises substantial enough to reward them for the extra effort and responsibility?

- Do promotional raises get all the employees into the range of the new job? Check to see that women employees are treated the same as males in promotional increase percentages. In some companies women always fall below the range after a promotion and men always fall above. This should not be allowed to happen.

Different rules may be needed for overseas-based employees if you are competing with pay policies in other nations. Many countries have a tradition of giving everyone a raise on the same date. In areas of high inflation, it is necessary to give raises more frequently than you would in the United States.

Do you periodically check policies and philosophical objectives with top management to be sure your practices and procedures are on target?

Performance Appraisal

- Have performance standards been established in advance and communicated to the employees?

- Are appraisals conducted by persons who are knowledgeable and trained? Do the raters have written guides, so they know for what they are supposed to be looking?

- Have appraisal forms been carefully reviewed? Revise forms every few years to keep them up-to-date with current human resource practices.

- Do you regularly check performance reviews to determine that they are bias-free with respect to employees' age, sex, race, length of service, and so forth—both in the same jobs and company wide?

- Do employees have access to a formal appeal procedure? Any appeal procedure should have at least three appeal steps ending with the highest local authority (vice-president, president, etc.).

Administrative Procedures

- Do you have a written salary policy?
- Have you communicated to supervisors and employees what is expected of them on the job?
- Does your policy fully comply with applicable laws and regulations?

What works in other companies will not necessarily work for your organization. Not many companies have been built successfully by copying what others do in salary management. Give your pay system a competitive edge by tailoring it to the career needs of your employees as well as company strategies and objectives. Add some innovative and distinctive elements and encourage employees to achieve their career goals while working to assist the company in achieving profit objectives.

It is important to take random samplings periodically to see whether your system is working. See if performance is reflected in merit increases and promotions. See if the company is as productive as it can be and that you have done everything you can to tie corporate and employee objectives together.

Three Areas to Push for Better Cost Control

How can we control human resources costs in the future? There are three specific areas where we can make real progress, where we can tie HR costs to the productivity of the organization. They are:

- workforce control
- salary planning
- benefit cost control

Understand from the start that cost control does not always equate to cost minimization. We all know, in purchasing capital equipment, consumer goods, or employee services, the cheapest is not necessarily the best value.

What we must learn to focus on is the value we receive from these massive expenditures. To that end, we must use the analytic tools and processes we apply to other investments. For instance, although it makes sense to cut costs when business slows, the real question such actions raise concerns long-range planning. How are these cost-cutting decisions made? What are the long- and short-term benefits of various actions? How will they affect competitive positions? Why have some staffs been allowed to grow to unwieldy levels?

The overriding question is: How can companies develop an appropriate strategy to optimize human resources costs? Without an ongoing strategy, important decisions become ad hoc, reactive, and all too often, in the long run, more damaging than helpful.

How to Identify and Measure Human Resources Costs

Aside from the most obvious human resource costs like compensation and benefits, there are many other costs that have to be measured and reviewed when a company wants to pare down HR expenditures. Look at how the company is organized . . . the number of levels of management, the number and cost of HR policies and practices, the timing of a layoff, and the next expected upturn in your business.

The key is to establish an ongoing monitoring process to track costs over a period of time and not simply say "now is the time to cut costs" and restructure without a thorough review of the overall HR function. Most organizations look at these organizational effectiveness issues to ensure:

- the organization structure is lean and there are not too many levels of management

- policies and practices are consistent with corporate strategy and in keeping with the organization's strategic plans

- policies are cost-effective and are not too bureaucratic

- the company's competitive position is enhanced by its human resources policies and the organization structure

- management understands salary and benefit costs and only implements cost reduction programs and layoffs when they are needed, and then only with as little impairment as possible to the culture and environment

- management provides ongoing training and development programs to ensure employees are as knowledgeable and productive as they can be

- management communicates up and down . . . at all levels of the organization openly and candidly and encourages two-way communications processes.

Three Case Examples of Cost Analysis

With the right methods, companies can understand HR costs and control them in a rational way.

Case one: A manufacturing organization competes with other companies in three related aspects of its business:

1. raw material production,

2. processing, and

3. end product manufacturing.

The company competes against large organizations. It tends to have a large staff, hierarchical structure, generous benefits, plant locations in major cities, and rather high compensation practices.

In the bulk processing of the product, however, the company also competes with small, owner-operated processors who have small staffs, minimal benefits, and flat organizations. Recognizing this, the company wanted to know what specific human resources practices were costing, expressed in dollars-per-pound of production, and how these costs compared to the competition. Analysis showed that many practices were preventing the company from becoming a low-cost producer and raised questions about its efficiency. For example, should the company continue to have relatively uniform compensation and benefits policies for all of its businesses? Further, should there be a vice-president level, let alone large and powerful staff functions? Should pay and benefits be as high as they are? The information about the effect of these practices lead the company to confront all the issues.

Case two: A company was concerned about the number of service and maintenance personnel in a cable TV operation. Analysis showed that the company had fewer such people-per-thousand installed bases than its competitors. The investigation also indicated that, increasingly, the competitive edge in this industry would be based on demonstrated ability to provide service. Consequently, the client established a plan to charge a greater proportion of its HR costs to the service and maintenance staff.

Case three: How can you best conduct a comprehensive analysis of human resource costs? And how can this analysis lead to management action? The key here is to focus on the organization: its size, its composition, and the costs associated with its workforce. You must ask and answer difficult questions: How many management layers are needed? Where should staff be placed? How much staff? How efficient is its operation? For example, an oil company asked us to determine the human resources cost competitiveness of all its staff functions, including the costs of purchasing outside services. The goal was to help begin a planning process that would make staff functions more productive.

Analysis focused on the functions performed in the corporate and two major business areas of the company. This helped the company measure its overall human resource cost competitiveness. Further, it provided insight into the causes of the noncompetitiveness that was found. Causes such as problems associated with the number of employees, the mix of employees, the average cost-per-employee, and the organization of specific functions.

The company's total annual staff costs were higher than for its peer companies; the systems function, in particular, was noncompetitive. Taking into consideration the use of outside consultants, only the accounting function showed lower costs than in the peer companies. The company explored whether the centralization of the system's function had any impact on its costs. In the sample, two companies had totally centralized the systems function, only one had a totally decentralized function, and three companies were somewhere in the middle. Although analysis indicated that the company might be able to reduce costs by centralizing some of its systems functions, this was certainly not the whole answer.

The company looked at the mix of employees and discovered that the organization compensated staff positions slightly lower than its competitors. However, the problem was not compensation, it was the number of people and low ratio of nonexempt to exempt employees. The organization was over staffed in middle-management positions.

The company's costs for the staff functions—except for accounting, were out of line with their competitors. These noncompetitive costs came in spite of lower compensation for exempt employees. The key reason for the higher staff costs is the higher number of employees involved in these functions. Contributing to these noncompetitive costs is the underuse of nonexempt employees; there was also an indication of over staffing at exempt levels.

These examples illustrate how management can begin to gain control over human resource costs. This process addresses the issue much more effectively than simple headcount reduction. The key is, first, to measure the organizational and HR cost elements that most clearly affect business performance; and, second, to implement a cost monitoring process that continually examines the costs of organization and human resources policies, and how these costs compare with competitive norms.

Developing a human resource cost strategy can become the basis for human resources planning decisions. By creating a baseline study and then monitoring developments periodically, management can strengthen the linkage between its strategic plans and its HR practices. The company can break the pattern of overbuilding staff during the good times and then reducing it in more competitive times.

Although a quantitative, database-oriented approach to controlling people costs is the heart of HR cost containment, HR managers cannot lose sight of the most visible elements of HR costs: pay and benefits. These areas carry very important implications—not just for today's compensation management, but for tomorrow's HR planning.

HOW TO PROVIDE ADEQUATE COMPENSATION FOR MULTINATIONAL EMPLOYEES

Concerns for overseas compensation policies are heightened for Fortune 500 firms, where over 474 of them have international operations. Overseas operations are not limited to the largest corporations in the United States.

There are over 3,500 other companies doing business around the world according to the United States Department of Commerce.

As most multinational corporations (MNCs) have American employees in a variety of countries, there should be a variety of compensation arrangements to provide for total compensation in each country. Because of local tax regulations, exchange controls, and salary structures no one type of compensation program will address all the concerns an expatriate will have about salary and benefits.

Determining Method of Payment

The general method of payment used by MNCs, and their expatriate compensation policies, are basically the same worldwide. But the procedures used in payment vary country by country.

Base salary ranges for overseas positions generally remain the same as for their United States based counterparts. Most organizations use the "balance sheet" approach to compensation of expatriates. The balance sheet approach is basically a philosophy that the home-based executive must neither gain nor suffer financially because of an overseas assignment. Employees of MNCs who move overseas usually do receive a much larger compensation package, however, because of all the allowances, premiums, and perks.

In addition to base pay, an American executive working overseas is paid an overseas premium that is not particularly related to what it costs the employee to live overseas. The premium is more job-related and designed to compensate the expatriate for the added responsibilities placed on the employee. An example of added duties and responsibilities is the need that frequently arises to be host or hostess to local dignitaries. It is also paid to compensate the executive for living in less than comfortable surroundings.

The most common method of computing an overseas premium is to base it on a percentage of the employee's base pay. Some firms pay a fifteen-percent premium, some much more depending on the geographic region and the discomfort or danger with which the executive employee may be forced to live.

Most United States companies also provide for education and language training allowances, entertainment allowances and club memberships, housing allowance, relocation allowances, and one-time expenses incurred in travel to the new assignment, cost of living allowances, tax equalization allowances, and dollar devaluation adjustments.

The cost of maintaining an employee overseas generally amounts to at least two to three (or even more) times that of the base salary. When companies are in a "cost reduction" mode there are many categories they review for cutting overseas operational costs. One of them, of course, is in the total number of expatriates and the other is in the compensation and benefits costs.

As the president of one local MNC put it, "we are attempting to control the number of expatriates that we have on our payroll rather than cutting compensation packages. We still need good people and we want to fairly compensate them . . . we just don't need as many people now as we used to."

Ten Ways to Cut Expatriate Staff Costs

There are ten basic ways to curtail expatriate costs without dislocating your employees or your overseas operations.

1. Conduct an overall review of the number of expatriate positions needed and eliminate those positions identified as marginal or nonessential.

2. If you have local nationals in certain locations, intensify the training in preparation for taking over jobs of expatriates.

3. Encourage single employees to accept overseas assignments rather than employees with large families.

4. Institute a regular audit of expatriate expenses, compensation, allowances, and so forth. Institute policies and procedures to curtail unnecessary or nonessential costs and expenses.

5. Reduce premiums in countries that are not hardship locations, such as Great Britain, Canada, and Germany. Put a cap on all premiums.

6. Use lump sum incentives that do not increase base pay, but do provide incentives where they are needed, as often as needed.

7. Do not allow pyramiding of premiums, expense allowances, and incentives. Most organizations today pay only one type of premium, a hardship allowance but not a foreign service premium, for example.

8. Negotiate when you can with the host country to curtail income taxes and other foreign service taxes. Plan relocations to take advantage of local tax laws.

9. Regularly review your expatriate home management program. Consider establishing housing and utility cost limits. Establish maximum amounts for shipping and storage reimbursements.

10. Administer all your expatriate policies as written and resist the temptation to provide more for "special circumstances" or every relocation will become a special case.

Most companies with overseas locations have expatriate policies but not all companies monitor them, or audit actual costs on a regular basis. More human resource executives are getting involved in expatriate expenditures and actual costs in order to improve the "bottom line." Expatriate expenditures are an important element in the overall compensation program of any multinational organization.

NEW TYPES OF INCENTIVES SOME COMPANIES OFFER EMPLOYEES

Included in the new multiple compensation strategies being employed by some organizations are a variety of perks that have not been seen before, at least in most companies. For example, as computer literacy is such a valuable asset and not all companies have the time or money to individually train employees, more companies are providing financial incentives to help employees purchase their own personal computers.

Financial Incentives Offered to Help Employees Purchase Personal Computers

The DuPont Company has made arrangements with Digital Equipment Corporation and Hewlett-Packard to offer discounts of twenty to thirty percent on selected personal computers and other equipment to its full time United States employees. DuPont is doing this not only to help employees, but to motivate them to become more computer oriented on their own.

Employees at McDonnell-Douglas are also offered computer discounts with the added incentive of interest-free loans. MDC negotiated with Wang, IBM, and Digital for discounts averaging around twenty-five percent. MDC then offers twenty-four-month interest free loans permitting employees to borrow up to eighty percent of the purchase price or $4,000, whichever is less.

Large Cash Prizes and New Cars Offered by an Insurance Company

Another new perk offered by at least one large insurance company, Executive Life Insurance Company in Los Angeles, is large cash bonuses and new cars. Cheryl Wada, Chief Operating Officer of Executive Life, gave one of her assistants a $10,000 cash prize and another got a new car. Ms. Wada feels that liberal bonuses are one reason Executive Life is one of the fastest growing firms in the industry.

A Home Away from Home

Honeywell employees that are travel-minded have an economical alternative to escalating travel costs. Honeywell has started a home exchange program in the United States and overseas. The home exchange program is not officially sanctioned by Honeywell, but employees carry it out on their own. The

Honeywell newsletter called WORLD acts as a clearing house for employee swaps and there has been an overwhelming response. This may not actually be a company offered incentive, but it is popular and seems to be working.

Incentives to Get Employees to Take Assignments Overseas

Some companies are having to offer larger incentives to get employees to take overseas jobs, especially in the middle east or other areas where civil unrest is a problem. Incentives range from large cash bonuses up front, to bigger housing and servant allowances, big security payments to keep the employee from being a target for terrorists, and so forth. American executives in Latin American countries receive significant additional compensation and perks.

The whole area of compensation and benefits is changing dramatically. Huge layoffs in many industries in the mid and late 1980's created a situation where many companies scaled-down their pay levels. As certain jobs now become more difficult to fill we are seeing a willingness to isolate those jobs from the general salary structure and pay higher salaries to selective positions. This practice although more common today, would never have been considered only five years ago. . .and as most HR managers know, it will create problems down the line. The whole idea of multiple compensation policies and practices has come to be accepted through necessity, and a need to deal with rapid change in company structure, profitability and competitive pressures.

Balancing Corporate Needs with Employee Rights Issues and Workers' Attitudes

CHAPTER 3

Significant changes are occurring in the workplace, and you as Human Resource Director are riding the forefront of these changes. Few professions have the potential that the human resources field has for reaching a high status in both the public and private sectors. Don't overlook the opportunities that are available—opportunities to help employees reach a higher level of productivity and personal fulfillment and to help your company become more effective and profitable in terms of human effort and economic return.

Dramatic growth patterns are building. Thousands of corporations are planning to double the size of their workforce in the next ten years, and small businesses are emerging and growing at an even faster pace than large corporations. According to the Small Business Administration, over eighty percent of all new jobs created are created by small businesses.

Along with this renewed growth have come problems evident in the economic recovery. The recovery has set organizations and their employees on a collision course. Organizations want to retain new-found profits and old prerogatives in dealing with their people. Employees who made concessions during the recession want their piece of the pie, and further, they want more job security. Employees are becoming more vocal and assertive about their rights, their benefits, and their compensation. Congress got into the action also when it passed the 1984 Tax Act, and now no benefit is tax free unless specifically excluded by the tax code.

Executive compensation, golden parachutes, perks, and bonuses are the subject of wide discussion; pay-for-performance programs for both workers and management are seen more frequently in corporate strategic plans.

Labor and Management—Mutual Interest Bargaining

Labor and management, with their long history of going head-to-head over economic issues, are eliminating the hammer-and-tongs approach and trying harder to cooperate. In order for America to survive in the world market, labor and management must recognize that their real opponent is foreign competition—not each other, and move quickly to mutual interest bargaining.

An even more important reason for labor and management to foster a more cooperative environment is that the nature of work in America has changed from heavy goods and production (primarily machine-based) to service- and information-oriented white collar, and public service occupations.

In these new occupations, productivity is greatly influenced by the individual's motivation and mental contribution. Both labor and management must concentrate on new, more creative approaches to productivity and then cooperate to apply these new approaches if they are to work.

Employment Relationships Are Changing

In addition, employment relationships are changing. If you want to remember what the jobs of today are like and how people work together in the industrial environment . . . take a quick look. The computer is about to make some jobs and management relationships obsolete, or at least very different. Top executives of many organizations are refusing to admit that automation of the office will change the way they manage. Computers are making human resource departments as we have known them nearly obsolete with teleconferencing, video-conferencing, telephone mailboxes, as well as more sophisticated computer-based information systems, training programs, and robotics—just to name a few of the new systems and products.

As times and conditions change, so do workers' attitudes and lifestyles. Today, workers demand more of their jobs and their employment arrangements. They want more chance to develop and apply their skills, more flexibility in meshing their work and off-work lives, and, perhaps more important, a greater voice in their work, their working conditions, benefits, and work schedules.

MEETING THE DEMANDS OF THE NEW WORKER

Each generation of worker brings to the job a different set of demands and a specific work ethic. What are the demands of the new worker? There are really two levels of new worker in the workforce today.

The first level of worker deals in knowledge, not goods and services. Most knowledge workers are lawyers, analysts, planners, engineers, editors, programmers, and so forth. These new knowledge workers are too intelligent to be managed with the old traditional methods. Todays workers are imaginative, creative, and original; they engage in complex problem solving, not bureaucratic drudgery or dull routine. Unlike generations before them, they are not docile and obedient and they have little tolerance for boredom. They want interesting work and a job that provides psychic and social stimulation.

Brain power is the corporation's key competitive resource, and the evolution of management practices needed to deal with today's first level workers has not kept pace with the challenge of harnessing their brain power.

One key to attracting and retaining these top level workers is to give them meaningful work immediately and to let them provide a fresh perspective to the corporation. Challenging nonrepetitive work is essential. For example, companies that have moved to a matrix management mode frequently give special projects of significant importance to new, perhaps younger professionals and fast trackers who appear to have the qualities needed to succeed in challenging situations. Previous thinking was to give those significant assignments only to long-term, previously challenged employees. Now, many organizations realize they have to challenge these new younger workers early in their careers with the company in order to retain some of their sharpest high potential people.

The second level of worker today is the level of worker just below these well-paid professionals. It is the level that makes from $15,000 to $30,000 a year and deals primarily with lower level information and data processing work. Clerical, data entry, accounting technicians, market analysts, nurses, computer programmers, training specialists, and teachers.

This group comprises one-third of the largest generation in history. These workers are in a slot between top professionals and the laboring ranks . . . some in service jobs, others in lower level corporate positions. These workers are not the young-urban-professionals. They have made it to white collar jobs but don't make the money or command the top positions. This group works hard but they are not as obsessed with their careers. They want to make more money but the almighty dollar and the vice-president's job are not their only aims in life. Many of these young people have been disappointed to find that a college degree and a white collar job do not guarantee affluence or even financial security. Over half of them have some college training but find that it has little application to their jobs.

This class of professional white collar worker feels left out, but they make up a huge segment of the workforce and human resource managers who are recruiting and trying to retain these workers need to spend more time in communicating with them.

They want to feel more "a part of the organization" for which they work. They see their higher level professional counterparts being wined and dined . . . getting on the fast track, and they feel left out of this process. These lower level white collar workers are the backbone of American industry today and they feel disenfranchised. We need to bolster our human relations skills in addressing their needs.

The dual-career couple, the single mother head-of-the-household, the over fifty worker who wants to keep working until age seventy, the new younger nonprofessional worker, and the middle manager whose job has been eliminated through office automation all bring new challenges to organizations. Can organizations that need creative, committed people afford to ignore any one of these groups? They will make up over ninety percent of the workforce in the next decade.

CREATIVE IDEAS FOR MANAGING THE NEW WORKFORCE

There is a far larger implication to all of these changes in the workplace and we may overlook it in the day-to-day struggle to "get the job done." There is a corporate and managerial identity crisis that is intensifying. Corporations are breaking up, buying each other, merging, growing, and shrinking—all in very short time spans. They are centralizing, decentralizing, hiring, and laying off in spans of less than a year.

Managers who are used to managing in the industrial society where mass production, mass marketing, mass distribution, and masses of workers were all motivated by uniform policies and procedures and by uniform compensation and benefits, are having trouble managing in a workplace that progresses at a much more rapid pace. Old managerial assumptions are no longer valid, and new, more creative ideas are needed.

People come to work today with an acute awareness of their professional, ethnic, racial, sexual, religious, and individual differences. Where they once fought to be integrated into society, they now fight to maintain their individual identities. Managers and corporations have not as yet addressed this issue . . . have not learned to cope with this new diversity of values, lifestyles, and needs.

We are all struggling to be successful in an environment we no longer recognize and are not sure how to cope with. We struggle to relate to a new workforce with new values and goals and demands. We find ourselves with few tools. What an opportunity for the human resources manager—the forward-thinking human resources manager who welcomes change and ambiguity—to come through with creative, effective solutions to these new problems.

The Most Effective Way to Deal with the New Worker

Most companies are looking for ways to deal with workers of all ages, backgrounds, ethnic origins, and so forth. The answer to the variety of problems that arise with this diverse workforce is to institute a variety of communications programs that target all areas of your employee population and provide effective up and down communications networks throughout the organization. Today, corporate communications must be honest and forthright, must include sharing of organizational goals and motivations, and must be defensible, but written in a style that doesn't sound like "you're in the army now!".

Ten Examples of Corporate Communications Programs

1.   One corporation holds monthly discussion groups with employees on new books that have a business theme the company would like to

communicate. The company provides the books and gives employees time to read them. The meeting is held at the end of the month and is lead by a different executive each time. The employees give one hour of their time, and the company pays the employees for an extra hour the evening of the group meeting. The company furnishes a box lunch.

Management believes these discussion groups help them get better acquainted with each other . . . they also help the organization get their work-related messages across to management and professional people in a more palatable and interesting way.

2. Several corporations have installed hotlines from time to time to allow more upward communication when there are labor problems or when a department seems to have problems and management can't get a handle on them. Install a telephone with an answering machine in an area that you can lock, ensuring complete confidence on the part of the caller. Have the telephone accessible day and night so the employees can call after hours. Issue a special bulletin telling employees about the hotline and advising them that they can call at any hour during the next thirty to sixty days (you decide how long the hotline will be in action). Tell employees they can call the hotline number and tell company management about any problems they are having. If they want a specific answer, they can leave their names and departments. If they don't want answers, but just want to let management know about problems, they can remain anonymous.

Handle the information you get on the hotline in a proprietary manner . . . use it to make *positive* changes . . . not to try and find a culprit if the information is negative. The manner in which you use the hotline will dictate its success.

3. Start an excellence-oriented employee newsletter. Employees want to know what is going on around the company. Don't just use it as a way to say happy birthday to people (although that is a good idea), but use it to tell employees about company plans, new products, marketing problems, or opportunities. Include new ideas and trends, and discuss hard issues like dealing with AIDS in the workplace. Employees want hard data. Involve them in information gathering and give lots of employees opportunities to contribute. You may also want to try a corporate news video if you have people on staff who can produce it for you. Send the video to all locations.

4. Institute company meetings two or three times a year where the CEO and other executives make presentations on current problems

and opportunities, and where employees are encouraged to participate. Have other management, professional, and lower level employees make presentations at these meetings.

5. Implement an organizational overview presentation and present it once or twice a year. By overview I mean ask each department to prepare and give a short twenty minute presentation about the department and how it works . . . its interfaces and a bit about the specific problems that department faces and how it deals with them. Use employees at various levels to moderate the program.

6. Encourage company-sponsored athletic events where employees participate and communicate in a relaxed atmosphere. Ask employees to plan the events and give them paid time as work load and budget allows.

7. Update the service award program idea by making the awards more personal. Ask the top executive, president, or vice-president to go to the employee's department and personally present the award. Give awards the employee can use rather than a service pin that will just get thrown in a drawer. The new lower-level white collar professional worker is more turned on by a Springsteen tape or a video cassette than a collar pin for one year of service.

8. Include second language (usually Spanish) articles in your newsletters or other company periodicals. Plan ethnic covered-dish lunches. All employees came from another country at some point . . . these ideas help you assimilate a variety of ethnic cultures in a positive way and foster more dialogue between cultures in the workplace.

9. Build an audio and video cassette tape library on a variety of subjects, such as stress reduction, quitting smoking, foreign languages, meditation, exercise, health, diet, and cooking, and make the tapes available to employees. You can also provide tape machines for employees to borrow or rent. Include tapes and videos from your company newscasts if you have them. Company video newscasts can also include messages on personnel policies and procedures, labor issues, and so on.

10. Include employees from all levels of the organization on committees, task forces, and panels that are part of your various programs. One of the common complaints of these new white collar nonprofessional workers is that they do not get to participate in special activities. They feel only the young-urban-professional-MBA gets the "goodies."

EMPLOYEE RIGHTS: HOW DOES YOUR COMPANY SIZE UP LEGALLY?

Unions in America are on a decline, but employee dissatisfaction with the boss-worker relationship in most companies shows up in surveys, in polls, and in a growing volume of court suits.

Executives feel pretty good about the decline in unions, and in their ability to decertify unions, but what is happening in actuality is a union-free environment that is starting to move toward a legalized environment. Even though there has been a move to defuse government entities like OHSA, EEOC, and the Civil Right Commission, the move has not done much to squelch the new job rights movement that is being fueled by the baby-boomers as they take over the workplace. States are also stepping in to take up employee causes. Many states are passing laws protecting whistleblowers (those employees who report violations of law by employers) . . . whether they be hazardous materials laws or retirement laws. Nineteen states have already said that companies may not force workers to retire at any age.

Key Federal and State Laws That Protect or Impact Employees

Following is a review of the growing number of laws and court rulings that protect workers, or impact employers. Basic protection against discrimination in hiring, promotion, and discharge is granted by:

- Civil Rights Act of 1964
- The Age Discrimination in Employment Act of 1967; and the 1978 and 1986 amendment disallowing mandatory retirement
- State and local laws, some of which add protection for marital status and sexual orientation

Sex discrimination in pay is prohibited by:

- The Equal Pay Act of 1963
- Federal court decisions requiring equal pay for comparable work

Funding, vesting, and other standards for pensions and other benefit plans are set by:

- The Employee Retirement Income Security Act of 1974; state laws

National minimum wage, forty-hour work week for regular pay, and other working conditions are set by:

- The Fair Labor Standards Act of 1938; state wage and hour laws (all states)

Company ability to discharge and discipline employees for union activity is limited by:

- The National Labor Relations Act of 1935; the Railway Labor Act of 1926.

Employee rights are being expanded at the state and local level by:

- right-to-know laws requiring companies to divulge information on hazardous substances used in the workplace (twenty-five states)
- laws protecting corporate and government whistleblowers (twenty-one states)
- court decisions eroding employment-at-will doctrine (thirty states)
- laws prohibiting any mandatory retirement age (nineteen states)
- laws requiring notice of plant shutdowns and severance pay for affected workers (three states)

Employee privacy is protected by:

- limits on data about individuals that the government can disclose to employers (ten states, plus the Federal Privacy Act of 1973)
- laws limiting use of polygraph tests for job applicants (twenty-seven states); giving employees access to their personnel files (nine states); restricting use of arrest records in hiring process (twelve states)

Standards for a safe and healthful workplace are established by:

- the Occupational Safety and Health Act of 1970; twenty-four state laws
- the Federal Mine Safety and Health Act of 1977

Regulations regarding the hiring of aliens:

- The Immigration Reform and Control Act of 1986

Regulation of pension accruals and pension participation (and other provisions):

- Omnibus Budget Reconciliation Act of 1986

Regulations pertaining to taxation of employee compensation and benefits:

- The Tax Reform Act of 1986

Landmark Cases in Human Rights at Work

As the huge body of case law sets the stage for managing human rights in the workplace, companies are beginning to get the idea that we had better change the way we manage. Otherwise we will become handcuffed in our ability to deal with the day-to-day issues that face us at work and we will not be able to exercise any independent judgment in managing our people. Following are some of the landmark cases.

Weiner vs. McGraw-Hill Inc.—New York, 1982
McGraw-Hill recruited Walton Lewis Weiner from Prentice-Hall. One of the incentives mentioned, Weiner later claimed, was McGraw-Hill's job-security policy, stated clearly in the company's employee handbook. Weiner was dismissed eight years later for "lack of application."

Decision: The influential New York Court of Appeals declared that the combination of factors cited by Weiner would have the force of a contract obligating McGraw-Hill not to fire without just cause.

Toussaint vs. Blue Cross & Blue Shield—Michigan, 1980
When Charles Toussaint was being interviewed for a job at Blue Cross & Blue Shield, he asked about job security. He said he was told he could stay with the company "as long as I did my job." He was given a handbook that said the company fired employees for just cause only. Five years later he was let go—without cause.

Decision: Employees can use printed company statements and proof of oral assurances of job security, said Michigan's highest court, to establish a contractual right to be fired only for just cause.

Pugh vs. See's Candies Inc.—California, 1981
After 32 years with See's Candies, Wayne Pugh had risen from pot washer to vice-president. The company had just completed its most successful season. He was called into the president's office and told his services were no longer needed. When he asked why, Pugh charged, he was told to "look deep within himself."

Decision: From the length of employment, the series of promotions, and the lack of criticism, a jury could reasonably conclude that the company had obligated itself to deal with Pugh only in good faith.

Petermann vs. International Brotherhood of Teamsters—California, 1959
A union's business agent was called to testify before a legislative committee. His boss, he said, told him to lie when asked certain questions. He didn't, and he was fired.

Decision: An appeals court declared: "It would be obnoxious to the interests of the state and contrary to public policy and sound morality to allow an employer to discharge an employee on the ground that the employee declined to commit perjury."

Monge vs. Beebe Rubber Co.—New Hampshire, 1974
Olga Monge operated a machine at $1.84 an hour. When a job opened in the shop that paid $2.79, she applied for it. Her foreman said that if she

wanted the promotion, she would have to be "nice" to him. She wasn't interested—and she was fired.

Decision: A dismissal motivated by bad faith is a ground for an employee to bring suit.

Fortune vs. National Cash Register Co.—Massachusetts, 1977
NCR reduced a salesman's rank the day after he placed a $5 million order.

Decision: There was enough evidence to indicate that the company took the action to pay him as little as possible in commissions. An employment contract contains an implied term that the employer will act in good faith.

Woolley vs. Hoffman-La Roche—New Jersey, 1978
Hoffman-La Roche lost confidence in Richard M. Woolley and fired him. Woolley sued. On May 9, 1985 New Jersey's highest court changed the law that for a century in New Jersey said companies had an absolute right to fire workers. In 1985 the court ruled that Hoffman-La Roche could be held to job security assurances implied in its employee personnel manual.

Meritor Savings Bank vs. Vinson, 1986
Probably the most significant court case relating to sex harassment in the workplace. It involved an employee named Mechelle Vinson who was hired at a branch bank of Meritor Savings Bank in the Washington D. C. area. Vinson claimed that over her four years of employment she had "constantly been subjected to sexual harassment" by her supervisor. She testified that he had made repeated demands upon her for sexual favors. There were several important points made by the court, but two key issues should be noted.

1. EEOC guidelines and the decision of the Supreme Court in this case both note that sexual misconduct constitutes harassment whether or not it is directly linked to the grant or denial of an economic benefit.

2. The EEOC guidelines which the Supreme Court cited favorably in its opinion, hold an employer responsible for acts of supervisors without regard to whether or not the employer was given any additional notice of the alleged wrongdoing.

TERMINATION-AT-WILL: CAN YOU STILL FIRE AN EMPLOYEE ANY TIME YOU FEEL LIKE IT?

Some courts say no and some states, twenty-three of them in fact, have recognized exceptions to the employment-at-will doctrine. Many courts and legislatures have stated that employees cannot be fired for disobeying an order that violates public policy. The Texas Supreme Court has ruled that a company cannot fire a worker for the sole reason that the employee refused to perform an illegal act.

One of the landmark cases on termination at will is the Hoffman-La Roche case. Back in 1978, Richard M. Woolley was fired by Hoffman-La Roche, Inc. The company said that it had "lost confidence in him," and asked him to resign. Woolley refused to resign and the company fired him. Woolley sued the company. For years the state of New Jersey (like most states) had held that companies had an absolute right to fire workers at will.

On May 9, 1985, seven years later, the highest court in New Jersey changed the law. It ruled that Hoffman-La Roche must be held to assurances of job security implied in its personnel policy manual.

After that 1985 ruling, New Jersey joined the states of California and Michigan in court decisions that declared broad new limitations on the power that employers have to dismiss employees.

When Is Firing Unjust?

Court rulings vary from state to state, but here are some general interpretations:

- Implied good faith: Employers have been held liable in cases where the general "breach of fair dealing" or malice has been shown, like firing workers to avoid paying earned sales commissions, pensions, and so forth.

- Implied employment contract: Promotions and raises, job longevity with advancement, and the absence of negative work evaluations have been seen as establishing a contract, demanding substantiation for fire.

- Other implied contracts: Statements in personnel handbooks and job applications, and even oral assurances about job security during recruitment, have been construed as binding.

- Public policy: "Whistleblower" cases—in which an employee was fired after reporting wrongdoing of a company or refusing to participate in a criminal act—have been ruled unjust. So have terminations caused by an employee's filing a claim for workers' compensation or going on jury duty (which is not mandatory in all states).

How to Protect Your Company from Litigation: Eleven Recommendations

A typical scenario for costly litigation involves a long-time employee who received yearly salary increases and whose personnel file is full of good performance reviews and no written warnings for poor performance. The employee is fired for no obvious reason . . . given some off-the-cuff reason like "you just aren't the person we need for that job." If the employee is not performing and is given written performance warnings and the company provides a reasonable opportunity to improve, the company stands a better chance of winning a lawsuit.

Following are eleven recommendations for avoiding costly litigation and employee complaints.

1. Before interviewing and hiring new employees, review all personnel documents including employment applications and personnel policy manuals to be sure they do not imply continued employment or employment for a fixed duration.

    Add statements to your written materials and say something like . . . "employment is for no fixed duration," and "These documents are not to be construed as employment contracts." Have your Legal Department review the revised manuals to ensure their legality.

2. Have both old and new employees review your employee handbook and work rules. Have them sign a form that says they understand the rules and the handbook, and that they agree to abide by the rules. Further, the statement should indicate that the employee understands that infractions may lead to discipline and/or discharge.

3. Meet with supervisors and managers and make sure they understand the rules and interpret them correctly. Be sure no one in authority makes promises the company does not intend to keep.

4. If discipline is necessary, be sure it is carried out in an even-handed manner by all supervisors and managers. Monitor disciplinary actions and follow up to make sure all actions are carried out according to your policies and procedures.

5. Use progressive discipline. Give an employee the opportunity to correct poor behavior, improve poor work performance, and so forth. Your policy should include one verbal warning, one or two written warnings, and possibly a suspension before final termination. Use your best judgment for your company's particular circumstances. Whatever you decide to use, however, should be uniformly administered.

6. In order to avoid unnecessary discipline and termination, utilize a formal program of regular employee performance reviews. Put them in writing with a copy to the personnel file and be sure to give the employee a copy. Employees need to know where they stand on an ongoing basis so there are no surprises and no abrupt terminations. Standardize disciplinary procedures and be sure that everyone follows them to the letter.

7. Also standardize your method of grievance handling and make sure all supervisors and managers understand and use your grievance procedures. Fair, impartial hearings and due process correct many injustices and protect rights, such as freedom of inquiry, conscientious objection, and privacy.

    It is a good idea to get the employee's side of the story with a witness present and to check it out before you take action.

8. Implement a standard personnel policy on how personnel files are to be handled. Review current files with an eye to fairness. How are files maintained? Can the employees review their files? Some states have regulations stating that employees can see their files. Who else can see an employee's personnel file? What is maintained in the personnel file? Never let a supervisor write up an employee without giving the employee a copy of the document.

    Review the files as though you were a hearing examiner or a judge in a discrimination case. How would you feel about what was in the files? Are they fairly maintained?

9. Make sure that reasons for promotion and demotion or termination are valid and fair.

10. If you have doubts about a personnel action, seek legal counsel either from an on-staff or an outside attorney.

11. Never block a terminated employee's future employment. Bad references and off-the-cuff remarks can lead to charges of libel, intentional infliction of emotional distress, and loss of income.

    Don't give a poor employee you terminated glowing references either. Adopt a policy of only confirming dates of employment and give no other information to prospective employers.

BIG BROTHER IN THE WORKPLACE? THE GROWING DEMAND FOR PERSONAL PRIVACY

Employees tend to underestimate how much their companies know about them. They do not realize what is in their personnel files, or who has access to the files. Even though seven states have passed laws that give the employees the legal right to inspect their personnel files, many employees never ask to look at them.

How Private Are Personnel Records?

In a survey of 2,047 workers in the retailing, automotive, aerospace and manufacturing industries, it was found that twenty-nine percent did not know whether their personnel files contained information about their personal assets and home ownership, and nearly one-quarter did not know whether their employer kept information about employees' religious affiliations. (Most employers do.) When employees did think their company kept information on them, they were frequently wrong as to what type of information it was.

Workers tend to underestimate how much their employers know about their health. Most companies keep records of illnesses, physical examinations, blood tests, and disabilities for which they claim insurance coverage. Most employers also know if employees have mental or stress problems because insurance plans pay a portion of the doctor's bill. Some companies even use this information to make decisions on promotion or termination, although they shouldn't follow this practice. You should help top management decide on a specific privacy policy for the company and then see that it is fairly and uniformly administered.

The Trend Toward Respecting Employee Privacy

Business has begun to pay attention to employee privacy. Corporations like United Technologies, IBM, Cummins Engine, Northrup Corporation, General Tire & Rubber, SmithKline, and Chase Manhattan Bank have implemented formal policies limiting both the data that will be put into employee personnel files and the access to information. In addition, employees are assured that they can see their personnel files and correct any mistakes in them.

Northrup Corporation must gather much more personal information than the normal company because of the need to complete security clearances on every employee. Northrup requires that data gathered for federal clearances be retained in separate files from the regular personnel files.

The Privacy Act of 1974

The Privacy Act of 1974 was enacted to "provide certain safeguards for an individual against an invasion of personal privacy." This law was passed December 31, 1974 and went into effect in September, 1975. It represents the major federal legislation dealing with personal privacy and indicates the probable direction of future privacy legislation.

The Privacy Act of 1974 does not apply to private industry. Rather, it is limited to the federal government and specifically applies to all executive departments, the military, independent regulatory agencies, government corporations, and government-controlled corporations such as the Federal Reserve Bank. In addition, any private business or state or local government that contracts with one of the agencies listed above is considered a part of that agency and is thus also covered during performance of that contract. The

Privacy Act does not pertain to Congress, governments of territories or possessions, the District of Columbia, or the federal courts.

The Privacy Act also established the Privacy Protection Study Commission. The Commission made a thorough study of current policies and practices and then issued thirty-four recommendations pertaining to all employers. The key ones are listed below.

General Recommendations on Maintaining Employee Privacy

Employers are requested to periodically and systematically review their personnel recordkeeping practices. This review should specifically consider:

- the number and types of records an organization maintains on employees, former employees, and applicants
- the items on each record maintained
- the uses made of information in each type of record
- the uses of information within the organization
- the disclosures made to parties outside the organization
- the extent to which individuals are aware and informed of the uses and disclosures of information in the records kept about them

After the above review of an organization's current practices, the Commission recommends that policies be set forth. Specifically, the second recommendation is that employers articulate, communicate, and implement fair information policies by the following means.

- Limit the collection of information about individuals to that which is relevant to specific decisions.
- Inform individuals of the uses to be made of such information.
- Inform individuals as to the type of information being maintained about them.
- Adopt reasonable procedures to ensure the accuracy, timeliness, and completeness of information about individuals.
- Permit individuals to see, copy, correct, or amend records about themselves.
- Limit the internal use of records.
- Limit external disclosures of information, particularly those made without the individual's authorization.
- Provide for regular review of compliance with articulated fair information practice policies.

Fairness of recordkeeping practices constitutes the majority of the Commission's recommendations. In fact, twenty-six of the thirty-four recommendations deal with fairness.

The Commission also stated that personnel and payroll records should be available internally only on a need-to-know basis and that employers who provide voluntary health-care services should set up procedures that severely limit the use of this medical information in making employment decisions.

The Privacy Protection Study Commission made a strong case for voluntary compliance by private industry, because legislation to protect the privacy of employees would entail a wide variety of disadvantages for the employment relationship. The Commission feels a voluntary approach should be tried before legislation becomes necessary. Most businesses have taken the hint and are complying with privacy recommendations voluntarily.

COMPANY-REQUIRED MEDICAL EXAMS

For years companies have required preemployment physicals and medical examinations of current employees. Many companies were lax in the methods of retention of these records and in the number of people throughout the organization they allowed to have access to them. Employees who thought this information was confidential and available only to their immediate supervisors began to find out this was not the case. Now lawsuits occur more frequently as employees begin to fight for their rights to privacy.

Case Example: Williams Pipe Line Company versus Oil, Chemical, and Atomic Workers

In 1982, an award was handed down by Arbitrator Preston J. Moore that established a procedure for management to use to avoid privacy problems in company-required medical exams.

Williams Pipe Line Company wanted to begin a program of physicals for those employees exposed regularly to petroleum products. The company wanted to know if an employee became unfit to continue working—and it wanted to collect data for use in setting safety and health policies.

The employees' union represented the point of view that the results of medical examinations are traditionally a private matter. Could management require the exams; and how could it collect the information it needed and still respect the employee's right of privacy?

In presenting its case to the arbitrator, management explained why it wanted to require physical examinations.

- Required exams would benefit the employees by detecting health problems at no cost to the employee.

- According to the company, some parts of the exam were needed to comply with federal safety requirements.

- Because the employees were exposed to petroleum products, there might be health problems.

- The company's cost for medical care benefits would be reduced through an ongoing preventive program.

- The company could reduce the possibility of litigation if health problems could be detected early.

Employees speaking through their union had one primary concern: Could they be assured that management would not begin discharging people on the grounds that their medical exams showed they had problems that might affect their work?

The arbitrator set out a procedure to give management the information it needed and to assure employees their right to privacy.

1. Medical information not related to an employee's job would be communicated by the physician only to the employee.

2. Aggregate information—data without names—would be supplied to the company for its use in setting safety policies.

3. If a medical exam showed a danger to the employee taking the exam or to others on the job, the physician would advise the company's industrial hygienist. Management would be entitled to know of such a danger—but would not be given the details of the employee's examination.

Who would conduct the examinations? In the Williams case, the company's own physician. Someone outside the company could be retained, however, and the same procedures used to safeguard privacy. Does management have the "right" to demand that its employees take physical exams? It does, whether the employer is a private company or a government agency.

When Use Turns to Abuse: Medical Records and Their Effect on Promotions

Employers who base hiring or promotions decisions on medical records are asking for trouble. More and more employees and prospective employees are suing organizations that deny them jobs or promotions based on information received from a medical examination. The only time a company can really justify denying a job or a promotion to an employee who has a handicap is if the handicap will keep the employee from doing the job safely. For example, an employee who is severely physically handicapped might not be able to perform a factory job on an assembly line without endangering himself and others.

On the other hand, an employer must act if there is reason to believe an employee is handicapped through the use of alcohol or drugs and the medical examination confirms those suspicions. If the employer does nothing, serious liability questions will be raised if there is an on-the-job accident that hurts the impaired employee or other employees.

There are also many questions raised about promotions that may have been lost because employees utilize the company medical plans for psychotherapy, drug rehabilitation programs, treatment of AIDS or other social disease. Many companies have been known to look at medical records before giving promotions. Employees in some companies have sued and won on the basis of an invasion of privacy.

In a large manufacturing company in the Midwest, Jane Bronson was in line for a promotion. Jane had outstanding performance appraisals and was a steady worker. Before making the promotion her boss checked her personnel file . . . there were no problems. He also decided to check her insurance claim forms and other medical data. To his surprise, he found that Jane had been submitting insurance claims for psychotherapy. He gave the promotion to someone else. Jane, expecting the promotion, was upset and hurt, and could not understand why she had been passed over for a significant career advancement.

In an attempt to cut medical expenses, organizations are receiving price breaks on insurance costs by processing their own medical claims. This puts a great deal of information in the hands of the employer, or, more specifically, personnel people. In the past personnel managers in some organizations misused this information. There are cases where employees have lost promotions because their medical records reflected claims for abortion, psychotherapy, and for taking advantage of employee assistance programs for problems of sexual preference, or for drug or alcohol abuse.

Medical records often contain mistakes and typographical errors. The employees should have a right to see their medical records and to correct any errors. A rough indication of the frequency of errors can be gleaned from data released by the Medical Information Bureau, Inc. (MIB), a Boston-based organization that acts as a clearinghouse for medical and some nonmedical information gathered by more than 750 insurance companies. MIB receives annually between 6,500 and 7,000 requests for disclosures; an average of 124 to 149 of these requests are from people inquiring about making corrections. These are the types of abuses the Privacy Protection Study Commission has tried to eliminate, and many organizations are following more straight privacy protection guidelines.

MORE BIG BROTHER IN THE WORKPLACE: COMPUTER MONITORING OF EMPLOYEES

Employers use computers to monitor the work habits of two thirds of the thirteen million video-terminal operators in the United States today. According to the National Association of Working Women, bosses monitor workers' terminals to keep track not only of how much work they produce but also how often they leave their desks and how many telephone calls they make.

Most grocery chains today monitor the productivity of checkers. It has been reported that one of the major airlines monitors the number of calls taken by its 6,000 ticket agents, the number of seats sold, and the average call handling time, and that not meeting group goals can result in suspensions. Most telephone companies monitor operators' calls.

Some executives feel that computer monitoring of employees is counter-productive and that it causes undue stress and a few organizations have discontinued the monitoring activity. For more information on worker rights refer to a book by Joel D. Joseph entitled *Employees' Rights in Plain English*, 1985 published by National Press, Inc., 7508 Wisconsin Ave., Bethesda, Md. 20814, $6.95 paperback. The author is a lawyer who has represented workers in disputes on subjects ranging from discrimination on the job to safety in the workplace, drug testing, and lie detector tests.

MANAGING HOMOSEXUALITY IN THE WORKPLACE: A GROWING ISSUE

In the last few years, homosexual workers have become more open about their sexual preferences and more vocal about their treatment on the job. Organizations still, in most instances, refuse to talk about the issue of homosexuality; and now with the subject of AIDS on everyone's mind the issue of the health of homosexual workers is a serious consideration for management and employees alike. In the past, homosexuals have been denied an opportunity to work and live in a normal society, but today a body of case law is developing as homosexuals increasingly litigate in an attempt to secure what they consider to be their constitutional rights.

There are only a few cities and states in the United States where homosexuals are free from employment discrimination. They have no legal recourse under Title VII of the 1964 Civil Rights Act. Few employment contracts or labor union rulings have recognized homosexuals as people to be granted equal rights . . . the equal rights fight is just beginning.

There were a flurry of court cases in the 1960s in the public sector that upheld dismissal of homosexuals because homosexual acts "indicated poor judgment that might affect the national interest" . . . or because "continued service would disrupt efficiency." In one case, Scott vs. Macy, Scott was dismissed from civil service employment on the basis of an investigation disclosing "convincing evidence of homosexual conduct which is considered contrary to accepted standards of morality."

The big question raised in the Civil Service is the Security Clearance issue; and in the private sector, over 2.2 million workers are subject to the Defense Department's Industrial Security Clearance Program. In the past homosexuals have, as a rule, been denied security clearances.

Relevant law in the areas of employment discrimination and employee rights in general, and, in particular, the area of employment of lesbians and gay males, is confusing and incomplete, but we have to try to understand the part we play as human resource professionals in the employment of homosexuals. The Fifth and Fourteenth Amendments of the Constitution state that "no governmental entity, official or agent may deprive a person of liberty or property without due process of law, nor may he or she deprive any person of the equal protection of the law." There are years of litigation in the public sector and so far homosexuals have had the most success in this area.

The whole subject is a difficult one for both sides—the homosexual employee, the human resource manager, and the organization. Homosexuals who have been subjected to inquiry, investigation, gossip, attention, and prejudicial comments regarding sexual orientation or related issues may have cause of action under the law for violation of constitutional, statutory, and common-law right to privacy.

Human resource managers should be concerned about equal treatment, about the right to privacy, and about wrongful discharge issues. We must stay current in this emerging body of case law.

Wrongful Discharge in a Sexual Preference Case: Three Points to Consider

An at-will employee whose employment is involuntarily terminated because of sexual preference may have a cause of action for "wrongful discharge." There must be a preexisting recognition of "wrongful discharge" as a cause of action in the jurisdiction where the case is filed. Important factors in a wrongful discharge suit include:

- the length and quality of the employee's service
- the equities of the situation, including possible unfair treatment of the employee
- policy considerations leading to the likelihood that the discharge will be termed "wrongful."

Extending Benefits to Same-Sex Partners: Still an Open Issue

In one case, Brinkin vs. Southern Pacific Transportation Company and the International Brotherhood of Railway, Airline, and Steamship Clerks, plaintiff Lawrence Brinkin challenged the enforcement of a provision of a collective bargaining agreement between his employer and his union. The provision at issue granted a three-day paid funeral leave to a married employee upon the death of his/her spouse, but denied plaintiff the same benefit when his same-sex family partner of eleven years died.

The issue of fringe benefits comes up frequently in homosexual employment, but no lawsuits have yet succeeded in obtaining extended benefit coverage for lesbian or gay family partners. This issue will become an important one in the next few years as more case law dealing with homosexuals tests the rights of employers to deny equal benefits.

Homosexuals and Social Attitudes

Law is a fluid thing—changing constantly in response to social policy and the demands of those whom it affects. A number of factors appear to be operating that may influence the direction of homosexual case law.

- changing attitudes toward homosexuals by many people and institutions

- rapid changes in life styles and mores in general, coupled with the greater willingness of homosexuals to admit sexual preference

- increasing militancy of homosexuals

- court cases upholding the private but controversial actions of teachers and public sector employees

- increasing use of the judicial test of establishing a direct link between conduct, sexual preference and job performance

- an increase in the number of court cases won by homosexuals

Because top management in most organizations will not discuss the problems of an ever-increasing number of homosexual employees, it will be up to human resource managers to implement fair policies and to counsel with homosexual employees as well as management when problems arise.

The recruiting and selection of people covers *all* people: people of all races, men and women, handicapped people, and homosexual employees. Our style of human resource management and our ability to fairly deal with this broad spectrum of employees will be a part of the measure of our worth to an organization.

Homophobia: Facing the Fear of Homosexuality at Work

The word "homophobia" comes up quite often these days. Homosexual groups use the term. It refers to a fear of homosexuals that seems to be quite common in "straight" people who have not been exposed to homosexuals in the past.

In most cases today, managers are still using the old traditional methods of management, and there are no frames of reference for managing the homosexual employee because homosexuals were in the workplace "closet" for so long. When traditional methods of management techniques were taught, it was unheard of to address the issue of homosexuality.

Our philosophy of management should be to treat all employees— regardless of color, race, handicap, or sexual preference—in the same manner. We must, however, manage differences, including personality and behavioral differences. Good managers have a sensitivity to these differences and a knack for effectively dealing with them to achieve organizational success.

Recently, there has been a proliferation of training programs aimed at helping male managers learn to deal with the "new woman" manager. Some companies are instituting programs to help straight managers learn to work with gay employees.

THE DUAL-CAREER COUPLE: HOW TO HANDLE THEIR SPECIAL NEEDS

Today, almost fifty percent of the workforce is made up of women and in many households both people must work. This means that there are now more dual-career couples than ever before in America.

The pressures on working couples have brought dramatic changes in the way they run their homes and finances, raise their children, and build their family life. The emergence of the dual-career couple has also brought a dramatic change in the way companies treat employees, and in the benefits, policies, and procedures companies have. Many companies now include day care, flexible working hours, job sharing, and other new benefits in their employment package.

Dual-career couples have so many issues to deal with that they must take a sensitive, proactive approach to career and home life in order to be successful in both areas.

The key issue and the most important skill that career couples have to deal with is open, give-and-take communication on all issues they face. They must be able to talk to each other, to be open and display a willingness to compromise, and to work together to establish a relationship that allows room for more than one career. Managing the dual-career couple also takes skill and a great deal of sensitivity to their problems. Human resource managers should plan programs especially for dual-career couples and take into consideration their special problems.

Managing the Dual-Career Couple

- Be open minded and flexible.
- Talk to them and get them to talk in order to help them resolve problems.
- Draft new policies on anti-nepotism that allow you to resolve problems and still employ working couples.
- Provide either child care assistance or child care referral.
- Provide flexible benefits.
- Provide workshops on conflict resolution, listening, etc.
- Be sensitive to specific trouble areas—when giving one employee a poor performance appraisal—you may have to explain to a spouse.
- Provide transplacement when relocating a married employee whose spouse works. Transplacement means helping your relocating employee's spouse find a job. You're really relocating two people.
- Don't get upset if the woman wants to retain her maiden name—your computer can handle it.

Transplacement for Dual-Career Couples

The new buzzword in relocation is transplacement. The number of dual-career couples has risen so significantly that a new corporate benefit called transplacement is common in most large organizations. Companies pay consultants to help the spouse of an employee that is being transferred find a job in the new location.

Transplacement helps employees cope with the disrupting effects of being moved to another city and recognizes the rights of spouses with jobs to continue working.

If your company moves many employees on an ongoing basis, you may wish to conduct a workshop for the employees and their spouses before you relocate them. A workshop might include the following.

- *Looking on change as opportunity*—Help employees focus on the positive side of change and relocation. Highlight the needs of the transferring couple and allow them to discuss the concerns they have in relocating.
- *Focusing on their dual careers*—Show the employee who is transferring

to what new career path he or she can aspire. Help the spouse look at career opportunities by focusing on long-range goals and providing information on jobs in the city where they will be relocating.

- *Assist with résumé development*—Help the spouse of your transferring employee develop a résumé or update a previous résumé.

- *Review job search skills*—The spouse may need to review and update job search skills, write marketing letters, and prepare for employment interviews. Use videotaped practice sessions for interviewing if possible.

- *Show continuing concern and support*—Both people need a support system and someone they can call on when things don't go right. Even the best planned relocation has bugs in it. Provide the ongoing support they both need. Give them advice, telephone numbers, and assurance that they can call on the Human Resource Department at any time for help.

MINORITY DISCRIMINATION: BOYCOTTS ARE GAINING GROUND

Minorities are boycotting products more frequently today when they perceive that companies are guilty of discrimination. There have been at least twenty-three such boycotts nationwide and they have been effective.

Case Example: The Adolph Coors Company

One company that was hit with a minority boycott is the Adolph Coors Company, a brewery in Golden, Colorado. The Adolph Coors Company will put about $325 million into black-owned businesses over the next five years under a major new trade agreement between the brewery and national black leaders. Most of the money will be spent in the form of investments in black-owned banks, new black distributorships, and advertising in black-owned publications and broadcasting stations.

The NAACP and other black groups agreed in return to help foster understanding of Coors and its products in the black community. About eight percent of Coors sales are to blacks. The company has over $1.1 billion in net sales.

The agreement contained the provisions that Coors will:

- put $325 million into black businesses over the next five years
- increase its level of black employees, both in lower-level jobs and in management positions, to correspond to the percentage of blacks living in the areas where Coors operates plants

- increase the number of black-owned distributorships they use nationally from one to twenty, and grant financial, operational, and sales assistance to qualified black owners to assure their success

- donate a minimum of $500,000 annually to black national, regional, and state organizations, with at least one-third of those funds provided to black colleges in the form of internship and scholarship programs.

Coors also signed a pact with Hispanic business and community leaders to spend $325 million for Hispanic businesses. The agreement was signed by Peter H. Coors, President, Sales, Marketing and Administration in agreement with six Hispanic organizations. The agreement basically includes the following.

- Hiring enough Hispanics at its Golden plant to match the percentage of Hispanics living in the Denver metropolitan area. Currently 8.5 percent of Coors' 9,000 employees are Hispanic. The area percentage was 10.7 percent in 1980, according to the United States Census Bureau. Twelve percent of the company's new hires will be Hispanic until the company reaches the goal.

- Investing eight percent of its available cash in banks owned by Hispanics and investing eight percent of its pension fund through Hispanic investment firms. Eight percent of its money in insurance companies will go to Hispanic agencies or companies.

- Buying eight percent of its supplies from Hispanic companies.

- Trying to appoint twenty Hispanic distributorships in the next five years, and setting aside five million dollars for investments in unspecified projects. Some of those projects may help finance Hispanic distributorships. There are now eight Hispanic-owned distributorships.

- Donating at least $500,000 a year for the five-year life of the agreement to the Hispanic community. At least a third of the funds will be used for education.

These minority boycotts, and the corporate agreements that end the boycotts, have become almost commonplace. They are another signal that today's workers are not happy with the old status quo and won't sit still for what they consider to be unfair treatment.

Fortune magazine reported that even though a damper has been put on affirmative action and EEO, most organizations are going to continue to implement their AAP programs. Most organizations feel it is in their best interests to include all workers equally.

SEX AND SALARY: THE SHIFT TOWARD COMPARABLE WORTH

> When one sees that dog-pound attendants, mostly men, are paid more than child-care center employees, mostly women, I believe it is time for a serious questioning of what our society values.
>
> Rep. Geraldine Ferraro (D-NY)

The issue for working women in the 1970s and 1980s has been a straightforward "equal pay for equal work." In the 1990s, is is going to be "comparable worth." The gears have shifted to a subtler concept of equal pay for work of equal value. In other words, if a secretary is as valuable to an organization as a truck driver, pay them the same. Equal pay isn't working because a majority of women who work are in low-paying jobs and there is no place for them to go. They are not moving up in most organizations, and they now make up almost fifty percent of the workforce.

Comparable worth gets little but abuse in Washington, but at the local level, six states—Idaho, Iowa, Minnesota, New Mexico, South Dakota, and Washington—have some form of pay-equity rules. Six states have as-yet-unimplemented policies, and thirty-four other states have studies under way.

But pay equity is probably dead in Congress for the next several years. Even so, Senator Dan Evans says he discovered ten years ago, while governor of Washington, that male zookeepers were earning more than female child-care specialists. "We paid people more for taking care of our animals than for taking care of our children," Evans, a Republican, told the Joint Economic Committee recently. Urging governments at all levels to take the lead in upgrading the salaries of underpaid women, Evans said pay equity in public jobs could induce private industries to review their own pay classification systems for evidence of sex discrimination.

More personnel directors are attempting to equalize wages where unwarranted differentials exist. The whole comparable worth issue is a significant and far-reaching one, and one that must be addressed, looking at the realities of our free enterprise system.

Unions have had all kinds of settlements that have amounted to comparable worth settlements. More companies are looking at their male and female salaries for various jobs and trying voluntarily to remedy obvious disparities.

Combating the Sex-Based Wage Discrimination Claim

Employers should examine wage practices to minimize possible liability for intentional discrimination and be ready to prove compliance with Title VII in the event they are hit with a sex discrimination suit. The United States Supreme Court's ruling in *County of Washington vs. Gunther* is worth reviewing.

The Gunther Guidelines

In *Gunther*, the Court held that wage discrimination claims that ordinarily would be precluded under the Equal Pay Act's requirement of equal work could be pursued under Title VII. Employers, the Court ruled, could be held liable for "intentional wage discrimination" even where the jobs performed by women are not substantially equal to those performed by men. Noting the "prompt action" to correct intentional discrimination may "completely avoid back pay liability," Blumrosen suggests that employers take the following steps:

- Eliminate sex-segregated jobs. The concentration of women in traditionally female jobs is the reason for virtually all wage discrimination claims of a class nature. An employer's conscious decisions to desegregate traditionally male and female jobs would be protected from claims of reverse discrimination by EEOC's Affirmative Action Guidelines.

- Review job evaluation and market data. Most large employers have used job evaluations to set wage rates, and the evaluation systems used may provide employees with grounds for arguing that the systems were based on intentional discrimination. Consider the following questions when reviewing the wage setting process:

    (1) Was the job evaluation free of factors that might have carried sex discrimination?

    (2) Did the evaluation process result in different jobs, some of which are predominantly held by women, receiving similar total scores? As evidence of intentional discrimination, employees may cite the existence of certain jobs that have been rated the same for internal analytical purposes, but are compensated differently. To avoid such potential problems, employers should examine the total evaluation process to ensure that such pay differences are attributable to factors other than sex.

    (3) How was the internal ranking of job meshed with market rate considerations? To achieve internal equity and a good fit in the labor market, a job evaluation system relies on an internal ranking of jobs and a wage survey that compares the organization's pay scale to those in the appropriate labor market. When the internal equity analysis is conducted, if women's jobs are devaluated, the result may be cited as evidence of intentional discrimination. The argument of intentional discrimination may be less persuasive if market rate considerations are incorporated before the internal equity analysis evaluation takes place.

- Minimize liability under the Equal Pay Act. An employer's exposure to liability in an EPA action has increased as a result of the *Gunther* decision. In the future, an EPA suit may well be coupled with a Title VII suit on behalf of women in other "female" jobs who are claiming that their pay rates are related to that of the EPA complainants. Thus a violation of the EPA with respect to one group of workers may serve as the basis for a claim of intentional discrimination by other groups.

- Issue a formal policy statement. Employers would be well-advised to publish a formal policy statement, as part of the job evaluation review process, emphasizing the company's position on wage discrimination issues.

- Determine any current effects of past discrimination. Wage discrimination complainants have sought to prove that, in the past, one employer had deliberately devalued "women's" jobs due to sex, and that this devaluation could be traced into the present. To counter the risk posed by such claims, an employer should review the history of wage rates to determine if any period of overt discrimination existed and if the wage relationships established during that period still exist. If the discriminatory relationships persist, the employer should determine whether they can be justified on grounds other than sex.

How to Know if You Have a Comparable Worth Problem

It would be prudent for all organizations to take comparable worth seriously at least in terms of ensuring their compensation programs do not discriminate. Here are certain actions that can be taken to ensure fairness. Review your current programs:

- Eliminate separate job evaluation plans for males and females.
- Eliminate double-standard salary ranges. Example: a company has one job—assembler. Management has one salary range for women and another for men. The male range is higher. That's discriminatory.
- Review current job evaluation practices. Look at them with particular emphasis on equity and objectivity of administration; support for evaluation factors that might appear to be sex biased; techniques for comparing widely different jobs; and documentation of procedures for collection of community wage rate data.
- Consolidate and simplify existing evaluation plans. Conglomerates and highly decentralized companies should examine the different evaluation plans that have grown up, with a view to reducing their number.

- Conduct special studies of jobs in which women predominate (women represent sixty-five percent or more of the population). Other types of analysis can also be undertaken. New methods of job evaluation may emerge out of this multidimensional analysis.

- Develop data to prove the economic and business necessity of valuing jobs in a certain way. Under Title VII, statistical evidence of disparate impact shifts the burden of proof to the employer, who then must show that lower market rates for some traditional women's jobs are justified.

- Speak out on the policy issues. Public policy in this area is still being formulated. Comparable worth and job evaluation are too important to be left to narrow specialists, and companies should be heard from on the subject.

- Comparable worth is an important issue. Even if federal policy and the courts do not support the concept, employers can expect private groups and individuals to continue to press it. Companies that can devise innovative ways of addressing the underlying social problems will save themselves money and earn dividends in good will.

Because comparable worth has been "beaten down" in the past doesn't mean it will go away—comparable worth is an issue that will keep heating up until it is finally accepted, because of the huge number of women working in low pay jobs.

Hay Management Consultants' Advice to Clients on Comparable Worth

Hay Management Consultants provide the following advice to clients regarding comparable worth.

Given our analysis of the issues in comparable worth, and within the existing climate of uncertainty and controversy, our advice to employers is as follows:

1. Base the compensation system upon clear and complete definitions of specific jobs. These jobs must be so designed and defined as to not restrict participation for or to any protected class unless one can demonstrate a necessary and irrefutable occupational requirement.

2. Identify the extent to which each job or job family or occupational family is dominated by a protected class. The common definition of "dominated" is 70% or more. Where domination exists, determine whether it stems from business necessity or is simply a matter of custom or convenience or indifference. In the latter instances, we recommend actions to reduce or remove the

domination. One well-known attorney has gone so far as to suggest that, when openings in male-dominated jobs appear, not only should the openings be posted but that female employees be specifically invited to apply; rejection of the invitation by a female should be recorded in her own hand. This sounds extreme to us. More suitable actions to balance the workforce might include focused external recruiting, in-company training or subsidized external training.

3. Where many employees hold the *same* job, whether this job is dominated by a protected class or not, test for *equal pay* for *equal work*. This is the law. It would also be prudent to test for equal pay in jobs that are very similar, although not equal, and where one or more are dominated by a protected class. At least one federal district court has found illegal discrimination in such an instance without using job measurement or task analysis.

4. Where the organization says that it has no job evaluation plan and that it uses a strictly market-pricing system, do the descriptions of grades of job families suggest or indicate some *de facto* form of job measurement? For example, slotting jobs that could not be market-priced into the pay scale could be labeled "whole job ranking," a technique recognized in all the textbooks as a specific method of job evaluation. Because it is a crude method, it would be particularly difficult to explain and defend.

5. Test the job evaluation process to determine if the results are repeatable as, for example, by committees with various combinations of knowledgeable members. Where protected class job domination is common, involve members of such classes in the job evaluation process.

6. Identify specific labor markets from which current and prospective job holders are typically drawn.

This material was excerpted, with permission, from Hay Management Consultants' special report, *Linking Employee Attitudes & Corporate Culture To Corporate Growth & Profitability, 1984*.

EQUAL EMPLOYMENT OPPORTUNITY ISN'T DEAD—COURT CASES, NEW LEGISLATION, AND JUSTICE DEPARTMENT OPINIONS KEEP IT ALIVE

Even though there has been a push in recent years to eliminate goals and timetables in affirmative action plans, most companies have opted not to eliminate the gains they have already made and to keep goals and timetables in effect. In fact, in 1986 the Supreme Court upheld affirmative action plans.

The Justice Department Takes Action

In 1986 the Justice Department took a major step to accept race-based hiring goals, following the lead of the Supreme Court. Companies support affirmative action. In a survey, 95 percent of 128 large companies said they would use hiring and promotion goals even if the government stopped requiring them, and in May of 1986, the National Association of Manufacturers voted a new endorsement of affirmative action. Most businesses understand and accept goals and timetables, because they feel they are the right thing to do.

New Legislation in the Cable Industry

Until 1985, there had been no new legislation in the affirmative action arena. In a surprise move in September 1985, Congress enacted an amendment to the Cable Act of 1984, which directs cable operators with six or more employees to meet specific requirements for equal employment opportunity compliance. The Federal Communications Commission (FCC), the federal regulatory agency for television, radio, and other communications industries, has been charged with monitoring EEO compliance in the industry. The first reporting requirements under the new amendment took place in May of 1986, with little fanfare. However, few cable companies were ready and trained to carry out compliance.

An astute cable industry employee, Eve Sandavol, who had been in the human resources department of Mile High Cable Company in Denver for several years, had the expertise and desire to help cable firms comply with the new Cable Act Amendment and formed a consulting company in Denver called New Visions.

She provides the following information for cable companies who need to comply with the new amendment and be prepared for FCC monitoring of their affirmative action plans.

> Cable operators are required to report their status on EEO requirements to the FCC EEO Enforcement Branch on an annual basis. Failure to report or to comply can result in sanctions which include fines or decertification of the company's operating license.
>
> The thrust of the cable EEO legislation is unique in the monitoring process as well as in scope. Monitoring of EEO compliance will include the annual reporting process as well as conducting actual on-site reviews. Each cable system will be reviewed at least once in five years by FCC EEO Enforcement Branch staff.
>
> The scope of the legislation is of particular significance. Virtually every aspect of human resource management is covered by the regulations and will be monitored to insure non-discrimination in the workplace.
>
> In accordance with the legislation, cable companies must report

information concerning their policies and practices in regard to the following areas of employment:

Recruitment, hiring, and selection

Promotions and transfers

Training and development

Employment practices

Job design and job progressions

Pay practices

Performance evaluations and standards

Termination and turnover data

Management and supervisory accountability standards

In addition, the regulations require cable operators to actively pursue conducting business with minority and female enterprises.

Supreme Court Guarantees Job in Maternity Leave

In another surprise move, hailed as a major victory for women, the Supreme Court upheld a California law on January 13, 1987 that granted pregnant employees the right to a four-month unpaid leave to have a child and guaranteed that they would get their jobs back when they returned to work.

Women and minorities have made tremendous inroads in the past twenty years. I don't think anyone in business wants to see a country-wide backsliding that would inevitably give way to new unrest and a lowering of employee morale. We have to be impressed at where we have come in terms of EEO legislation in twenty years. Also, when we look at affirmative action rulings and presidential orders, we see that tremendous energy has gone into bringing affirmative action into the workplace. To backslide now would be a tremendous waste.

CORPORATE SOCIAL RESPONSIBILITY
AND ORGANIZATIONAL CHANGE

When I read about all the groups that want a piece of the corporate pie I have to ask myself, "What is the obligation of business to society?" Especially when we read about companies who make large commitments to putting revenues back to work in their communities and to supporting a great many other philanthropic groups. Should business performance be evaluated in some part on the basis of social performance and social responsibility? Is the corporation a vehicle for the redistribution of income—a community benefactor?

I think we would all agree that the social impact of corporations is very important, but we must also agree there has to be a happy medium.

Perhaps more corporate responsibility for change and changing attitudes should lie with the human resource executive. I think we have to teach ourselves not to close our minds prematurely to the novel, the surprising, the seemingly radical. We have to try harder to fight off the close-minded idea killers who squelch any new suggestion on the grounds that it is impractical. There are those who will always defend what now exists as "best" . . . no matter how unworkable it is. If we don't help our organizations accept change willingly, it will be forced on us by government legislation, or minority boycotts, or the huge numbers of working women who now fall below poverty levels in pay.

In this chapter, we have talked about employee rights, about termination-at-will, privacy issues, homosexuality, dual-career couples, comparable worth, and new employee attitudes in general. Five years ago these were subjects rarely discussed. Today they are issues we must deal with and tomorrow they will be "old hat." How difficult they are for us to deal with will be the measure of our own ability to accept change.

In the book *Innovation,* by Richard Foster, director of the consulting firm of McKinsey & Company, managers are shown how to gain the attacker's advantage by spotting and capitalizing on the technologies of the future . . . and then abandoning them before they become obsolete. When new technologies are launched, they almost always outstrip competition, but then eventually reach a point of diminishing returns. This same scenario can be detailed for human resource management techniques, procedures, programs, and attitudes. The most successful human resource managers are the ones who understand this theory of innovation and can apply it effectively to HRM in their own organizations.

FIFTEEN OTHER ISSUES AND THEIR POTENTIAL IMPACT ON HUMAN RESOURCES

In addition to the more macro-issues, here are fifteen issues that will impact the human resource function over the next three to five years.

1. There is a trend toward increased corporate absorption of the professional infrastructure. So far this important trend has only been analyzed piecemeal, profession by profession; but it is becoming clear that more major corporations are pulling in house a variety of functions normally done by outside professionals—legal, accounting, stock trading, etc.

2. Corporate employee social services are a growing benefit area,

primarily in response to increased pressure from employees—promoting day-care assistance, physical fitness, employee assistance programs to combat alcoholism, employee counseling services, legal services, and there is an increased emphasis on the family and family needs.

3. Today corporations are developing a role in our society far beyond their traditional functions, and this new role will greatly impact the human resources function. Functional lines between types of enterprises are blurring, as conglomerate corporations increase in relative importance and as financial institutions diversify into each other's territories.

    Retailers like Sears now own their own banking and insurance operations. General Electric and Sears have both formed their own trading companies like the huge Japanese trading combines. If they grow to the size of Japan's Mitsubishi, for example, and there is further industry deregulation, we could be managing human resources for a whole new breed of megacorporation.

4. We are seeing many new benefits trends . . . what workers want in benefits, flexible benefits, cost-containment programs, and cost sharing of benefits. We have to continually monitor the benefits function in order to stay up on the latest developments.

    For example, today over ten million workers have basic legal services such as wills and over-the-phone legal advice. It has been the goal of most employers during the past two or three years to stop the spread of non-wage fringe benefits, yet new ones are popping up all the time. Company paid legal services are on the rise. The United Auto Workers have negotiated a plan covering 635,000 workers. Also covered are some employees at General Motors, American Motors, and Chrysler. There are now over 3,000 prepaid legal plans offered around the country.

5. Office automation has eliminated entire layers of management at many organizations. Among these are the FMC Corporation, a Chicago based producer of machinery and chemicals; Hercules, Inc., a Wilmington, Delaware, chemical company; and Citicorp's North American Banking Group. Human resource directors more and more will be called on to provide retraining and outplacement services.

6. Training and development activities will have to include new elements like computer literacy, bilingual education, retraining, etc. Human resources departments that aren't creatively scoping the

future trends in their fields will be left behind because this area is changing so fast.

7. In the early 1990s, fifteen million people will be working at home. Unions are fighting this trend, but it is a stampede. With the advent of the computer and the new entrepreneurial spirit in the country today, work at home will be a growing demand of the workforce. We will need policies and procedures and benefits to manage the work-at-home employee.

8. Middle-class workers will need to hold two jobs to maintain their desired life styles, so there will be more two- and three-job families. This will increase the need for more programs about stress and dual-career problems.

9. We are becoming an older society, but we address the needs and issues of an older society very poorly in most organizations. Older workers are becoming more vocal and more active politically.

   There are approximately sixty million people over sixty, and by the early 1990s there will be thirty-one million people over the age of sixty-five in the United States. A vast percentage of these people will want to continue to work past age sixty-five, and for business this means that the surge of twenty-five- to thirty-five-year-olds who want to succeed and move ahead quickly in their jobs will be greatly curtailed.

   Corporations will have to upgrade recruiting and retention programs to appeal to older workers because they will need older workers badly in the future.

10. It has been projected that by 1990 over seventy-five percent of the women in America will be working outside the home. Right now over sixty percent of married women with children work outside the home. More often now these jobs are the mainstay of a family's livelihood; and the Census Bureau counts nearly six million homes in which wives earn more than their husbands.

    Women will want more of the pie as time goes by . . . higher pay, comparable pay, more flexible hours, a bigger say in types of benefits offered, etc. Human resource managers must address these issues very soon to be prepared for some serious activity in this area.

11. New types of jobs and new career fields present a challenging opportunity for the human resource manager to counsel young people just preparing for a career and for older people who need to make a career change.

12. Business and personnel management ethics will be more carefully

scrutinized by employees. Certainly the majority of human resource managers are ethical in their dealings with employees. But the ethics surrounding denial of promotions, performance appraisals, terminations, and all actions that affect an employee's future with an organization will be more closely scrutinized.

13. With the advent of the microcomputer, technicians—instead of engineers and designers—will be able to design elaborate and futuristic facilities and all types of designs for industry. The United States Department of Labor estimates there will be fifty-five million information workers in 1990. That is an increase of ten million people who will be working with some type of computer.

14. The rise in the number of minorities in the workforce will create the need for management to better understand and successfully interact with ethnic and cross-cultural groups. There are 28.6 million black Americans, who account for 12.1 percent of the population. Americans of Spanish origin have increased their numbers in the United States by 61 percent and now number over 16 million. Americans of Spanish origin are expected to outnumber black Americans in this decade. Asian Americans, the fastest growing group, jumped 128 percent in one decade to total 3.5 million.

Bilingual education, the ability to speak at least one other language, probably Spanish, will be a new emphasis for the human resource manager and all professionals in the field. We are already seeing a number of advertisements that require applicants to speak and write Spanish.

15. CEOs, managers, and supervisors will have to learn a new way of managing people—a more cooperative, participative, and open style. They will be managing more dual-career couples who met and mated at work, more homosexual couples, and a wider variety of age groups.

An Up-Beat Philosophy of Human Resources Management

The changes that are occurring in HRM may boggle the mind of the old-fashioned personnel administrator, but they excite and challenge the energetic forward-thinking human resources manager or director who views change as an opportunity to actualize creative ideas.

Benefit Programs: How to Make Them Work and Achieve Maximum Advantages for Your Company

CHAPTER **4**

Because this chapter covers so many current issues in the benefits area, it is organized differently from the other chapters. You will note that this chapter has a special introduction and eight main parts:

Part A: An Analysis of Employee Benefit Provisions in the Tax Reform Act of 1986

Part B: What You Should Know about COBRA, the Consolidated Omnibus Budget Reconciliation Act of 1985

Part C: A Look at Innovative New Benefits Some Companies are Offering

Part D: Flexible Benefits

Part E: Pension and Retirement Benefits

Part F: Medical Cost Containment

Part G: Calculating the Cost of Benefits

Part H: Employee Benefit Communications

These eight benefit areas have changed dramatically and many of the important changes are covered in this chapter in a succinct and simple format. Included are the changes that have occurred as a result of the Tax Reform Act of 1986 and the Consolidated Omnibus Budget Reconciliation Act (COBRA).

INTRODUCTION

We are all well aware that employee benefits are undergoing significant change. These changes have complicated administration but at the same time, they have provided some advantages for both employees and employers.

Some HR people feel, for example, that flexible benefit programs better meet the needs of today's family, which is more likely to be a single mother head-of-the-household, or an empty nester with grown children, than the family of the 1950s: a male with two children and an unemployed spouse.

Flexible benefit plans have become very popular in mid-size and in larger organizations. Employees appreciate them and tend to migrate toward companies that make flexible programs available. On the other hand, however, some companies have found out through mergers and acquisitions that benefits are a high priority item in pricing a deal. Most executives involved in mergers or acquisitions in the past few years overlooked benefits as an issue in a pre-buy-out review. Not so now. Today savvy executives have discovered that benefits rank next to product liability in affecting the price of an acquisition, merger, or leveraged buyout, and the biggest companies in the buyout game, like W. R. Grace and Company, have teams of experts in the areas of management, financial, legal and human resources that thoroughly review each area prior to consummating a deal.

Although flexible plans are popular, the United States Treasury Department has put a damper on them by issuing restrictions. Treasury guidelines state that employees must choose before the end of each year how much they want to contribute to the benefit spending program for the following year. If the total amount of allowable benefits is not spent during the year, the employee forfeits whatever is left.

The Treasury Department is also concerned about equity between highly paid executives and those at the lower end of the income scale. It has moved to set up rules to make certain that the higher paid employees are not receiving an unfair advantage from the plan. Most benefits experts feel the new restrictions may slow down development of flexible benefits plans, but that ultimately they will remain popular and grow over time. This chapter provides a review of flexible benefits programs and tells how one well-known benefits consultant suggests they be instituted.

This chapter also covers trends in health and medical benefits. The whole area of health care is changing and a new health care system is taking shape at the urging of business and government, the two most significant users. Satisfied with the quality of health care in America, but dissatisfied with the price, these groups are changing their purchase strategies in an attempt to keep future cost increases within manageable limits.

For example, the Federal government implemented a prospective payments program for Medicare, a dramatic departure from the previous method of reimbursing hospitals for the full cost of caring for Medicare patients. Under this new method, hospitals are paid a fixed amount for each of 467 diagnostically related groups, called "DRGs." If a hospital's actual costs are less than the fixed amount, it keeps the difference. If they are more, it pays the extra costs from its own funds. The objective is to encourage hospital efficiency.

Some organizations are changing the structure of their group health plans and buying less costly delivery systems. Health Maintenance Organizations (HMOs), Individual Practice Associations (IPAs), and Preferred Provider Organizations (PPOs) are all further explained in this chapter.

Medical benefits are also changing because of more creative and innovative applications of technology and services. Some new ideas in cost cutting relate to delivery and location of services. These include:

- birthing centers that might become a new corporate benefit (this chapter provides information on companies using them), and

- the hospital-in-the-home concept that is also catching on with organizations that take hospital cost cutting seriously.

The broad scope of employee medical benefits now covers the entire area of employee health, including mental health and combating the problems of drugs and alcohol. This chapter describes Employee Assistance Programs (EAPs) and reviews another new trend that companies are using to handle organizational problems. This trend is the use of management psychologists instead of the traditional management consultants for organizational development and organization change strategies.

Walter T. Crane, President and CEO of Crane, Dignum, and Bolton Insurance Agency of Boston, Massachusetts, felt a new corporate culture was necessary in order to enhance expansion objectives. Instead of looking for a traditional management consultant, Mr. Crane hired Westman Associates, a Boston, Massachusetts group of management psychologists. Retaining the services of a psychologist is a practice that is beginning to gain wider acceptance in the business world, although it is still a sensitive issue among many executives.

Retirement Counseling

This chapter also covers preretirement counseling. Many leading companies are launching programs to make employees aware of all the choices they will face when their working days are over. Until a few years ago, retirement was a simple process. A retiree was called into the company's personnel department and given a few basic facts about Social Security and pension benefits.

No longer. Today many companies, well aware of the innumerable pitfalls awaiting the unprepared retiree, are making preretirement counseling a new and vital benefit for employees—just as important to many of them as their insurance and pensions.

The more reasonable companies now offer corporate-wide, multi-hour, seminars that, in the aggregate, involve thousands of employees, and usually their spouses. Inside and outside experts offer advice about every conceivable aspect of retirement: financial planning, estate planning, maintaining health, deciding where to live, getting a post-retirement job, handling legal questions, finding ways to use suddenly increased leisure time happily and productively. The sponsoring companies offer no one solution in any of these areas; instead, they see to it that employees are made aware of the wide range of choices they will face. CBS, Inc. is one company that decided to provide preretirement counseling to employees. Their program was so successful, they decided to market it to other organizations. The CBS program is reviewed in this chapter.

Employee Stock Ownership Plans

Nearly everyone today has heard of Employee Stock Ownership Plans (ESOPs) but many people still do not know what they are. Tax benefits have enhanced the ESOP as a financing tool, one that becomes particularly handy when a company wants to raise capital or take itself private in a leveraged buyout.

We are all interested in increasing profits. A study done for the New York Stock Exchange shows that publicly traded companies in which employees own ten percent or more of the stock tend to have a higher operating margin than other companies. About 5,000 companies now have ESOPs. The key elements of ESOPs and leveraged buyouts appear in this chapter.

TWELVE SIGNIFICANT FORCES RESHAPING BENEFITS PROGRAMS IN AMERICA

In addition to the high cost of employee benefits, other forces are reshaping programs. These forces will forever alter the structure, levels, and makeup of organizational employee benefits programs in all organizations.

Here are twelve of the most significant forces behind these changes.

1. Accelerating medical costs have mandated serious cost-containment programs in nearly every organization, and preferred provider organizations and cost containment coalitions are growing.

2. The demographics of the workforce are changing . . . workers are getting older. Health costs are higher for this group, and retraining is becoming a big issue because older employees want to remain in the workforce and mandatory retirement has been eliminated.

3. The changing pension scene now includes pension equity for women, extension of benefits for workers after age sixty-five, and so-called pension asset reversions or "raids" by many corporations that have taken place in the past three years, causing thousands of retired workers and those getting ready to retire to become concerned. Older workers are becoming more vocal and proactive in the employee rights areas.

4. Demands of the contemporary worker for different benefits, like child-care assistance, health/fitness programs, flexible working hours, and so forth are changing employee benefits programs.

5. Flexible benefits programs and flexible compensation in general have increased in popularity.

6. Companies are taking more responsibility for the mental and physical well-being of employees by providing formal Employee Assistance Programs. EAPs help management handle one of the most serious health problems on the job: substance abuse.

7. There is a surge in ESOPs (Employee Stock Ownership Plans) and a trend toward employees buying their ailing companies. In fact, ESOPs and IRC Sec. 401(k) plans are the fastest growing benefits. ESOPs have experienced a 2,000 percent growth in the past ten years.

8. The taxing of fringe benefits and the Tax Reform Act of 1986 put a new light on employee benefits and perks.

9. The lack of funding of retiree fringe benefits on the part of many companies is thought by some to be a ticking "time bomb." More attention is being paid now to the potential liabilities employers create when they promise post-retirement health and life benefits. These escalating liabilities are estimated by some experts to be in the trillions of dollars, and they are complicating mergers and acquisitions.

10. The new Financial Accounting Standards Board (FASB) rules for the first time require companies to report certain information on retiree benefits in their annual reports, and it appears there are only a handful of companies funding retiree fringe benefits. The new FASB rules will impact the benefits area over time.

11. Over the past fifteen years, government intervention in the employee benefits area has been unprecedented with the passage of the Employee Income Security Act, the Pregnancy Disability Act, Amendments to the Age Discrimination in Employment Act, the Health Maintenance Organization Act, the Consolidated Omnibus Budget Reconciliation Act of 1985, and the Tax Reform Act of 1986. In addition, courts have stepped in, setting precedents with such decisions as the Bethlehem Steel decision where a Federal judge ruled the company had to give a retiree the higher medical benefits promised when he retired. Bethlehem Steel had cut back on medical benefits for retirees.

12. Some experts, although unwilling to talk about it, fear that the morass of benefit problems, underfunding, tax laws, accelerating costs, and the demographics of our population will eventually result in a new emphasis on socialized medicine.

Nine Trends and How They Are Affecting Benefits

Employees are changing their life styles so quickly today that most ordinary benefits programs offered by companies are not well-suited to the average worker anymore.

People marry, divorce, share homes without marriage, pass up or postpone parenthood, and so forth. Companies are beginning to wake up to the fact that traditional fringe benefits don't fit the needs of the contemporary worker. So, more companies are looking at new types of benefits to attract and retain the smart, contemporary employee.

There are nine important trends transforming the traditional benefits offered by organizations.

1. More and more women are entering the job market. Many of these women are single heads of household and desperately need benefits for themselves and their children. It has been projected that by 1990 over seventy percent of the women in America over age sixteen will be working.

2. Marriage is not the norm anymore. In the 1970s, seventy percent of all households were maintained by married couples. Today, the figure is only sixty percent, and the Census Bureau predicts that figure will drop to fifty-five percent by 1990.

3. Because of the number of working mothers, work spans are not continuous. Working women frequently take sabbaticals during their childrens' early years.

4. More couples are remaining childless, and many couples are opting for only one child.

5. The average household is no longer made up of a working father and a stay-at-home mother.

6. Contemporary workers are more vocal in demanding that their needs be met, and the standard benefits package does not meet their needs.

7. Benefits cost containment has organizations looking for ways to cut benefits where they can, and some companies are cutting basic benefits in order to offer the new benefits contemporary workers want, and more companies are charging employees for part of their benefits costs. Companies have to consider that today's workforce is characterized by a variety of situations, and plan for benefits that take into consideration an employee's obligations—not only to a spouse and at-home children, but possibly to a former spouse, children living elsewhere, or a live-in, nonmarried partner.

8. There is a new emphasis on family life and the quality of family life. It is not just the emphasis on the need for day-care by the working mother; for example, the father too is concerned about the quality of child care in those employee households where there is a traditional family unit.

9. Workers are opting to work beyond age sixty-five, which is changing company benefits obligations.

Organizations are being confronted with the problems of changing life styles and the issues of people's relations to each other. Personal relationships are more important, and the fact that one spouse or live-in partner has group medical coverage makes people more vocal about wanting to change other benefits rather than just accepting double medical coverage that is not going to be used. More people will ask for cash rather than having the company pay premiums for insurance that they don't need.

Family patterns were clearly changing all through the late 1970s and early 1980s, but employers did not see these changes. Now, many employers are being forced to consider new types of plans. Demographic changes are also creating pressures for new types of benefits, and companies are responding.

Two-career families, especially those with professional and/or managerial women, are becoming more intelligent about wanting to have more of their income tax sheltered. This means that they want employers to purchase services with before-tax dollars that formerly came out of the family budget.

In the future, companies will more frequently be faced with the decision of providing group medical coverage for a live-in same sex "family" member.

Today's more sophisticated employee also realizes that currently many company benefits run counter to some people's needs. For example, group life insurance coverage is normally tied to an employee's salary, giving the least coverage to young workers with big mortgages, young children, and spouses who have limited earning power—while executives whose major child-rearing and home-buying expenses are behind them, get the most dollar protection.

New Benefits Offered by Some Companies

Even though some companies are cutting back on benefits as costs escalate, many periodicals like *The Wall Street Journal* and *Business Week* are reporting that companies are offering innovative *new* benefits. Following is a chart showing some of these programs and what employee population is receiving them.

Benefit	For Executives	For Managers	For All Employees
Employee assistance programs	X	X	X
Dental insurance	X	X	X
Prepaid legal services	X	X	X
Financial planning	X		
Day care subsidies	X	X	X
Nannies	X	X	X
Parental leave	X	X	X
ESOPs	X	X	X
Company car	X	X	
Vacation apartments in Hawaii and Vail	X	X	X
Private museum showings	X	X	X
On-site MBA training	X	X	X
Paid adoption	X	X	X
Plot of land for farming	X	X	X
Coverage of parents under health plans	X	X	X
Home health care	X	X	X
Mental health care	X	X	X
Health/fitness programs	X	X	X
Physical exams	X	X	X
Free lunches	X	X	X
Company-subsidized housing	X	X	X
Self-defense training for women	X	X	X
Country Club membership	X		
Lunch Club membership	X	X	
Meditation and self-hypnosis training to aid in reducing stress and to stop smoking	X	X	X
Courses in speed reading, memory, creativity, etc.	X	X	X
Cash gift when new child born	X	X	X
Psychological counseling	X	X	X
Lending libraries including audiocasettes and videos	X	X	X
Vision insurance	X	X	X

Part A

An Analysis of Employee Benefit Provisions in the Tax Reform Act of 1986

ANALYSIS OF EMPLOYEE BENEFIT PROVISIONS IN THE TAX REFORM ACT OF 1986

The following analysis is provided by Charles D. Spencer and Associates, Inc., Chicago, Ill. and covers Qualified Retirement Plans, Section 401(k) Plans, Distributions, Loans, Withdrawal, IRAs, Employee Stock Ownership Plans, Welfare Benefit Provisions and Cafeteria Plans.

The 1986 Tax Reform Act affects nearly all employee benefit plans— both those that provide retirement benefits and those that provide welfare benefits.

Years are likely to pass before the ramifications of the benefits provisions are completely understood. Three major themes run through the benefits provisions, however, and benefits experts in the government are likely to adhere to these notions when writing regulations in the future.

Most simply put, the benefit provisions strive for consistency across different types of benefit plans, firm guidelines that make tax-advantaged benefits equitable across salary lines, and standards for retirement plans that insure the use of these benefits for retirement.

Thus, a new definition of highly compensated is adopted, and this definition is consistent across all benefits. New discrimination rules are adopted for welfare plans, and these rules are similar to those for retirement plans. New distribution and withdrawal rules limit the nonretirement uses of qualified plans.

This booklet analyzes in detail those provisions of the 1986 Tax Reform Act that affect employee benefit plans. The information is taken from the Conference Committee Report, which accompanied the final bill as it came up for a vote in the House of Representatives and the Senate, and the language of the law itself.

Following are the primary effective dates for the 1986 Tax Act's employee benefit provisions.

Plan or taxable years after Dec. 31, 1985:

- ability of money purchase plans to reallocate forfeitures;
- extension for educational assistance plans;
- extension for group legal plans.

Plan or taxable years after Dec. 31, 1986:

- definition of highly compensated, including $200,000 cap;
- top heavy plan accruals;
- changes in the IRC Sec. 415 limits;
- new nondiscrimination rules for Sec. 401(k) plans;
- Sec. 401(k) loan and hardship withdrawal restrictions;
- repeal of ten-year forward averaging, replaced by a one-time five-year forward averaging;
- 10% penalty tax on pre-age 59 1/2 distributions;
- maximum limit on annual qualified plan distributions;
- expiration of tax-credit ESOPs (on Dec. 31, 1986);
- ESOP distribution requirements and extension of put option for stock bonus plans (applies to stock acquired after Dec. 31, 1986);
- changes in rules for individual retirement accounts;
- deductibility of health insurance for self-employed;
- $5,000 limit on dependent care plan benefits.

Plan or taxable years after Dec. 31, 1987:

- welfare plan nondiscrimination rules, if rules are issued before the end of 1987; otherwise the effective date is three months after rules are published between Jan. 1, 1988, and Sept. 30, 1988, or if rules are not published, Dec. 31, 1988.

Plan or taxable years after Dec. 31, 1988:

- qualified retirement plan coverage tests;
- retirement plan minimum participation standards;
- changes in integration rules;
- changes in retirement plan vesting schedules;
- Sec. 415 $200,000 limit;
- nondiscrimination tests for existing 401(k) plans for tax-exempt entities and state and local governments.

Other Effective Dates

The repeal of the three-year recovery method for calculating taxable distributions is effective for annuity starting dates after **July 1, 1986.**

For plan terminations on or after Jan. 1, 1986, the 10% excise tax on asset reversions is imposed for reversions after **Dec. 31, 1985.**

The changes in the calculations of amounts available to be cashed out in a lump sum distribution are effective on the **date of enactment.**

Reduction of maximum age requirement from 25 to 21 for simplified employee pensions is effective on the **date of enactment.**

The penalty for defined benefit plan overfunding is the **date of enactment.**

QUALIFIED RETIREMENT PLANS

"Highly compensated" is defined as a 5% owner; an employee paid at least $75,000 annually; an employee in the top-paid 20% who is earning at least $50,000 annually; and any officer of the employer (excluding "name only" officers, as defined in IRC Sec. 416(i)) who received annual compensation in excess of 1-1/2 times the Sec. 415 defined contribution dollar limit. The dollar amounts of compensation shown here are to be indexed in the same manner and at the same time as the Sec. 415 dollar maximums.

Benefits may not be based on compensation in excess of $200,000 per year.

This definition of "highly compensated" does *not* replace the Sec. 416(i) definition of "key employee" which applies to plans determined to be top heavy.

The new definition is effective for plan years beginning after Dec. 31, 1986.

Coverage Requirements

In lieu of the present-law 70%/80% test, the Act requires a retirement plan to satisfy *one* of the following coverage tests, effective with plan years beginning after Dec. 31, 1988:

1. 70% of all nonhighly compensated employees must be covered under the plan.

2. The ratio of nonhighly compensated employees covered under the plan must be at least 70% of the percent of highly compensated covered under the plan.

3. If the plan qualifies under the present-law fair cross-section test, then the average benefit (as a percentage of pay) provided to nonhighly compensated employees must equal at least 70% of the average benefit provided to highly compensated employees.

If the employer also maintains a Sec. 401(k) plan, elective deferrals under that plan are taken into account in applying the coverage tests.

New 50 Employee/40% Test

Minimum participation standards.   Small employers will be particularly impacted by another rule. If an employer has more than one plan, it can no longer rely upon comparability as defined in Rev. Rul. 81-202 to qualify each plan under the Code. Instead, each plan will have to benefit no fewer than the lesser of 50 employees or 40% or more of all employees.

The new 50 employee/40% test would be effective for all plan years beginning after Dec. 31, 1988.

The Act provides a transitional rule that mitigates the impact of the new minimum participation standards. Under the transitional rule, plans that do not comply after the effective date must be merged or terminated by the end of the first plan year. In those instances, the actuarial present value of the accrued benefits must be calculated using an interest rate no lower than a specified rate. If there is an asset reversion as a result of the required merger or termination, the excise tax penalty will not apply.

Integration Rules

Defined benefit offset plans may not reduce a participant's benefits by more than the lesser of

(1) 50% (it is now 83-1/3%) of the benefit that would have been accrued; or

(2) 0.75% of the participant's final average compensation multiplied by the participant's years of service with the employer (not to exceed 35 years).

Defined benefit excess and step-rate plans face a 200% or 0.75% test. Two situations are applicable. First, for benefits attributable to any year of service, the maximum excess percentage of compensation is the lesser of—

(1) 200% of the base benefit percentage, or

(2) the sum of the base benefit percentage and 0.75%.

Second, for total benefits, the maximum excess percentage of compensation is the lesser of—

(1) 200% of the base benefit percentage, or

(2) the sum of the base benefit percentage and 0.75% multiplied by the participant's years of service (maximum of 35 years).

Defined contribution plans face a similar 200% rule. The excess contribution percentage cannot exceed the lesser of 200% of the base contribution percentage *or* the sum of the base contribution percentage and the old age benefits FICA tax percentage applied to employers at the beginning of the plan year (but not reduced below 5.7%).

Integration changes are effective for plan years beginning after Dec. 31, 1988.

Top-Heavy Accrual Rule

Another provision involves the benefit accrual rule used for calculating whether or not a qualified plan is top-heavy. The Conference Committee report expresses concern that some plan sponsors are using artificially accelerated benefit accrual rules for nonkey employees to take the plan out of top-heavy status.

To correct this, the Act requires the use of only the fractional accrual rule method (IRC Sec. 411(b)(1)(C)) when the top-heavy determination is being made. Any of the three methods can be used during actual operation of the plan. This provision would be effective for plan years beginning after Dec. 31, 1986.

Sec. 415 Limits

The Tax Reform Act adopts the Senate version, keeping the present $90,000 maximum for defined benefit plans and the present $30,000 maximum for defined contribution plans, subject to the following modifications, for plan years beginning after Dec. 31, 1986;

- In the event of retirement prior to age 65, the $90,000 must be actuarially reduced. The present floor of $75,000 at age 55 is repealed, resulting in a reduction to $67,500 at age 62 and $37,800 at age 55.

- After the year 2003, when the age of unreduced Social Security benefits begins to increase, reaching age 67 in 2022, retirement at 65 under a qualified plan would be considered *early* retirement and the actuarial reductions would apply. Thus, in projecting Sec. 415 maximums for an individual retiring at that time, the dollar limit for retirement at age 62 would be $54,900 and $30,600 for retirement at age 55.

The preceding provisions would not apply to plans of tax-exempt entities.

- The availability of the $90,000 maximum would be conditioned on completion of ten years of participation, rather than ten years of service. This would reduce the incentive to adopt a plan to provide maximum benefits for highly compensated or key employees who are close to retirement.

- The defined contribution dollar limit of $30,000 would be frozen until the defined benefit limit reaches $120,000; it would then be adjusted in tandem with the defined benefit maximum but at a 1:4 ratio.

- The Sec. 415 cost-of-living adjustment will be indexed using the present-law Consumer Price Index.

- All employee contributions are to be included in determining the annual addition under a defined contribution plan. However, a special exception would apply to contributions made by nonkey employees for retiree medical coverage; these would not be counted against the 25% of compensation limitation.

Vesting Requirements

The Tax Reform Act reduces the number of alternate minimum vesting schedules to four:

1. 100% after five years of service (5-year cliff).
2. 20% after three years of service, 20% per year thereafter, with 100% after seven years.
3. Retaining the present top-heavy plan 2/20 schedule, resulting in 100% vesting after six years.
4. Modifying the present top-heavy alternative of 100% after three years' service to 100% after two years.

Class year vesting as currently defined by IRC Sec. 411(d)(4) would be eliminated.

The effective date for the vesting schedules would be plan years beginning after Dec. 31, 1988.

Profit-Sharing Carryover

Under the new profit-sharing carryover rules, contributions in excess of the 15% deduction limit can be carried forward to future years and deducted when the plan sponsor's contribution is less than 15%. However, the deduction in any year cannot exceed 15% (instead of 25% as under existing law). No longer will plan sponsors be able to "save" percentages to be used in future years; the excess contribution must exist prior to utilizing the carryover.

This provision is effective for taxable years beginning after Dec. 31, 1986. Unused pre-1987 limitation carryforwards may be used in future tax years, but only up to 25% of compensation.

Two-Plan Deduction Limit

When a defined benefit plan and a defined contribution plan are being used, the deduction for contributions to both plans cannot exceed 25% of compensation. However, exceeding the 25% limit is permitted if it is necessary to meet the minimum funding standards in defined benefit plans. When that occurs, no contribution to the defined contribution plan can be deducted.

This 25% limit applies to all combinations of defined benefit and defined contribution plans. Under prior law, if the defined contribution plan was a money purchase pension plan, the 25% limit could be exceeded.

Contributions that exceed the 25% limit may be carried over and deducted in future years when the contributions are less than 25%.

This provision is effective for taxable years beginning after Dec. 31, 1986.

SEC. 401(k) PLANS

The Tax Reform Act of 1986 establishes a $7,000 cap on elective deferrals to a Sec. 401(k) plan. The employer may make additional non-elective contributions on behalf of participants up to the IRC Sec. 415 defined contribution limit, which includes the $7,000. Effective date: taxable years beginning after Dec. 31, 1986.

The present 401(k) coverage requirements are reduced under the new nondiscrimination tests to provide that the average elective deferrals for highly compensated employees may not exceed—

(a) 125% of the average deferral percentage for all other employees, or

(b) 200% of that deferral percentage up to a two percentage point spread.

Those limits compare to the current 150%/250% plus three percentage points alternatives. Under those current tests, the point at which the lower-paid two-thirds makes elective deferrals of 6% or more is the point at which the 150% ratio becomes more advantageous for the upper one-third because the three percentage point spread limit under the 250% plus three alternative can be exceeded.

Under the new test, the lower paid will have to make elective deferrals of 8% or more before the highly compensated can make elective deferrals under the 125% alternative without regard to the two percentage point limitation on the spread between highly compensated deferrals and lower paid deferrals.

For example, a company has one highly compensated person and ten nonhighly compensated employees. If the average deferral for the ten employees is 3%, the highly compensated employee would be limited to the greater of 3.75% (3% × 1.25) or 5% (3% × 2.0 = 6%, not to exceed 3% + 2% = 5%). However, if the deferral rate for the ten employees were 9%, the highly compensated employee would be limited to the greater of 11.25% (9% × 1.25) or 11% (9% × 2.0 = 18%, not to exceed 9% + 2% = 11%).

These tests are effective for taxable years beginning after Dec. 31, 1986.

With respect to *any* qualified plan that conditions employer matching contributions upon employee contributions, such as a thrift plan, the Act adopts the same 125%/200% plus two percentage points test to limit the amount of employer matching contributions for highly compensated employees.

Tax-exempt entities and governmental employers may not establish 401(k) plans for their employees. However, plans of tax-exempt entities adopted prior to July 1, 1986, and plans of state and local employees adopted before May 6, 1986, are grandfathered. Such plans have to comply with the new nondiscrimination tests and Sec. 415 dollar cap for years beginning after Dec. 31, 1988.

DISTRIBUTIONS, LOANS, WITHDRAWALS

Under current law, a lump sum distribution that meets the requirements of IRC Sec. 402(e)(4) is entitled to ten-year forward averaging tax treatment. That portion of the lump sum attributable to employer contributions made prior to Jan. 1, 1974, is eligible for capital gains tax treatment.

The Tax Reform Act would repeal the special ten-year forward averaging provisions, effective after Dec. 31, 1986, and substitute a one-time five-year averaging election by plan participants who have attained age 59-1/2.

Amounts attributable to years prior to 1974 will continue to receive capital gains treatment if the distribution takes place in 1987. For distributions in subsequent years, only the following ("phaseout") percentages of the pre-1974 money will receive capital gains treatment:

Year	Phaseout
1988	95%
1989	75%
1990	50%
1991	25%

A transitional rule allows plan participants who have attained age 50 by Jan. 1, 1986, to make either the one-time five-year averaging election or to retain ten-year averaging and be taxed at 1986 rates, with the capital gains portion (pre-1974 accumulations) of their lump sum distributions grandfathered at the present-law maximum 20% rate.

Distributions in whatever form received prior to age 59-1/2 will be subject to an income tax penalty of 10% of the amount so distributed, effective for years beginning after Dec. 31, 1986. As under present law, no penalty will apply to pre-59-1/2 distributions made on account of death, disability, or separation from service, but the Tax Act modifies that last condition to apply only if the distribution is a life annuity or life expectancy payout.

Distributions made prior to March 15, 1987, if attributable to separation from service in 1986 and taxable in 1986, are grandfathered under present law so that the life payout requirement will not apply.

The Act also permits early withdrawals without penalty in the case of early retirement after age 55, and for amounts used to pay medical expenses to the extent deductible under IRC Sec. 213, which has been amended to permit such medical expense deductions to the extent they exceed 7-1/2% of adjusted gross income.

Payments made pursuant to a Qualified Domestic Relations Order (QDRO) are free of penalty tax, regardless of age.

Commencement of Benefits

Benefit payments or distributions must commence no later than April 1 of the calendar year following the year in which the participant attains age 70½, whether or not actual retirement occurs. This rule covers all participants, not just 5% owners as is the case under present law. Benefits may be distributed as a lump sum, life annuity or annuity with survivorship options, or under the life expectancy method.

Failure to comply with the benefit commencement rule or with the minimum distribution requirement will result in a 50% excise tax penalty on the difference between what was actually distributed and what should have been distributed.

The penalty does not apply to individuals who are not 5% owners and who attain age 70½ by Jan. 1, 1988; nor does it apply to those who made an election before Jan. 1, 1984, under TEFRA Sec. 242(b), to postpone distributions beyond the age 7-½ starting date (IRS Notice 83-23).

Contributory Plans

If a participant has made nontaxable contributions to a plan and receives a distribution in the form of an annuity after the "annuity starting date," the present three-year recovery method of calculating the taxable amount is repealed. Under that method, no tax is paid on the amount of annuity payment equal to the participant's own contributions, if received within three years. Subsequent annuity payments are fully includible in taxable income.

The result of repealing this provision is, effective with annuity starting dates after July 1, 1986, that all annuity payments that include employee contributions or "investment in the contract" will be taxed under the exclusion ratio method, where a fraction is derived representing the amount attributable to the participant's investment in contract, and then a second calculation is performed based on the appropriate life expectancy table.

For distributions not received as an annuity, such as under the life expectancy method, a fractional method will be used derived from the ratio of the employee's investment in contract to the total value of accrued benefits or total value of the account balance. That pro rata approach applies to distributions commencing before the annuity starting date.

Limit on Annual Distribution

If a participant receives an annual distribution from *all* qualified plans in which he participated (including IRAs, ESOPs, and Sec. 403(b) tax sheltered annuities), in excess of 125% of the defined benefit Sec. 415 dollar maximum—or $112,500 in 1987—such excess will be subject to a 15% excise tax penalty, effective for taxable years beginning after Dec. 31, 1986.

However, benefits accrued prior to Aug. 1, 1986, are grandfathered, but only if the value exceeds $562,500. The law and committee report are unclear about the actual application of this grandfather provision.

However, if the $562,500 threshold might be exceeded, benefits should be valued as of Aug. 1, 1986. For the grandfather provision to apply, the individual must elect it on an annual tax return, in a manner prescribed by the Internal Revenue Service, for taxable years ending before Jan. 1, 1989. To further confuse the issue, if the grandfather election is not made, the $112,500 limit is changed to "the greater of $150,000 or $112,500 (indexed)." Four types of distributions are excluded from this limit:

(1) distributions rolled over to an IRA or another qualified plan,

(2) amounts attributable to employee contributions,

(3) amounts payable to another individual pursuant to a qualified domestic relations order, and

(4) distribution on account of the death of the individual. However, if the "death exclusion" is used, the excess amount will be subject to a 15% increase in the applicable federal estate tax.

Rule for Nongrandfathered Distributions

For lump sum distributions not eligible for the grandfathering above, there is another rule. If the participant elects income averaging taxation of the lump sum distribution under Sec. 402(e)(4), such lump sum will escape the excise tax penalty to the extent that it does not exceed five times $112,500 or $562,500.

For example, if a participant receives a lump sum distribution of $400,000, no excise tax would be payable since $400,000 does not exceed $562,500—five times $112,500.

The special rule applies only to the lump sum. Any annuity payments received in addition to the lump sum in the example above would be subject to the 15% penalty.

Loans Tightened

Under current law, a participant may receive a loan from a qualified plan of $10,000, or 50% of the value of his accrued benefit or account balance, up to a maximum of $50,000. These limits apply to the aggregate of outstanding loans.

The Act reduces the $50,000 maximum by the highest outstanding loan balance during the preceding 12 months, and limits housing loans to purchases of a principal residence of only the participant.

Under the Tax Reform Act, the loan must be repaid in approximately equal installments over a period of not more than five years. "Balloon" payments are prohibited. The five-year repayment schedule does not apply to loans used for the purchase of the personal residence of the participant. Interest on loans, except for mortgage interest, is not deductible by the participant.

Sec. 401(k) Hardship Withdrawals

Hardship withdrawals under Sec. 401(k) plans are limited to the participant's elective deferrals. However, the present-law definition of "hardship" is retained: heavy and immediate financial needs of the employee which cannot reasonably be met from other resources. The 10% premature distribution tax and rules apply.

The loan and hardship withdrawal restrictions are effective for taxable years beginning after Dec. 31, 1986.

IRAs, MISCELLANEOUS PROVISIONS

Effective for taxable years beginning after Dec. 31, 1986, no IRA deduction will be allowed to individuals covered under qualified retirement plans if such individuals have more than $35,000 in adjusted gross income in the case of a single taxpayer or $50,000 if married and filing a joint tax return.

For individuals with adjusted gross income below $25,000 (single) or $40,000 (married), the full IRA deduction is retained whether or not covered under a qualified retirement plan.

If adjusted gross income falls in the $10,000 band between those limits, the IRA deduction is reduced on a pro rata basis—for example, $20 of IRA deduction for each $100 of adjusted gross income.

Nondeductible IRA contributions up to the present $2,000–$2,250 limits are permitted, with the interest earned on such contributions accumulating on a tax-free basis until withdrawn. For individuals with existing IRAs who can no longer make deductible contributions, the opportunity for tax-free earnings may provide sufficient incentive to continue IRA contributions on a nondeductible basis.

Taxpayers not covered under a qualified retirement plan are entitled to the full IRA deduction, irrespective of earned income.

With respect to spousal IRAs, the requirement that the spouse have no earned income for the year in order to participate has been repealed, effective for years beginning after Dec. 31, 1985, thus allowing a spousal contribution to be made as late as April 15, 1987, for the 1986 tax year.

Asset Reversions

A nondeductible excise tax penalty equal to 10% of the amount of assets reverting to the employer is imposed, effective for reversions occurring after Dec. 31, 1985, so long as the termination date of the plan is on or after

Jan. 1, 1986. The Act refers to cash or property received by the employer "directly or indirectly" from the plan.

An exception to the excise tax penalty is made if the assets reverting to the employer are transferred to an ESOP invested in securities of the employer. However, this special exception expires for reversions received after Dec. 31, 1988.

Money Purchase Plan Reallocation

Under the Tax Reform Act, money purchase pension plans would be able to reallocate forfeitures to the accounts of remaining paricipants in a nondiscriminatory fashion. By this amendment, the Act makes uniform the treatment of forfeitures under all defined contribution plans.

The Conference Committee report emphasizes that this is a permissive rule; money purchase plans may still use forfeitures to reduce future employer contributions or administrative expenses if they so desire. The effective date would be plan years beginning after Dec. 31, 1985.

Cashing Out Accrued Benefit

Under present law, an employer may make a lump sum distribution of a participant's accrued pension benefit if the present actuarial value of the accrued benefit is less than $3,500. In making that determination, the terms of IRC Sec. 401(a)(11) mandate the use of an interest assumption that does not exceed the rate published by the PBGC for plan terminations. That requirement also applies to the automatic survivor annuity under Sec. 417 if the present value of the accrued benefit exceeds $3,500.

The Conference Committee, as a means of discouraging the cash-out of accrued pension benefits, extends the required use of an interest assumption no greater than the PBGC termination rate to participant cash-outs and survivor annuities, for calculating present values to $25,000. For lump sum conversions over $25,000, an interest rate no greater than 20% higher than the PBGC rate may be used.

For example, if the PBGC single-employer plan termination rate is 7.5%, that is the maximum rate that can be used to calculate the lump sum conversion of accrued benefits up to $25,000. The rate for amounts in excess of $25,000 can be no more than 20% higher than 7.5%, or 9.0% in this example.

Effective date is the date of enactment.

Penalty for Overfunding

Effective after Dec. 31, 1986. Under the Act, the Treasury is given discretionary authority to determine the "correct valuation" of a defined benefit pension plan. To the extent that there have been excessive deductions based on an overstatement of plan liabilities, H.R. 3838 provides for a graded penalty tax on the difference between the correct valuation and the valuation on which the tax deduction was claimed, allowing for a 49% "honest disagreement" differential:

Valuation Claimed As % Of Correct Valuation	Penalty Tax Applied
150% but not more than 200%	10%
200% but not more than 250%	20
More than 250%	30

The penalty tax is applied under IRC Sec. 6659A in addition to the tax imposed on any disallowed deductions. The penalty tax does not offset the imposition of appropriate excise tax penalties.

This provision is specifically aimed at the assumptions used to maximize deductions under professional corporation plans. In a series of letter rulings issued in 1985 and early in 1986, the Internal Revenue Service made it clear that it would disallow deductions based, for example, on 5% pre-retirement and 5% post-retirement interest assumptions for a two-doctor pension plan with a normal retirement age set at 55 and the plan assets invested in a 13% GIC. The objective of these letter rulings has now been codified.

Employee Leasing

The rules for employee leasing arrangements under IRC Sec. 414(n) have been considerably tightened.

A leased employee will not be considered an employee of the recipient employer if the leasing organization provides a retirement plan contribution on behalf of that employee equal to 10% of compensation, compared to the present-law 7-1/2% "safe harbor" contribution.

In addition, two conditions have to be met:

1. The leasing organizations must cover 100% of its employees under at least a 10% of pay plan. Employees who earn less than $1,000 for the year do not have to be covered.

2. If more than 20% of the "individuals performing substantial services for the recipient organization" are leased employees, the 10% safe harbor contribution may *not* be used.

Recipient organizations that have no top-heavy pension plans and use only a de minimus number of leased employees are exempt from the employee-leasing recordkeeping requirements.

That exception essentially frees large companies that use a limited number of "temporaries" from the strictures of Sec. 414(n). The Tax Reform Act changes are aimed, once again, at the small professional corporation that establishes a pension plan for its principals and effectively excludes its lower-paid employees by "leasing" them.

Technical Amendments to REA

The 1986 Tax Reform Act contains a number of technical corrections to the Retirement Equity Act of 1984, which established rules for distributions under qualified retirement plans as joint and survivor annuities and preretirement survivor benefits. These are generally effective Jan. 1, 1987, except for collective bargaining agreements when the effective date is July 1, 1988, or the expiration of the current agreement. The following is a summary of the major changes:

1. For simplified employee pension, the maximum age requirement is reduced from 25 to 21 years of age. This provision takes effect on the date of enactment.

Survivor Benefit Requirements

2. The amendments clarify that the qualified preretirement survivor annuity rules apply in the case of death before the annuity starting date, and the qualified joint and survivor annuity rules apply in the case of death on or after the annuity starting date.

3. For transferee plans, only transfers made on or after Jan. 1, 1985, are affected. If separate accounts are maintained for the transferred assets, then the transferee rules apply only to the transferred assets.

4. For participants who separate from service prior to death, the amount of the qualified preretirement survivor annuity will be calculated from the actual date of separation from service, rather than the date of death.

   The amendments also clarify that a plan exempt from survivor benefit requirements is not required to provide for payment of a participant's nonforfeitable accrued benefit upon the death of the participant, unless the participant and spouse have been married at least one year on the date of death.

5. A waiver of spousal consent must include the option to name a designated beneficiary or to relinquish all rights to name such a beneficiary. Beneficiary designations may not be changed without consent of the spouse. Also, no portion of an accrued benefit can secure a loan unless the spouse consents.

6. The period for giving notice of the right to waive a qualified preretirement survivor annuity is a reasonable period after the date of hire for a person hired after age 35. The same reasonable period applies to a participant who separates form service before age 35.

Qualified Domestic Relations Orders

7. Distributions to a spouse or former spouse generally will be taxable to the spouse. However, distributions to any other

alternate payee (such as a child) generally will be included in the gross income of the participant. This provision is applicable to distributions after the enactment date of the tax act.

8. The definition of earliest retirement age for domestic relations order provisions is the later of age 50 or the earliest date benefits are payable under the plan.

Other Provisions

9. The amendments clarify that a plan will not qualify if it distributes, as a lump sum, amounts greater than $3,500 without the consent of the participant or the spouse.

   The law also makes clear that rules for cash-outs of accrued benefits apply only to vested, accrued benefits. These rules do not apply to dividend distributions from employee stock ownership plans.

10. A plan administrator is required to notify participants of eligibility to roll over plan distributions.

11. A waiver of a survivor benefit is not treated as a transfer for purposes of gift tax provisions.

12. For benefits payable as a joint and survivor annuity, the annuity starting date is the first day an amount is received as an annuity. In all other cases, the annuity starting date is the date all events have occurred which entitle the participant to the benefits.

13. Owner-employees would be allowed to borrow from qualified plans if a prohibited transaction exemption is obtained.

ESOPs

The payroll-based ESOP tax credit (PAYSOP) is repealed for compensation paid or accrued after Dec. 31, 1986. This refers to the 1/2 of 1% of covered payroll used to buy stock for participants. PAYSOPs may be terminated and accounts distributed. This provision overrides the rule that accounts must remain in the plan for 84 months (seven years).

Most ESOP provisions in the tax bill relate to small, closely held businesses rather than to ESOPs in large, publicly held companies. However, the new minimum coverage and participation standards for qualified plans apply to all ESOPs.

Excise taxes on asset reversions. The Act imposes a 10% excise tax on asset reversions from terminated defined benefit plans. An exception to the 10% excise tax is made for amounts transferred to an ESOP. The exception for ESOPs expires after Dec. 31, 1988.

Diversification. Any participant age 55 and with ten years of *participation* (not service) in an ESOP may elect to diversify annually up to 25% of the participant's account balance (50% after age 60). The ESOP is required to offer at least three investment options during an annual election period and to complete the diversification within a specified period. Diversification rights apply to stock acquired after Dec. 31, 1986.

Limits on contributions.   The limit on contributions so that no more than one-third of the contributions can be allocated to officers, shareholders, and the highly compensated has been modified to conform to the new definition of highly compensated.

Independent appraisals.   Privately held ESOP companies will be required to use an independent appraiser for annual stock valuations.

Put options.   The put option requirement (company agrees to buy back the stock) for distributions when the stock is not readily tradable is extended to all stock bonus plans.

Distributions.   Unless a plan provides that a participant may elect a longer distribution period, the plan is to distribute in five years or less. The period is extended one year for each $100,000 that the participant's account balance exceeds $500,000. The employer is required to provide security for the installment payments and credit a reasonable rate of interest. Benefits must begin no later than one year after the *later* of:

—the plan year in which the participant retires, dies, or is disabled;

—the fifth plan year following the year in which the participant terminates; or

—the first anniversary of the date on which the securities acquisition loan was repaid.

These provisions apply to distributions attributable to stock acquired after Dec. 31, 1986.

With regard to early distributions, ESOPs are exempted for three years from the 10% excise tax on distributions from pension plans before age 59-1/2. ESOPs are not excluded from a 15% excise tax imposed on "excess distributions" from pension plans of over $112,500 annually.

The distribution requirements and the extension of the put option to stock bonus plans apply to stock acquired after Dec. 31, 1986.

1984 ESOP Incentives Retained

Generally, the four types of incentives for ESOPs added to the 1984 tax law are retained and in some cases improved.

1. *Deduction for dividends.* Employers receive a tax deduction for cash dividends paid on ESOP shares that are passed through to participants. The tax deduction is expanded to include dividends used to repay ESOP loans that were used to acquire the securities on which the dividends are paid.

2. *50% interest exclusion.* The exclusion of 50% of the interest earned by a lender to an ESOP has been expanded from banks and insurance companies to include regulated investment companies (mutual funds). The exclusion is applicable also to loans to an employer who within 30 days transfers an equal amount of employer securities to the ESOP and such contributions are allocated to participant accounts. This would also apply to refinancing loans used to acquire employer securities after May 23, 1984. The rules apply to loans of seven or fewer years.

3. *Tax-free rollovers.* Generally, there are no changes in present law on taxfree rollovers of gain derived from sale of stock to an ESOP, provided the ESOP then owns 30% of the stock or more. (See technical corrections to 1984 law.)

4. *Estate tax.* No curtailment of present law on assuming the payment of estate tax by an ESOP upon the purchase of stock from an estate. The 1986 provisions would also permit an exclusion from the gross estate of 50% of the qualified proceeds from the sale of employer securities by the executor of an estate to an ESOP until 1992. Stock received from the qualified retirement, stock option, or incentive plan is excluded.

Technical Corrections Clear Up 1984 Ambiguities

A major provision of the ESOP incentives of the 1984 tax law was the provision for a tax-free exchange under IRC Sec. 1042 upon the sale of qualifying securities to an ESOP. After the sale by the stockholder or stockholders, the ESOP must own 30% of the company stock, and the shareholder must reinvest the proceeds in securities of another unrelated company.

The Tax Act clarifies that in the case of the death of the individual who sold qualifying securities to the ESOP, the executor of the estate may elect to defer recognition of gain if proceeds are invested by the executor in qualified replacement property.

The 30% ownership test applies to the total number of shares in each class of stock other than preferred or 30% of the total value of all stock.

If family members (ancestors, descendants, spouses, brothers, or sisters) are members of the ESOP, the stockholder cannot elect Sec. 1042 treatment for any stock in which they would receive a distribution. Also prohibited is a distribution to a 25% stockholder. Assets allocable in lieu of these securities may not inure for the benefit of the prohibited group.

The Technical Corrections provision clearly applies the rule to the taxpayer who elects nonrecognition treatment. An excise tax is applied for failure to conform to the Sec. 1042 nonrecognition rules.

WELFARE BENEFIT PROVISIONS

The 1986 Tax Reform Act establishes a new IRC Sec. 89 for welfare benefit plans, which essentially does the following:

1. establishes new eligibility and benefits nondiscrimination rules applicable to group term life plans and accident or health plans (insured or non-insured),

2. allows employers to elect these rules to cover certain other plans,

3. establishes a special benefits rule for dependent care assistance programs,

4. establishes uniform definitions of employer, highly compensated employee, compensation, and excludable employee,

5. permits satisfaction of nondiscrimination rules on a line of business or operating unit basis.

Statutory employee benefits generally are accident and health plans under Sec. 105(e) and group term life plans under Sec. 79. Group legal services plans, educational assistance plans, and dependent care are statutory employee benefit plans only if the employer treats them as such.

All welfare benefit plans are subject to five basic rules, which are as follow:

1. the plan must be in writing;

2. the employee's rights under the plan must be legally enforceable;

3. the employer establishes the plan with the intent to maintain it indefinitely;

4. the plan must provide for reasonable notification to employees of benefits available under the plan;

5. the plan must be maintained for the exclusive benefit of the employees.

Failure to comply with these five basic qualification rules will result in the value of the benefits provided (rather than the value of the coverage) being included in the employee's gross income. This will apply to all employee participants.

Insurance-type plans include only group term life plans and accident and health plans. In the case of self insurance, the employer provided benefit is the value of the coverage and is not limited by the actual disbursements made by the employer.

Inclusion in Tax

Assuming the five basic rules are complied with, statutory employee benefit plans that discriminate will cause "the discriminatory excess" to be includible in the gross income of the highly compensated employees.

For group life plans, the value of the discriminatory excess is the greater of the cost of the coverage under Sec. 79 or the actual cost of the coverage.

The discriminatory excess is defined as the amount of employer contributions that would have had to have been made as after-tax employee contributions from the highly compensated employees in order for all of the nondiscrimination tests to be satisfied.

The discriminatory excess will be allocated as includible in income to highly compensated employees beginning with employees with the greatest nontaxable benefits, up to the amount that will make the plans nondiscriminatory.

The employer is obligated to report the discriminatory excess to the employee. If this is not done, the employer will be liable for an excise tax at the highest individual tax rate on the total value of benefits of the same type.

Discrimination Tests

The new eligibility and benefits nondiscrimination tests apply only to statutory employee benefits, as defined above. No nondiscrimination rules apply to disability benefits to the extent that the benefits payable are includible in the employee's gross income.

Accident and health plans include those providing ancillary benefits such as dental and vision care. What is subject to the nondiscrimination rules is the value of the benefits, not the value of the contributions.

Present-law standards apply to dependent care, tuition reduction, group legal, educational assistance, and Sec. 132 fringe benefit plans. A special benefits test is added for dependent care. Employers may treat group legal, educational assistance, and dependent care plans as statutory employee benefit plans if they wish.

Definitions of highly compensated employees, compensation, excludable employees, and employer apply to all of the above-mentioned plans, whether or not they are subject to the nondiscrimination tests.

Eligibility Tests

Statutory employee benefit plans must satisfy three requirements to meet the new eligibility test:

1. Nonhighly compensated employees must constitute at least 50% of all the employees eligible to participate in the plan(s) being tested.

    This requirement is satisfied if the percentage of eligible highly compensated employees is not higher than the percentage of eligible nonhighly compensated employees. For example, if all employees are covered by a plan in which 11 are nonhighly compensated and 15 are highly compensated, because 100% of each group is covered, the 50% required is deemed to be satisfied. Comparable plans (see below) may be aggregated for this test.

2. At least 90% of all the employer's nonhighly compensated employees must be eligible for a benefit that is at least 50% as valuable as the benefit available to the highly compensated employees. All plans of the same type are aggregated for this test. Available salary reduction amounts are not taken into consideration for this test. For accident and health plans, employees and spouses may be tested separately for this 90%/50% test.

3. A plan may not contain any provision that by its terms discriminates against the nonhighly compensated. This means that the facts and circumstances of the individual situation will be taken into account in determining whether a plan is nondiscriminatory.

Benefits Test

To satisfy the new benefits test, the average employer-provided benefit received by nonhighly compensated employees under all plans of the employer of the same type must be at least 75% of the average employer-provided benefit received by highly compensated employees. Plans of the same type means plans providing benefits excludable under the same IRC section.

The average employer-provided benefit is defined as the total benefits divided by the number of employees.

In applying the benefits test, employers may aggregate different types of benefits. Aggregation must be of all plans of a type. However, when testing accident and health plans, other types of plans may not be aggregated with those health plans. When testing plans other than health plans, health plans may be aggregated with those other plans. Thus, group life and group legal may not be aggregated when testing for health plans, but group life and group health may be aggregated when testing for group legal plans.

A special benefits rule is established for dependent care plans under IRC Sec. 129. The average employer-provided benefit received by the nonhighly compensated is required to be 55% (as opposed to 75%) of the benefit provided to the highly compensated. In plans that are funded through salary reduction, employees with compensation below $25,000 are disregarded.

Alternative to Benefits, Eligibility Tests

The Tax Reform Act provides a single alternative test for insurance-type plans that may be used in lieu of the eligibility and benefits tests.

Under this alternative, a group life or accident and health plan must benefit at least 80% of all an employer's nonhighly compensated employees. Individuals must receive coverage under the plan; eligibility to receive coverage is not considered benefiting under the plan. An employee who waives coverage or elects to contribute thus is not covered under the plan. Comparable plans may be aggregated. A comparable plan is one that is at least 95% as valuable as the employer plan providing the largest benefit.

In general, this alternative test will be used primarily by employers with a single plan for all employees. If an employer offers two or more plans, passing the test will require that all plans be substantially the same (95% as valuable). The line of business exception (see below) may be used for this test.

Special Rules for Health Plans

For purposes of the benefits test, employers may disregard employees and spouses and dependents who are covered for core benefits under another employer's accident and health plan. This rule applies only to accident and health plans. Core benefits do not include benefits from a salary reduction medical reimbursement plan, a "low-level non-elective medical reimbursement plan, or a disability plan." Noncore benefits include coverage for dental, vision, psychological, orthodontia, and elective cosmetic surgery benefits.

For purposes of the alternative 80% test and the 50% component in the 90%/50% test, coverage for employees and coverage for spouses and dependents may be tested separately.

Certain employees may not be disregarded. These are highly compensated workers whose coverage under an accident and health plan is in excess of 133% of the average benefit provided to the nonhighly compensated.

In general, annual sworn statements are required to determine whether employees have spouses and/or dependents and/or are covered under other plans. Rules are to be written that allow valid samples of employee sworn statements.

In the absence of sworn statements, in the case of nonhighly compensated employees, it is presumed that they do not have other coverage and that they do have spouses and/or dependents. It is presumed that highly compensated employees are covered under another plan and do not have spouses and/or dependents.

Valuing Benefits

The value of coverage provided by a health plan shall be determined in future regulations. These rules will include standard types of coverage involving representative groups and will allow adjustments for the specific plan and group involved.

The cost of group term life coverage will be considered as the amount under Sec. 79(c) for an individual at age 40, adjusted for compensation. Coverage in excess of $50,000 may not be disregarded.

For other types of benefits, the employer-provided benefit is defined as the value of the benefit, not the value of coverage as above.

In order that employers need not value every accident and health plan, the law sets up a special rule that allows a plan to pass the benefits test if the percentage of nonhighly compensated employees who benefit is not less than 75% of the percentage of highly compensated employees who benefit. For example, assume an employer has ten health plans, and nine of them pass this 75% rule. The employer may then aggregate with the tenth plan only those number of plans needed to satisfy the benefits test, and only that group of plans need be valued.

Highly Compensated Employees

In general, the definitions of compensation and highly compensated employees are those adopted for qualified retirement plans (see the chapter on Qualified Retirement Plans). One clarification applies to welfare plans, however.

When family coverage is treated as a separate benefit in an accident and health plan, the family member rule is modified. In these cases, where a family member normally would be aggregated with the highly compensated, such family member shall be treated as a nonemployee family member.

Excludable Employees

The following employees may be excluded:

1. employees who have not completed one year of service (in the case of a health plan providing core benefits, six months of service);
2. employees who normally work less than 17-1/2 hours per week;
3. employees who normally work less than six months during the year;
4. employees included in collective bargaining agreements;
5. employees who have not attained age 21;
6. certain nonresident aliens.

The exclusions must apply to all plans of the same type. For cafeteria plans, all benefits under the plan shall be treated as of the same type.

Line of Business Rule

Both the eligibility and benefits tests may be applied separately to separate lines of business or operating units, as defined in Sec. 414(r).

A line of business or operating unit shall not be treated as separate unless it has at least 50 employees. However, more than one line of business or operating unit may be aggregated. A safe harbor rule states that the line of business rules will be satisfied if "the highly compensated employee percentage" of the line of business or operating unit is (a) not less than one-half, and (b) not more than twice, the percentage of all employees who are highly compensated in the entire company. For example, if the highly compensated make up 10% of all employees, a line of business or operating unit that has between 5% and 20% highly compensated employees will satisfy this safe harbor.

All employees, including those headquarters employees who may work in several lines of business or operating units, must be considered as working in one specified line of business.

A separate operating unit must be operated in a significantly separate geographic area from another operating unit in the same line of business.

Separate lines of business and separate operating units will be determined on a case-by-case basis, using the facts and circumstances in each case. Bona fide business reasons must exist for separating lines of business and operating units. The conference committee report specifies that annual reporting requirements will be established for employers to explain their positions in determining separate lines of business.

Effective Dates

The welfare benefit provisions generally take effect for plan years beginning after Dec. 31, 1987. However, if regulations are not published by that date, the rules take effect on the earlier of Dec. 31, 1988, or three months after rules are published.

Collectively bargained plans negotiated after March 1, 1986, have until the earlier of the end of the agreement or Jan. 1, 1991.

Other Provisions

Self-employed individuals may deduct up to 25% of health insurance payments.

Tax-favored status for educational assistance and group legal plans is extended for two years, until the end of 1987. The educational assistance cap is raised to $5,250, but it is not indexed. The tax exclusion for dependent care assistance is limited to $5,000 per year.

Funding for retiree health benefits may not take inflation into account.

CAFETERIA PLANS

The 1986 Tax Reform Act retains the present-law eligibility test for cafeteria plans and retains the concentration test. Thus, each type of benefit available is subject to its own applicable nondiscrimination rules and to any applicable concentration test.

For example, group term life insurance benefits under a cafeteria plan must satisfy eligibility and benefits tests applicable to group term life plans.

If a cafeteria plan does not satisfy the cafeteria plan eligibility or concentration test, benefits under the plan are taxable.

Definition Modified

The definition of cafeteria plan is changed to mean a plan that meets the requirements of the new IRC Sec. 89 and under which

(a)   all participants are employees,

(b)   the participants may choose

    1.   among two or more benefits consisting of cash and qualified benefits, or

    2.   among two or more qualified benefits.

The new definition means that even plans that offer choices just among nontaxable benefits must now conform to the Sec. 125 cafeteria plan rules.

Other Definitions

Qualified benefit means any benefit excludable under the tax code, except for tuition reduction, educational assistance, and Sec. 132 fringe benefit plans. Qualified benefit includes Sec. 79 benefits above $50,000 and can include any benefit provided for in regulations.

Uniform definitions of highly compensated employees, excludable employees, and employee apply.

Certain educational institutions may include paid-up post retirement life insurance in a cafeteria plan.

The cafeteria plan exception to constructive receipt applies for purposes of FICA and FUTA taxes. This exception does not extend, however, to Sec. 401(k) benefits offered under a cafeteria plan. Thus, FICA and FUTA taxes will be payable on elective deferrals under 401(k) plans but not on the choice of other benefit plans available under the cafeteria plan.

What You Should Know About COBRA, The Consolidated Omnibus Budget Reconciliation Act of 1985

What You Should Know About COBRA

The Consolidated Omnibus Budget Reconciliation Act of 1985 (COBRA) significantly changes the way employers handle health care coverage for older workers. Charles Newcom, a partner of the Denver law firm of Sherman & Howard provides the following overview of COBRA:

> The Consolidated Omnibus Budget Reconciliation Act of 1985 (COBRA) requires employers with twenty or more employees to give employees and dependents who are covered by an employer-sponsored health care plan the option to continue their health plan coverage at group rates for substantial periods of time after certain "qualifying events" that would otherwise result in an employee's or dependent's loss of coverage. An employee has a right to choose continuation coverage if he or she loses group health coverage because of a reduction of hours of employment or the termination of employment (for reasons other than gross misconduct).

> Such continuation coverage is for an 18-month period. The spouse of an employee covered by a group health plan has the right to choose continuation coverage for three years, if the employee dies, if the employee's employment is terminated (for reasons other than gross misconduct) or the employee's hours of employment are reduced, if the spouse and the employee are divorced or legally separated, or if the employee becomes eligible for Medicare. Likewise, a dependent child of an employee covered by a group health plan has the right to continue coverage for a three-year period if the employee dies, if the employee's employment is terminated (for reasons other than gross misconduct) or the employee's hours of employment are reduced, if the parents are divorced or legally separated, if the employee becomes eligible for Medicare, or if the dependent ceases to be a "dependent child" under the terms of the group health plan.

The employee or dependent has sixty days from the date he or she would otherwise lose health plan coverage to exercise the continuation coverage option. If continuation coverage is selected, the employee or dependent may be required to pay for the continued coverage (at group health plan rates). This new law applies to group health plans for plan years beginning on or after July 1, 1986, except for plans maintained pursuant to collective bargaining agreements. In the case of collectively bargained plans, COBRA does not apply to plan years beginning before the later of (a) the date on which the last collective bargaining agreement relating to the plan terminates, or (b) January 1, 1987.

It is anticipated that COBRA will impose significant administrative and record-keeping burdens on employers, because employers are required to notify employees and their spouses (if any) who are covered by health care plans that they will have the option to continue health care insurance coverage after a qualifying event occurs. This notification must be given as soon as COBRA applies to the plan. COBRA also requires employers to notify each employee and his or her spouse as soon as they are covered by the employer-sponsored plan that the option to continue health care coverage will be available following a qualifying event. Employers also must notify their plan administrators that qualifying events have occurred, within thirty days after such qualifying events occur. The employee or dependent is responsible for giving notice of a divorce, legal separation, or a dependent child's loss of coverage.

It is imperative that employers comply with the requirements of COBRA. Among other penalties, a covered employer who fails to provide a required health care continuation option will be *denied a tax deduction for the expenses it incurs in maintaining all of its group health plans.*

Also employers with twenty or more employees must offer active employees and their spouses age 65 and over (including those over age 70) the same health insurance coverage that they offer younger workers. The employer plan must be the employee's or spouse's primary plan unless the employee or his or her spouse elects to be covered only by Medicare. Before the enactment of COBRA, this requirement did not apply to persons over age 70.

Following are sample forms that can be used in complying with COBRA.

Sample COBRA Letter to Employees

September 29, 1986

Dear

Effective October 1, 1986, you and your eligible dependents may continue participation in the firm's group medical and dental plans even though certain events occur which would otherwise cause loss of coverage. This continued coverage is provided by the Consolidated Omnibus Budget Reconciliation Act (COBRA), a new Federal law enacted on April 7, 1986. This notice is intended to inform you, in a summary fashion, of your rights and obligations under the continuation coverage provisions of the new law.

HOW THE LAW WILL APPLY:

1. Your coverage can be extended up to 18 months if one of the following "qualifying events" occurs:

   - your employment with the firm terminates for any reason (including voluntary resignation or retirement) other than gross misconduct, or

   - your working hours are reduced to a level at which you would no longer be eligible for coverage;

2. Coverage for your eligible dependents can be extended up to 36 months if one of the following "qualifying events" occurs:

   - they are covered under the plans and you die while still employed, or

   - you and your spouse become legally separated or divorced, or

   - a dependent child reaches maximum age for coverage, or

   - your spouse or dependents are under age 65 when you become eligible for Medicare and are no longer an active employee.

THE FULL 18 OR 36 MONTH EXTENSION WILL NOT APPLY IF:

- All employer-provided medical or dental plans are terminated.

- You do not pay your required premium in a timely manner.

- You or your dependents become (an employee) covered by any other group medical and/or dental plan.

- Your former spouse remarries and becomes covered under another group medical and/or dental plan.

- A dependent becomes eligible for Medicare. (Medicare eligibility terminates coverage only for the Medicare-eligible individual.)

How to Obtain This Continuation Coverage

You or a family member must notify the plan administrator if a divorce, legal separation, or child loses dependent status under the Plan. You must notify the plan administrator of the employee's death, termination of employment or reduction of hours, or Medicare eligibility. The plan administrator will, within 14 days of receiving notification, inform you or the dependent of the right to choose continuation coverage. You do not have to show that you are insurable to choose continuation coverage. Please note that prompt notification is extremely important. You will have at least 60 days from the date you would otherwise lose coverage to inform the plan administrator if you want continuation coverage. If you do not elect continuation coverage, your group health plan coverage will end.

YOUR COST FOR CONTINUATION COVERAGE

You will be charged the full cost of coverage under the group plan in which you are enrolled. We will no longer pay a portion of it. You will also pay a 2% administrative charge. (Note: This may still be less expensive and provide better coverage than an individual health policy.)

You may pay for the continuation coverage on a monthly basis. You must make your first payment within 45 days after the date you elect the continuation of this coverage. Subsequent payments must be made to the Office Manager by _____.

THIS DOES NOT AFFECT YOUR NORMAL CONVERSION PRIVILEGE

You will still have the option to convert your group coverage to individual coverage. If you first elect continuation coverage under our group plan(s), your election period to convert to an individual policy will be the last 180 days of your continuation coverage. If you do *not* wish to continue coverage under the group plan(s), you must make your conversion election for individual coverage within 30 days of the date your regular group health coverage ends. The new continuation coverage option under our plan does *not* apply to life insurance. If you wish to convert your group life insurance to individual life insurance, you must elect to do so within 30 days of the date your regular group life insurance coverage ends.

If you have any questions about either the conversion option or the continuation coverage option, please call or write:

(Insert name of your carrier)

Also, if you have changed marital status, or you or your spouse have changed addresses, please notify the plan administrator at the above addresses.

Sincerely,

Sample Notice to Provide Terminating Employees

The Consolidated Omnibus Budget Reconciliation Act of 1986 requires that employers offer certain categories of individuals the opportunity to continue in the employers group health insurance plan within sixty (60) days of becoming eligible. Coverage may continue for eighteen (18) or thirty-six (36) months depending upon category of eligibility.

Who is covered	Situation	Duration of Coverage
1. Employee	Termination other than for "gross misconduct" or reduction in hours	18 months
2. Family members	Death of employee	36 months
3. Spouse	Divorce or legal separation from employee	36 months
4. Dependent child	For a child who ceases to be a dependent under terms of the health plan	36 months
5. Spouse	Employee reaches age 65 and makes Medicare primary health insurer	36 months

The cost to you is   % of the current premium cost to
It is your responsibility to remit each month's premium to the Office Manager no later than the first of each month. Failure to do so will result in cancellation of coverage.

_____ I decline coverage
_____ I elect coverage   _____ Monthly premium
_____ Category applies to me

Please print name of individual(s) covered.

_____   _____
_____   _____
_____   _____

_____   _____
Date   Signature

A Look at Innovative New Benefits Some Companies Are Offering

CHILD CARE: MEETING THE NEEDS OF WORKING PARENTS

Day care, once only a family problem, has become an employer problem now that so many women are working outside the home. According to a recent Census Bureau report, there will be 10.5 million working mothers of children under age six by 1990. Because of single-parent or two-income family situations, the difficulty has steadily increased. In addition to total day care, families must also solve the problem of before and after school supervision, and the sick child who must stay home from school or day care facility.

Over half the women in today's work force have children under the age of six. Increasingly, organizations from banking to manufacturing, health care to transportation, are having to confront the issue of working parents and their child care needs. This is especially true of the clerical work force, for whom working is less of an option than an economic necessity.

On the employer's side, there is obviously tremendous impact both financially and emotionally. This brings up some questions. How does corporate supported child care affect the recruitment and retention of quality clerical workers? What new benefits are there in the child care area and are these programs effective?

The Results of a National Survey on Child Care and the Clerical Workforce

Adia Personnel Services, based in Menlo Park, California, has been in the business of providing clerical and word processing temporary and permanent employees to organizations since 1972. They recognized the problems of child care for working mothers before it became a full-blown corporate problem, and conducted an indepth survey in 1985-86.

In order to obtain a viable sample, Adia surveyed 445 employers and 238 clerical workers in 30 states, and the anonymous survey results were tabulated

Table 1 □ Impact Of Child Illness/Day Care Problems

	Has No Impact 1	Has A Little Impact 2	Has Some Impact 3	Has A Great Deal Of Impact 4
Child Illness			3.4	
				3.6
Babysitter/Day Care Problems			3.1	
				3.4

☐ = Employers

■ = Clerical Employees

by an independent market research firm. The tables in this section show the results of this comprehensive survey.*

There are many different options for corporate day care assistance. Some companies have in-house facilities; some provide cash vouchers to assist employees by paying a portion of the tab. Following are some statistics about child care costs.

Potential Child Care Costs

Some of the potential cost factors included in corporate owned and managed day care centers at first glance are considerable.

Space: Capital expenditures for land and building utility fees, taxes and insurance. Equipment: Classrooms, outdoor playground, office furnishings, telephone, kitchen equipment.

Staff: Administrator, teachers, aides, clerical, custodial, cook, driver, substitutes. Salaries and benefits.

Supplies: Teaching supplies, food, maintenance, office and clerical, postage.

Transportation: Van or bus may be needed for transportation to special activities and for carrying supplies.

Miscellaneous: Legal fees, accounting costs, liability insurance, medical consultations, training, and education costs for teachers and staff, emergency funds.

---

* Reprinted with permission of Adia Personnel Services, P.O. Box 2768, Menlo Park, CA 94026.

Table 2 □ Impact Of Day-to-Day Child Care Needs

	Has No Impact 1	Has A Little Impact 2	Has Some Impact 3	Has A Great Deal Of Impact 4

Child care after school or child care facility closes
 2.8
 3.1

Child care before school or child care facility opens
 2.6
 3.0

Transportation of child to and from school/day care
 2.6
 3.0

Checking on child at home before and/or after school
 2.6
 2.8

▨ = Employers

■ = Clerical Employees

Start-up funding for a company owned day care center can run from $50,000 to $150,000 depending on the availability of space, cost of space, or the necessity of rental of an outside facility. Yearly operating budgets can run from $40,000 to $250,000 depending on the number of children served, the wages in the area of the facility, and so forth. Many companies that have facilities charge a nominal fee to employees who use their services. Some charge as low as $25.00 per week, some charge a flat 10 percent of the employee's gross weekly salary.

Companies may lose money on the actual facility, but feel they come out ahead in employee goodwill, lower absenteeism, higher productivity, and a greater ability to attract good people.

How One Company Offset a High Employee Turnover Rate with Day Care

Permacraft, Inc. surveyed employees and found that child-care problems were at the root of high absenteeism and turnover rates plaguing the company in the late 1970s. In June 1986, the company opened a twenty-four-hour day-care facility. Eighty-five percent of Permacraft's 650 employees are

Table 4 □ Company Employment Problems Affected By Child Care

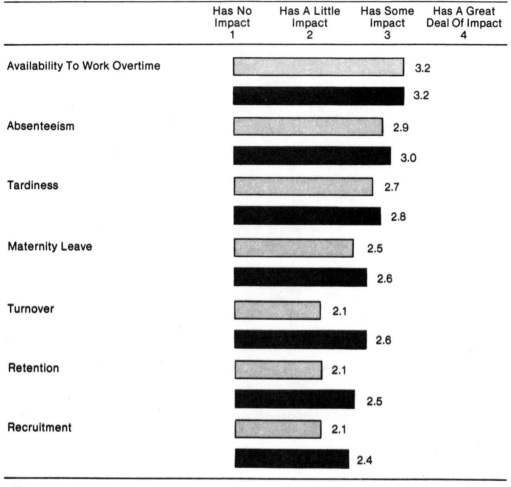

	Has No Impact 1	Has A Little Impact 2	Has Some Impact 3	Has A Great Deal Of Impact 4
Availability To Work Overtime			3.2	
			3.2	
Absenteeism			2.9	
			3.0	
Tardiness			2.7	
			2.8	
Maternity Leave		2.5		
		2.6		
Turnover		2.1		
		2.6		
Retention		2.1		
		2.5		
Recruitment		2.1		
		2.4		

▨ = Employers

■ = Clerical Employees

women, many of them single parents with young children. Turnover was their biggest problem. They had 250 people in 1980 and wrote 900 plus W2s; which indicates that they turned every job in the plant over three times.

In 1986, Permacraft built a new plant and included a quarter-million dollar, 6,600-square-foot child learning center. The company pays one-half the $50-dollar-per-week tuition for its employees and gives free care to those who work overtime.

Not every company has the time, interest, or resources to get into the

Table 6 □ Child Care Benefits Offered/Considered

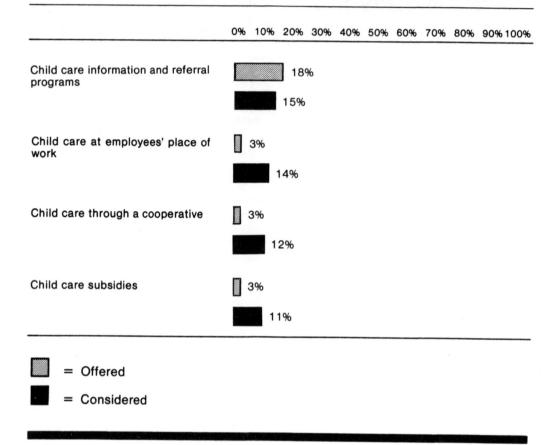

child-care business. But a recent study by the National Employer Supported Child Care Project in Pasadena, California, reveals that the number of companies with child-care programs has increased almost 400 percent. The study refers to a pool of corporate human resource executives, 67 percent of whom report that their companies expected to provide child-care benefits within five years.

Seven Ways to Introduce Child-Care Services in Your Company

There is a broad spectrum of child care services available for meeting the needs of working parents. Some possibilities for corporate involvement are:

1. On-site day care centers, right at the office or plant. These most often are offered by hospitals, high-technology companies, and family-owned businesses. They are wonderful for nursing mothers

Table 7 □ Benefits Preferred By Clerical Workers/Parents

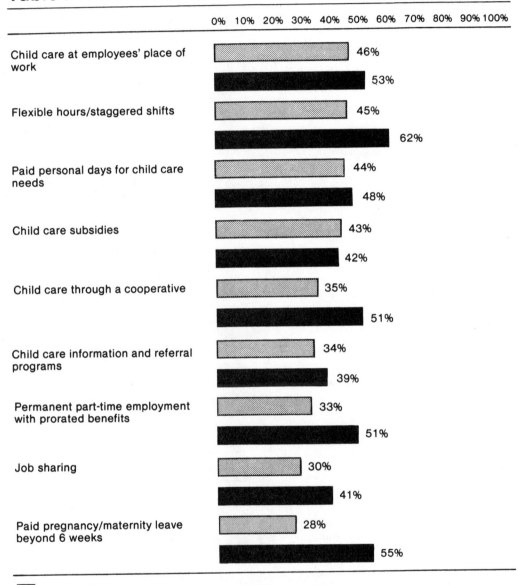

0% 10% 20% 30% 40% 50% 60% 70% 80% 90% 100%

Child care at employees' place of work — 46% / 53%

Flexible hours/staggered shifts — 45% / 62%

Paid personal days for child care needs — 44% / 48%

Child care subsidies — 43% / 42%

Child care through a cooperative — 35% / 51%

Child care information and referral programs — 34% / 39%

Permanent part-time employment with prorated benefits — 33% / 51%

Job sharing — 30% / 41%

Paid pregnancy/maternity leave beyond 6 weeks — 28% / 55%

▨ = Clerical employees with children would find *most* helpful

■ = *All* Clerical workers would like to see offered

and parents who work irregular hours, but inconvenient for employees who have a long commute. Many companies consider on-site centers too great an expense and are looking to other forms of help.

2. Employer-purchased slots of community day-care centers. The com-

Appendix 1

☐ Attitudes And Opinions of Employers And Clerical Employees Regarding Child Care, Family Responsibilities And Work

	Disagree Completely 1	Disagree Somewhat 2	Neither Agree/ Disagree 3	Agree Somewhat 4	Agree Completely 5

Child care problems make it difficult for some employees to work overtime — 4.6 / 4.7

Women's jobs are more affected by child care and family responsibilities than are men's jobs — 4.4 / 4.6

The mother generally has the major responsibilities for child care and family needs in the home — 4.4 / 4.4

More women with child care responsibilities would work part-time if they could afford it — 4.3 / 4.4

Employees should have the choice among a variety of benefits that can be tailored to their individual needs — 4.1 / 4.4

Mothers and fathers should play an equal role in caring for children even if it means taking some time away from their jobs — 4.2 / 4.2

The cost of child care is too high for most clerical and other non-managerial employees to afford — 4.0 / 4.4

Government should provide more incentives to business to provide child care subsidies or programs — 3.8 / 4.3

☐ = Employers

■ = Clerical Employees

Appendix 1 (continued)

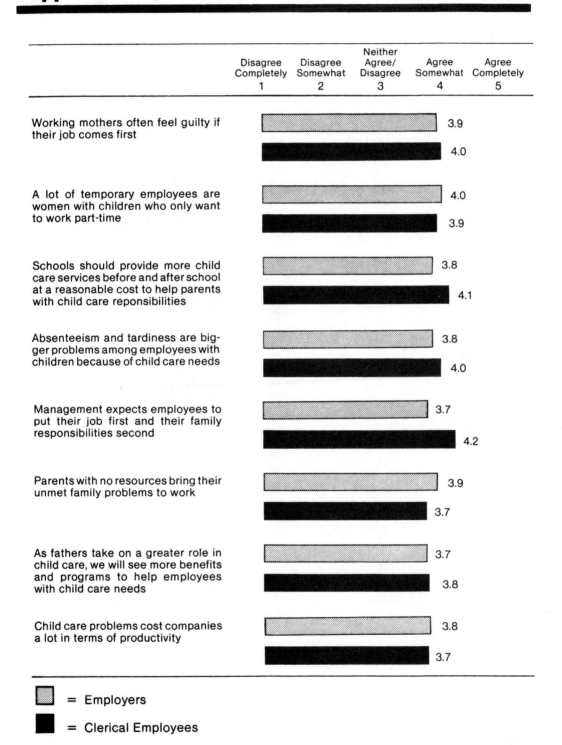

	Disagree Completely 1	Disagree Somewhat 2	Neither Agree/ Disagree 3	Agree Somewhat 4	Agree Completely 5

Working mothers often feel guilty if their job comes first — 3.9 / 4.0

A lot of temporary employees are women with children who only want to work part-time — 4.0 / 3.9

Schools should provide more child care services before and after school at a reasonable cost to help parents with child care reponsibilities — 3.8 / 4.1

Absenteeism and tardiness are bigger problems among employees with children because of child care needs — 3.8 / 4.0

Management expects employees to put their job first and their family responsibilities second — 3.7 / 4.2

Parents with no resources bring their unmet family problems to work — 3.9 / 3.7

As fathers take on a greater role in child care, we will see more benefits and programs to help employees with child care needs — 3.7 / 3.8

Child care problems cost companies a lot in terms of productivity — 3.8 / 3.7

= Employers

= Clerical Employees

Appendix 1 (continued)

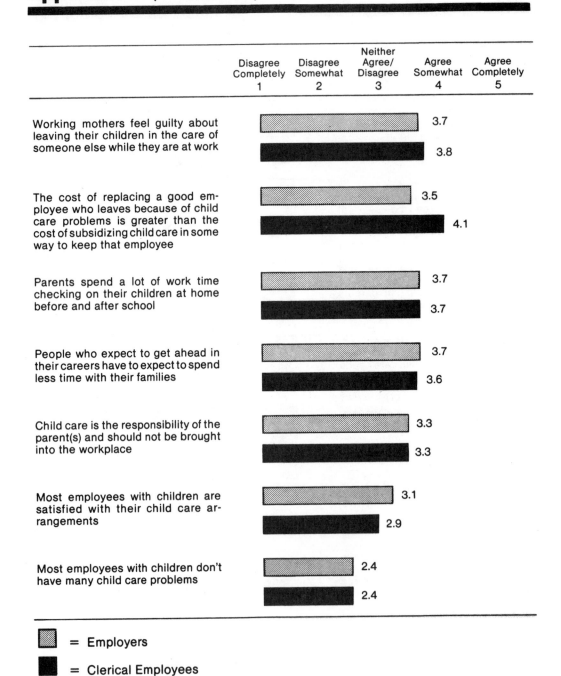

	Disagree Completely 1	Disagree Somewhat 2	Neither Agree/ Disagree 3	Agree Somewhat 4	Agree Completely 5

Working mothers feel guilty about leaving their children in the care of someone else while they are at work
3.7
3.8

The cost of replacing a good employee who leaves because of child care problems is greater than the cost of subsidizing child care in some way to keep that employee
3.5
4.1

Parents spend a lot of work time checking on their children at home before and after school
3.7
3.7

People who expect to get ahead in their careers have to expect to spend less time with their families
3.7
3.6

Child care is the responsibility of the parent(s) and should not be brought into the workplace
3.3
3.3

Most employees with children are satisfied with their child care arrangements
3.1
2.9

Most employees with children don't have many child care problems
2.4
2.4

▨ = Employers

■ = Clerical Employees

pany buys a certain number of places every year and gives them to the children of employees. Company may pay the full price (generally in the area of $75 to $125 a week) or share the cost with employees.

3. Employer subsidies to the day-care center itself. Employers may give only start-up funds or they may give annual subsidies. Employees pay for the day care, but company gifts help keep the cost at acceptable levels.

4. Day-care vouchers. An employee is allowed a certain amount of money for day care, which he or she can spend at any accredited center in the community.

5. Flexible benefits. More and more companies allow employees a certain sum of money toward a cornucopia of fringe benefits they want. A working mother might choose day care, and "pay" for it by foregoing a cash bonus or dental plan. Or she may choose to have her taxable pay reduced by the amount of the day-care cost—an approach that allows her to finance day care with pre-tax dollars.

6. Information and referral programs to help employees find care for their children. These often are the first steps that companies take, before providing direct financial help.

7. *The day care consortium* is popular with companies that are located in the same area and have the same day care problems. In fact, some think the consortium idea is the most cost effective approach. It allows companies to pool resources by funding geographically convenient day care centers and sharing the financial and administrative responsibilities. Some examples of consortiums are the Urban Affairs Corporation Center of Houston, Texas, that includes fourteen companies, and the Broadcasters Child Development Center, in Washington, DC that includes five radio and television stations.

One or more of these day care alternatives may fit your needs. The best way to decide which alternative is best for you is to establish a task force that should include management, labor representatives (if you have a union), and employee/parents to look into the feasibility of day care assistance for your company. It is also a good idea to ask your legal people to be a part of the task force if you have them on staff.

Child Care Task Force Assignments

Some of the actions the task force might take in investigating the feasibility of child care assistance include the following.

1. Assess current needs in your organization. How many people would use the center? How many children would be involved?

2. Evaluate the current community services. Find out what already exists, and how good it is. Do the available services already fit the needs of your employees?

3. Consider hiring an outside consultant to help analyze needs and costs, and the best way to deliver services to those employees who will be using the service.

4. Evaluate all the data from the task force and the consultant (if you hire one) and make a presentation.

5. Review the task force results with employees and communicate the information through memos, posters, and group meetings. Communication should be ongoing if you implement a plan.

Company funds for day care are tax-deductible to the corporation and not counted as income for the employee. So it is cheaper for the company to provide day care than it is for workers to finance it themselves.

Several states also provide tax credits to companies that make day-care payments.

If the decision is made to implement a child care assistance program be sure your planning process is effective. Also, try to interview management of a company who is currently involved in child care assistance before you implement your own program in order to see firsthand what the program entails.

The United States Department of Health and Human Services completed a research project designed to help employers explore whether child care might make sense for their companies. This study provided the following information:

- *Turnover.* Sixty-five percent of employers who had collected such statistics reported that child care helped reduce costly employee turnover. Estimates of actual dollar savings in this area in one year ranged from $25,000 to over $2 million.

- *Recruitment.* Eight-five percent of respondents reported that offering child care benefits helped them attract qualified new workers. Some found that many prospective employees applied for jobs in their companies specifically because of such benefits.

- *Morale,* worker satisfaction, commitment, and motivation were all positively affected by child care programs, according to a substantial majority of the companies surveyed.

- *Public relations.* The company image was greatly enhanced, 85 percent of the companies reported. Many received repeated media mentions as "good places to work," and continue to be cited as examples of community-minded, caring organizations.

- *Productivity*, while often difficult to measure, was higher as a result of child care benefits in about half of the companies that were surveyed.

- *Absenteeism* was measurably down in 53 percent of the responding firms. A substantial number also claimed notable reductions in tardiness.

Nanny Care – A New Trend

Another new trend in the child-care area is Nanny-care. Terri Eurich of Denver, Colorado, started the National Academy of Nannies, Inc. and cannot provide all the nannies for which she has orders. According to Barbara Lansbaugh, the Academy's marketing director, there will be a new program soon for corporations to provide a "Nanny Benefit" as part of a corporate flexible benefit program. Nannies are usually more expensive than regular day-care, but if corporations make a certain amount of money available to employees for day-care, they can choose the type of day-care that best addresses their particular need.

Here are two resources for additional information on the subject:

The Child Care Action Campaign, a nonprofit corporation under the direction of Elinor Guggenheimer, can provide answers on twenty-four topics. Write: CCAC, 132 West 43rd Street, New York, NY 10036; or call (212) 354-5669. Send a self-addressed, stamped envelope.

Or send for *Child Care and the Working Parent*, a $15 loose-leaf book prepared by Karol Rose and Barbara Adolf; the address is Children at Work, Inc., 569 Lexington Avenue, New York, NY 10022.

ADOPTION BENEFITS: AN INEXPENSIVE PLUS FOR EMPLOYEES

More and more companies are including adoption assistance in their benefits package. Why? Because it is a fairly inexpensive benefit and it makes employees happy.

Pitney Bowes in Stamford, Connecticut, is one of the growing number of American companies offering adoption benefits. IBM, Xerox, and Hallmark Cards also offer it.

The benefits generally range from $800 to $1,000 per child, but some companies pay the same amount that an employee would receive through a medical plan for a normal delivery. In most cases, taxes are withheld from the check containing the adoption benefit.

At IBM, eighty percent of the legal, maternity, and agency fees involved in an adoption are reimbursed, with a maximum payment of $1,000. Since IBM added adoption benefits, more than 2,000 couples have been reimbursed.Xerox and Hallmark both pay adoption expenses up to a maximum of $1,000. Foote Cone and Belding, which has offered an adoption benefit for about ten years, reimburses employees for the same amount of money they would receive for a normal delivery, around $2,200 or $2,300.

PARENTAL LEAVE

Today, over 2,300 companies offer employees parental leave in connection with the birth or adoption of a child. Although this benefit is becoming more common, small companies with less than 100 employees normally cannot afford to provide such a leave. These small companies are moving more readily to flexible use of vacations and sick leave and providing flexible benefit plans. Parental leave is not yet a common part of every organization's benefit package, but it is gaining acceptance as more women join the workforce.

In 1986 The Parental and Medical Leave Act was introduced by Representative Pat Schroeder of Colorado in an attempt to create a national parental leave policy for both mothers and fathers. The Act would establish parental leave for the birth, adoption, or serious illness of a dependent son or daughter. Employees would be permitted to take up to 18 weeks unpaid leave over a two-year period with no penalty to their health insurance coverage, benefits, or seniority. The Bill was introduced in the House but never reached the Senate. The number of working parents is increasing and the possibility of a new emphasis on parental leave as a national mandate will undoubtedly grow.

PREPAID LEGAL SERVICES: A LOW-COST BENEFIT

Although most employers have been looking for ways to cut benefit costs, many have added a new benefit—prepaid legal services. This is a low-cost benefit. Several labor union contracts currently provide for legal benefits. In 1982, the United Auto Workers negotiated a plan covering 635,000 workers and retirees at General Motors, American Motors, and Chrysler. The National Education Association offers legal plans to seventy-five percent of their 1.6 million members, and about ten million workers, both union and non-union, are covered by some style of legal plan.

There are about 3,000 legal plans offered around the country. One such plan is provided by Nationwide Legal Services, Inc., of Hartsdale, New York. Nationwide administers five different prepaid plans involving 40,000 emloyees. Nationwide assigns the client to a lawyer who is selected from a pool of attorneys on a rotating basis.

How Do the Plans Work?

These lawyers provide over-the-phone advice and basic services including help with wills, real estate closings, uncontested divorces, consumer disputes, and personal bankruptcies.

How is the Plan Administered?

The UAW self-administers the plan and handles about 120,000 cases a year. Other companies choose to hire an outside group like Nationwide Legal Services, Inc.

Do Employees Like and Use the Plans?

Most workers like the plans. Surveys of the 110,000 member New York-based District Council 37 of the American Federation of State, County, and Municipal Employees have turned up complaints in less than one percent of the 50,000 cases handled since 1977. In this case, the union itself administers the plan using sixty staff lawyers.

What Do the Plans Cost a Company?

Chrysler Corporation pays $50 an hour for covered services and employees pay $45 an hour for additional work if they need it. The lawyer probably charges private customers $75 to $100 per hour.

The UAW plan costs General Motors Corporation about $60 a year per employee, or about 3¢ an hour of the average total compensation of $22 an hour. Nationwide's plan for the Westchester County New York Civil Service Employees Association costs $20 per year per worker.

CHARGING HEALTH CARE SERVICES: A GROWING TREND

Did you know you could charge your hospital or clinic stay to your American Express card? The number of health-care services and treatment alternatives made possible by new medical breakthroughs are steadily increasing. So are the number of ways to pay for these services.

If you or any member of your family needs emergency room treatment and you have an American Express card, just identify yourself and hand over your card. Then, when checking out of a hospital, if you find that a gap exists between what your health insurance pays and the amount due, you can charge the difference at hospitals that accept the American Express card.

More and more, patients are being asked to pay up front for services that are covered by medical insurance. A credit card is a convenient way to pay for these charges. If you develop a health problem while traveling, you don't have to worry if an out-of-town check will be accepted. You can visit any participating clinic, doctor, or dentist and charge the services.

A recent poll conducted for American Express by an independent research organization indicated the charging of health-care services is one of the benefits cardmembers wanted most. They have responded by expanding the number of health-care professionals and organizations that take the card. These include individual physicians and dentists and those practicing in groups, hospitals, clinics, and other professionals such as psychologists, optometrists, and nutritionists.

Here are a few hospitals who take the card:

Humana Hospital, Inc. and Medfirst, all locations

Emory University Hospital, Altanta

Cedars-Sinai Medical Center, Beverly Hills

Massachusetts Eye and Ear Infirmary, Boston Michael A. Reese Hospital, Chicago

Dallas Medical and Surgical Clinic, Dallas Presbyterian Hospital,

Dallas Hospital of the University of Pennsylvania, Philadelphia

You may write or call American Express in New York for a more complete list.

BIRTHING CENTERS: A COST EFFECTIVE ALTERNATIVE TO HOSPITALS

The number of children delivered each year outside hospitals has increased thirty percent and totals more than 35,000, according to the National Center for Health Statistics. Birthing centers, which can cut delivery costs in half, account for about 10,000 of these births and are capturing a substantial share of the eight billion dollars a year delivery business. The National Association of Childbearing Centers (NACBC) near Philadelphia says there are 133 birthing centers shown in its records.

A comparative cost study by NACBC showed that deliveries in birthing centers cost less than half (forty-seven percent) what comparable care for a normal delivery in a hospital costs—$801 in a center versus $1,713 in a hospital. The average hospital stay for obstetrical cases nationally is 2.7 days, 3 days in many hospitals, and that the average fee is $2,200, but can climb to $5,000.

Several major corporations specifically call for birth center coverage in their employee health plans for cost containment. These corporations include Rockwell International, Pittsburgh; Atlantic Richfield, Los Angeles; Bank of America, San Francisco; Eastman Kodak, Rochester, N.Y.; and E. I. du Pont de Nemours, Wilmington, Del. Dale Stratton, assistant director of compensation and benefits for du Pont, which covers birth center charges for 36,000 employees in twenty states under Blue Cross/Blue Shield Plans, says, "It would seem that birth centers are more cost-effective than a hospital stay, if in no other way than based on duration of stay."

FOUR KEY AREAS OF HOME HEALTH CARE

The prognosis for home health care is excellent. The major trends—a growing elderly population, technological advances, hospital cost-cutting attempts, and increasing patient distrust of institutional care—seem to set the stage for growth that rivals any new industry in recent memory. Market researcher Frost & Sullivan Inc. estimates the home health and self-care market hit $6.4 billion in 1983 and will soar to $18.3 billion by 1990.

The key factor likely to aid home care is solidly entrenched. The federal government has a prospective payment plan for diagnosis-related groups, under which hospitals are reimbursed a set amount for an illness regardless of their actual costs. In a scramble to cut costs, hospitals will tend to speed up discharges, which means that people leaving hospitals will need more care than in the past.

Home is not just for the mildly ill. Home Health Care of America states that forty percent of its business is derived from cancer patients and advertises its ability to handle people with AIDS. Patients immobilized in traction are being treated at home. Home health care is divided into four segments:

1. infusion therapy, where fluids are administered intravenously, through the nose, or directly into the intestine. Basic nutrition, antibiotics, painkillers, chemotherapy, and dialysis are provided.
2. personnel companies, providers of nurses, health aides, and therapists.
3. durable medical equipment manufacturers that sell walkers, wheelchairs, oxygen concentrators, plus aids for daily living that enable the handicapped to function more effectively.
4. Self-care products, including diagnostic tests, many based on monoclonal antibody technology.

Many organizations are seriously considering this viable alternative to long hospitalization in cutting medical costs for employees who will need long-term care. Home health care provides a definite cost saving over time.

SEVEN BENEFITS OF EMPLOYEE PHYSICAL FITNESS PROGRAMS (PFPs)

Private industry has become increasingly interested in the physical fitness of employees, and more organizations are investing in various types of exercise facilities. One study reports that over 100,000 private companies in the United States have invested in physical fitness programs for their employees.

Studies have attempted to determine the monetary value of health/fitness programs, but it is difficult to do a cost/benefit evaluation. The following benefits have been identified by some organizations, however.

1. People with higher levels of fitness tend to have lower medical claims. An estimated thirty-one million dollar reduction in medical claims nationwide could be expected if all adults were of at least average physical fitness.

2. People with higher levels of physical fitness tend to have reduced incidence of coronary heart disease.

3. Workers taking part in physical activity miss fewer days through respiratory and non-respiratory disease than those not engaged in physical training and sports.

4. The duration of sickness of individuals practicing physical exercise is less than that of sedentary employees.

5. Unfit workers are two to three times more vulnerable to industrial accidents than their active colleagues.

6. A fit work place means millions of added days to worker productivity.

7. Fit workers have a higher production capacity—approximately five percent higher.

Fitness programs range from simple aerobics programs with no special equipment to highly sophisticated weight lifting equipment, swimming pools, and fitness instructors. They range in cost from a few hundred dollars to several thousand dollars.

If you want to install a fitness program, find a company in your area that has one and review their program. Most companies will share information on this subject.

Some companies that have fitness programs are:

Exxon

Mobil Oil

Kimberly-Clark

Manville Corporation

Xerox

Chase Manhattan Bank

Johnson & Johnson

Pepsico, Inc.

Time, Inc.

Sperry Corp.

Coors Brewery

ENCOURAGING MENTAL FITNESS WITH PAID SABBATICALS

Many employers are finding that granting workers extended leave to "recharge their batteries" pays off. Sabbaticals are in place today in companies like McDonald's, Rolm Corporation, Tandem Computers, and IBM.

McDonald's officials say that sabbaticals substantially raise productivity, creativity, and morale. Available to every full-time employee, the leave consists of one eight-week stint at full pay for every ten years of full-time service.

"The sabbatical allows long-term employees the opportunity to reflect on their jobs and their careers away from the daily pressures of work," says a spokesman for the fast food chain. "It's not so much a reward for past performance as it is an investment in the future."

Ten-year-old Tandem Computers established a sabbatical program in 1979 after employees voted for it over two other benefits—profit sharing and a retirement plan. Executives at the Cupertino, California, company created the sabbatical program because they recognized that many employees had been working flat out during Tandem's early period of high growth and needed a chance for an extended period of leave time to refresh themselves.

As a result, all of Tandem's 4,000 United States employees are eligible after four years with the company—and every fourth year thereafter—to take a six-week sabbatical in addition to normal accrued vacation time. So far, seventy-five employees have taken their second sabbaticals.

Most companies let employees do whatever they want while they are away. At the Rolm Corporation in Santa Clara, California, employees can take either twelve weeks off with full pay or six weeks off at double pay after six years on the job. Leave takers are encouraged to step back from their work routines, have some fun, and relax.

SUBSTANCE ABUSE: WHEN TO BEGIN AN EMPLOYEE ASSISTANCE PROGRAM

Someone you know may be doing it right now. Actors and writers do it, doctors and lawyers do it, football players do it, law enforcement officers do it, and many employees do it . . . it's called "substance abuse," and it costs our American economy over $28 billion a year.

Industry has been turning to Employee Assistance Programs for relief from this crisis for several years, but now the EAP is changing and becoming broader in its scope. A recently survey by the National Institute on Alcohol Abuse and Alcoholism shows that of the Fortune 500 manufacturing companies and 50 top banking, insurance, utility, transportation, and financial organizations, there is widespread acceptance. Over 57 percent of the Fortune 500 companies have reported they have alcoholism programs.

Today's EAPs deal with a broad spectrum of employee problems that affect productivity and profitability. EAPs differ in their scope of services provided and costs per employee; however, there seems to be a universal opinion that their rate of return far exceeds their cost. There are well over 8,000 EAP programs nationwide, and today the EAP concept has expanded to include mental and emotional problems.

Ten Key Ingredients of a Successful EAP

A review of current literature, and discussions with EAP managers strongly indicate that there are ten key elements critical to the success of an EAP.

1. *Management backing*: Without support at the highest level, key ingredients and over-all effect are seriously limited.

2. *Labor support*: If the company has a union, there is strong evidence the EAP cannot be successful if it is not backed by the union.

3. *Confidentiality*: Anonymity and trust are crucial or employees will not use an EAP.

4. *Easy, Confidential Access*: For maximum use and benefit. Also, the EAP office should be located where management and the employees cannot monitor usage.

5. *Supervisor training*: is crucial to employees needing understanding and support during program use.

6. *Labor representative training*: a critical variable is employees' contact with labor if you have a union.

7. *Insurance involvement*: occasionally assistance alternatives are costly and insurance support is a must if the company is not paying the total cost.

8. *Breadth of service components*: availability of assistance for a wide variety of problems (e.g., alcohol, family, personal, financial, grief, romance, medical, drugs).

9. *Professional leadership*: from a skilled professional with expertise in helping. This person must have credibility in the eyes of the employee.

10. *Follow-up and evaluation*: to measure program effectiveness and overall improvement.

There are some basic components of all EAPs.

1. A positive policy that establishes the specific methods used to become involved in the EAP is important. The policy should define in layman's terms how the program works.
2. Supervisory training in use of the EAP is very important. Supervisors are the key link between the employee and the EAP and must be trained in handling the various problems that most frequently arise.
3. The employees need educational programs regarding the EAP.
4. Counseling and clinical services must be provided on an ongoing basis.

The overall success of an EAP depends also on two key ingredients.

1. *Confidentiality*. The respondents indicated satisfaction with this factor of the EAP. No EAP can expect to be worthwhile unless the individual anonymity of each participant and his family is protected.
2. *Referral*. It is crucial to an EAP that participants are willing to refer fellow employees when assistance is needed. Fellow employees are the best advocates of an EAP.

Two Main Types of EAP Structures

According to Kenneth J. Fisher, ACSW, psychotherapist and EAP consultant in Denver, there are generally two types of EAP structures—each having certain advantages and disadvantages that should be reviewed by any company considering the establishment of an Employee Assistance Program.

In-House Programs: These are programs in which a company hires a person or group to work exclusively (or at least primarily) with its own employees. Examples: Mountain Bell, United Airlines.

- Advantages: Employees become acquainted with one person who provides information and referral services. This person generally has the freedom to circulate to various departments of a company in an informal manner. This creates high visibility and level of usage for the program.

- Disadvantages: Some employees prefer anonymity and resist utilizing a resource that can be viewed as a part of the management structure.

Out-of-House Programs: These are programs in which a company contracts with another company to provide employee assistance services. Services provided are often more comprehensive and sometimes even include ongoing therapy services.

- Advantages: These programs offer a greater feeling of anonymity and confidentiality. Offices of the EAP provider are usually located away from the company facilities, and the EAP staff does not usually have an informal relationship with company personnel.

- Disadvantages: Communication between company management and the EAP can become an additional burden to the company unless careful planning is utilized to anticipate issues that may arise.

Some companies that have EAPs are:

IBM & Rolm Corp.

Hewlett Packard

International Telephone and Telegraph

Chemical Bank

Blue Cross and Blue Shield

Mountain Bell

United Airlines

The subject of employee assistance programs is covered more fully in Chapter 9—including a sample EAP program and personnel policy.

Part D

Flexible Benefits

WHY FLEXIBLE BENEFITS MAY BE THE BEST CHOICE FOR YOUR ORGANIZATION

If management decided to start a program—

- How would it be administered?
- What would it cost?

Kwasha Lipton, consultants in employee benefits, offers two key reasons for considering flexible benefits . . .

- First, the workforce has changed so dramatically in the last ten years that today only one out of every five employees is married with a non-working spouse at home. Yet that "traditional unit" is still the basis for most companies' benefit plans. As the figure below depicts, the number of working women will continue to grow faster than the total labor force.
- Second, the cost to management of most benefits, and especially health care benefits, is rising so quickly that there is a growing need to involve the employee in some arrangement that will help contain benefit costs to the organization.

How to Operate a Flexible Benefits Program: Three Main Phases

If your management group were to decide in favor of flexible benefits, you would need to know how to set up the program. In an article in its *Newsletter*, titled "Flexible Benefits—Why They Should Be Considered," Kwasha Lipton Employee Benefits Consultants offers the following example of how a flexible program might be implemented.*

To illustrate the administrative feasibility of a flexible benefits program, an outline of how a program can operate from year to year is described below. It has three principal phases—

---

* Kwasha Lipton, Employee Benefit Consultants, Fort Lee, NJ 07024. Reprinted with permission.

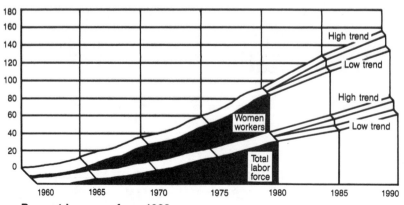

Percent Increase from 1960
Source: Bureau of Labor Statistics

(1) **communication**—the solicitation and confirmation of each employee's annual elections;

(2) **payroll**—the application of each employee's credit allowance with his election; and

(3) **benefit administration**—the recognition of the elections in premium payments to insurance carriers and in claim processing.

Phase 1: Communication
In the fall of each year, employees are required to make all of their elections for the next calendar year. They are first given individual statements listing —

a. the options they have in effect in the current year;

b. the options available to them next year; and

c. their credit pool for the next year.

The credit pool is determined for each employee on the basis of his applicable factors (e.g., service, dependent status, and pay)—and is stated as a percentage of base pay, or as a dollar amount, or as a combination of the two, depending on how the credit pool is defined in the program.

After the election forms are returned and checked for consistency, the employees are again given individual statements confirming their elections for the next year, as recorded in the system.

In effect, the procedure is a two-step personalized benefit statement. The statements can be as simple as the underlying program design.

Phase 2: Payroll
The credit pool determined each year for each employee is prorated over the number of pay periods during the year. Deductions are made from the credit allowance each pay period based on the employee's elections, and

any remaining balance is added to current pay or transferred to the capital accumulation plan, as applicable.

Social security and tax withholding—A balance added to current pay or transferred in the form of IRA-type deductible employee contributions is reflected in Social Security and withholding taxes—except where the employer has elected not to withhold tax on deductible employee contributions, as the law permits.

A balance transferred in the form of employer contributions to a Section 401(k) salary reduction plan is not so reflected—except where it exceeds the nondiscrimination limit for the plan, in which case it would be transferred as a nondeductible employee contribution or added to current pay.

Vacation—Deductions for extra vacation elections are recorded in a bookkeeping reserve and used when the employee takes the extra vacation.

Phase 3: Benefit Administration

In determining premiums to carriers and in processing claims, the procedures can be the same as those used under the present plan except for the addition of one further variable, i.e., which optional plan of benefits applies.

A program should allow prospective changes to be made during the year for legitimate cause, e.g., if a spouse's employment situation changes, causing a need for previously unelected dependent health coverage.

In such situations, the employee can change the entire package of elections for the balance of the year—or, if that is too burdensome administratively, the employee can change only the one coverage impacted by the legitimate cause and adjust the cash option, or salary reduction accordingly.

Kwasha Lipton sums up the cost-benefit picture this way:

In the normal set of circumstances, a company should not expect the adoption of a flexible benefits program to yield immediate cost savings. It is more likely that, at least initially, the company's cost will be higher than it would have been under a continuation of the conventional benefit package. The higher cost is likely to result from –

(1)   a wider application of the existing subsidy for dependent health care coverage;

(2)   the impact of 'anti-selection'

(3)   an expanded administrative burden.

Cost savings, or return on investment, come later and, unfortunately, will be very difficult to measure—since the savings are expected in the intangible forms of –

(1)   greater employee relations value per dollar of benefit cost

(2)   lesser growth in future costs than what the growth would have been in the absence of a flexible program.

Management's choices can keep costs down.   In the area of dependent coverage, management can adopt a philosophy that will be consistent with its cost objectives. It can decide, for example, to provide full coverage, or to require the employee to use credits or take a reduction in pay in order to get full coverage.

Increased costs may also result from the anti-selection that can arise in a flexible program. Anti-selection is an insurance industry term referring to a practice whereby people will tend to exercise self-interest when purchasing various coverages. They will elect the benefits that they expect to use the most.

To avoid management having to pay for greater use of coverage than is expected, Kwasha Lipton advises making each benefit option self-supporting. That is, the group's actual experience for that option can be built into the cost to the employee. If the use of an option is heavier than anticipated, the number of credits needed to purchase that option can be increased.

In all, the administrative costs of a flexible benefits program are significant, but are not so burdensome that they outweigh the advantages that will accrue from installation of a flexible program. Kwasha Lipton points out that it is not necessary to take on a full program at once. The flexible approach can be introduced gradually into each of a company's present benefit plan. In addition to helping management contain costs, the flexible approach—as more companies adopt it—will become an increasingly important element of the compensation program needed to attract and retain good employees."

- Kwasha Lipton, Employment Benefit Consultants, may be contacted at 2100 North Central Road, Fort Lee, New Jersey 07024. Telephone (201) 592-1300.

How Flexible Benefits Work at American Can Company

American Can was one of the first companies to go flexible, and its plan has since become the archetype for many others. Installed in 1978, the broad-based program offers salaried employees (now over 12,000) choices in five areas: life insurance, medical benefits, disability income, vacation, and a combination of retirement and capital accumulation. In drawing up the plan, Canco first shrank the basic benefits in each area to what it felt was the minimum everyone should have. Then, to compensate employees for what they had lost, it gave each one a certain number of flexible credits based on age, pay level, length of service, and family status. Employees can use those credits to repurchase benefits, invest them in other benefits, or bank them for future use. They can also get more benefits than the plan provides by buying them through payroll deduction.

American Can's program served as a model for two other organizations—Morgan Stanley and Northern States Power—but each added variations. Morgan did not automatically shrink benefits—they left it up to each employee to shrink the benefits they chose as being less important to their current needs. Northern States Power allows employees to use soft-dollar credits (vacation time) to buy hard dollar benefits (medical care). They also cut vacation time down from three to two weeks for everyone who qualified and let them buy back their third week and use the credit in other areas. In other words, an employee that was eligible for three weeks vacation would now only have two weeks and could use the third week they had earned as credit for other benefits.

All three companies plan to add benefits. American Can expects to offer financial planning; Morgan Stanley proposes to integrate a profit sharing plan; and Northern Power plans to add cash as a benefit alternative. (If employees don't use benefits, they can elect to receive cash instead.)

Most experts don't look on flexible benefits as a panacea, but feel that they do provide employees with a variety of choices; and companies that offer them find it is easier to attract and retain good people.

If you decide to implement a flexible benefits program the most important action to take is to hire a benefits consultant that is well versed in installing flexible benefits programs. Three of the most experienced consulting companies are:

Hewitt Associates
100 Half Day Road
Lincolnshire, IL 60015

Mercer-Meidinger-Hansen
1050 17th Street
Denver, CO 80265

Kwasha Lipton
2100 North Central Road
Fort Lee, NJ 07023

Part E

Pension and Retirement Benefits

TWO POPULAR EMPLOYEE BENEFITS

401k Pension Plans

This is one of the most popular tax-deferred retirement plans around today. In fact, it is estimated that one out of three taxpayers participates in one, and eighty-five percent of the Fortune 1000 Companies have one. So far, they have not replaced defined benefit plans. Companies are offering the 401K plans in addition to their regular pension plans and not "sweetening" the original plan.

The 401k acts as a tax shelter. Employees can set aside a portion of their wages tax free until they retire. They can start drawing money out after retirement. Under most 401k plans employers contribute a matching amount, usually fifty percent of the employee's contribution.

How Does the 401k Plan Work?

As with most profit-sharing plans, the first step is to set up a trust through an insurance company, bank, brokerage house, or attorney. The next step is designing the actual plan—how much money employees will contribute, where the money will be invested, and who will administer it. Companies that sell the program to small business, such as Connecticut General and Massachusetts Mutual, do everything.

In order to benefit the lower level employees, there is a built-in limitation on how much upper-tiered management can contribute to—and benefit from—the plan. Your employees determine their contributions through a vote, and, as an employer, your contributions are restricted by tax law.

You should anticipate spending anywhere from $20 to $25 in administration costs for each employee enrolled in the plan, plus another $1,500 to $2,000 for a one-time flat fee that some consultants charge for installing the 401k.

How Exxon Launched Its 401k Plan

When Exxon installed a 401k, they knew there would be communications problems, so they carefully planned installation. Their campaign started with the design of a distinctive logo, then came a series of posters: the first had just eight words, the second and third had nine, and the fourth poster had thirty. Then came the first major communication: *a letter from each unit's employee relations manager.* Along with that came the required prospectus and a highlights folder. That piece had 700 words of text and one chart.

Presentations were made to employees throughout the country. The presentation text was backed up with a nine-minute slide tape, so that even if local presenters made variations in the text, certain information went through in the way corporate wanted the story told.

Handouts for employees included worksheets.   The latter led employees step by step through the calculations, so they could see how the plan worked and how it would affect them. They could take them home and work on them at their leisure.

To back up the worksheets, employees received a forty-four-page booklet. Presenters for the local meetings also had a list of questions and answers supplied by corporate, and support material appeared in print media going regularly to employees.

Because changes in the tax law have altered the benefits of 401k plans from time to time, it is a good idea to review your plans with a qualified pension plan consultant or tax attorney. See Part A of this chapter for more details.

Employee Stock Ownership Plan (ESOP)

One of the hottest benefits around today is the Employee Stock Ownership Plan, because other fringes are being eliminated or curtailed by firms whose profits are sagging. Many companies have instituted ESOPs because the cost is minimal.

Some firms that have ESOPs are: AT&T, Sears, General Motors, Control Data, Dayton-Hudson, May Department Stores, Frontier Airlines, and many more. Sears' ESOP covers 300,000 employees including those employed by Allstate Insurance Company, one of their subsidiaries.

One reason the ESOP is such a good employee benefit is because it is free to the employee and nearly free to the employer also, because it is financed by a federal tax credit.

How ESOPs work:

Basically, a company puts some of its stock into a trust for its employees— all of them or at least a large class, such as salaried workers. Specific amounts of stock are earmarked for each eligible worker either on a flat, per-capita basis, or in proportion to the employee's pay. Every year, the company makes another contribution; at the same time, each person's share of the pot also benefits from the reinvestment of dividends.

The law says that the stock must remain in trust for at least seven years; usually it will stay there until the employee dies, retires, or leaves for any reason.

ESOPs are so popular that the Association for Workplace Democracy in Amherst, Massachusetts, believes that within the next ten years, twenty percent of all American employees will be beneficiaries. The Employee Stock Ownership Plan Association in Washington, DC estimates there are already approximately 6,000 ESOPs nationwide.

There are some potential problems with ESOPs, and the federal government loses over $2.5 billion in taxes annually, according to the Office of Management and Budget.

In addition, serious issues of fairness have arisen in ESOPs set up by such companies as Blue Bell, Inc., an apparel manufacturer, and Raymond International, Inc., a construction firm. In large leveraged buy-outs such as these, three separate interests—managers, outside investors, and employees—frequently split up ownership by bargaining for shares on the basis of their investments. But the employees are many times represented only by an ESOP trustee who is often a company official. Critics say that this procedure usually lets management and outside investors take extra-generous portions of stock and voting control at the workers' expense . . . many times not giving employees a voice in the decisions even when their pension plans are terminated.

Advocates, however, say that ESOPs are a powerful tool in raising productivity. The National Center for Employee Ownership (NCEO) recently studied 360 high-technology companies, and concluded that those sharing ownership with most or all employees grew two to four times as fast as companies whose employees do not own stock. In the study of 52 employee-owned companies in all industries, NCEO found that the best performers were those that made the largest stock payments to their workers' ESOP accounts.

As is the case when installing any complicated benefit, it is a good idea to review current tax law and to seek the assistance of a qualified benefits consultant.

How One ESOP Leveraged Buy-Out May Have Actually Hurt Employees

The leveraged buy-out of Parsons Corporation by its Employee Stock Ownership Plan, one of the largest ESOP transactions in United States history, is now raising serious questions among company employees, pension experts, and financial planners.

Parsons employees think they may have gotten the short end of the deal. The Labor Department is investigating the $518 million buy-out of the international engineering and construction company's public shareholders at $32 a share after the agency received protest letters from at least three employee groups. Just before Parsons announced that it was considering going private, its stock was trading at about $27.50 on the New York Stock Exchange.

The Labor Department says employees have charged that the company executives who designed and implemented the buy-out will get $19 million out of the transaction, while the employees' future retirement funds have been loaded with hundreds of millions of dollars of debt. Employees also were angered that some Parsons executives had received stock through options and other awards for as little as $1 a share, and would be cashing out at $32 a share. The Chairman, William E. Leonard, received $5.6 million for his 175,207 shares.

Encouraged by tax breaks in the 1984 tax law, interest in employee stock ownership plans has picked up. The plans are being used increasingly to take companies private . . . in some cases the employees save their jobs (as in the Frontier Airlines buy-out), but in other instances it is a way to avoid a takeover of the company. Watch closely updates in tax law on ESOPs.

For the next seven years, Parsons employees who retire are guaranteed to receive at least $32 a share. After that, value of the shares will depend on how well the company does. Some employees are worried about the future value of their shares because they have been burdened with $518 million of debt.

One executive described the Parsons buy-out . . . "Parsons employees have all their eggs in one basket . . . but they don't have control of the basket."

Other people who are involved in buy-outs, like Frontier Airlines, are having second thoughts. Big pay cuts have made them wonder if they did the right thing. The buy-out did save their jobs.

The ESOP is still a popular benefit, but we won't know how good a deal the leveraged buy-out is for some employees for several years.

Some companies that have gone through ESOP leveraged buy-outs are: Fastener Industries, Inc., Jeannette Sheet Glass Corporation, Janco Corporation, Bofors, Inc., Blue Bell, Inc., Raymond International, Inc.

WHAT YOU SHOULD KNOW ABOUT PENSION AND RETIREMENT BENEFITS

Pension Welfare Obligations

If you have an employee pension or welfare benefit plan, you should be aware of the following obligations:

Under ERISA you must:

- make plan information easily available.
- protect your plan assets from mismanagement or misuse.
- give employees the right to appeal denial of claim for benefits.
- prohibit interference with attainment of your employee rights.
- assure you provide employees an environment free from harassment in exercising their rights under ERISA.
- give employees the right to sue in federal court.
- give employees the right to assistance from the government in such cases.

ERISA also protects the interests of participants in most private employee pension benefit plans and their beneficiaries by:

- setting standards for eligibility for pension plan participation.
- safeguarding rights to pension benefits.
- protecting from inadequate plan financing.
- providing protection of pension benefits in the event of plan termination or merger.
- providing survivor pension to spouses of retirees in some cases unless the participant elects otherwise.
- protecting from alienation or assignment of benefits.

Plan Information that Employers Must Make Easily Available to Participating Employees*

- the summary plan description within 90 days after a person becomes a participant or beneficiary, or within 120 days after the plan becomes subject to the reporting and disclosure provisions of the law.
- a summary of any change in the plan description or a summary of a material modification in the terms of the plan, within 210 days after the end of the plan year in which the change is adopted.
- an updated summary plan description every five years integrating all amendments, if there have been any; and, if no amendments have been adopted, another summary plan description every ten years.
- a summary of the annual report within nine months after the end of the plan year.

---

* From the Department of Labor Publication, "What You Should Know About the Pension and Welfare Law," a Guide to the Employment Income Security Act of 1974.

The administrator must furnish automatically to each pension plan participant:

- a statement upon termination of employment of the nature, form, and amount of deferred vested benefits.

- a statement of total benefits earned and the percentage of such benefits that are vested upon termination of employment or a one-year break in service.

- a written explanation before the annuity starting date of the terms and conditions of any joint and survivor annuity and the effect of electing against such an option.

The administrator must furnish to any pension plan participant or beneficiary, within thirty days of written request, a statement of total benefits accrued, accrued benefits that are vested, if any, or the earliest date on which the accrued benefits will become vested. This statement need not be furnished more than once in a twelve-month period. The administrator must furnish to any participant or beneficiary within thirty days of written request, and for which a reasonable charge may be made:

- the latest updated summary plan description

- the plan description Form EBS-1

- the latest annual report Form 5500, 5500-C, or 5500-K

- the documents under which the plan was established or is operated

- terminal reports, if any

If a claim for benefits is denied, the administrator must furnish an explanation in writing to the participant or beneficiary whose claim has been denied.

The administrator must make available to any participant or beneficiary at the principal office of the administrator and other places:

- the plan description Form EBS-1

- the latest annual report Form 5500, 5500-C, or 5500-K

- the documents under which the plan was established or is operated, such as the bargaining agreement or trust agreement

The Internal Revenue Service will furnish to the Social Security Administration information on deferred vested benefits of plan participants who have terminated employment during a plan year before retirement. The Social Security Administration will keep the information on deferred vested benefits to provide to employees involved and their beneficiaries upon request and automatically when they apply for social security benefits.

Employees who are "interested parties," as defined by Internal Revenue Service regulations, must be notified of a request to the Internal Revenue Service for a tax qualification of a plan. Tax qualification gives tax benefits to a plan, the employer, and the employees participating in the plan. "Interested parties" have the right to see the application for approval and to see the supporting documents.

The plan descriptions, annual reports, and any other documents filed with the Secretary of Labor must be made available for public inspection. The reports filed with the Department of Labor under ERISA may be examined in Room N-4677 of the department at 200 Constitution Avenue N.W., Washington, DC. Copies of documents may be purchased at a cost of 10¢ per page. For further information, telephone (202) 523–8771.

Department of Labor Publications on ERISA

Often-Asked Questions About the Employee Retirement Income Security Act of 1974 is a twenty-eight page booklet, geared to answer questions of workers, employers, and plan administrators affected by ERISA.

Reporting and Disclosure: Employee Retirement Income Security Act of 1974 is a sixteen-page booklet that outlines and explains how the Act's reporting and disclosure provisions affect workers and their beneficiaries, employers, and plan administrators. It covers the reports plan administrators must file with the United States Government (not only the Labor Department, but also the Internal Revenue Service, and the Pension Benefit Guaranty Corporation), information administrators must disclose to participants and beneficiaries, exemptions and alternative methods, descriptions of the reports, and recordkeeping requirements.

Fiduciary Standards: Employee Retirement Income Security Act is an eleven-page booklet that outlines the fiduciary provisions of the law and includes a list of Labor Department releases on fiduciary standards as of the date of publication.

Coverage Under the Employee Retirement Income Security Act of 1974 is a twelve-page booklet that outlines the types of welfare and pension plans and the types of benefits covered by ERISA, and specifies those plans that are exempt by statute and by regulation.

Identification Numbers Under ERISA (Publication 1004), a publication jointly developed by the Department of Labor, the Internal Revenue Service, and the Pension Benefit Guaranty Corporation, explains which identification numbers are to be used on certain reporting forms required by each agency under ERISA.

These booklets may be obtained free of charge from Labor-Management Services Administration, United States Department of Labor, 200 Constitution Avenue N.W., Washington, DC 20216, telephone (202) 523-7222.

CHANGES IN PENSION FUND FINANCIAL ACCOUNTING STANDARDS

Some experts are calling the new pension fund financial accounting standards issued by the Financial Accounting Standards Board (FASB) almost revolutionary. They go into effect over a period of three years. FASB Statement 87 appears to have a widespread effect on businesses that go beyond even pension matters. Some experts say that almost twenty percent of all United States businesses will have to make a record of pension liabilities. The main thrust of the new standards require companies to elevate minimum unfunded pension liabilities (not assets) from footnote status to the balance sheet along with related intangible assets or reductions in equity.

Although some human resource directors may not have FASB reporting responsibility, it is a good idea to maintain an effective knowledge base about the overall reporting requirements in the benefits area. It appears that the new standards will at a minimum, result in lower employer contributions to pension plans, accelerate the shift from defined-benefit to defined-contribution plans, increase accounting costs in maintaining the plans, and perhaps enhance takeover appeal of small publicly held businesses with overfunded pension plans.

Human resource directors must not only be concerned with compliance with the new standards, we must also continue to be concerned about profitability and continuing to provide attractive retirement benefits to employees. Whether you have an accounting expert on staff monitoring FASB compliance, or you use an outside consultant, it will pay you to keep on top of this new area of reporting responsibility.

For a succinct overview of the new FASB statements contact the Denver office of Mercer-Meidinger-Hansen, 303-629-6767.

KEY ASPECTS OF THE TWO MAJOR QUALIFIED RETIREMENT PROGRAMS

Because of the aging workforce, retirement programs are of more significant interest to all human resource professionals today. James Frohne, consulting principal with Mercer-Meidinger-Hansen, provides the following easy-to-understand explanation of retirement programs.

There are three general types of retirement programs. These are called "Defined Contribution Plans," "Defined Benefit Plans," and "Supplemental Retirement Programs." An employer may sponsor one of either type, or one of each, and sometimes a combination of the three.

1. Defined Contribution Plans

Defined Contribution Plans are plans in which the plan document defines the contributions to be made, but does not specify the resulting benefit. One or more individual accounts are maintained for each participant, and the benefit at retirement (or earlier termination of employment, disability, or death) is simply the balance in the participant's account(s). Vesting—or ownership in employer provided balances—ranges from full and immediate to schedules requiring from five to ten years of service (for example, twenty percent for each year of service). The Tax Reform Act of 1986 (TRA '86) accelerates the maximum vesting schedules allowed. In addition, full vesting is usually granted in the event of disability or death, and in any case on retirement at age sixty-five.

Vesting schedules for plan years beginning after December 31, 1988 must grant full vesting within five years of service, or follow a schedule that credits an employee with twenty percent each year after two years, up to 100 percent after seven years of service.

Advantages

Simplicity: The concept is similar to a savings account and is therefore readily understood and appreciated by employee participants. Communication efforts are more likely to be successful and can more readily focus on the plan's special provisions such as vesting or participant directed investments, as the basic plan concepts are easily understood.

Cost Control: A major advantage to the employer or plan sponsor is the fact that plan costs are controlled as defined in the plan document. There will be no surprise cost increases to create additional problems in an already difficult financial period.

Liability Control: As there is no promise of benefits beyond the assets existing in the plan's trust at any time, the employer or plan sponsor is not exposed to any liability for benefits promised, but not yet funded.

Disadvantages

Benefit Adequacy: Especially for those who retire during a Defined Contribution Plan's early years, benefit levels may be seriously inadequate simply because there has not been enough time for contributions and investment income to accumulate to a sufficient level.

Investment Risk: Even for participants who retire after a significant length of service under a Defined Contribution Plan, benefit levels may be inadequate. By definition, benefits are limited to individual account balances, and these are subject not only to the persistence and significance of contributions made, but to investment performance as well. In the absence of employee directed investment alternatives, the plan's trustee/administrator will bear increased fiduciary responsibility for investment return (for example, the "prudent person" rules). Even with employee directed investment alternatives, poor choices are possible, and retirement during depressed economic times will frequently mean retirement with depressed and inadequate retirement benefits.

There are a number of different major types of Defined Contribution Plans currently in existence. Following is a brief description of each of the most common, in simplest form. Many plans are combination plans that contain features from several of the basic types.

Five Types of Defined Contribution Plans and What They Offer

Profit Sharing Plans: Under this type of Defined Contribution Plan, the employer decides each year what amount to share with employee participants (generally limited to a maximum tax deduction of covered payroll). Such contributions are generally allocated to individual participant accounts on the basis of pay, but the formula may also consider length of service to a limited degree. Forfeitures resulting from the termination of participants prior to attainment of a fully vested status are reallocated among remaining participants. Contributions and investment income are not taxable to participants until payment from the plan is made, and then the advantages of five-year averaging may apply. Contributions made by the employer are tax deductible by the employer when made within the limits provided by current tax law.

Savings (Thrift) Plans: A Savings Plan is a Profit Sharing Plan under which employees contribute a percentage (frequently any whole percentage of pay on an after-tax basis and the employer commits to matching a portion of each dollar (assuming profits are available). Refer to current tax law for specific percentages. TRA '86 has imposed a new discrimination test for these plans to ensure that there is reasonable relationship between the amount of benefits provided for highly compensated employees, as compared to all other employees.

Salary Reduction Section 401k Plans: As mentioned earlier, this is a plan that is similar in most respects to a Savings or Thrift type of Profit Sharing Plan, except that employees elect to have their pay reduced by the amount of their elected contribution, and the employer then transmits these amounts to the plan for the employee as an employer contribution. Employer matching contributions, if any, are made in addition to the amounts of employee elected payroll reductions. The result is a tax savings to the employee, as his contributions are made on a pre-tax basis. In addition, since employee elected payroll reductions are effectively converted to employer contributions, the percentage of covered payroll employer tax deduction limit is more likely to come into play. Also Social Security taxes must be paid on payroll reduction amounts. There are special tests that must be satisfied annually to ensure that there is a reasonable relationship between the amount of benefits provided on a tax-favored basis for highly paid, as compared to all other employees.

ESOP (Employee Stock Ownership Plans):   This is a Defined Contribution Plan similar to a Profit Sharing Plan, except that plan assets are primarily invested in employer stock, and benefit distributions are entirely in employer stock.

2. Defined Benefit Retirement Plans

Defined Benefit Retirement Plans are distinguished from Defined Contribution Plans primarily in that the plan document defines the benefit to be paid rather than the contribution to be made. As such, under a Defined Benefit Plan, an individual participant does not have an individual account(s). Instead, each participant has an accrued benefit at any point in time that is generally based on length of service and pay history. The accrued benefit is expressed as a number of dollars of deferred income on a monthly or annual basis, generally to be paid commencing at retirement (usually age sixty-five).

Vesting in the accrued benefit means that additional service with the employer sponsoring the plan is not required in order to receive benefit payments at retirement. Vesting is generally more restrictive than in Defined Contribution Plans, the new TRA '86 rules will also apply to Defined Benefit Plans. Because of this, and the fact that benefit values are determined on the basis of actuarial factors that are heavily age related (due to the deferred nature of benefit payments), it is generally true that a Defined Contribution Plan will be more favorable to participants who terminate service early, than a Defined Benefit Plan because a Defined Benefit Plan generally favors longer service career emloyees. Death benefits are mandated by law once vesting is attained, and benefits are frequently provided for participants who become disabled as well.

The basic definition of a Defined Benefit Plan results in different advantages and disadvantages than the Defined Contribution Plans. Some major advantages and disadvantages are:

Advantages

Benefit Adequacy: Benefits are always adequate, by definition, because the plan is subject to minimum funding standards set by law, and the contribution amount is determined on an actuarial basis rather than discretionary basis (as in a profit sharing plan).

Investment Risk: There is no investment risk for the employee. Benefits are determined by formula, and investment gains or losses affect the amount of contribution required of the employer. In fact, accrued benefits (up to certain relatively high limits) are guaranteed by the Pension Benefit Guaranty Corporation (PBGC), which is funded by mandatory employer premium payments. No such insurance exists for Defined Contribution plans.

Disadvantages

   Complexity: Defined Benefit Plans are relatively complex in concept, and participants generally find it difficult to understand and appreciate their benefits.

   Lack of Cost Control: Not only are annual employer contributions mandated at minimum levels under the Employee Retirement Income Security Act of 1974 (ERISA) without regard to profitability, but the amount of contribution is subject to the plan's actuarial experience (including investment performance) and can fluctuate significantly over time.

   Employer Liability: A Defined Benefit Plan is a significant long-term commitment, and the employer is liable within limits (thirty percent of net worth) to the PBGC for vested benefits even in the event the plan is adequately funded. Recognition of Defined Benefit Retirement Plan liability on corporate books is required per statement of Financial Accounting Standards No. 87 for certain employers.

How the Four Main Types of Defined Benefit Retirement Plans Work

The various types of Defined Benefit Retirement Plans are described in terms of the type of formula used to determine participant benefits. The most prominent types are outlined briefly below.

Flat Dollar Plans: The benefit formula in Flat Dollar Plans describes the benefit as a number of dollars multiplied by years of service. Such plans are commonly adopted for groups of blue collar workers, and they are most popular with union groups. Increases in the dollar amount of benefits are frequently required to maintain the purchasing power of benefits due to inflation.

Pay-Related Plans: In Pay-Related Plans, the benefit formula is related to the participant's pay history as well as his service. The benefit can be a function of the entire history of pay, as in *Career Average Pay Plans* or, more commonly, it is related only to the pay level over a period (usually five years) of time just before retirement, as in a *"Final Average Pay Plan."*

Integrated Plans: Defined Benefit Plans may be "integrated" with Social Security benefits, and most salary related plans are. The concept of integration results from the fact that Social Security retirement benefits heavily favor lower paid employees. Also, Social Security contributions made by employees are matched by the employer so that Social Security is effectively a part of the employer's retirement program. In an effort to produce employer provided benefits that, when combined from both sources (the private plan and the employer portion of Social Security), represent a more level percentage of pay across all pay levels; an Integrated Plan provides higher benefit credits on pay above the Social Security level. In relatively few cases, known as *Excess Only* Pay Plans, this is accomplished by providing no benefit credit for pay below a certain level (related to Social Security). In *Step Rate* Plans, the benefit credit on pay above a certain level (such as the Social Security wage base) is higher than the credit on pay below that level. Most common is the *Social Security Offset* Plan, in which the benefit formula is based on total pay and then is reduced by a portion (usually not more than fifty percent) of the participant's primary Social Security benefit.

Floor Plans: A final type of Defined Benefit Plan, the Floor Plan is really a combination of a Defined Benefit Plan and a Defined Contribution Plan. In the classic case, a profit sharing plan is adopted and is viewed as the primary retirement vehicle. However, in recognition of the problems that could develop for some employees with regard to inadequate benefit levels, a Defined Benefit Plan is also adopted—which is expected to pay benefits only infrequently. The benefit formula in the Defined Benefit Plan is reduced by the monthly or annual income that could be provided by the profit sharing balance. Thus, if that balance is low for whatever reason, the employee will still retire with a floor benefit under the Defined Benefit Plan.

As with Defined Contribution Plans, employer contributions to Defined Benefit Plans are tax deductible within limits to the employer, and are tax deferred to the employee until received (as is investment income). There are many requirements relating to coverage, non-discrimination, and maximum benefit levels, to name a few. Generally speaking, these requirements are spelled out in ERISA and subsequent federal legislation (ADEA, TEFRA, DEFRA, REA, TRA '86), and the requirements are usually more complex for Defined Benefit than Defined Contribution Plans.

3. Supplemental Retirement Programs (SERPs)

Due largely to the limitations in benefit levels that may be provided to employees in qualified retirement programs, nonqualified retirement plans have become quite common. These plans generally provide for benefits above the mandated maximum levels and are specifically permitted in ERISA for a select group of highly paid management employees. Funding such plans, known as SERPs (Supplemental Employee Retirement Programs), is significantly different from funding qualified plans. In general, any assets set aside for such a plan remain corporate assets and are, therefore, subject to corporate creditors. This, of course, puts the employee participant at substantial risk and is a significant disadvantage. Contributions to such a plan are not tax deductible to the employer until the benefit is paid and become taxable income to the employee.

INCOME REPLACEMENT: HOW TO DETERMINE WHAT EMPLOYEES NEED FOR A COMFORTABLE RETIREMENT

Any retirement program should provide benefits at an appropriate level. Benefits below this level will not meet employee needs, and benefits above this level represent a loss of employer funds that could have been more appropriately used for other purposes. A great deal of time and effort has been spent in an effort to define in concrete terms just what the appropriate benefit level is for a retirement program.

Perhaps the best answer is given in terms of income replacement. In essence, the question of appropriate benefit level is restated as what income replacement level is appropriate for a career employee at retirement. Most employers would consider their retirement program successful if career employees (thirty to forty years of service) were able to retire with the expectation that income from Social Security and their retirement program would permit continuation of the lifestyle attained during the period of perhaps five years immediately prior to retirement.

Table 4–7 shows one of many possible developments. The case considered is that of a couple retiring in 1985 at age sixty-five with final earnings in the year before retirement ranging from $10,000 to $200,000. The results of this analysis are set forth in column (15), which shows that employees earning from $10,000 to $30,000 will need a retirement plan that provides from three percent to twenty-three percent of pay in addition to Social Security benefits. Those earning from $35,000 to $75,000 will need from twenty-seven percent to forty-three percent, and those earning more will need from forty-eight percent to fifty percent. As might be expected, these results reflect the fact that Social Security benefits are more significant for those in the lower pay levels. If the benefit plan being considered is a Defined Contribution Plan, it is necessary to consider what level of life annuity could be provided by the expected balance at age sixty-five. On an approximate basis, divide the balance by a factor of nine to determine the amount of life annuity (for example, $90,000 would provide about $10,000 per year for life under current interest rates and life expectancy tables).

When deciding to enter into any retirement program, an employer should review impending tax law changes with their plan consultant.

Table 4-7
1987 Spendable Income Analysis
Retirement Benefits Needed by a Couple Retiring at Age 65 to Maintain Pre-Retirement Living Standard

	(1) Final Earnings Before Retirement	(2) Federal Income Tax*	(3) Estimated Work-Connected Expenses**	(4) 1987 Social Security Tax	(5) Estimated Personal Savings, Insurance Premiums, State and Local Taxes	(6) Estimated Retirement Income Required (After Taxes) (1) – (2) thru (5) Amount	(7) % of Pre-Retirement Gross
A	$ 10,000	$ 268	$1,165	$ 715	$ 273	$ 7,579	76%
B	15,000	996	1,340	1,073	819	10,772	72
C	20,000	1,746	1,515	1,430	1,365	13,944	70
D	25,000	2,496	1,690	1,788	2,047	16,979	68
E	30,000	3,135	1,865	2,145	2,730	20,125	67
F	35,000	3,772	2,040	2,503	3,549	23,136	66
G	40,000	4,696	2,215	2,860	4,368	25,861	65
H	50,000	7,076	2,565	3,131	6,006	31,222	62
I	60,000	9,610	2,915	3,131	8,106	36,238	60
J	75,000	14,072	3,440	3,131	11,247	43,110	57
K	100,000	21,510	4,315	3,131	16,641	54,403	54
L	125,000	29,383	4,625	3,131	22,107	65,754	53
M	150,000	37,564	4,625	3,131	29,341	75,339	50
N	175,000	45,745	4,625	3,131	36,510	84,989	49
O	200,000	53,927	4,625	3,131	43,680	94,637	47

* 1987 rates, two exemptions of $1,900, itemized deductions = 15% of gross (or standard deduction = $3,760, if more).

** Transportation, meals and clothing.

	(8)	(9)	(10)	(11)	(12)	(13)	(14)	(15)	(16)	(17)
	Estimated Retirement Income Required	1987 Taxable Social Security Income	1987 Non-Taxable Social Security Income	1987 Total Social Security Income***	After Tax Income Required In Addition To Non-taxable Social Security (8) − (10)	Pre-Tax Income Required to Provide Amount In Column (12)****	Pre-Tax Income Required Other Than Social Security		Total Gross Retirement Income From All Sources	
							Amount (13) − (9)	% of Pre-Retirement Gross	Amount (11) + (14)	% of Pre-Retirement Gross
A	$ 7,579	0	$ 7,416	$ 7,416	$ 163	$ 163	$ 163	2%	$ 7,579	76%
B	10,772	0	9,630	9,630	1,142	1,142	1,142	8	10,772	72
C	13,944	0	11,844	11,844	2,100	2,100	2,100	11	13,944	70
D	16,979	0	13,194	13,194	3,785	3,758	3,785	15	16,976	68
E	20,125	0	13,644	13,644	6,481	6,481	6,481	22	20,125	67
F	23,136	0	13,950	13,950	9,186	9,186	9,186	26	23,136	66
G	25,861	0	14,166	14,166	11,695	11,904	11,904	30	26,070	65
H	31,222	0	14,202	14,202	17,020	18,117	18,117	36	32,319	65
I	36,238	0	14,202	14,202	22,036	24,018	24,018	40	38,202	64
J	43,110	3,721	10,481	14,202	32,629	36,481	32,760	44	46,962	63
K	54,403	7,101	7,101	14,202	47,302	55,745	48,644	49	62,864	63
L	65,754	7,101	7,101	14,202	58,653	71,761	64,660	52	78,862	63
M	75,339	7,101	7,101	14,202	68,238	85,406	78,305	52	92,507	62
N	84,989	7,101	7,101	14,202	77,888	99,143	92,042	53	106,244	61
O	94,637	7,101	7,101	14,202	87,536	112,988	105,887	53	120,089	60

*** Married couple, same age. Benefit for single person is ⅔ of the amount shown.
**** Based on two $1,900 exemptions; 15% deductions (or standard deduction = $6,200, if more).

187

POTENTIAL DRAWBACKS TO PRIVATE PENSIONS

Pension Security and the "Defined Benefit" Plan

The federal government has changed policies that relate to private pensions, and these changes are causing some big headaches. The government has encouraged the "Defined Benefit" Plan. This is the Plan where a company promises to pay a specific pension to the employee after retirement. It works well for an employee who works for one company during his/her entire working life. The problem is, however, that companies merge, go out of business, and so forth; and people don't work for one company long enough to vest for a pension. The average time an employee works for one company now is seven years for males and five years for females.

Although over forty million people work for companies that provide defined benefit plans today, a shrinking number will work for their company long enough to collect a pension. If the company falls on hard times and has to take bankruptcy, like Braniff Airways, monthly pension payments can drop as much as fifteen percent to thirty percent or be lost altogether.

Even if you work for a financially healthy company, you can lose. The laws now allow companies with overfunded pension plans to terminate them, and after they pay off their pension obligations, the company can keep the difference. Over ninety United States companies announced intentions to terminate their pension plans and take back over $1.1 billion in surplus assets. In addition, the media have reported numerous stories over the past few years about unions and union leaders tapping pension funds and being accused of embezzlement and fraud.

What about ERISA? The Employee Retirement Income Security Act does provide insurance administered by the Pension Benefit Guarantee Corporation. Every employer is assessed the same premium per employee, regardless of benefits provided by the pension plan. Current trends in pension security, however, are as troubling as trends of a few years ago with the Social Security system . . . trends that still continue. It is conceivable that unless a new method for managing pension funds is found, both private pension funds and the Social Security system could be financial disasters.

Pension Asset Reversion: Legal and Ethical Implications

Another fairly common practice in large corporations today is the pension asset reversion. Pension funds used to be in trouble, but with higher interest earnings many pension funds are "fat"—their assets are multiplying faster than their liabilities, and they are irresistible targets for top executives whose companies have not been profitable.

Companies are not required to retain assets in their pension funds over and above their actual pension liabilities, so the so-called "pension asset reversions" are legal, but most companies keep them as quiet as possible because retirees tend to look on pension funds as their private property. They feel the company should not be able to "raid" pension funds for cash.

Many companies have used pension asset reversions as a routine management tool. One such company, AMF, Inc., took a $100 million reversion. Through a series of setbacks and some poor timing on buy-outs, AMF found itself in a financial crunch. The AMF pension fund was fat and too big to ignore. AMF's actuaries found assets of the fund so far in excess of the Plan's ongoing needs that they could have actually stopped paying into the fund for five years. AMF used the $100 million to pay down their debt.

Actually, more than 300 companies have replaced older, rich pension funds with new ones, claiming more than $3 billion. The Labor and Treasury Departments have cleared up some of the weak guidelines on reversions, and now more companies like AMF that have terminated pension plans have purchased annuities to satisfy existing liabilities. Companies must now design new plans that will fully vest all ongoing participants. Many HR people, Congressmen, and corporate executives, feel there is an ethical issue here, and it is undoubtedly one to watch closely in the coming years.

The Traditional Pension May Be a Thing of the Past

Mention pension benefits in a group and you are liable to start a long discussion and more than a few arguments. There have been six federal tax bills in the last six years and pension experts pass themselves coming and going in the halls of government. Companies and their human resources experts are going through future shock with their benefit programs. If you are a courageous or short-tempered employer, you may just say to heck with it—I'm just going to give employees a salary increase and let them get their own benefits. That may be a drastic approach but companies are, in a way, moving to "monetize" their benefits through defined contributions, personal retirement accounts, and other employee benefits. And, it is a fact, employees are certainly watching their private retirement benefits more closely.

HOW TO HANDLE PRERETIREMENT COUNSELING

The working population is steadily aging, and today there are a record 45.7 million Americans between the ages of forty-five and sixty-five, an aging population that must deal with retirement options that can be quite complex. In the past, most employees were left to their own resources and spent little time planning for retirement. It was one of those things frequently put off "until tomorrow." In the mid 1980's inflation scared many employees nearing sixty-five and wondering if they could afford to retire. Companies began worrying also—about how their older employees would be able to handle retirement, both financially and emotionally. Some companies have started preretirement education programs and they are very successful.

How CBS, Inc. Successfully Developed Its Preretirement Program

There is a lot of variation in the scope of preretirement programs being offered by organizations. Some give only information that the law requires and call it "preretirement planning." However, most companies voluntarily go much further. The more responsible companies now offer corporate-wide seminars that involve thousands of employees and their spouses. Not only are companies heavily involved in preretirement counseling, but several organizations have developed programs they offer other companies on a fee basis. One such company is CBS, Inc. Honora Zimmerman, Seminar Leader for the CBS preretirement program, describes the benefits:

> In 1980, CBS developed its Pre-Retirement Education Program (PREP) and offered the three-day seminar to its employees aged 58 and over. The response of the over 1000 participants to this popular program was very positive. After an analysis of the marketplace and examination of the changing demographics of the workforce, CBS decided to market the seminar outside the corporation. Minor modifications were made to the seminar to give it broader appeal; and New Beginning, the CBS preretirement seminar, was launched in 1984.

> New Beginning is a two-day seminar program conducted by CBS personnel and consultants. The "total package" approach allows for complete flexibility and customization for any organization. The package includes unlimited consultations with New Beginning personnel before the actual seminar. These meetings can assess needs, clarify goals, and provide any needed assistance with public relations, publicity, and other communications needs within the company. When needed, informal briefings can be conducted by New Beginning personnel. All of these pre-seminar functions are designed to inform all client company personnel about the upcoming program and to allay any fears or reservations about preretirement education. The New Beginning package also includes assistance in selecting prospective participants and communicating with them about the program. The seminar can be conducted at the client company training facility or an appropriate off-site conference center or meeting room.

> Throughout the two-day training, a wide variety of methods and media are employed to inform pre-retirees (and their life partners) about the major issues they will face in retirement. Group interaction and participation is encouraged in order to foster a sense of mastery, confidence, and good will. The major topic areas (or modules) are:

> - Personal financial management (budgeting, investing, saving, planning)

- Social Security/Medicare
- Pension, insurance, and other company benefits
- Health maintenance, wellness, sexuality, nutrition, health problems in aging
- Lifestyles
- Hobbies
- Second careers
- Volunteerism
- Where to live, to move or not to move
- Living as a single
- Continuing education
- Changing roles in mid-life

At the end of the two-day seminar, all evaluations are tabulated and the results shared with the client company. As a further follow-up to New Beginning, all participants receive a free first year membership to A.A.R.P. and regular retirement newsletters from New Beginning.

Why Is Preretirement Education Important?

The 1981 Harris study on aging in America strongly supported the conclusions of several other studies regarding the importance of preretirement planning. Those who are most content in retirement are almost always those who had planned for this important life phase. There is a close correlation, of course, to retirement happiness and financial, physical, and emotional well being. Those who had planned ahead and devoted time, thought, and effort to these aspects of life reported a greater degree of retirement fulfillment than those who had not planned at all.

An increasing number of employers have come to recognize the value of preretirement education. Human resources personnel are attracted to the potential increase in loyalty, productivity, and higher morale—not only among the preretirees, but also in the ranks of their younger colleagues. By offering a complete education program in seminar format, employers can provide peace of mind and greater self-esteem to their experienced and mature work force. At CBS, the preretirement education program is valued more than a farewell dinner and gold watch. The client companies that purchase the New Beginning Pre-Retirement Program from CBS will undoubtedly experience similar results.

You can contact CBS, Inc. at 51 West 52nd Street, New York, New York 10019, telephone (212) 975-4321, for additional information on their program.

Where to Look for More Information on Preretirement Programs

An excellent information resource is the American Association of Retired Persons (AARP) in Washington, DC. If you are thinking of offering a preretirement program, call AARP or one of the companies that is currently offering one and review the pros and cons they have experienced before you proceed.

Other companies that have preretirement programs are:

Honeywell

Sun Company

Bankers Life and Casualty Company

American Telephone and Telegraph Company

Union Carbide, Ciba-Geigy Ltd.

Equitable Life Assurance Society

Raytheon Corporation

Kimberly-Clark

Consolidated Edison Company

California Federal Savings and Loan

One of the keys to an effective preretirement education program is the successful communication of the benefits that will be experienced from participation. A second key is the inclusion of the employee's spouse. All the companies I talked to who have implemented preretirement programs say they are very successful. The employees who go through the programs find them so helpful they don't know what they would have done without them. In fact, many employees now sponsor ongoing networking and communications programs after retirement.

Part F

Medical Cost Containment

THE RISING COST OF EMPLOYEE BENEFITS

Cost containment of medical benefits is a key issue in every organization. I interviewed over fifty organizations and human resource people and compiled the following list of major areas where they felt medical benefits could be contained.

FIFTEEN WAYS TO CONTAIN MEDICAL COSTS

1. One of the best ways to cut costs in a responsible manner is through a utilization review, which basically is an organized effort to promote peer review by physicians to ensure cost-effective delivery of required health care services. (See the next section for more detail on utilization reviews.)

2. Review claims by health care providers and challenge the ones that look out of line. A claims audit will compare employee usage with the norms for hospitals, doctors, and druggists in your area and isolate overcharges, unusual activity, or excess treatment. Some large organizations, like Caterpillar, retain a full-time physician to handle questionable practices or fees.

3. Educate your employees to buy smarter. *Prevention* magazine recently reported that the principal cause of rising health care costs is that the consumer feels entitled to the most expensive treatment money can buy when it is paid for by someone else. One company, Reliance Electric, will pay the full cost of an employee's surgery if the person gets a second opinion. If not, the company only covers eighty percent.

   NCR offers employees two health insurance plans: one that pays ninety percent of the bills, another that pays eighty percent but includes a dental plan.

4. Get corporate executives involved with insurance companies, hos-

pitals, and doctors. The executive can ask pertinent questions, show an interest in costs, and has the leverage of choosing other providers if costs are too high.

5. Look into the feasibility of self-funding or self-insuring. Ask an expert about self-funding or self-insuring. There are many experts in the field—the accounting group of Coopers & Lybrand is one.

6. Consider redesigning your plan. Review possibilities for redirecting care delivery from hospitals to less expensive settings, like birthing centers for delivery of a baby.

7. Form or participate in an already established employer coalition. In five years the number of coalitions has grown from just a handful to over 150. About one-third of these groups now has a full-time staff. Health care coalitions are groups of employers dedicated to serious dealing with the medical establishment. Collectively they have enormous clout. There are health care coalitions in most large cities.

8. Ensure that your organization uses coordination of benefits to contain the cost of health insurance and to avoid overlap and duplication in payments. Married employees who both have insurance coverage should be told to claim only on the primary plan.

9. Look into the feasibility of establishing your own insurance company. A combination of federal and state regulations combine in some areas to make this a possibility, and companies are doing it successfully.

10. Some companies are shifting health care premium payments to employees to cut their costs. According to a survey by the International Foundation of Employee Benefit Plans, companies that shift the cost of benefits to employees are doing very little to curb escalating health expenses. Shifting the cost burden to employees can in fact increase taxes for entitlements under Social Security, Unemployment Compensation, Workers Disability Compensation, Medicare, and Medicaid. However, more companies today are asking employees to pay a portion of their health care coverage.

11. Use an HMO (Health Maintenance Organization) that puts the emphasis on preventive medicine. An HMO provides medical care either directly with its own staff, or indirectly by contracting for medical services in exchange for a predetermined, prepaid fee.

12. Review the feasibility of using a Preferred Provider Organization (PPO). PPOs are a group of physicians and/or hospitals who agree to cut your insurance premiums, doctor's fees, and hospitalization

charges by fifteen to twenty percent without sacrificing quality of care. More information on PPOs is provided later in this chapter.

13. Put an increased emphasis on preventive care. Health and fitness programs, yearly physical examinations, and emphasis on nutrition and exercise are all important. Install a pilot program to assist employees in identifying and managing health problems. You can assign a human resource person to look at costs and logistics of a fitness program for your company, or you can hire an outside consultant to do that for you.

14. Closely monitor claims to determine if there are certain people, departments, or other groups that are heavy users of medical insurance. Then determine not only if there are any abuses, but whether or not advance fitness measures can be taken. For example, if there are an unusually high number of injuries from lifting in your warehouse, what can be done to eliminate them?

15. Hire a health care consultant who can advise you on the cost/benefit of your plans. Hire one who has experience in both the medical and administrative side of the business.

FOUR COST-CONTAINMENT PROGRAMS AND HOW THEY WORK

1. Health Maintenance Organizations (HMOs)   In 1973 Congress passed the Health Maintenance Organization Act with emphasis on preventive medicine. An HMO provides medical service either directly with its own staff or by contracting for medical services in exchange for a predetermined, prepaid fee.

In recent years some HMOs have gone under but the ones that have survived and most of the new ones are doing well. Many people now prefer them to the personal physician approach to medical care.

Most companies now give employees the option of using their personal physician or choosing an HMO. The important thing to watch in choosing an HMO is to make sure it has a facility that is convenient to a majority of your employees and one that has office hours that are compatible with yours. If you are deciding on an HMO, ask for the names of other companies that are using the plan and call the companies to find out how they rate the service.

How They Work   If you work for a company employing 25 or more workers that has an existing health plan and the company is approached by a qualified HMO, it must offer the prepaid HMO option. With an HMO, you must go to their clinic and to the doctors on their staff. You have a primary physican who usually sees you first when you have a medical complaint.

The primary doctor will prescribe treatment or, if necessary, refer you to a specialist, or hospitalize you in one of the hospitals affiliated with the organization. If that doctor is not on duty during an emergency, you are referred to a substitute.

Coverage varies among HMOs, but generally it covers physician and surgery charges, as well as routine visits, physical examinations, laboratory work, X-rays, and anesthesia. Some plans also cover psychiatric care.

An alternative to a centralized HMO is called an Individual Practice Association (IPA). IPAs are arrangements in which doctors choose to practice from their own offices. If your doctor belongs to an IPA, you have the convenience of prepayment (like an HMO) without the inconvenience of changing doctors. The inconvenience of separate medical bills is mostly eliminated, but you and your doctor must choose medical facilities affiliated with the IPA plan.

2. Preferred Provider Organizations   PPOs are groups of physicians or hospitals who agree to cut your insurance premiums, doctor's fees, and hospital charges by fifteen to twenty percent without sacrificing the quality of care. PPOs are being launched all over the United States by major insurance companies like Blue Cross and Blue Shield and Firemen's Fund. One reason for their popularity is the current "glut" of doctors and empty hospital beds due to competition from outpatient centers and free-standing surgical facilities. PPOs are similar to HMOs. The major difference is that you see a private physician in his or her office. If you require hospitalization, you use a participating facility. All of your costs are covered, and the administering firm arranges for monitoring the quality of care.

You are free to see any provider in the approved group. If you need services from specialists outside the PPO, your PPO will normally pay seventy percent to eighty percent of what they would have paid the PPO physician . . . unlike an HMO, which covers none of your expenses outside the HMO.

In deciding whether or not to offer a PPO, there are certain factors you should consider.

- Choose a PPO plan that offers *hospitals and physicians that are convenient for your employees.* If employees have to travel long distances, they may not use them.

- If you have plants and offices in other locations, *check the extent of the PPO's coverage in these locations.*

- Compare the *services* provided in your current health care plan with those offered by the PPO.

- Identify the *benefits offered that might provide an incentive* for your employees to participate in the PPO. If you do make one available, check regularly on employee acceptance and participation in the program.

- *To assure long-term cost effectiveness*, be sure there is constant claims review by the PPO or an outside claims reviewer.

- Request that the PPO demonstrate its *financial strength* and ask for a list of the health care providers who are under contract.

- Check the *PPO's previous experience* with claims processing and timely claims payments, along with its actuarial expertise.

- Ask whether the PPO has *liability/malpractice insurance* to cover you in case of an adverse court judgment resulting from a policyholder's suit.

- Get *references* from other firms that have contracted for the PPO's services. Also, ask whether the PPO is *registered with any regulatory agency*; if so, check with the agency to assure that the group is properly licensed as well as to determine whether any complaints against the group have been filed.

PPOs have been established in over thirty states so far, and they are a growing alternative to more expensive medical care.

Some companies that have PPOs are:

Reynolds Aluminum

Philip Morris

Eastman Kodak

Sperry

Honeywell

Motorola

3. Health Care Coalitions   HCCs are also growing in popularity. They are basically groups of companies that band together to discuss hospital costs as a group with hospitals they all use. The idea is that they have more clout in cutting costs as a group than each has alone. One Health Care Coalition was formed in Arizona when hospital rates soared twenty-two percent in one year. The Coalition included Sperry Corporation, Honeywell, Motorola, and Garrett Corporation. They successfully lobbied the State Legislature for a uniform hospital billing system to allow comparison shopping.

Many other companies are collectively exercising their muscle by forming coalitions to purchase medical services and curb health care costs. There are approximately 100 such coalitions in the United States today.

One such coalition, called *The Coalition for Cost-Effective Health Services*, includes Blue Cross of Central Ohio, the Franklin County Hospitals, and local employers. They have joined together to publish a cost comparison guide for twenty-four common diagnoses at ten hospitals in the Columbus, Ohio area. The guide is based on 5,300 cases and lets consumers and employers shop for the best prices among local medical centers.

The coalition of employers started the project and began compiling data. Coalition members included health administrators, benefits managers and medical representatives, Blue Cross, and local hospitals. They began assembling data for the two dozen most common and high volume diagnoses. The guide is updated every six months. It has already provided some interesting comparative data. A heart bypass in one hospital is $13,600; in another, it is $21,000.

Employers post the price guide for employees to use and encourage them not to use the higher priced centers. They monitor quality of service to ensure high-quality care. Because the guide has been so successful, they are considering publishing a national guide.

There are health care coalitions in Michigan, Colorado, California, Pennsylvania, and other states. While all the coalitions are trying to bring down the cost of medical care, their tactics vary.

In Denver, about twelve employers contract with the six hospitals run by Presbyterian/St. Lukes Medical Center and with a physicians' group. Based on the volume of business done by the hospital, the employers get a discount of between five and seven percent. Doctors who give discounts of between five to twenty percent receive quick payment and hospitals are assured a stable patient load.

Most employers agree that if the medical field does not do something to curb costs, the government will have to step in and no one wants that. Many coalitions consist solely of businesses. Doctors and hospitals are joining reluctantly. They want to preserve the status quo, but it is becoming quite obvious that costs are out of hand.

In the past few years, the federal government has reduced the percentage of costs it will reimburse hospitals for treating Medicare patients. Hospitals are making up this lost revenue by increasing charges to private insurers who are generally employers. This trend is costing employers an extra five billion dollars according to the Health Insurance Association of America.

Most people think it will take health care coalitions about five years to affect the nation's total health spending, but they will eventually make a dent in the rising health care costs.

4. Utilization Reviews: Four Key Areas to Consider   A utilization review is an organized effort to review all health care services. The review may be conducted by a physician, an insurance carrier, or a third-party administrator and ensures cost-effective delivery of health care services. Audits, management reports, and controls are involved in a utilization review. There are basically four key areas considered in a utilization review.

1. *Outpatient vs. Inpatient Treatment*—Benefit expenses will be reduced substantially if hospital room and board charges can be eliminated. In this area, utilization review norms concentrate on whether a person is being admitted as an inpatient in situations where outpatient treatment would be proper.

2. *Preadmission Testing*—When a hospital stay is required and major surgery ordered, preadmission testing should be done to confirm the physician's diagnosis.

3. *Admission/Discharge*—Length of stay is an important factor of each claim. A reduction of one or two days can result in a substantial overall saving on each claim. It also reduces the risk of unrelated infection, which is becoming a new and serious threat.

4. *Ancillary Services*—Eliminating standard work-ups when they are not necessary and providing only appropriate ancillary services can have a significant effect on total charges.

As mentioned above, the utilization review is usually conducted by either an insurance carrier, a doctor, or a third-party administrator. Reviews done by an insurance company are carried out after the fact so they cannot improve on management; however, they are useful in looking at claims experience. A third party administrator or doctor can provide a more unbiased and current perspective.

Calculating the Cost of Benefits

WORKSHEET FOR USE IN CALCULATING THE COST OF BENEFITS

With the cost of benefits escalating each year, it has become more important to calculate the cost of your benefit programs on a regular basis. The average cost of benefits today is about thirty-seven percent of payroll, but it varies from almost twenty-five percent to fifty percent. Calculating the costs is easier than most HR managers realize.

Following is a benefits cost analysis form used to calculate benefits for C&F Enterprises, Inc., a Denver-based firm.

The first form is a two-part benefits cost analysis form. To begin with, you need to know the average number of full-time employees. This can be determined on a weekly, monthly, quarterly, or annual basis, or any other time period for which you keep employment data. Secondly, you need to know the normal hours paid per period per employee. The base period should be the calendar year, but you can use any other period of time that would be best for you. Multiply the number of employees by hours worked to arrive at the total hours paid per period. The last element is the total base payroll. Be sure to exclude overtime and any part-time or temporary payments from the total base period. (If part-time employees receive *exactly* the same benefits as full-time employees, they could be lumped in with full-timers; otherwise, separate calculations should be made for part-timers.)

BASE PERIOD PAYROLL

1. Average number of full-time employees   _____
2. Normal hours paid per period per employee   _____
3. Total hours paid per period
   (multiply item 1 × item 2)   _____
4. Total, base period payroll   _____

The next step is to make a list of your benefits and indicate dollar amounts for each. The list below is not meant to be all-inclusive, and you may want to delete some benefit areas or add others. Remember: Follow the same approach from year to year so you can analyze the full impact of cost changes. The groupings by type of benefits may be changed to agree with your approach to benefit calculations.

BENEFITS CALCULATION WORKSHEET
PART I

BENEFITS	COST		
	Net	Per Employee	% of Payroll
Legally Required:			
F.I.C.A.	$_____	$_____	_____%
Workmen's Comp.	_____	_____	_____
Unemployment Comp.	_____	_____	_____
TOTAL	$_____	$_____	_____%
Qualified:			
Pension	$_____	$_____	_____%
Profit Sharing	_____	_____	_____
E.S.O.P.	_____	_____	_____
401 K	_____	_____	_____
TOTAL	$_____	$_____	_____%
Nonqualified:			
Medical	$_____	$_____	_____%
Dental	_____	_____	_____
Life	_____	_____	_____
STD	_____	_____	_____
LTD	_____	_____	_____
TOTAL	$_____	$_____	_____%
Pay for Time Not Worked:			
Vacations	$_____	$_____	_____%
Holidays	_____	_____	_____
Illness	_____	_____	_____
National Guard	_____	_____	_____
Jury Duty	_____	_____	_____
Paid Personal	_____	_____	_____
TOTAL	$_____	$_____	_____%
Other			
Tuition Refund	$_____	$_____	_____%
Adoption Reimbursement	_____	_____	_____
Health/Fitness Club	_____	_____	_____
TOTAL	$_____	$_____	_____%
TOTALS—ALL ITEMS	$_____	$_____	_____%

The second part of the form shows you how to find benefit cost as a percentage of payroll by using one of two methods. (These two methods are the most commonly used by employers when reporting benefits costs.)

- The first method ignores pay for time not worked. This means you deduct pay for time not worked from the total net benefit cost. The resulting benefit cost as a percent of payroll includes everything except that category.

- The second method includes pay for time not worked as an employee benefit. The only difference here is you leave that cost in the total net cost, but deduct it from the total base payroll. If you didn't deduct it from the base payroll, it would misrepresent the percentage of benefits cost as a percent of payroll.

Be sure to compute the cost using both methods so you can see the discrepancy between the two figures. There is no right or wrong approach—but be careful if you compare your results with those of other employers, and make sure you're both using the same method.

Shown below is a second type of form used to express benefit costs in a slightly different way. Calculate the total net cost by year for several years. This allows you to compare individual benefit areas and total benefit costs from one year to the next. Once again, this type of comparison allows for quick analysis and may well point out certain aspects of your benefits costs that you hadn't been aware of before.

Here is another form used in the "paid time not worked" area.

In addition, here is a form that shows the total benefit cost by year. You decide how you want to define total cost (for example, including paid time not

BENEFITS CALCULATION WORKSHEET

PART II

BENEFIT COSTS AS % OF PAYROLL

Total of items in net cost column   = a
Total of pay for time not worked   = b
Total base period payroll   = c

Ignoring "pay for time not worked"

$$\frac{(a - b)}{c} = \underline{\hspace{4cm}}$$

Including "pay for time not worked"

$$\frac{a}{(c - d)} = \underline{\hspace{4cm}}$$

worked or excluded it). *Note*: By listing your total cost, your net cost, and your employee cost, you can get a very accurate picture of benefits cost. It is a good idea to accumulate data for a few years and then try to project future costs.

Benefits consultants can perform these calculations for you very quickly, but if you want to do them on your own, these worksheets and instructions will be helpful.

INDIVIDUAL BENEFITS BY YEAR

	19___	19___	19___	20___
Employees*	___	___	___	___
Payroll*	___	___	___	___
Profit Sharing	___	___	___	___
Medical	___	___	___	___
Life	___	___	___	___
STD or LTD	___	___	___	___
Social Security	___	___	___	___
Unemployment Compensation	___	___	___	___
Worker's Comp.	___	___	___	___
TOTAL	___	___	___	___

* Full-time permanent employees/payroll (exclude part-time employees/payroll and overtime)

PAID TIME NOT WORKED

	19___	19___	19___	20___
Vacations	$___	$___	$___	$___
Holiday	___	___	___	___
National Guard	___	___	___	___
Jury Duty	___	___	___	___
Coffee Breaks	___	___	___	___
Personal Leave	___	___	___	___
TOTAL	$___	$___	$___	$___
Cost Per Employee	___	___	___	___
Cost as a % of Payroll	___%	___%	___%	___%

TOTAL BENEFIT COSTS

Base Period	Total Cost	% Change	Net Cost	% Change	Employee Cost	% Change
19	___	___	___	___	___	___
19	___	___	___	___	___	___
19	___	___	___	___	___	___
19	___	___	___	___	___	___
20	___	___	___	___	___	___

Part H

Employee Benefit Communications

EMPLOYEE BENEFIT COMMUNICATION

Communicating the Value of Employee Benefits

There are many ways to communicate employee benefits. One way is to use an employee letter. An employee benefits letter is not only good business and an important public relations tool, but a crucial part of your overall employee communications effort.

Most companies distribute benefit letters in January because they send them out with the employee's W-2 form. A sample benefits letter used by John L. Shea Associates, Inc., a west coast communications firm, appears in Figure 4–1. Employees look for items such as gross wages paid, medical benefits, payment for vacations and holidays, and all the other benefits your company provides.

Organizations make a big investment in fringe benefits with the expectation that the benefits will assist employees and their families. It is also hoped that employee fringe benefits will promote positive employee behavior and increase morale, but unless organizations translate the level of coverage of all of these benefits and communicate their actual cost, employees will not understand or fully appreciate their value.

Benefits do not motivate people to be more productive—in the long run, cash compensation is the best motivator. However, the peace of mind and security that an employee feels as a result of having benefits goes a long way toward retaining committed and dedicated employees. The benefits letter is one of the most effective tools for communicating the tremendous value of fringe benefits. Most companies computerize benefit information because that is the most effective method of providing individualized data.

Five Items to Include in Your Benefits Letter or Statement

- Provide personal data and revise that data for each employee on a yearly basis.

- Reflect group benefits by event. This makes information more understandable in terms of what happens when a person terminates, dies, or retires.

- Show the actual dollar amount or the eligibility requirements for each benefit.

- Estimate the value of the total benefit program and relate it to total compensation.

- Easily project benefits out, for example, on a pension or retirement plan.

Important Tip: If you use computerized benefits information, try not to use technical language that employees will not understand. Computerized statements have some latitude in the language, style, content, and format. It is also important to check with a benefits expert before you issue a statement to ensure that your benefits letter includes all the information you are required by law to provide.

Five New Ways to Communicate Employee Benefits

Most organizations look for new ways to communicate the value of their benefits programs. Here are five communications ideas your company might find useful.

1. Produce a benefits video. Provide an innovative show on how your benefits plans work and what they cost per employee and totally. Show the video in the lunchroom at noon or during coffee breaks. Make the show fun—don't use a talk-down approach or preach.

2. Have posters made the depict certain benefits such as day-care assistance, fitness programs, recreational activities, and so forth. Post them in high traffic areas.

3. If you have an employee newsletter, reserve a section each month that discusses some benefits area, or usage of benefits by employees. Perhaps a picture of an employee receiving a benefits check, or coming home from the hospital.

4. Start a booster club for employees who are ill. Ask other employees to volunteer to visit them or send cards. Call it the Benefits Booster Club, or give the program a name that employees will equate with your benefits program.

5. Have a contest for employees to guess the total cost of benefits for the whole company for one year and for each employee. Give a nice

<u>A SAMPLE EMPLOYEE COMPENSATION AND BENEFITS LETTER</u>

JOHN L. SHEA & ASSOCIATES, INC.
Communications Consultants
14327 Hollywood Boulevard
Los Angeles, California 90069

Date

Employee's Name _____

Address _____

_____

Dear _____:

  Enclosed are your W-2 forms showing the amount of taxable income you received during 19_____. Listed below are your gross wages and a cost breakdown of the many wonderful fringe benefits that you enjoy. In addition to the money you received as wages, the company paid benefits for you that are not included in your W-2 statement. These are fringe benefits that are sometimes overlooked. In an easy-to-read form, here's what _____ paid to you in total compensation and benefits in 19_____.

Section A—Paid to you in your W-2 earnings $_____
Vacation Pay   _____
Holiday Pay   _____
Funeral Pay   _____
Jury Duty Pay   _____
Military Pay   _____
Accident and Sickness Benefits   _____
Regular Earnings   _____
Overtime Earnings   _____
Allowances   _____
Suggestion Award(s)   _____
Service Award(s)   _____
  GROSS WAGES $_____

Section B—Paid for you and not included in your W-2 earnings
Company Contribution to Stock Purchase and Savings Plan $_____
Company Contribution to Pension Plan   _____
Company Cost of your Hospitalization Payments   _____
Company Cost for Dental Insurance   _____
Company Cost of your Life & Accidental Death Insurance   _____
Company Cost for Social Security Tax on your Wages   _____
Company Cost of the premium for Workers Compensation   _____
Company Cost for the Tax on Wages for Unemployment Comp.   _____
Company Cost for Tuition Refund   _____
  TOTAL COST OF BENEFITS NOT INCLUDED IN W-2 EARNINGS $_____
  TOTAL WAGES AND BENEFITS $_____

  We hope this summary gives you a better idea of the total salary and benefits being provided to you and your family. If you have questions on your benefits, please call our Benefits Coordinator on ext. 100.

Sincerely,

Director, Human Resources

prize, a VCR or a television to the one who comes closest to the exact number. Don't allow employees who work with benefits to enter or to tell other employees the costs. Take the benefits employees who can't enter the contest to a special lunch.

New Training Techniques in Human Resource Development

CHAPTER 5

Human Resources Development (HRD) has become big business. The American Society for Training and Development estimates that companies are spending an astounding $60 billion a year on formal courses and general training programs for workers. And that's only the tip of the iceberg. ASTD figures it costs organizations another $180 billion annually for unstructured training like learning on the job, orientation, and so forth.

John Naisbitt and Patricia Aburdene in their book, *Re-Inventing the Corporation*, talk about the corporation as university. They say that universities are becoming more like businesses and that businesses are becoming more like universities. It's true. Corporations have begun to realize that in order to attract and retain the best people they must devote time and money to developing those people who are the "cream of the crop," the ones who will be the future leaders in their organization. Not just at the top but all through the company.

Another excellent study on corporate education is a study by the Carnegie Foundation. They report that over eight million people are learning within corporations. This is about the same number as are enrolled in institutions. The Carnegie Report states that there has been a transformation of corporations into institutes of life-long learning. Some organizations can even grant degrees. In fact, there are over eighteen corporations that award degrees and eight more companies will do so in the next three years.

Because high-technology companies and universities must keep technical people up to date on state-of-the-art technology there must be effective continuing education programs being developed all the time. For this reason, companies and universities must commit to help each other.

Human Resources Development is a whole new "whiz-bang" ball game! Television, videos, compact discs, and games are just a few of the training devices available to human resource directors today. When television was new it was exciting and dynamic and it opened a new era in education. We put trainers in front of the camera and they became "talking heads." They used flat formats and boring scripts in the early days. It has taken time, experience, and a lot of creativity and imagination to get to the training videos and computer-based training activities we are now using. Today, computer-based training (CBT) is "old hat," but it continues to be the most effective training activity implemented in the last decade. CBT techniques are growing in

211

sophistication and the tools are becoming more powerful. New programs reflect significant progress in simulations and visual presentations. Much of what is being done today on PCs could not have been done just a few years ago without dedicated hardware and authoring language development tools that cost hundreds of thousands of dollars.

There are many forces working on HRD today, and these forces are the impetus for development of hundreds of new training products and ideas.

TWENTY-FOUR FORCES RESHAPING THE HRD FUNCTION

The information age has forever changed the field of training and development. Forces impacting the HRD function are

1. the need for computer literacy at all levels of an organization
2. the changing demographics of the workforce
3. need for retraining huge numbers of workers displaced in corporate cutbacks
4. need to match individual career plans to company goals
5. a growing demand for self-reinforced learning available twenty-four hours a day
6. the demand for long-distance training and communication links to service international operations
7. the need for development that is interruptible without critical deterioration of the learning experience
8. a continuing desire on the part of corporations to analyze the cost-benefit of training
9. the escalation of training costs
10. a strong focus on learning processes rather than job content (i.e., the process of time management, decision making, etc.)
11. a fundamental change in value systems and motivational factors of employees
12. the deemphasis on one-on-one leadership as we now know it and a new emphasis on remote leadership
13. a need for new ways to provide feedback and rewards during learning processes that are ongoing through the maturity of projects
14. a tremendous increase in the need for interactive training systems (hardware seems to be outstripping courseware)
15. the need for software that is compatible with a variety of systems

16. the continued deterioration of workers' math, reading, and writing skills, due to the increased use of calculators and computers

17. Organizational development efforts are changing drastically because interventions are more often on a one-on-one simultaneously with large numbers of people. Consultants will be instantly available via the computer either preprogrammed to respond to certain situations, or live for instant consultation.

18. training for a growing number of people who must interface with the media.

19. Because organizations need increasingly sophisticated types of training programs, videos and video disc packages on a variety of subjects are needed.

20. There is a growing demand for games that train people. We have become enchanted with games and games can simulate specific work situations. They facilitate the learning process.

21. There is an increased interest in ESP and the use of intuition in training.

22. The popularity of teleconferencing is growing and training will be essential for many managers.

23. The growing need for sophisticated training methods has made the "Star Wars" type training done in the military catch on in the private sector.

24. There is a growing need to attract more young people to replace retiring workers and this will spur training companies to plunge into music video with a corporate look.

Organization survival has become as dependent on the human resource and organizational development functions as it has been on sales and marketing. The idea is not to sit back and hope that the HRD function is pushed by the tide. The overwhelming odds are that it won't be. That is why an organization has to be proactive, rather than reactive, taking the lead in the development of its people.

HOW TO IDENTIFY KEY HRD NEEDS IN YOUR COMPANY

To be effective, HRD programs must respond to the training and development needs of the whole organization. Organizations are constantly responding to change, and even when people understand and accept change, they do not always have the skills and abilities they need to adapt to it and to manage it.

For example, a large cable television company purchased a chain of small cable stations in the southeastern United States. These smaller companies were profitable and successful, and the parent company wanted to maintain that positive business environment. To manage these operations, the company promoted a star salesman from the field into the top executive position. The company did not provide any specific development program for the new executive. The CEO didn't feel it was necessary in view of the salesman's past track record in marketing and sales.

The new executive had been an outstanding individual contributor; a salesman with a great deal of enthusiasm, a good personality, and a willingness to work hard. He had not managed a company, or even an entire department before. The skills he needed were management skills, planning, organizing, controlling, as well as the personal skills of mentoring, crediting, reinforcing, correcting, leveling, and so forth.

Without a specific individual management development program to help him, the new executive became frustrated at his inability to get things done through others, and to motivate his people. The overall effectiveness and profitability of the organization began to slip, and each quarter they showed a loss in customer base, and in advertising sales. One year later the company was showing huge losses and the executive was replaced. Given the salesman's background and personal experience the outcome was predictable, but no one had stopped to think about it in advance and identify his specific development needs. If the HR manager had stepped in to identify the different skills needed to be successful in the new position and to plan a development program, the outcome might have been different. The best way to find out what the various needs are in the organization is to interview key executives in each department. Here is a list of questions that can help you identify training and development needs.

Training Needs Checklist

1. What type of training do you feel your employees need? Why?

2. Are current training programs filling the needs of the organization at all levels?

3. What type of training would you like for your people? For yourself?

4. Does your organization effectively use the talents of all of its people?

5. Do managers in your organization integrate their personal goals with the business objectives?

6. Do your employees have opportunities for growth and actualization of their skills and abilities?

7. Do you know how to use meetings to resolve conflict and solve problems?

8. Have your employees had individual development experiences beyond their areas of specialty?

9. Are fast-track employees groomed for larger assignments?

10. What are the major problems your employees face? in their current jobs? in promotional assignments?

11. When a person is promoted, are training needs in the new job identified?

12. What do you think are the most common problems of managers in your company? Can they be eliminated through training and personal development programs?

13. What are the positive aspects of the company's training programs? Is there a need for improvement?

14. What percentage of your employee population participates in training and development programs? Why?

A TOP-DOWN APPROACH TO GAINING SUPPORT AT ALL ORGANIZATIONAL LEVELS

When the CEO and other top executives embrace the need for training and development at all levels of the organization, and they begin to articulate that need, the whole company feels more enthusiasm and commitment to HRD. If you need some structure to help you get started use the following list to identify organizational and departmental goals, and to use as a guide when you talk about the programs with the CEO.

Sample Objectives for HRD Programs

- Review and address specific problem areas in the company with the CEO and prepare to take advantage of training opportunities as they arise. Cross training may be one answer. Local university programs may be another.

- Provide the tools to assist managers in identifying their specific needs. A training needs analysis form might help, and a catalog of available training and development programs might facilitate the process.

- Show managers that their input is valuable and necessary for success. Include them in discussion groups and perhaps a training task force.

- Provide managers with a conceptual framework and a better perspective on the need for training in their particular areas. Provide specific examples of employee training needs where you know them. Outline a formal program and ask for the managers specific input and approval.

- Develop the desire to learn more about managing people. Help managers learn the basic principles of communication and behavioral psychology. Form a discussion group on this subject. Perhaps a series of brown-bag lunches.

- Help managers understand their environment, the corporate culture and the company's particular management style so they can pass that understanding onto employees.

- Build a strong management team by providing training in group dynamics and team building skills, eliminating the "we and they" philosophy that pervades many organizations.

- Provide an orientation to managers regarding the resources that are available to them. Train members to use these resources and to feel comfortable with them. Include managers in the program development process.

- Identify the high performing employees at all levels in order to have people ready to move up as they are needed. You first need to identify good people and then identify the specific training they need to grow in their particular career fields.

- Provide a forum where managers and other professionals can exchange experiences, solve mutual problems, voice concerns, and develop a communication network.

- A responsive human resource development program shows employees that the organization cares about their needs and wants to help them develop to their full potential.

These objectives should also assist the CEO in determining the depth of commitment to be made in the HRD function. Some questions a CEO might ask are:

1. How should I measure our HRD effort?
2. What are our overall HRD needs now? in the future?
3. How much emphasis should we place on HRD?
4. What has our expenditure on HRD been as a percentage of operating costs for the past two years?
5. What percentage of our budget is currently going for HRD? How much should be spent on HRD?
6. Have we done a cost/benefit analysis of current HRD programs?

7. Will a greater emphasis on HRD favorably impact our profits?

RETRAINING VERSUS DISPLACING THE WORKFORCE—HOW CALIFORNIA IS TAKING POSITIVE ACTION

With whole industries shutting down, thousands of jobs becoming obsolete, and entire levels of management being eliminated, retraining of the workforce is probably the most important training objective human resource people can have for the 1990s.

The state of California has devised a unique idea for retraining a large segment of its workforce. The program is administered by an agency called the Employment Training Panel (ETP). It is financed by unemployment insurance (UI) and represents the first use of such funds for a purpose other than providing benefits to the unemployed. It differs from other government retraining efforts by focusing exclusively on experienced workers who are either unemployed or soon to be displaced, rather than on new entrants to the labor force. This program is a new approach that assures retrained workers have a job to go to when the training is completed. An organization that hires and retrains workers is reimbursed for training expenses only if the job has lasted ninety days. ETP has been very effective. Since 1983, 27,000 people have enrolled for training in 212 projects for which ETP has allocated $94 million. Training costs come to $3,500 per employee for jobs paying an average of $7.82 per hour. To date 3,000 workers have been retrained and placed in jobs.

ETP is attracting national attention. The state of Delware has adopted a similar program. In New York, Governor Mario M. Cuomo proposed cutting the UI payroll tax and imposing a new tax to raise about $30 million for retraining.

In addition to training UI recipients, ETP helps employers retrain current workers whose jobs have become obsolete. These workers need retraining to be able to handle new technology. At Noel J. Brown Manufacturing, Inc. in Campbell, California, ETP granted $216,000 to retrain fifty current employees in higher skills. Contact your state government to see what funds may be available for an ETP program.

Case Example: Bank of America Retrains Rather than Lay Off Employees

The Bank of America in San Francisco spends $40 million each year to upgrade the skills of its employees. They are in the process of automating many functions in their California offices and upgrading the skills of employees. Because Bank of America has closed 130 branch offices, consolidating their operations, they could have laid off 2,000 employees, but they preferred to retrain them. ETP gave them a grant of $5 million to retrain their workers.

They feel that retraining instead of displacing workers makes economic as well as socially ethical sense.

Four Major Reasons Why Retraining Rather than Replacing Workers Is Good Business

1. Organizational productivity still relies heavily on people. About half of our national productivity growth comes from increases in individual skills and knowledge.

2. Even though unemployment lines continue to grow, there are shortages of critical workers from service workers to machinists and industrial engineers. The result is bottlenecks, higher prices, and lower quality in every area—both domestic and defense industries.

3. The lack of critical skills will worsen as the country continues to race into an advanced technological era with a population that just doesn't know how to operate in a high-tech environment.

4. Organizations are fast realizing that they have to invest in people because they can get only so much out of machines. The robot era has not materialized. We have no choice but to equip thousands of high-tech illiterate workers with new skills. We have to find new ways to train and pay for training of older workers, and women and minorities who are just now entering the labor force.

Most experts feel our economy will not thrive until there is a major effort on the part of government and private industry to upgrade the American labor force from top to bottom.

NEW WAYS TO TEACH WORKERS WHAT'S NEW: A VIDEODISC UPDATE

Employers are buying computerized systems to train nurses, waitresses, mechanics, repairmen, and jet pilots. These new systems make learning more interesting—and more fun because they respond to the student. They also save money because employees learn at work.

Most of the new teaching technologies are based on videodisc systems similar to those used at home on videodisc players, and on computer-generated graphics like those used in the movie *Star Wars*. These new systems move high-tech training a long way beyond the videotape machines used to teach workers in the 1950s.

The biggest improvement in videodisc systems is in the way they react to the student. The old videotape systems allowed students to control the pace and to test themselves. The new systems do a lot more: they let the student move through the subject at an individual learning pace. The system highlights errors and points the student back to review material that he hasn't understood. It lets a student skip material already mastered and keeps track of progress.

The hardware used to run these systems is typically Sony or Pioneer videodisc players, a personal computer such as Apple II or an IBM PC, and a video screen. Software is expensive and has to be especially created for each course. To produce one hour of instruction on a disc costs anywhere from $35,000 to more than $100,000, because it requires a production crew, a cast, and sets. Programmers can create computer-based training for $2,000 to $20,000 per hour of instruction, so the cost of interactive training is a deterrent unless the company can spread the cost of developing the software over the cost of thousands of trainees.

Case Example: The Ford Motor Company Videodisc System for Training Mechanics

Ford dealers have been sending their 40,000 mechanics off to some 38 Ford Motor Company training centers to develop and polish their skills and to learn about the many innovations in Ford's products. The average Ford mechanic gets over 22 hours of training per year, mostly to learn about new technologies. Ford feels they are being forced into developing new training delivery systems. They purchased 4,000 units of an interactive videodisc system from Sony. They liked the system and are testing newer systems now with more computer power to put in all their dealerships across the country.

Other large corporations with significant training needs are looking at similar videodisc systems because they have a tremendous storage capacity. One side of a single disc can hold over 54,000 pictures or pages of text, any of which can be retrieved within one second, and, unlike videotapes, videodiscs don't wear out.

Corporations are adopting interactive training for a variety of reasons. AT&T Information Systems, Inc., which makes and services communications and data processing equipment, will use the training to keep technicians up to date. Their new courses include how to install and maintain Dataphone II, their new sophisticated data communications systems. The old courses used to take at least seven days—the new technology lowers training time to three days, saving a great deal in technician training costs.

Case Example: The General Electric Interactive Program

General Electric uses interactive training to teach workers how to use big, ultra-expensive machines that cost too much to have sitting around in the classroom—jet engines, diesel locomotives, and so forth. The GE aircraft engine group is planning to put seventy-five percent of their hands-on-training budget into video disc systems. When video systems are combined with computer graphics, simulations of a jet cockpit or a tank turret can achieve vivid realism, complete with sound and sense of motion. Flight trainers used by generations of pilots have been upgraded to new altitudes of sophistication and realism.

The United States Defense Department is probably the largest user of interactive training. The old maintenance manual for a World War II fighter was contained in a 1,000 page manual. Today the manual for an F-18 fighter takes up to 500,000 pages, and high-tech systems are indispensable in both the instruction and maintenance of expensive planes.

Case Example: How a Human Resources Consultant Uses Computer Software to Improve Managers' Interpersonal Skills

Bob Rodwell, a human resources consultant in Minneapolis, uses computer software to help clients train their salespeople. He saw the application in sales and marketing but for a long time he didn't see the direct applications in honing his own skills of managing his employees. One of his employees was indispensable to the successful completion of a large contract. Bob was having problems with the employee and all his efforts at identifying the problem and eliminating it were futile.

Bob heard about a software product that asked a series of questions to be answered with a yes or no, and a few questions that asked for adjectives to describe the employee. After using the program and answering the questions, there was a final eight-page printout that told Bob what kind of manager he was, what kind of an employee he had and, further, suggested ways of handling the behavior problems he was experiencing. It provided some new approaches to use in addressing the problems, and they worked!

Bob found the software so effective he is recommending it to clients. Many new programs emphasize the participative management and entrepreneurial attitudes that are reflected in today's workforce. These programs are becoming so popular that it is expected sales of off-the-shelf training software for personal computers will jump from $15 million in 1984 to over $90 million in the early 1990s.

The Corporate Look in Music Video

More and more corporate training departments are taking on the music video look, as they try to train the thousands of entry level professionals that were raised on television and music videos. Stuart Sleppin, music video director with Teeman/Sleppin Enterprises, Inc. in New York City, has produced music videos for the United States Army and for such large corporations as Sperry and Dupont.

Music video doesn't have to be limited to contemporary pop; corporations can use jazz, classical music, and Broadway style show tunes—any kind of music that sends the corporate message and provides long-lasting retention power.

Music videos are just another new trend in corporate training and development.

Customizing Sales Training with Videotapes

There is a $600 million market for customized training programs and a new company in Denver, Colorado is ready to tap that market. If you are a human resource manager for an organization with a large sales force, you may be interested to know that Team Marketing Group, Inc. in Denver has the ability to customize your sales training effort.

Team Marketing has customized sales training for the Gates Rubber Company, ANR Freight Systems, Inc., Swedish Health Management Systems, and Affiliated Bankshares of Colorado, to name just a few organizations keeping up with the changing training scene.

There are lots of off-the-shelf video sales programs, but few of them are designed for exactly the message a specific company needs. A survey of the American Society for Training and Development in Washington, DC showed that fifty-two percent of the corporate trainers in the United States have never dealt with either customized or packaged training programs.

Companies that do use sales programs, according to ASTD, spend approximately $617.9 million on customized training materials. A Conference Board study on "Trends in Corporate Education and Training" showed that fifty-eight percent of companies surveyed had increased their sales training to some degree over the past five years.

A sales training video is expensive to produce, between $25,000 and $30,000 on average, but that normally includes field trips with the company's sales people, and special scripts tailored to the language of the industry and the style of the company.

Customized sales training is going video and human resource managers will need to know some of the basics of video scripting.

Tips on How to Write a Video Script and a Sample Page Layout

If you are in an organization that is beginning to use videos for training programs, you may need to know the basics of properly preparing a video script. Here are some tips to get you started, and a sample page layout provided by Pat Thompson, Thompson Associates, Inc., Denver, Colorado.

There are certain basic rules to follow for page layout when preparing a video script.

1. Begin a script by using an idea and language that grabs the viewer's attention.
2. Prepare viewers in the beginning for what is to follow.
3. Design the middle of the script to hold audience attention.

4. Avoid monotony and predictability.

5. Avoid the "talking head" or "chalk talk" syndrome.

6. The close should be brief and summarize what was covered in the video.

7. The program should be held to ten minutes or less.

8. Use a step-by-step page layout, or story board, to prepare the script.

9. To indicate a new scene, assign it a number and type it in capital letters at the left-hand margin.

10. Scene segments, which describe camera moves, stage directions, and any change of continuity within a scene are identified by letters. Indent scene segments a number of spaces from the left margin and type them in upper and lower case.

11. When writing dialogue, indicate the character's name in caps and center it over the dialogue. Indicate voice-overs by typing the name of the character followed by "*VOICE-OVER*" in brackets, all typed in caps and underlined on the right-hand side of the page. This keeps it separate from the rest of the dialogue.

12. Type camera moves or action in upper and lower case and set them in brackets.

13. Scene transitions are also typed in caps, underlined on the left-hand side of the page at the end of a scene.

14. Review a rough script and check locations for accessibility and believability. Also to view how the camera and the people will be able to move—lighting and illusion, and so forth.

In addition, here are four key words you need to know to work on a video script:

CUT-TO—This is the editor's direction to make an instant change from one picture to another.

FADE-OUT and FADE-IN indicate that one picture will gradually fade away to black, followed by the next scene gradually fading in . . . or, a slow or quick fade may be specified.

DISSOLVE—is a transition in which one picture fades out while the next simultaneously fades in, with no black in between.

The first couple of times you work with a video production crew you will need to know the basics and will certainly feel like a novice . . . which you are, but HRD professionals will be called on more and more frequently to produce sophisticated video programs, and with a few simple pointers you can plunge comfortably into the world of training videos.

SAMPLE PAGE LAYOUT

1. SCENE: A SEPARATE LOCATION OR CONCEPT, LIKE AN
ANIMATION SEQUENCE, DESCRIBED IN DETAIL.

   A.   Scene segments indicate parts of a scene.

   <u>CHARACTER'S NAME</u>

   This represents the spoken portion of your script.

   B.   Whenever you change cameras, you change scene
   segments.

   <u>CHARACTER'S NAME (VOICE OVER)</u>

   THIS IS NARRATION RECORDED SEPARATELY
   AND PLACED OVER THE VISUAL DESCRIBED
   IN SCENE 1.B.

<u>TRANSITION</u>:
   CUT, FADE, OR DISSOLVE

Figure 5-1

A sample page layout is shown in Figure 5-1. There are also college courses available around the country and The National Audiovisual Association, 3150 Spring Street, Fairfax, Virginia 22031 is a good resource. You can learn how to:

- plan a production
- write a script
- interact with a client
- produce graphics
- record a sound track
- generate computer graphics
- design CAI
- produce a slide/tape program

- produce a multi-image presentation
- produce video
- create interactive video
- present a video program

ELEVEN STEPS FOR ESTABLISHING A COMPUTER LITERACY PROGRAM FOR MANAGERS

What does computer literacy mean to you, knowing how to use a personal computer (PC)? speaking COBOL over tea and croissants? If all you want to do is get managers to feel comfortable using a PC, that's simple. Here are eleven steps for installing a computer literacy training program for managers using a PC.

1. Get all the free advice, training tools and information you can from the Company that sold you the PCs. There may be free classes or a representative of the computer company may come to your site if you have purchased a large enough order.

2. Talk to people in your organization who are experienced in using a PC and enlist their assistance with your training program.

3. Begin by asking managers to use the PC to perform a single job-related task. A spreadsheet exercise is a good place to begin.

4. After managers have mastered one simple task use two or more applications to perform related tasks. The novice manager now at least has some idea what a personal computer can do.

5. Start file and disc management. The manager may start·accumulating a store of information on disc, and now needs to learn how to manage electronic files. This step might include merging files from two or more discs, deleting files, and coming up with a file labeling system.

6. Start integrating the PC into the manager's everyday work routine. The manager should feel confident enough by now to let the computer take over simple routines.

7. Suggest managers include computer planning in larger projects and use it for more sophisticated planning programs. Ask the manager to review how the PC will affect budgeting and project scheduling.

8. Look at what effect, if any, the computer is having on support people. If it has taken away some of the dull routine work, redirect new projects and responsibilities to staff employees.

9. Start helping support staff personnel learn the systems and programs the managers are using on their PCs.

10. Identify additional ways in which the computer can help in other departments of the organization. Computer literate managers will share their ideas with other users and identify people in the organization who are developing special computer skills.

11. Add the requirement of computer literacy to each manager's job description and performance appraisal forms. There is more impetus to take action.

Executives at every level, including the CEO and Human Resource Directors, will need to know how to use personal computers. A simple training program like the one outlined above will get you started.

TELECOMMUNICATIONS—TRAINING BY TELEPHONE

"Hello Dallas, Hello Vancouver, Hi! Charlie! Welcome to the bridge and today's training session. Can you hear me all right? I hear you loud and clear and we're ready on this end." Those words and the cheery hellos introduce a training session via telephone that is becoming more popular with corporations who have many far-flung operations and who want to utilize expensive training programs over a wide area, where many employees have similar training needs.

Teleconferencing is becoming very popular and is an effective and economical way to reach widely dispersed groups of trainees. The "bridge" is one of several ways to connect trainees and instructors located at multiple sites for a training session conducted by telephone.

Who Uses Teleconferencing?

Many companies have found that telecommunications training is a time and money saver for them. It reduces the time and expense of travel. American companies spend $9 billion annually on the cost of moving trainees from place to place. Teleconferencing reaches employees in remote locations and trains larger numbers of people. The Iowa Department of Social Services uses AT&T's network services to provide orientation to 8,000 employees, and AT&T Communications uses its own technology to train over 25,000 employees.

Hewlett Packard says that it brings academic experts to the workplace by using satellite technology to import training and development from colleges and universities throughout the United States. Roche Laboratories says that it conducts teleconference workshops for one-quarter the cost of on-site seminars. In Hartford, Connecticut, the Travelers prepare field employees at forty-four sites around the country for a grueling six-hour stockbroker's examination via telephone, and the pass rate has increased from fifty percent to eighty-nine percent.

United Banks of Colorado present their product of the month and the necessary marketing training by telephone to thirty banks throughout Colorado. Some of the advantages United Banks sees are:

- Employees take responsibility for their own learning.

- Teleconferencing is a speedier way to disseminate information.

- As information is disseminated all at the same time and the same way, there is better consistency and less chance for miscommunication.

- Teleconferencing helps promote a sense of family and esprit de corps.

Cost is probably the main reason all of these companies use telecommunications in their HRD programs.

Case Example: How Bennett & Sloane, Inc. Set Up Their Teletraining Program

Bennett & Sloane, Inc. (a fictitious company) has approximately 4,000 employees scattered around the United States and Canada. They set up a pilot program to study the costs of training delivered by traditional classroom methods, bringing people to their headquarters from many locations. They also did some training with telephone and slides, with telephone and slow-scan video, and telephone with video cassettes. The interactive two-way telephone instruction with slide support was significantly less expensive than classroom teaching and more effective.

Planning Guidelines for Teletraining

Bennett & Sloane Training Director Jan Weberg provides these planning guidelines.

- Planning is as important in teletraining as it is for any other human resource activity. When you start your planning be sure to include supervisors and managers from areas from which you will be drawing students for the program.

- Set up the necessary facilities, determine locations, and ensure the facilities include the needed equipment and power. Both are important elements in your teletraining program success.

- Arrange for instructors that are well versed in telecommunications and teletraining.

- Determine the availability of teleconferencing equipment, such as omni-directional speaker microphones, the needed audiovisual aids, and bridge times.

- Assign responsibility to someone at each site to arrange the room, provide the equipment needed, distribute materials, provide for refreshments, if called for, and to be ready to display visuals on cue.

- Have discussions with managers about the employees who should attend. Make up an attendance list several weeks in advance.

- Develop written materials and exams several weeks before the classes are to start. Do a dry run—and try materials out to see that they will work as planned.

- Have a trial run of the teletraining program before the actual classes are to start in order to iron out any problems in advance.

As you plan the program and write training materials, here are a few added tips.

- Variety is the key to holding attention. Intersperse presentations with discussions, questions, quizzes, jokes, and so forth. Use an interesting mixture of visuals.

- Create programs with a lot of interactivity. This can be arranged by asking the teleconferencing operator to join pairs of sites. This interactivity also humanizes the training and makes it more meaningful to participants.

- Bennett and Sloane wants employees on the job at least part of each day, so they schedule training sessions for four hours at a time. "We keep the goals clear and the activities moving right along," says Weberg. "We are paying for on-line time and we want our employees to get the maximum amount of learning from each program."

- Weberg mails students materials and quizzes ahead of time so they can read them over before the on-line training sessions. This saves time and helps to ensure that students get involved.

- Evaluations are always requested of each participant and participants are encouraged to call about special problems to get them resolved.

- If the training materials are "company confidential," there could be a concern with security. Bennett and Sloane transmits encrypted digital signals, rather than scrambling analog signals, to avoid problems when material is confidential.

- There can be equipment failures. It doesn't happen very often, but here are some guidelines on what to do when there are such problems. Use high-quality equipment to avoid frequent breakdowns, check all equipment ahead of time, carry spare light bulbs for slide projectors and arrange for backup equipment in advance.

Teletraining is a wonderful new advance in HRD. Not everyone can afford it yet; you can spend from $100,000 to $900,000 depending on the equipment you choose and the distance between sites and training facilities, and the variety of material to be used. But many corporations feel it is considerably cheaper than old methods of on-site training.

Figure 5-2 shows how a teletraining program might work.

CROSS-CULTURAL AND BILINGUAL TRAINING: HOW TO INTERNATIONALIZE EMPLOYEES

One of the greatest challenges facing human resource managers and corporate executives in the HRD area today is the need to internationalize the American workforce. Multinational United States companies involved in international collaboration, joint ventures, mergers, and acquisitions on a world-wide scale have a serious problem. The problem is finding people who are cross-cultural and bilingual and who understand how to be effective in an environment that is foreign to them.

According to government estimates, more than 100,000 American nationals work overseas for United States-based corporations. The average cost of sending a manager to a foreign assignment ranges from $75,000 to over $150,000, and a conservative estimate is that 30% of the people transferred overseas don't work out and must be recalled. Systran, a Chicago-based international training company, maintains that a more realistic price tag for foreign transfers is $138,000 and adds that American corporations spend 53.3% more than budgeted for overseas transfers due to the high rate of washouts.

In a survey reported by R. L. Tung in *Key to Japan's Economic Strength: Human Power* (D. C. Heath, Lexington, MA, 1984), eighty United States corporations responded to their survey, and more than three-quarters reported that ten percent or more of the people assigned overseas had to be recalled or dismissed for poor performance. In this survey, the recall rate ran as high as forty percent.

The thirty-five Japanese companies responding to the survey reported failure rates below ten percent and no respondent's recall rate was as high as twenty percent. This isn't exactly conclusive research but it does mirror the batting average of two countries sending people abroad.

One reason Japanese companies enjoy a higher retention rate is because, before managers arrive at a foreign assignment, they are thoroughly prepared

Figure 5-2
TELETRAINING

Type	Technology	Delivery
AUDIO and AUDIO-GRAPHIC: One-way or two-way telephones, microphones or speakers.	Dial-access telephone	Direct dial to instructor.
	Dial-up teleconferencing	AT&T operator-assisted.
	A bridge	Linked lines leased from private companies that provide operator assistance or from AT&T that provides operators or allows direct dial.
	Dedicated network	Lines that permanently connect all training sites.
	Slides or overheads	Mail or courier
AUDIOVISUAL: Two-way telephone plus visuals.	Electronic blackboard, pen that sends drawings made on a pressure-sensitive slate to monitors at distant sites.	Telephone lines
	Slowscan or Freeze-frame that sends still pictures.	Telephone lines
FULL-MOTION VIDEO: One-way or two-way live or taped moving images may be with two-way audio.	Instructional Television Fixed Service	Special frequencies received at various sites by a frequency converter.
	Television	Satellite by transmitting digital and receiving analog or digital signals.
	Television	Satellite by transmitting digital and receiving analog or digital signals.
	Television	Microwave
	Videotape	Satellite or mail

for living and working in the country and in an alien culture. The Japanese treat the issue of culture shock in the same thorough way they treat the issues of productivity and quality.

Overseas assignments are made at least a year before Japanese employees depart for their new jobs. During that year, employees learn the culture and customs and the ways of doing business in their new country. Normally they learn the language as well. Japanese companies also use the mentor system. For the first year, new managers in overseas assignments have mentors to assist them in becoming acclimated. The mentors help newcomers to reshape skills and managerial techniques in order to be as successful as they can in the new assignment.

In the middle east, American managers have run into trouble because they don't understand that family comes first. Where American companies frown on nepotism, in the Arab world one's primary responsibility is to hire one's relatives. An Arab will hire a nephew before a stranger regardless of competence.

Americans also have problems with simple things like body language. The typical "thumbs up" gesture is offensive to Arabs, the left hand is considered unclean in many cultures. In some cultures, China, for example, there is no inhibition against staring, and most Americans are made uncomfortable by that.

Most cross-cultural experts think language training will receive a greater emphasis in schools as more and more companies require bilingual employees. Many multinational organizations maintain their own language training facilities and require at least a working knowledge of language and culture in all executives, spouses, and adult children going to overseas assignments.

The costs are high for extensive language training done outside a company's training facility. Inlingua charges $3,900 for four weeks including lodging, $5,700 for Berlitz, four weeks, nonresidential. An average college program can run as high as $2,500, evenings for six semesters. At Inlingua, 170 hours of private training over four months can run as high as $4,000. Berlitz, 300 hours of private training over six months, costs approximately $7,000.

Being bilingual does not mean a person is cross-cultural. Many people who can speak a foreign language are poorly equipped to understand and work in a foreign culture.

In the coming years, HRD efforts will highlight competence in international relations and companies that will be successful will be the ones that emphasize collaboration and provide in-depth cross-cultural and bilingual training.

Companies that Have Cross-Cultural and Bilingual Programs

Getty Oil Company

Sperry Corporation

Hewlett-Packard

Westinghouse

3M Company

IBM

Just to name a few. . . . also, nearly all large banks with overseas branch banks have programs.

For more information on training and international management programs contact The Society for Intercultural Education, Training and Research, 1414 22nd St. N. W. Washington, DC 20037, Phone (202) 862-1990 or the American Graduate School of International Management Thunderbird Campus, Glendale, Arizona, 85306, Phone (602) 978-7011.

USING BUSINESS GAMES IN TRAINING

The make-believe company that comes in a box—Sony's International Management Game is just one of the hundreds of new games used in business to simulate actual managerial problems. The Sony game introduces the student to the fundamentals of corporate planning, business strategy, and management expertise. The game is a three-day simulation that provides hands-on experience in running a business through roleplaying. It is a sophisticated game that includes simulations of a United States corporate headquarters with markets in Germany and Japan.

Some Corporations that Include Business Games in HRD

At Monsanto, SmithKline Beckman Corporation, and the Union Pacific Corporation, managers are going through "in" baskets stuffed with everyday managerial problems. Managers lobby superiors, delegate to subordinates, promote new ideas, pick holes in other people's ideas, and eventually find their way to a consensus.

At New York University, an imaginary medium-sized company bumbles through a myriad of problems such as bankruptcy, recession and products that don't sell. The company's fate depends on how well students in NYU's Graduate School of Business Administration play the "Management Decision Laboratory" computer game. The game is tough, complex, and simulates the workings of a real organization. Students participate in the game in lieu of writing a Master's thesis. By playing this tough computer game, students probably learn more about business than in all their other courses combined.

At Union Carbide, managers have to run a fictitious company called

Looking Glass, Inc., a simulation exercise that takes place at the Center for Creative Leadership in Greensboro, North Carolina. Managers have the opportunity to run a company for two and one-half days and are then evaluated on how successful they are.

The Boeing Company has a complex game called TOPEXEC. It is a permanent part of their annual aerospace industry manufacturing seminar for senior management. The game teaches leadership and management skills.

AT&T developed a game called Simile II that cost them approximately $70,000. They also developed games called "Relocation—A Corporate Decision," "Trebedies Island—The Economics of Monopoly Management," "Where Do You Draw the Line?", an ethics game, and "The Privacy Game."

Sometimes business games are just for fun. Bank of America hired a quiz show emcee to do a game show presentation of a psychological study that could benefit its managers in their employee relationships. He invented "The Great American Management Game." That effort was a great success and after that the emcee turned his game into a business. He now sells game-show gimmickry to corporations that want to jazz up their sales training and their new product line introduction. Some of his games are:

The Site Is Right, for American Airlines

Play It Safe, for Chevron

Eat the Clock, for Keebler Company

You Bet Your Life, for CNA Insurance

The Question and Answer Game, for the American Medical Association

There are many technical innovations on the horizon in computer games. Computers are getting cheaper and easier to buy, slide projectors and videotape recorders also greatly increase the capabilities of computer games.

Case Example: Hewlett-Packard's Business Game

At Hewlett-Packard's international headquarters in Palo Alto, California, an in-house simulation called DivSim, for Division Management Simulation, has been up and running for three years. It addresses a need among some of their functional managers for a better understanding of the steps they could take to respond to downturns in the economy. At a conference in Geneva, Switzerland, HP's manager of corporate training ran into an intriguing mainframe simulation. Developed in Scotland, it was used to teach economics to high-school kids. They can run a country's economy—vary government spending, interest rates, and the money supply—see what happens. HP enlisted the Scottish economist who had designed the simulation, turned the draft version over to HP's own people for modification and customization, and eventually had a very slick computer model of the Hewlett-Packard Corporation.

Four teams of seven players compete to ring up the highest marks on a complicated scoring system that considers factors such as profit generation and the shape the company is in at the end of a simulated five-year period in terms of assets, human resources, R&D projects in the works, and so forth. Each team has a general manager and six functional managers who head divisions corresponding to HP's. As one of the game's main purposes is to teach functional managers how the pieces of the company fit together and affect one another, nobody is allowed to play a real-life role.

In the high-tech industry, you grow up in one function. If you grow up in marketing, you won't have a thorough understanding of the problems of your counterparts in manufacturing or R&D. The point is to teach the interrelation of functions.

Because Hewlett-Packard has a no-lay-off policy, it is also vital that managers understand what to do when the economy goes sour. In DivSim, the economy—and demand for HP products—can go as sour as the trainer wants it to. And the lessons are many. For example, there is one about placing orders in anticipation of need versus real need. If you are back-logged on inventory when the economy goes down, you can really be in trouble. HP has more than $200,000 invested in DivSim.

Today there are several hundred such business games and about ninety percent of all M.B.A. graduates and management trainees have played one or more of them. The game-training scene is dazzling and growing glitzier by the hour!

If you are about to purchase one of these expensive training games there are some pros and cons to consider.

PROS AND CONS OF TRAINING GAMES

PROS

The majority of university studies that have been done on the value of games in training have been positive. The studies indicate that, for decision making and strategy implementation on the executive level, games are superior to lecture or simply using case studies.

Games are stimulating and fun—people like to play games to learn.

Their top attraction to business is their laboratory capability. Games permit business people to test-run new strategies and sometimes fail

CONS

The business game field is extremely disjointed and it may be difficult to identify the best game for your purpose.

The most complex games don't fit what many corporations feel to be their training needs.

In single-function skills training, games need to be made simpler in order to gain wider use.

without harming the company. They also allow the student to learn valuable lessons without having to take real-world risks.

Business uses games to run tests on lessons that should already have been learned.

Games are a good way to evaluate employees for promotion.

Younger people moving up through the ranks of corporations today are used to playing games. They relate to game-training much more than older workers.

Games can be purchased and run in house, which saves a corporation a lot of money in travel costs. It also allows the company to get the maximum return on dollars invested because the game is used over and over.

Some top management trainees perceive business games as a childish way to learn.

Because games illuminate weaknesses, some trainees fear bad performances will ruin their careers and they may shy away from them.

Up to now business games have been very expensive and this has curtailed their use to some degree.

Six Benefits of Using Games in Training Seminars

Games are seen as having primarily two values in a seminar, instructional and motivational. However, there are several additional values you should consider.

1. The process of learning through game-playing removes the HR trainer from the boring role of instructor and judge. The trainer is more of a guide and a resource than an authority figure.

2. Game playing to learn management skills allows the employee to take an active, rather than a passive, role.

3. Game playing keeps employees active and interested, and in a sense they are influencing their environment. This orientation favorably affects their personal attitudes toward learning.

4. Even slow employees participate actively in games and seem to gain confidence in their abilities as their scores improve.

5. Game competition stimulates employees to make an extra effort to learn. Employees also seem to gain a better understanding of usefulness of what they are learning.

6. Games force interaction among many people and enhance the use of interpersonal skills and team playing.

The *Training and Development Journal* maintains a bibliography of business games and training applications. Write: P.O. Box 5307, Madison, WI 53705 for more information.

A TRAINING TREND: "QUICKIE" SKILL-BUILDING SEMINARS

Corporate downsizing in the mid and late 1980s created a tremendous need in companys for development of professionals and management employees in areas that emphasize personal skills. When entire levels of management were eliminated the depth of skills was drastically trimmed in many organizations creating the need for a broad-based training activity on a slim training budget.

One of the fastest growing trends in corporate training is the "quickie" skill-building seminar on subjects not taught in college and not normally part of the regular training menu. Our company started offering the skill building seminars in 1985 in response to needs in the cable TV industry headquartered primarily in Denver. The seminars caught on and are now offered on a variety of topics essential to both employee and organizational success.

- Writing for Business and Career Success
- Speaking on Your Feet
- How to Get Your Ideas Accepted by Others
- Using Influence and Giving Advice
- Leveling: How to Tell It Like It Is
- Listening Skills
- Networking for New Business
- Performance Appraisal Training
- How to Increase Your Reading Speed
- Basic Negotiating Skills
- Identifying Management Style
- Identifying Your Corporate Culture
- When to Take Action and When Not to Act
- Understanding Corporate Politics and Working Successfully in a Political Environment

With a pared-down staff, most companies are cutting training costs so they like the "quickie" seminar. They realize that the short two-hour program will not drastically modify behavior. What the programs do is produce change and provide new ideas for employees to use on the job. For more information contact: Mary Cook and Associates, 2700 Youngfield Street, Suite 206, Lakewood, CO 80215.

USING ASSESSMENT CENTER METHODS IN SELECTION OF MANAGEMENT EMPLOYEES

Selection of management level employees is an important and difficult task. The assessment center method to succession planning provides a realistic and effective alternative to paper and pencil tests or a simple selection interview. Assessment center appraisals typically predict management potential much more effectively than general tests or relying only on a superior's personal appraisal.

Basically, assessment center methods consist of exercises that are simulations of lifelike management problems. For example, a common assessment center exercise is called the "in basket." The employee being assessed is asked to go through a stack of papers provided by the assessor, called the "in basket," and to take some action on each piece of paper in the stack. The employee is then assessed on the appropriateness of the decisions made and the actions taken in the exercise.

The assumptions underlying the assessment center method are that (1) successful managers possess some measureable behavioral skills that unsuccessful managers do not possess to the same degree, (2) these differences can be identified and measured, and (3) appraisers observing potential managers can identify and adequately evaluate these characteristics.

The appraiser's task is to:

- observe candidates in exercises
- record behaviors relevant to management skills
- classify behaviors into the areas to which they are relevant
- evaluate candidates on their skills and abilities
- integrate assessor evaluations into an overall performance appraisal

If you don't have an HRD manager on staff who can perform assessments for you, there are many consultants in the assessment field who can establish a program for use in succession planning. One company that does assessment for large organizations, including AT&T, American Airlines, Bendix Corporation, Boise Cascade Corporation, Consolidated Edison, RCA Corporation, and many others, is Development Dimensions, Inc., 7101 Wisconsin Avenue, Washington, DC 20014.

Information Resource Management: HR's New Responsibility in This Important Management Function

CHAPTER **6**

KEY ISSUES OF INFORMATION RESOURCE MANAGEMENT

We are learning that Information Resource Management (IRM) is as important as any other corporate capability. IRM includes the management of labor, capital, equipment, offices, and plants. As office automation and information technology push corporations into a new era, the management of information will be pivotal and corporations will be affected at every level. For the human resource manager, the challenge will be to develop training programs for a variety of audiences at all levels of an organization. IRM requires the constant upgrading of human resources and ongoing efforts to raise the level of computer literacy within the corporation.

Human resource managers have not had significant responsibility in the past for IRM, but the future will bring an increase in responsibility with the Management Information Systems (MIS) manager for employee communication and the training of employees in the understanding and use of information technology. In fact, as human resource managers become increasingly involved in Human Resource Information Systems (HRIS) themselves, they will provide role models for other departments to become more knowledgeable about IRM.

The key issues of IRM in relation to the human resource function are:

1. office automation and training,

2. how HR managers can help workers and executives meet the challenge of office automation,

3. planning and implementing HRIS,

4. providing the badly needed communications link between employees and management in the telecommunications area, and

5. being proactive in bringing about dialog between employees and management on two issues that are becoming crucial to both parties—the computer monitoring of employee productivity and the privacy of employee information in the HRIS and other personnel records.

How Workers and Executives Are Meeting the Challenge of Office Automation

There is currently one electronic keyboard for every three white-collar workers in America. In a few years, the ratio will be one-to-one. Computer literacy is a built-in requirement for most knowledge workers and executives today.

IBM is setting an example for its customers. A senior IBM marketing executive told a business group recently that IBM aims to install one personal computer work station for each of its office employees. IBM has 369,000 employees. A report published by International Data Corporation predicts that dollar sales of personal or microcomputers will surpass dollar sales of large mainframe computers this year.

Savvy executives are using office automation to flatten the bureaucratic pyramid by eliminating management levels and redefining work patterns. Office automation is not just a room full of secretaries typing on video display terminals. It is a matrix of new technologies that includes personal computers, electronic message and mailboxes, video conferencing, telemarketing, video training, computerized human resource systems, and so forth. The matrix comes together to form the total management system and that is how companies are run today and will be run even more efficiently in the future.

Human resource managers and senior executives who do not understand and cannot discuss office automation—who do not learn themselves how to access information and use computer generated data—will soon have to do so. It is a revolution. Computer technologies affect the flow of information throughout a company. They also significantly affect the way decisions are made, the organization's strategic plans, and the credibility of the human resource manager.

How Office Automation Has Changed Four Major United States Companies

Citicorp. One of the Citicorp's banking groups developed a sophisticated information system to improve customer service and to make sure market information is available for its corporate clients more quickly than had previously been possible.

This system has allowed the group to cut its staff by seventy percent, most of whom were clerical workers. This cut took them from 2,650 employees in three years to 2,150 employees.

FMC Corporation. FMC's Chicago plant produces machinery and chemicals. It has installed a voice mail system that allows salespeople and their regional and district sales managers to exchange messages and instructions at any time via telephone "mailboxes." FMC says that this system has allowed them to eliminate one level of management.

Allied Corporation. Allied, based in New Jersey, has consolidated all of its data processing, office automation, and communications departments into one department at its corporate headquarters. Its goal has been to integrate all of the technology into one overall office system, without creating major disruptions in the office. It provides training and conducts ongoing educational programs to help people better understand what part technology plays in their organization.

Cigna Corporation. This large, Connecticut-based insurance organization created a group called the Systems Division. Systems Division staffers are integrated directly into each of Cigna's four major operating groups. They help managers learn how to use personal computers and other office technology, and how the equipment and software can be applied to their work.

Resistance to Change—The Biggest Obstacle

Some top executives feel that in order to increase productivity, managers must overcome their own resistance to innovation. Interviews with top executives in several large corporations—most of whom are responsible for coordinating productivity improvements in their firms—show that many see available human and material resources as significant opportunities for increasing bottom-line results.

The executives identify a number of methods that have been instrumental in improving productivity. Among those mentioned most often are use of microcomputers, analyzing and modifying traditional work procedures, redesigning job responsibilities, experimenting with alternative physical layouts and machine configurations, more fully utilizing existing technology, and more actively eliciting ideas from their staffs.

All executives surveyed share the belief that substantial productivity gains can be made. Most, however, point to one major drawback; too many of today's executives are not comfortable with new technology and become reluctant to use it in their own areas. The majority attribute this reluctance to psychology. People generally feel they are doing a good job without computer technology and are reluctant to change.

The pressures on executives to provide management information systems as a part of the overall business and decision-making processes will intensify during the 1990s. Computer systems already play a pivotal role in business activities—they are already an integral part of corporate strategic planning. Unless a company's information capabilities can accommodate its business and human resource strategies, it may find itself with limited growth opportunities.

In order to put more emphasis on Information Resource Management, some organizations are creating a new corporate position called the "chief information officer" or "vice president of management information systems." This position is usually equal to the company's chief financial or human resource officers and is responsible for making sure that information (which is one of the company's most valuable assets) is properly collected, handled, distributed, and stored. Another important responsibility is to see that the company and all of its people learn to apply technology creatively to change the way business is done, in order to become more productive and to achieve a competitive advantage.

HUMAN RESOURCE INFORMATION SYSTEMS: A LOOK AT WHAT THEY ARE AND HOW THEY WORK

Most human resource departments today are already on the computer. At least, all large companies have installed Human Resource Information Systems (HRIS). Thousands of smaller companies, just starting to think about an HRIS, might save money by considering some mistakes that other companies have made in purchasing and installing HRIS.

Ten Common Mistakes Made When Installing an HRIS

1. Trying to solve every problem you think you have and attempting to address every function in the first phase of installation. You cannot install the perfect all-inclusive system immediately in a one-shot application.

2. Having only computer experts install the system. It is important that a human resource expert be part of the project team to install the system if you want it to work. It is also important that one person on the team be familiar with your company's products, services, and structure.

3. Building a customized HRIS instead of buying an already developed and tested package that includes all your specific needs. Another mistake many companies make when they buy a packaged system is to try to modify the package so much that they never get it up and running.

4. Some companies have tried to design their systems or modify the packages they buy, using the committee approach. The project team should be relatively small; downsize the team rather than enlarge it. You can't successfully design an HRIS by committee.

5. Not tying the personnel and payroll systems together. If possible, buy the two systems from the same organization. If each depart-

ment tries to buy and install its own separate program, they will not work well together.

6. Going wild with the number and complexity of the reports you want from HRIS. You will never get the system up and running if you spend months designing special complex reports. Buy a packaged system that already has most of the reports you need designed into the system, and make few report modifications.

7. Not securing management support from the top down to install an HRIS. Top management usually approves purchase of an HRIS and they want to see it installed quickly at a minimum of expense. Provide top management with a regular update on installation and remind them periodically of the benefits of the HRIS to return top-down support.

8. Not installing a user-oriented system. A good HRIS system is one that assists personnel and other users with all the needed information on interviewing and selection, administration, compensation, benefits, training, labor relations, and so forth.

9. Promising management that installation of the HRIS will allow you to eliminate jobs in your department. I have never seen a computerized personnel information system do that. For one reason or another, computer-based personnel systems rarely create opportunity for reduction of the workforce.

10. Losing control of the total project. As the human resource manager, you should always be in control of the installation project. Conduct regular meetings to review progress of the installation and use such tools as PERT Charts to track progress.

Six Stages in HRIS Planning

There are typically six stages in the evolution of a management or human resource information system. First, companies seem to take a reactive and reluctant approach to implementing their first systems, which reduce clerical costs and provide the minimum system necessary to conduct business in an efficient manner.

Second, they become more optimistic and opportunistic in an unconstrained way after they have their initial system up and running, expanding into many new applications where benefits are less obvious. In the third stage, companies impose tighter management controls over computer applications. Fourth, MIS and HRIS planning begin to take place within the context of regular business and human resource planning. Fifth, computer systems are integrated into all management functions. Sixth, the entire organization participates in planning for computer systems, using computer systems and in training the workforce to improve its knowledge and ability to effectively use the systems.

The human resource department plays a big role in an organization's move to automation by implementing its own HRIS and by instigating communication and training for automation throughout the entire company.

To Change or Not to Change—Performing the Needs Analysis

If you have had an HRIS for some time, and you need modifications, or even a new system, do the following.

1. Perform a structured step-by-step needs analysis for modifying an existing HRIS. The needs analysis should include a statement of objectives and what you want to accomplish. It should also include a list of users that will be affected by the modifications.

2. Produce an overview of your requirements when you have identified them. Use a function-by-function summary of activities performed and systems support that will be required. List common interfaces.

3. Compile a detailed list of requirements that adds to the list of functional needs and further itemizes the needs by clerical, professional, and executive staff.

4. Compile and prioritize a list of user needs. Review cost versus benefit and any other pertinent evaluation strategy to rank system functions. This list can serve a two-fold purpose: (1) to manage the requests of prospective users and (2) to provide a basis for evaluating software.

5. Compile a preliminary dictionary of data. Itemize and describe each element of data that users need from the HRIS. You don't need any special computer expertise in order to do this. Use in-house expertise to make sure the analysis is user-oriented.

6. Review your objectives. Make them general and all-encompassing, and limit them to five or six major goals of the HRIS. If you and the users cannot agree on the overall objectives, chances are good that the entire project could fail.

7. Have the project team identify all the users and interview them. Provide a user list by functional breakdown, whether the function is centralized or decentralized, and then talk to key people.

8. Prepare a statement of each function's needs followed by a list of specific recommendations.

9. The last step is to prepare a list of data elements together with some approaches that you think will work in installation of the HRIS.

This whole program will take several weeks, but if you want to be sure your system modifications will be successful, you should go through this or some other comprehensive process before you make any modifications to your HRIS.

Guidelines for Purchasing HRIS Software

There are so many Human Resource Information Systems and subsystems available today that a review of all of them is impossible. Also, they change so quickly that a system someone recommends one day may not be available the next. There are, however, some good stable HRIS programs that have become standards in our field and they are listed on the following pages.

(*Note*: I do not personally recommend the systems listed nor do I guarantee that they will do the job you want done. This is simply a representative list of companies and software that might be of interest to human resource managers. Some of them have been recommended by other human resource managers, some have been advertised in trade journals and magazines. The list is intended to serve as a resource.)

Vendors of Micro Human Resource Information Systems

Product	Vendor	Environment
Applicant Tracking	Comshare, Inc. P.O. Box 1588, 3001 S. State St. Ann Arbor, MI 48106	IBM PC, IBM PC-XT; Radio Shack TRS-80
Delta Employment Systems	The Adalcar Group, Ltd. Buckminster Place Ext. 561 Union Ave. Framingham, MA 01746	Apple II, Apple II Plus, Apple III; IBM PC
Employee Contribution Accounting and Reporting System	BISS Suite 275 6620 Harwin Drive Houston, TX 77036	IBM PC, PC-XT; CP/M, CPM/M-86
Pension Planning Administration	American Micro Dynamics Suite 760 4000 MacArthur Blvd. Newport Beach, CA 92660	CP/M-based systems
Personnel Autominstrator	Information Breakthroughs, Inc. 415 West Main St. Wyckoff, NJ 07481	IBM PC, PC-XT, CP/M-based systems

Vendors of Micro Human Resource Information Systems

Product	Vendor	Environment
Personnel Manager	Radio Shack 1800 One Tandy Center Fort Worth, TX 76102	TRS-80 Model I TRS-80 Model II
Personnel, Payroll, and Benefit Accrual System	Retail Concepts, Inc. School Haus Square 245 South Main St. Frankenmuth, MI 48734	Four Phase
Personnel Search	Radio Shack One Tandy Center Fort Worth, TX 76102	TRS-80 Model II
Placement System	Computer Depot, Inc. 961 Penn Ave., South Bloomington, MN 55431	CP/M operating systems
Social Security Calculation Systems	A. S. Hansen, Inc. 1080 Green Bay Road Lake Bluff, IL 60044	IBM PC, Apple II
The Management Edge	Human Edge Software Corp. 2445 Faber Place Palo Alto, CA 94303	IBM PC
Thoughtware	Thoughtware Suite 1000A 2699 S. Bayshore Drive Coconut Grove, FL 33133	IBM PC, PC-XT
Total Personnel System	Execu-Flow Systems 2013 Morris Ave. Union, NJ 07083	Cado C.A.T.

Mini and Mainframe Human Resource Management Systems

Product	Vendor	Environment
ABS Payroll/Personnel	Applied Business Systems 4350 Upper Soda Road Dunsmuir, CA 96025	Data General: Nova, Eclipse (RDOS)
Employee Information System	Tres Computer Systems, Inc. 16775 Addison Road Dallas, TX 75248	IBM: System/ 370, 303X, 4300; PCMs (DOS, DOS/ VS(E), VS1 MVS)
Employment Management System	J&K Computer Systems, Inc., Suite 115 1819 S. Dobson Road Mesa, AZ 85202	IBM: System/ 34,/38 (SSP)
Payroll/Personnel System	International Programming Laboratories Corp. 385 S. Main St., Box 2330A Providence, RI 02906	IBM: System/ 34,/36,/38
Pension and Lump Sum System (Plus)	National FSI, Inc. Suite 452B 500 South Ervay Dallas, TX 75201	Wang 2200 series
Personnel Recruitment	Whelan Associates, Inc. Gwynedd Plaza, A/E Center Box 650 Spring House, PA 19477	IBM: Series/1
Personnel 2000	MSI Software Inc. 64 Enterprise Road Hyannis, MA 02601	IBM: System/ 34,/38
Profiles/3000	Comshare 3000 P.O. Box 1588 Ann Arbor, MI 48106	Hewlett-Packard
Xerox Employee Information System for IBM Computers	Xerox Computer Services 5310 Beethoven St. Los Angeles, CA 90066	IBM: System/ 370, 3000, 4300; PCMs (VS1, MVS, DOS/VSE, SSX/VSE)

Mini and Mainframe Human Resource Management Systems

Product	Vendor	Environment
H/R Plus (Personnel)	McCormack & Dodge Corp. 560 Hillside Ave. Needham Heights, MA 02194	IBM: System/370, 3000, 4300; PCMs (DOS, DOS/VS(E), VS1, MVS)
Human Resources Management	Software International Corp. One Tech Drive Andover, MA 01810	Wang: VS, IBM; Hewlett-Packard; HP 3000; DEC: VAX, Data General; MV; Sperry; System 80, 90; ICL (All associated operating systems)
Human Resources Management System (HRMS)	Noble Lowndes International, Inc. Three Park Ave. New York, NY 10016	IBM: System/370, 303X, 308X, 4380; PCM (DOS/VS(E), VS1, MVS)
INSCI/80	Information Science, Inc. 95 Chestnut Ridge Road Montvale, NJ 07645	As supplied on a turnkey basis by vendors
INSCI Human Resource System	Information Science, Inc. 95 Chestnut Ridge Road Montvale, NJ 07645	IBM: System/370, 303X, 4300
Interactive PIRS (Personnel Information Retrieval System)	Resource Software International, Inc. 330 New Brunswick Ave. Fords, NJ 08863	Hewlett-Packard: HP 3000 (MPE)
ISI On-Line Applicant Tracking System	Integral Systems, Inc. 165 Lennon Lane Walnut Creek, CA 94598	IBM; Hewlett-Packard; Prime
ISI On-Line Human Resource Management System; Personnel System	Integral Systems, Inc. 165 Lennon Lane Walnut Creek, CA 94598	IBM; Hewlett-Packard; Prime

Mini and Mainframe Human Resource Management Systems

Product	Vendor	Environment
MSA Human Resource Management System	Management Science America, Inc. 3445 Peachtree Road, N.E. Atlanta, GA 30326	IBM: System/ 370, 3000, 4300; Burroughs: medium, large systems; Honeywell: Level 66; Sperry: 1100 Series (DOS, DOS/VS, VS1, MVS)
MSA Payroll/Personnel Management and Reporting System	Management Science America, Inc. 3445 Peachtree Road, N.E. Atlanta, GA 30326	IBM: System/ 370, 3000, 4300; Honeywell: DPS 8; Burroughs: B 2700 through B 7700; Sperry: 1100 (All associated operating systems)

Other Vendors

Following is a list of additional software vendors that market HR software, general administrative software or custom designed software

Product	Vendor	Environment
Management Software	Arthur Anderson and Co. 69 West Washington St. Chicago, IL 60602 (312) 580-0033	
Cyborg HR Management System	Cyborg Systems, Inc. Two N. Riverside Plaza, 21st Floor Chicago, IL 60606 (312) 454-1865	IBM: Honeywell; H-P; NCR; Burroughs, CDC; Data General; Prime; Univac; DEC

The HRIS and the Merger

One of the biggest headaches for human resource managers today is the HRIS after a merger. This is probably one of the most overlooked areas of administration during and after a merger. A good example is two large airlines that merged and found their two computer systems were incompatible. The two systems caused many time-consuming problems over several years and the human resource people had ongoing problems in their payroll and personnel processing activities.

If you are part of a merger and you are lucky enough to be in the dominant organization, you may be able to say, "We'll do it our way—use our system, and work with the human resources people from the other organization in bringing their data onto our HRIS." If you are lucky, your system is comprehensive enough to handle the numbers of people effectively.

Companies that are the dominant organization, however, and that insist on doing it "their way" have lost talented data processing people from the new organizations because of their inflexibility. Really good data processing people today can write their own tickets almost anywhere and don't have to live through a takeover.

In fact, businesses' demand for trained computer analysts and programmers is fast outstripping the supply, according to a National Science Foundation study. It predicts that business will need as many as 604,000 computer specialists in the next three years, while only 466,000 of them will be in the workforce. So think twice before alienating any good computer people in a merger.

It is a good idea to set up a task force of people from both organizations, with managers from all functions, to tackle the huge task of an HRIS integration.

SOME INNOVATIVE WAYS COMPANIES USE HRIS

Company user groups are good sources of innovative approaches to human resource information systems. If you start an HRIS and you cannot find a good user group, start one of your own by calling other companies in the area and networking. Most companies that have microcomputer systems have been innovative in using them to their best advantage.

Case Example: Polaroid Profiles Personnel Trends

Polaroid prevents the loss of talented staff by monitoring wage and labor issues and talent availability for promotion on its HRIS. They analyze internal pay and compensation data in relation to surveys of pay scales in comparable companies, using an IBM personal computer. They also review job categories to monitor which ones may become obsolete, and they use their system when they are going to have force reductions in the workforce.

Scenarios can be worked through the computer, using compensation and benefits costs, seniority and age, and so forth in order to choose the most advantageous approach to use in a layoff.

Polaroid also developed a model to use on merit increases based on what they knew of the past history, how often their people were given merit increases, what their projected costs would be.

COMPUTER MONITORING OF EMPLOYEE PERFORMANCE

As mentioned earlier computers are used to monitor performance of employees. Companies like Giant Foods and AT&T Communications have tried performance-monitoring programs. These programs are becoming more and more unpopular with employees.

Organizational Analysis by Computer

SMC Hendrick, Inc. of Framingham, Massachusetts, a division of Science Management Corporation, has developed a unique, automated method of gathering data on managers that will pinpoint effectiveness, and provide suggestions for improving productivity. There are several factors that make this method unique including

- The initial organizational analysis is accomplished by use of a computer that generates more data than most clients have ever gathered on their organization before.
- The process requires that a group of key executives called coconsultants, who are collectively knowledgeable about all facets of the business, work with the Hendrick consultants to analyze the results of the computer generated reports.

Where most consultants spend eighty percent of their time gathering data and twenty percent analyzing it, in this program it is just the opposite. Hendrick uses the computer to reduce the time the research takes. You can learn exactly where your money is being spent and whether or not you have been managing it effectively. You will learn if your ratio of managers to workers is unbalanced and what level, if any, needs to be cut.

This is a very comprehensive organizational analysis that has been used by several organizations, including Pitney Bowes and Polaroid Corporation.

USING THE COMPUTER TO FORECAST SALARY PROGRAM COSTS

The computer can be used to provide a realistic overview of a proposed wage and salary program. Organizations spend so much money on compensation programs that it makes good sense to try to project costs as accurately as possible.

You need to gather some information.

- average rate per employee
- number of increases per year
- change in rate for each employee
- total cost of program changes by activity, by quarter and by function
- change in average rates per employee

For purposes of this discussion, we provide a simple example, but we can't guess at all the variables that will come into play in any given organization. There are different types of payrolls, seasonal and temporary employees, shift differentials, and so forth. But for discussion purposes, the following model is used.

Simulation of Wage/Salary Costs

Constant Employees
1. Beginning Rates (Jan. 1–Dec. 31)
   $6 \times (20,000) =$ $120,000
2. Merit Increase (Jan. 1–Dec. 31)
   $6 \times (2,000) =$ 12,000

Total for Constant Employees $132,000

Deletion
1. Beginning Rates (Jan. 1–June 30)
   $1 \times (20,000) \times 1/2 =$ $ 10,000
2. Merit Increase (Jan. 1–June 30)
   $1 \times (2,000) \times 1/2 =$ 1,000

Total for Deletion $ 11,000

Replacement
1. Beginning Rates (July 1–Dec. 31)
   $1 \times (20,000) \times 1/2 =$ $ 10,000
2. Merit Increase
   None—Employee Not on Roll on Jan. 1   0

Total for Replacement $ 10,000

Total Wage/Salary Cost $153,000

Because simulation gives the human resource manager a feel for the process, it is a valid rehearsal for the overall salary program.

As you build a simulation model, you can establish files that correspond to actual employees. The number of employees in each file can vary depending on the size of your workforce. You can use the actual rate of each employee in order to make your simulation as real as possible.

THE TELECOMMUTING REVOLUTION: WHAT IT MEANS TO HUMAN RESOURCE MANAGEMENT

Managing human resources at remote sites by telecommuting is a growing management activity, and future possibilities for growth are significant. Shortages of skilled personnel, the continued need to boost productivity, the necessity to stay competitive, and the growing expense of office space and employee expenses all converge to make telecommuting a vital management tool in the future. There are already over 21 million American households conducting some portion of their business at home, and many of them utilize PCs.

In most organizations the human resource manager is the main contact and ongoing communications link between the employee, the supervisor, and the company in the telecommuting chain. The telecommuting work environment has become one of the most sought-after work benefits of this decade, especially among working women who have started their families and who want to work at home. Women almost make up fifty percent of the workforce today, and that figure is growing.

In most cases telecommuting reduces turnover, provides a valuable new labor pool, cuts overhead, and is viewed as a long-overdue management response to employee needs. In fact, telecommuting has so much promise for workers of the future that experiments are springing up all across the United States. Some companies currently experimenting with telecommuting are: Control Data Corp., Walgreens, McDonald's, Mountain States Telephone and Telegraph, Pacific Bell, and Continental Illinois National Bank and Trust Company, to name just a few.

There are pros and cons about telecommuting, not the least of which is the feeling of isolation that some workers feel when they start working at home after years in the corporate environment. Some managers don't always like telecommuting because it makes supervising an employee more difficult. The other big issue with employees is that some companies are refusing to provide their regular benefits to homebased workers, preferring to treat them as contract labor. This issue is heating up and unions are beginning to get involved. The cost of establishing a telecommuting work arrangement for one employee is minimal. It costs approximately $1,700 per employee to install a computer terminal and a communications hookup to the home. One company, Freight Data Systems in Inglewood, California, grew from three to twelve employees in one year. They were unable to expand their office space, so the president decided to use telecommuting; most of his employees now work at home. The company eliminated the position of office manager to oversee workers and instead pays a bonus to employees who can complete projects in record time. Freight Data Systems President, Joseph Taussig, says that he paid for his telecommuting system in five months.

Telecommuting is an extremely important trend for the handicapped who could not work at all if not for telecommuting. Bill Banks is a computer programmer for Trends, Inc. in Chicago. He is a quadriplegic who utilizes a breath-operated wheel chair and punches terminal keys with a clothes pin held between his teeth. Telecommuting has opened his world and allowed him to be self-supporting.

Case Example: Fair International, Ltd.

Fair International, Ltd. is a company whose entire workforce works in their homes. This computer software company saves a great deal of money by not having expensive offices. They have one computer in a small office and all of their 600 employees communicate directly with that computer.

There are some drawbacks, naturally. Working at home requires discipline, and it is more difficult to supervise home workers. Fair International hires only people with at least four years in telecommuting to ensure they have the ability to adhere to a strict deadline. Another difficulty is that some organizations such as banks and brokers are concerned with the confidentiality of work they send to Fair International, but after years of experience with the organization and their people, customers feel safe about the issue of confidentiality.

Most human resource managers find it easy to recruit the necessary computer skills because telecommuting is seen as a real employee benefit. For a more in-depth review of telecommuting, refer to *Telecommuting: How to Make It Work for You and Your Company*, by Gordon and Kelly, Prentice-Hall, 1986.

ROBOTS VERSUS PEOPLE: THE IMPLICATIONS OF A MECHANICAL WORKFORCE

The Census Bureau has reported that American industry has produced 5,535 robots. The Census report found that seventy-five United States companies are engaged in production of robots with shipments of 5,535 machines valued at $357.7 million. If current growth trends continue, the United States robotics industry could have production of $1 billion in the 1990s.

The country's preoccupation with lower production and service costs compared with human labor makes robots a more viable consideration in many industries. The average labor cost in the United States is about $15 per hour, while the average cost of a fully utilized robot is less than $5 per hour. Inflation can be expected to increase the cost of human labor intensive products, while escalating technological advances might even further reduce the cost of robots.

There is some fear naturally on the part of employees who could be replaced by robots; however, people in the robotics field say that unemployment increases due to robotics would be more than offset by job opportunities in the growing robotics industry, and in manufacturing in general. Most experts also feel that robots will free employees to perform more meaningful, interesting work.

Human resource managers will have to be concerned with retraining the workforce, especially people who are replaced by robots. Another significant issue in human resource management (HRM) will be the need for human resource people. Our own function will be drastically affected by the introduction of robots into the workforce.

It is estimated that about fifty percent of the HRM function can be directly linked to local, state, and federal regulations—collective bargaining, safety and health, EEO, overtime laws, and so forth. With a significant increase in robots at work, that activity could drop in a drastic way.

The HR functions of job descriptions, job analysis, compensation and benefits, and training and development would all be heavily impacted in a company that makes a significant change from a human to a robotic workforce.

Strategic planning for human resources through the 1990s must take into account that there are estimates that one million jobs in United States heavy industry may be eliminated by robots by 1990. General Electric alone is stepping up its use of robots for spray-painting and other repetitive jobs and plans to replace about one-half of their 37,000 appliance assembly workers with robots. The Ford Motor Company and other car companies are in the process of installing robots in thousands of their repetitive low level jobs.

More small to mid-size companies are opting not to hire full-time human resource managers. As I monitored this trend in the mid-1980s, I saw a niche in the market for consultants who can provide the needed human resource or administrative personnel functions on an "as needed" basis to small and mid-size businesses.

Preliminary market research provided a list of over 500 companies in the Denver area alone that were operating without a full-time human resource manager. These companies, when contacted, were very open to using the services of a consultant rather than hiring a full-time personnel administrator or human resource manager.

The significant issue here is that you will need to watch closely two situations that will heavily impact your employment in the next five to ten years:

1. The robotics revolution is going to drastically impact on the number of people hired into repetitive blue collar jobs. As fifty percent of the human resource function deals with local, state, and federal regulations, and programs that address regulation, there will be a significant trend toward smaller human resource staffs.

2. Because the largest area of growth in employment will take place in small and mid-size businesses in the next decade, employment of human resource managers will decline. More and more small and mid-size companies are maintaining lean staff levels and hiring outside consultants to handle personnel matters on an "as needed" basis.

Human resource consulting on an "on-call" basis is a new and effective way of addressing personnel problems for small and mid-size companies. In my own consulting firm, Mary Cook and Associates, we go into a small company, organize the personnel function, set up recordkeeping procedures, write their personnel policies and employee handbook, and train someone on their staff to maintain all the necessary records. Then we leave—we are not on their payroll full time. However, we are available anytime we are needed to step in and assist with any type of personnel or human resource problem.

COMPUTER LITERACY—WHAT YOU DON'T KNOW COULD HURT YOU

Management consultants, Booz, Allen, and Hamilton, Inc., reported in the *Wall Street Journal* that ninety percent of the roughly ten million executives and professional managers in the United States today are computer illiterates. Even with all the press about personal computers and the rush to "own your own," we still have a whole generation of executives and middle managers who cannot use a microcomputer.

There are many reasons: Some executives feel it's beneath them, "doesn't suit the executive image." Some managers are intimidated by the computer's ability to point out their mistakes. Some male managers think sitting in front of a computer terminal makes them look like a low level technician, and women executives who use computers are constantly asked if they also take dictation.

Most human resource managers feel the best way to overcome computer fear is through planned training that includes all managers and provides personal tutoring where necessary. The overall framework for training in computer literacy might include four key items.

1. Assessment of training needs at all levels, with concentration on the managerial level.

2. Design of training programs that meet the needs of all employees, taking into consideration specific user requirements.

3. Implementation of training programs.

4. Ongoing evaluation of training programs by human resource managers and by users at all levels.

Computer Training Programs for Executives

Consultants in Denver with the CPA firm of Pannell Kerr Forster, have worked with many organizations to implement training programs for professionals and executives on the use of microcomputers.

In order to meet their own staff needs and the requests of their executive clients, Pannell Kerr Forster decided to employ professional microcomputer trainers and establish an in-house program. Structuring the curriculum to offer training on the most commonly used computers, a classroom was designed to be conducive to personalized training. No more than six students were in each class to ensure individualized attention. While the training facilities were available at PKF's offices, frequently individuals and organizations were provided training at locations more convenient to them.

The most popular classes are:

Selecting and Introducing Microcomputers   This session presents a disciplined methodology for choosing between computers on the market. Executives are shown how to determine their needs and compare them with the capabilities of available hardware and software. Planning for operations, training, and troubleshooting procedures is explained.

Hardware and Peripherals   The CPU (processor) is often a small fraction of the cost of a computer. Printers, disk storage, communication boards, and a myriad of other devices are required to make a working system. This session examines some of the equipment options and provides the decision maker with a detailed understanding of the alternatives for enhancing and increasing the value and usefulness of their system.

Part of this session includes a comparison of the major CPUs on the market, such as IBM PC, XT and AT, Apple, and TRS from Radio Shack.

Operating Systems   This session describes and evaluates different operating systems, such as MSDOS, DOS 3.3, TRSDOS, and the CP/M family. File structures, command languages, and libraries are discussed. In addition, Unix, the operating system that may become the most widely used in the world, is explored.

Word Processors A comprehensive comparison of the most popular word processing software is reviewed. Hands on training is provided to the student on the use of function keys, creating letters, paragraphs, reformatting, underlining, and spell checking capabilities.

Electronic Spreadsheets This session explores the various spreadsheet programs commercially available. From Lotus 1 2 3 to Multiplan, the student receives training on setting up tables, rows, columns, and formulas, and how to verify the spreadsheet.

Integrated Software Examining the popular integrated programs is the objective of this session. The students are trained on their choice of *Symphony*, *Jazz*, and other software after they have a clear understanding of which would be best for their needs.

Accounting Systems While there are literally hundreds of accounting programs on the market, only a few are sufficiently mature for the students to consider. This session examines several of these programs from CYMA, MBSI, SBT, MCS, and Timberline to aid the students in selecting a program best for them. After selecting the program, the students are trained in its particular use.

Micro-Mainframe Relationships Despite claims to the contrary, friendly micro-mainframe interfaces are a technical challenge. This session reviews the technology, capabilities, and limitations, and so establishes the framework for products currently on the market. Significant new applications are offered by integrating micros and mainframe technology. Examples of micro-mainframe links employed in a variety of industries and functions are presented.

Telecommunications and Local Area Networks (LANS) Local area networks allow low cost microcomputers to share high cost resources—large capacity disk storage, high speed printers, and so on. They allow interconnection of individual machines for electronic mail, program swapping, and file transfer.

This session examines the problems related to local networking of microcomputers and assess available software and peripheral boards of microcomputers.

In addition to the above courses, individuals may request other topics and a combination of several of the more popular sessions. This has proven to be an excellent method for many executives to prepare themselves for their business needs without loss of time.

Pannell Kerr Forster also converted education into ongoing support for the executive. Follow-up calls were handled after the training class. Installation assistance and ongoing support were provided as a means of ensuring that what was taught in the classroom were placed in actual operation by the executive.

There are hundreds of consultants across the United States who can provide microcomputer training to executives. Pannell Kerr Forster is only one organization that has seen a need and provided a good product.

PERSONAL PRIVACY VERSUS THE COMPUTER AND THE HRIS

As more and more personal information on employees is entered into the corporate computer, legal and ethical issues are being raised. In fact, human resource executives, academic experts, congressional committees, and business people have all expressed concern that the use of computers to gather personal information about people may outpace the legal safeguards.

In America, the two most significant gatherers of information on people are the federal government and the individual's employer. Federal laws provide protections against governmental abuses under the concepts of constitutional rights, due process, equal opportunity, individual rights, and safety. Also, government falls under public scrutiny, especially by the press and the television media. The laws that provide safeguards and legal restrictions on government information, however, do not regulate private employers.

Employers can gather all the information on employees they want. There are no controls over employer recordkeeping, virtually no legal limits on the information that an employer may gather, and no limits on the disclosure of that information to others.

Laws have been passed in some states stating that employees have a right to see their personnel files and may request the company change any information that is in error.

Medical records are another major concern of employees. Even though a doctor takes the Hippocratic Oath, agreeing not to disclose medical information on patients, third party payments and personnel data banks make confidentiality impossible.

Most human resource people can tell horror stories about medical information being used to make a decision on an employee's suitability for promotion. Most human resource people will tell employees not to use medical benefits to pay for psychotherapy if they want to move up in an organization. This is certainly a privacy and an ethical issue that will be challenged in the future.

Employees sign away their rights to privacy when, for example, they sign a medical claims form that says, "I authorize any licensed physician, medical practitioner or other person to disclose information." When you hurriedly sign this statement, you may not realize it, but you are knowingly granting access to any and all medical information in your personnel file.

The issue of personal privacy versus the corporate computer is heating up and employees are beginning to question the invasion of privacy threat of personnel data systems.

Three Steps to Avoid Invasion of Privacy Lawsuits

It is absolutely essential today to implement corporate privacy policy guidelines. There are three steps you can take to implement workable guidelines and avoid costly litigation in the privacy area.

1. Publish a privacy policy or statement regarding your computer system. Include such areas as controls on operating practices, access of data subjects, and usage control by data subjects. This statement should cover both the system's impact on individual employee privacy, and the effect of privacy regulations on the system.

2. Construct a comprehensive privacy plan for all computer systems. A plan will ensure that all necessary privacy controls are integrated into the design of the system. For an existing system, the plan should cover changes in programs, equipment, and procedures.

3. Train employees who work in data systems and in human resources how to handle personal information on employees. Make your privacy policies and procedures well known to all operating personnel and to all employees.

Employees who work with personal information on employees should understand the legal and ethical considerations of employee privacy. Also, employees want to know how their personal information is being treated; because of past abuses, many employees do not trust their employer to maintain confidentiality over personal information. Smart corporate management is open and above-board with employees—telling them exactly what is maintained, where and how it is maintained, and they communicate privacy policies openly to employees.

Privacy and Home Based Employees

As we have discussed in other chapters, many employees are working at home using computers and telephones. Television used to be just a device for bringing news and entertainment into the home, but now people hook up their televisions to computers, cable systems, and telephones and are creating new technology called interactive home media or *hometech*.

Cable is primarily used today for commercial programming, but cable companies are exploring new services that will transform cable into a tremendous network of data available on a daily basis. We will be able to receive electronically stored news, classified ads, yellow pages, weather reports, and stock quotations, and perform interactive transactions such as banking, shopping, making airline reservations, and even have remote medical diagnosis. There will also be monitoring of home security, energy use, opinion polling, and special communications for home workers.

All of this tremendous technical capability also creates privacy dangers that have been largely overlooked. Our old traditional concepts of individual privacy do not account for the new realities of interactive home media.

As more employees choose to work at home and as more companies provide these arrangements, human resource managers must take responsibility in addressing the important issues of both personal privacy and corporate security.

Protecting the Privacy of Computerized Personnel Records

Most automated personnel systems have protections and safeguards built in, but many human resource information systems that were developed years ago contain information that is contrary to privacy and affirmative action regulations today. You must ensure that the HRIS is cleansed of old, obsolete data. An automated personnel records audit is one way of doing this.

I recommend to my clients that every change that goes into the system trigger a profile printout that is given to the employee in order to allow updating and cleansing of wrong information on a regular basis.

There has been an increased use in the last few years of HRIS data in court cases. Most of the time it is used in discrimination cases. Plaintiffs can gain access to the HRIS data through legal processes and attempt to use the data to prove discrimination. The data from computerized systems may be given more credence by a jury and may, therefore, be difficult to rebut.

In the case of Adams versus Dan River Mills, Inc., a case involving alleged racially discriminatory employment practices, the court ordered the defendant, Dan River, to supply the plaintiff with a computerized master payroll file, as well as printouts for the W-2 forms of defendant's employees. The court reasoned:

> The plaintiffs stated that they need the current computer cards or tapes and the W-2 printouts in order to prepare accurate, up-to-date statistics which will be relevant to determining whether or not discriminatory practices have occurred. Furthermore, the plaintiffs contend that the use of this computerized data is the most inexpensive and reliable method which can be used since making the necessary studies with human labor is not only extremely time-consuming and expensive, but also is more susceptible to error.

Because of the accuracy and inexpensiveness of producing the requested documents in the case at the bar, this court sees no reason why the defendant should not be required to produce the computer cards or tapes and the W-2 printouts to the plaintiffs.

A plaintiff's attorney can use inaccuracies in a computerized system to weaken a company's defense against an employment discrimination claim. It could also be embarrassing for the human resource department to be the focal point in a lawsuit where the employee-related database they designed, developed, and maintained becomes a helpful tool for a plaintiff.

It becomes more obvious every day how important the management of the human resources information system is. The responsibility transcends just the departmental personnel files.

Recruiting the 1990s Workforce

CHAPTER 7

RECRUITING THE NEW WORKER

Corporations are spending unprecedented sums on ads to persuade the public that they are okay and to entice the new worker. The camera sweeps a Colorado mountain terrain from snow capped peaks to clear mountain lake with wildflowers in bloom, sun shining on the handsome face of Mark Harmon. In his hand an ice cold Coors beer brewed with clear rocky mountain spring water. Who wouldn't want to work for a company with that healthy, young American image? A company like that would have to treat their employees well. And, most people feel they do. They have great benefits, and good wages, but they have had serious labor problems in Coors country and the expensive ad campaigns in the media are placed to help them eliminate an image problem that plagued them for several years. The Coors ads portray the company as a champion of democratic values, something the new worker relates to.

How do we attract this new worker? What kind of a recruiting program do we need? How do we advertise to get their attention? Can we really define our recruiting market? We are learning that out of the masses of baby-boom and post baby-boom workers is emerging this new class of individual who is challenging the establishment, the politicians, and their supervisors and managers.

This "new collar" class of worker is important to us—they are not blue collar, not all white collar, they are in between, and corporations need them now and will even more so in the future. The baby-boomers alone comprise one-third of the biggest generation in our history. In our post-industrial economy, they are the successors to the traditional blue-collar workers, they are working between professional jobs and the laboring ranks. They are in information and service jobs, and they have a different work ethic. They work hard, but they want time and the money to play. They are not as upwardly mobile in their personal objectives as they are driven by the desire to make enough money to enjoy life.

The more we learn about these new workers, the easier it may be to recruit them. Pollsters calculate this so-called new-collar worker is about thirteen percent of the electorate and they have spending power of 327 billion dollars a year. They are from twenty-one to forty years of age and make anywhere from $18,000 to $30,000 per year. These are the workers for which human resources people are hunting. This is the workforce we have to attract. They are not the upper class, well off yuppie. They are the hard working less affluent backbone of the country today and they are a deeply individualistic generation—difficult to motivate and difficult to manage.

This new worker accounts for fifty-one percent of the clerical workers, fifty-two percent of the blue collar workers, fifty-seven percent of computer operators, and sixty-three percent of all technicians, according to government statistics.

They work hard but they are not obsessed with their careers. They love their leisure time. They read *TV Guide* and *People* magazine according to some pollsters and their favorite TV shows are *Cheers, Hill Street Blues, The Bill Cosby Show,* and *Monday Night Football.* A lot of these young Americans have struggled to get a few years of college, some have college degrees but they are now disappointed to find that a college degree and a white collar job do not guarantee high incomes or financial security. They are still struggling to make ends meet. Some have had to move back to their parents' homes because they cannot afford apartments or condominiums and cannot scrape together the down payment on a home of their own.

Many of these new workers feel left out of the working establishment. They haven't moved up in organizations like yuppies have. Organizations don't "court" them and many corporations don't even seem to be communicating with them. How do we attract and retain them? One of these new workers gave me some clues.

> Let me be candid with you and share my ideas about improving my job . . . the way I do my work. Let me participate in the "workings" of the Company. I would like to be on some committees or a task force when the need arises . . . be more involved. Interview me for your newsletter. Let me share some of the new ideas I'm learning in the college courses you are paying for me to attend. Let me learn more about other jobs in the company so I can practice new skills. Include me in some of your meetings occasionally—and, by the way, I need more money, I'm not affluent. I'm having trouble making my car payments and keeping an apartment. I buy everything at discount stores and budget to the penny. Another $3 or $4 per hour would make a real difference in my budget. I have two weeks vacation but no money to go anywhere. I can afford only an occasional movie, concert, or football game.
>
> —A PC operator in a subsidiary of a large Telephone Company

A PROFILE OF THE 1990s WORKER

The following profile can help you develop a workable recruiting plan. You will need to be open-minded in order to attract the best workers—the people you will need in the future will not necessarily work the same hours you use now, or under the same policies and procedures you have had in the past.

The 1990s workers may

- work shorter hours and a shorter work week.
- work at home.
- work part time.
- share a job with another person.
- ask to work early evenings to share babysitting with a working spouse.
- request help with baby sitting because he or she is a single parent and works the night shift.
- get an extension of company benefits for a same-sex partner, because they are homosexuals.
- be retired from one job and seeking a second career.
- be over fifty.
- be handicapped.
- meet their spouses on the job and/or participate in at least one work romance.
- work together with a spouse in the same company and possibly in the same department.
- bring a child to work if the job can be done effectively with a child present—or bring the child to a corporate day-care center.
- have to change careers and be retrained at least twice in a lifetime.
- lose at least one job either through merger, or to a computer or robot.
- be healthier because of health and fitness programs offered on the job.
- participate in a van or carpool, or ride a bus.
- use a personal computer on the job.
- own company stock through an ESOP or other profit-sharing program.
- own a share in the company through a leveraged buyout.
- make less on an hourly basis than workers doing the same jobs in the 1980s.
- not join a union as quickly as workers did in the 1960s and 1970s.
- be more outspoken on personal rights issues like privacy and termination-at-will.
- want more say in the way his job is done.

- refuse to take lie-detector or other controversial types of tests.

- be more likely to have tried and/or used drugs.

- be a white collar rather than a blue collar worker—the so-called new collar worker.

- be bilingual—probably Spanish speaking.

- have legally or illegally immigrated to the United States.

- be a member of a minority group—Asian, Hispanic, or Black.

- be a two-income family member or a single-parent head of household.

- want more development opportunities and benefits that promote personal growth.

- want comparable pay for work of comparable worth, an issue that won't go away as more women enter the workforce. An estimated seventy-five percent of all women over the age of sixteen will be in the workforce by 1990.

- insist on flexible benefits so that, in a two-income family, the benefits won't overlap.

- hold two jobs off and on through a lifetime in order to attain a desired life style.

This profile won't shock you . . . most HR managers have thought about the way the workforce is changing. The profile may, however, give you some new ideas or get your creative juices to flowing in order to find new ways to plan for and recruit the new worker.

FOURTEEN ADAPTABLE IDEAS FOR RECRUITING CAPABLE PEOPLE

1. Use job sharing as a technique to attract clerical, technical, and professional people to your company. Two part-time clerical or data processing people can do one job. You meet the needs of the person who can only work part-time, and you have two people who are trained on the same job.

2. Use odd-hour scheduling to attract clerical, technical, professional, or service and blue-collar workers, and even students. People working full-time jobs elsewhere who need extra work will be attracted to odd-hour scheduling. If they see how enlightened your management is in providing for employees' needs, they may be attracted to work for you full time.

3. Allow professional and clerical workers such as writers, typists, data

processing people who have a home computer, draftspeople, and others who can work just as well from home as from your office, to work at home and bring the work in at scheduled times. You can pay by the hour by asking them to keep time cards; you can pay a salary; or in some cases you can pay them as independent contractors. Adapt the method of payment to the individual and the company needs. As long as payment complies with all necessary regulations, you can be flexible.

4. Use retired workers for special projects. Whether they retired from your company or another company, if they have needed skills and abilities, they can do special projects at home or in the office. Use the local Over 40 employment service of your State Employment Office, or use your own retired workers. There is a distinct possibility that a critical worker shortage could occur in the 1990s.

5. Design and implement a retraining program so that employees whose jobs become obsolete can be retrained for jobs you have difficulty filling. It is important to do some advanced human resource planning and to keep revising the plan. If you don't, you won't know far enough in advance when certain jobs will become obsolete and retraining won't be carried out in advance of your critical needs.

6. Create an ad hoc committee in-house with engineers, accountants, and other professionals, the same types of people you are trying to hire. They can help you come up with new ideas for recruiting. They also can add a networking element with a variety of professional associations.

7. More than seventy percent of the women in the country today work outside the home. Be sure your ads and recruiting literature appeal to women. Ask women currently on staff for new recruiting ideas.

8. Set up a hotline for people who might be interested in a job with your company to call in and get information about specific jobs. Keep the hotline open during evening hours for people who work.

9. In every company there are people who, if given the chance to learn a new skill, could do so in a very short time. Can a data clerk learn a job one or two levels above the current assignment? Can a secretary learn a job as a report writer or a project coordinator? Can an order clerk learn new skills and become a warehouse or purchasing supervisor? Are you being creative and thoughtful in looking inside your own company for talent? An investment in training might bring a better return than recruiting costs. Look for tradeoffs.

10. Consider organizational change as an alternative staffing method. If you cannot hire a specific person, consider an alternative move. For example, one company had two managers in its data processing organization—one manager for business systems and one manager for technical mineral systems. They lost the mineral systems manager and could not replace that person immediately with another qualified individual. A discussion about organizational alternatives brought excellent results. They reorganized the data processing function. The manager of business systems had a good general background and knowledge of the mineral systems function, had a great deal of credibility with both groups, and was an excellent manager. When they were unable to find an experienced mineral systems manager, they decided to reorganize by putting both groups under the business systems manager and beefing up the technical mineral systems group by adding a geologist with a degree in data processing. The reorganization proved to be a good move and resulted in a more productive department.

11. Some companies have started paying middle managers hiring bonuses. Upfront bonuses, a perk once reserved for senior executives, has become a way to attract middle management. The perk helps combat inflation while not upsetting established compensation levels. The bonuses range from eight percent to twenty-five percent of a manager's first-year salary. With the pluses, there are, however, certain negatives on the front-end bonus. Unless deferred in some way, it has no holding power; and once paid, the candidate is free to walk away. Some companies also pay bonuses to employees who refer applicants. The bonus is awarded if the person is hired and stays for a certain period of time, usually three to six months.

12. Make an effort to recruit and employ handicapped workers. Forward-thinking companies like Control Data allow workers like technical writers to work at home while receiving employee benefits. There are more than thirty-five million Americans with some form of mental or physical handicap. The Xerox Corporation has an excellent program for employing disabled workers, and AT&T has developed a program to train managers of disabled people.

13. Let your employees who cannot work full time, women who quit to have a baby, or men or women who don't want to work full time come in on a part-time basis. One Denver accounting firm is filling several professional positions with former employees who want to work part time and it works very well for them.

14. Beef-up your networking activities through associations, clubs, and

local professional affiliations. The best sources of good people are personal referrals.

HOW TO USE ADVERTISING AND PUBLICITY TO ATTRACT THE NEW WORKER

The toughest problem in recruiting is always finding enough qualified candidates to interview for every job opening. We will have to be more creative and innovative in our recruiting techniques in the next few years in order to attract the best candidates. Advertising and publicity of the company are two good ways to recruit.

A recruiting ad to attract the new worker might read as follows:

> Wanted—PC operator with new ideas for improving our productivity. We have a participative management style and welcome employee involvement. Company sponsored activities encourage employee participation. Good wages and flexible benefits. Company paid educational assistance. Your skills and your mind are welcome at the XYZ Company!

When you run ads you want to spend dollars where they will do the most good. One way to do this is to take advantage of free market information. Knight-Ridder newspapers, for example, publish a *Recruitment and Market Information Manual* you can obtain free by calling their classified manager in Chicago at (312) 263-6270. This kind of information may help you save media dollars by showing how to target markets to reach the best prospects for specific jobs. The Personnel Locator Chart shown in Figure 7-1 gives you an idea about targeting areas for advertising specific job openings.

Other newspapers, magazines, television stations, and nationwide ad firms also provide resources and market data.

ADVERTISING FOR HUSBAND AND WIFE TO WORK TOGETHER: A NEW APPROACH TO AN OLD TABOO

For years companies have had a prohibition on employing husbands and wives to work together. Now some companies are actually recruiting husband and wife teams. As good workers become more difficult to find, organizations will have to be more open-minded in recruiting and selection. One company that has employed this new approach for advertising is La Quinta Motor Inns. Figure 7-2 reflects a fresh and new approach to recruitment advertising.

How One Company Uses Publicity for Recruiting and Public Relations

Betty and Don Bennett found a way to get $5,000 worth of free advertising for $500. They own several small businesses in Phoenix, Arizona under the

Figure 7-1: The Personnel Locator Chart

Put your recruitment budget to work in the markets where the prospects live.

KNIGHT-RIDDER NEWSPAPERS	AEROSPACE/AIRCRAFT/AIRLINES	AGRICULTURE	AUTOMOTIVE	BANKING/FINANCIAL	COMMUNICATIONS	CHEMICAL/CHEMICAL ENGINEERS	COMPUTER TECHNOLOGY/DATA PROCESSING	EDUCATION/UNIVERSITIES	ELECTRONICS	ENGINEERS	GOVERNMENT	HEALTH/MEDICAL	HOTELS/TOURISM	MILITARY INSTALLATIONS	MANUFACTURING (LIGHT)	MANUFACTURING (HEAVY)	OIL/GAS/PETROLEUM REFINING/ENERGY RELATED	RETAILING	RESEARCH	SHIPPING	STEEL	TEXTILES	TRANSPORTATION
AKRON BEACON JOURNAL	●		●			●		●	●	●					●	●							●
CHARLOTTE OBSERVER AND NEWS		●		●			●	●	●	●	●	●			●			●				●	●
DETROIT FREE PRESS		●	●			●	●	●		●		●			●	●		●	●	●	●		●
FT. WAYNE JOURNAL GAZETTE & NEWS SENTINEL			●					●							●	●							●
LONG BEACH PRESS-TELEGRAM	●				●		●	●	●	●		●	●	●	●	●	●			●			
MIAMI HERALD AND NEWS	●	●		●	●		●	●	●	●	●	●	●	●	●			●		●		●	●
PHILADELPHIA INQUIRER & DAILY NEWS	●		●	●	●	●	●	●	●	●	●	●	●	●	●	●	●	●	●	●	●	●	●
ST. PAUL DISPATCH-PIONEER PRESS	●	●					●	●	●	●		●			●								
SAN JOSE MERCURY NEWS	●		●		●		●	●	●	●		●		●	●			●	●				
WICHITA EAGLE-BEACON	●	●					●	●	●	●		●		●	●	●	●						
ABERDEEN AMERICAN NEWS		●					●	●				●			●								●
BOCA RATON NEWS							●	●		●		●	●										
BOULDER DAILY CAMERA	●					●	●	●	●						●		●		●				
BRADENTON HERALD		●							●				●		●					●			
COLUMBUS LEDGER & ENQUIRER														●								●	
DULUTH HERALD & NEWS-TRIBUNE								●				●	●				●			●			
GARY POST-TRIBUNE			●		●	●	●	●	●	●	●	●			●	●				●	●		
GRAND FORKS HERALD		●						●				●		●					●				
LEXINGTON HERALD AND LEADER		●				●	●	●	●	●	●	●	●	●	●		●		●	●			
MACON TELEGRAPH & NEWS	●	●				●		●		●		●		●	●							●	
PASADENA STAR-NEWS	●						●	●	●	●					●				●				
STATE COLLEGE CENTRE DAILY TIMES						●	●	●	●	●		●			●				●				
TALLAHASSEE DEMOCRAT								●			●						●						

Knight-Ridder Newspapers let you pinpoint target markets for professional recruitment programs. Use the Personnel Locator Chart above to find those key markets that allow you to achieve maximum impact and avoid wasted media dollars.

Reach the prospects where they live. Call Jim Moss, Knight-Ridder Newspaper Sales Classified Advertising Director in New York (212) 826-0500, Diane Clardy in Los Angeles (213) 876-8530, June Occhipinti in Chicago (312) 263-6270, or Paul Burley in Atlanta (404) 955-5086.

KNIGHT-RIDDER NEWSPAPER SALES, INC.

One Dag Hammarskjold Plaza, New York, N.Y. 10017

ATLANTA • CHICAGO • DETROIT • LOS ANGELES • MIAMI • MINNEAPOLIS • SAN FRANCISCO

National Classified Advertising Representative for Knight-Ridder Newspapers

Figure 7-2: Advertisement for Husband and Wife Recruitment

umbrella of Bennett Enterprises, Inc. The businesses have combined revenues of $12 million. The Bennetts will give an employee $500 for writing and having published a trade journal article. Trade journals go to the Bennetts' customers and have wide distribution. Typically a black-and-white ad costs about $1,500 for one full page.

If a magazine accepts an article from one of the Bennetts' employees, it usually runs two to three magazine pages. The Bennetts' employees have been published a dozen times in the last two years. Publication not only promotes the Bennetts' business but it gives employees recognition, encourages potential customers to call on the Bennetts, and helps them attract potential employees.

How Other Companies Use Publicity to Aid Recruiting

- The corporate employment manager of a major manufacturing firm published an article in a leading engineering publication last year, discussing the company's concern with improving career opportunities.

- A short article appeared in a computer trade journal recently, reporting that a major software corporation was about to launch a recruiting drive.

- A New York mail order company publicized an open house in local papers, noting in the press release that it had a policy of allowing part-time employees to choose work schedules that met their personal needs (it recruited more than 100 part-time workers for the Christmas rush).

- A journal sent to college placement executives carried an article by two human resource executives of a major telecommunications corporation, describing company studies on the managerial abilities of recently hired graduates.

Publishers have discovered that information relating to employment and careers gets high readership. This has made it easier to place articles and to get local newspaper coverage of recruiting events. Many newspapers publish career issues or supplements; some carry regular features on employment, including syndicated columns.

CREATIVE IDEAS FOR RECRUITING FOR THOSE HARD-TO-FILL JOBS: ADAPT ONE OF THESE APPROACHES TO YOUR COMPANY

Here are six relatively new recruiting ideas that provide companies with major sources of qualified labor.

Hiring the disabled
Hiring older workers
Hiring the dual-career couple
Job sharing
Using more temporary help instead of hiring permanent workers
Leasing instead of employing workers

All of these ideas have been used to some extent before—especially utilizing temporary help, but most of them are just now being tried in significant numbers. Although companies have said they do not discriminate against older workers or the handicapped, they certainly have not set any records in placing these groups on the job. Things are changing, however, and organizations, especially in the service industries, cannot find enough workers to fill their open positions. So, more and more companies are hiring handicapped people and older workers and they are finding these two groups to be committed and productive employees.

Nepotism used to be a dirty word in corporations. Policies forbid the hiring of husband and wife in the same company, and especially not in the same department. Those policies have fallen by the wayside in many companies today. They could not stay open without hiring relatives. In small towns where many people are related, manufacturing companies hire relatives and try to better manage any problems that arise out of a work relationship.

Why Hiring the Disabled Is Good Business

There are over thirty-five million Americans with some form of physical or mental disability. More than fifty percent of disabled people of working age who are not institutionalized are unemployed. Disabled people and their families constitute fifty percent of the poor in America. Over $110 billion is spent on disability-related costs, medical care, workers' compensation, and rehabilitation every year.

In the past, America has spent $10 on keeping disabled people dependent for every $1 spent on helping them get into the workforce and become self-sufficient. Many disabled people make good employees. The challenge is to recruit and hire the most capable and willing handicapped workers. The Xerox Corporation is one organization that does something concrete. When Gregory Kleisley, a Xerox employee, was permanently disabled in an accident at his home in Rochester, New York, Xerox provided sincere support and concern and told him that he would have a job when he was ready to go back to work. Kleisley is paralyzed from the waist down and confined to a wheelchair. Within five months of his tragic accident, Gregory Kleisley was back to work at Xerox.

How Disabled Employees Are Cracking the Managerial Barriers

There is a new trend in organizations. Disabled workers are starting to rise through the corporate ranks. In the past many employers refused to promote workers because they felt handicapped employees could not do the job, and that making handicapped accommodations to the workplace would be too costly. Some organizations felt that customers and employees would have an aversion to handicapped workers.

Larry E. Styron has received six promotions from American Express Company in New York City. He lost both legs in the Vietnam war. Michael R. Coleman who lost both hands in Vietnam uses prosthetic devices to do his job at IBM. General Motors, Hewlett Packard, and General Corporation of

Hartford, Connecticut are just a few companies that make concerted efforts to hire the handicapped.

Handicapped Litigation

Businesses that refuse to hire the handicapped may be facing more litigation from unhappy job applicants. The Rehabilitation Act of 1973 protects handicapped applicants and employees. Any company with a contract to sell at least $2,500 worth of goods and services to the Federal government must take affirmative action to employ and advance in employment qualified handicapped people. Hiring the disabled when they are qualified just makes good sense.

Screening in Handicapped Workers

Here are some ways to "screen in" qualified handicapped people.

- Ensure the job requirements don't "screen out" disabled workers.
- Ensure that all training programs include handicapped workers.
- Provide car or van pools for disabled workers or consider subsidizing a van pool.
- Ensure that your employment office is accessible to the handicapped, and that receptionists are trained in dealing with handicapped applicants.

Do's and Don'ts for Interviewing the Handicapped Applicant

The objective of any employment interview is to match an applicant's qualifications with the requirements of the job. Handicapped applicants are the same as any other applicants and don't require any special interviewing knowledge or skill. Look at the handicapped applicant as a person with abilities, strengths, and weaknesses, just like any other applicant.

- Handicapped people want to be treated normally. Don't avoid humorous situations that may occur.
- Don't tell the applicants you admire their courage. Don't sympathize with their problems—they don't want sympathy.
- Do maintain eye contact. Speak directly to the applicant, even if he or she is accompanied by another person.
- Do offer assistance if you see it is needed, but don't be oversolicitous.
- If you have trouble communicating, ask the applicant how you can best communicate in order to understand answers to your questions.

A Test for Executives—Do Your Job Requirements "Screen Out" the Handicapped?

Take the following test to see if you are inadvertently denying jobs to qualified handicapped applicants, and thereby denying your organization the opportunity to hire good people.

- Do job requirements screen out disabled people? Can such candidates qualify in spite of their disabilities?

- Do training programs offer full opportunities for handicapped workers?

- Do your disabled workers need car pools or special parking facilities?

- Is your firm's employment office accessible to handicapped job seekers?

- Have receptionists been given training in the basics of dealing with disabled visitors? They should know the rudiments of sign language, be able to guide blind people, and feel comfortable with people in wheelchairs.

- Have you developed contacts with local schools, colleges, and rehabilitation agencies? They can supply qualified disabled men and women for your job openings.

- Have you contributed equipment and machinery to local rehabilitation and training establishments so disabled people can get updated, hands-on training?

- Have you met with local educational and rehabilitation leaders to coordinate training programs with the company?

- Are all employee meetings fully accessible to handicapped workers? This includes ramps into meeting halls, sign interpreters for deaf employees and cassettes instead of printed material for blind men and women.

Eight Reasons for Employing Older Workers

Although most companies are making an effort to retrain employees whose skills have become obsolete, a survey of 322 human relations managers in the Fortune 500 companies polled recently shows that nearly half of them replace employees rather than retrain them. Corporations have not been quick to start retraining programs. This is changing, however, as demand for workers exceeds the readily available supply.

More than three-quarters of the companies reported they have been affected by technological or economic changes that have an impact on employees' job skills. An overwhelming eighty percent believe changes in required skills is an issue that will continue to influence the workplace. If organizations are to attract people they need in the next decade, retraining the workforce in America will have to become a serious priority.

A number of changes—in the workforce, within industries, in the attitudes of older workers, and in government policy—are making the workers more of an issue for corporations in the 1990s. First, it is clear that our society is aging. According to the United States Census Bureau, in 1982 about forty-nine million Americans were fifty and over (twenty-one percent of the population); by 2020 it is projected that there will be over ninety-one million in that age (thirty-one percent of the population).

The National Alliance of Business, provides the following information on new direction for an aging workforce.

Corporate managers have a number of different reasons for employing older workers in order to meet the human resource requirements of today's changing economy. Here are eight reasons why it is "good business" to attract and/or retain older workers.

1. Retaining Valued Employees   Perhaps first and foremost, employers often retain older workers because of their value to the business. This is particularly true if they have specialized skills (such as managerial, technical) that are difficult to replace. When there is a shortage of scientists and engineers, many companies will take steps to encourage the continued employment of their older workers in these professions. Predictably, many of the noteworthy employment initiatives for older workers have been targeted at white collar and knowledge workers in industries such as high tech. But, such initiatives can apply equally well to experienced, loyal, and productive workers in nontechnical positions. Job redesign, job transfer, and retraining programs are among the methods used to retain valued older workers.

2. Increasing Flexibility in the Workforce   For some time, particular firms have used older workers and others to help meet their labor demands during peak load seasons (retail stores during inventory and during Christmas, for example). However, one of the new realities of human resource management for virtually all firms in the changing economy is the challenge of coping with change—not just at certain predictable times of the year, but at all times. The stable era of a mass production economy with routine assembly line processes, steadily growing markets, slow moving technology, and limited foreign competition is gone. To avoid continuous swings in the size of their workforce, some companies maintain a smaller core workforce and use temporaries, part-time workers, job sharing arrangements, and other more flexible labor arrangements. Older workers and others who are willing to work in these new arrangements can be important resources for employers.

3. Stabilizing the Younger Workforce   For some companies with a younger workforce and high turnover, making use of older workers adds to stability. In some youth-dominated industries, such as the food services, older workers serve as role models for younger workers, demonstrating a strong work ethic, loyalty to the firm, and stability.

4. Supplementing the Younger Workforce   Demographics show that the number of young people entering the workforce will decline over the coming decades. Industries traditionally reliant on younger workers may need to adjust their recruitment targets, concentrating more on the expanding older labor pool.

5. Maintaining a Desired Public Image   Given the increased attention on issues of aging in recent years and the growing political and economic impact of older people, some firms have made efforts to retain or recruit older workers in order to maintain a positive image with the general public, in the communities where they do business, and with their own workforce. Firms using older worker options tend to be seen as more socially responsible and employee-oriented.

6. Attracting Older Consumers   Another increasingly important consideration for many companies is the attraction of older consumers to their products and services. There is an increased recognition of the economic capacity of older people (those fifty-five and over account for over one-fourth of all consumer purchases) and evidence of new strategies in product development, service, and marketing to tap that heretofore overlooked market. Thus, some industries, such as tourism (older Americans are a major part of the travel market), are recruiting and utilizing more older workers in the hope of attracting more older consumers to their products and services.

7. Responding to Government Policies   Some companies (approximately one-third according to a recent National Commission for Employment Policy study) report that involvement with older workers stems from their attempts to respond to government policies such as the Age Discrimination in Employment Act (ADEA), changes in the Employment Retirement Income Security Act (ERISA), or legislation eliminating mandatory retirement age. With the increase in the number of age discrimination suits, firms are becoming more sensitive in their management of older workers.

8. Gaining Experience in Managing the Older Workforce of the Future   Given the changing demographics of the workforce and the maturing of the "baby boom" generation, it is clear that we will have an older workforce in the decades ahead. Some firms—especially those with a long-term planning orientation—may seek to prepare for the future by gaining experience today in employing and managing older workers.

Figure 7-3

CIVILIAN LABOR FORCE BY SEX AND AGE
(Number and Participation Rate)

Men	Number (millions)	Participation Rate
45-54	9.8	91.2
55–64	7.1	70.2
65–69	1.1	27.4
70–74	.5	17.2
Women		
45–54	7.1	61.6
55–64	4.9	41.8
65–69	.7	15.1
70–74	.3	7.5

Source: Handbook of Labor Statistics, U.S. Bureau of Labor Statistics

Figure 7-4

PROJECTED CIVILIAN LABOR FORCE TRENDS,
1982 to 2000, By Age
(Number of Persons and as a Percent of Total)

All Ages	1982	1990	2000
16+	109.6 (100%)	122.3 (100%)	134.1 (100%)
18–24	21.4 (19.5%)	19.1 (15.6%)	19.7 (14.6%)
25–34	30.5 (27.8%)	35.0 (28.6%)	30.2 (22.5%)
35-44	22.3 (20.3%)	31.2 (25.5%)	36.4 (27.1%)
45–54	16.7 (15.2%)	19.3 (15.8%)	27.8 (20.7%)
55+	14.9 (13.6%)	14.1 (11.5%)	15.2 (11.3%)

Source: Howard N. Fullerton, Jr., "The 1995 Labor Force: A First Look," *Monthly Labor Review*, December 1980.

Figure 7-5

SOME STEPS FOR EMPLOYERS TO FOLLOW IN DEVELOPING OLDER WORKER EMPLOYMENT POLICIES

(1) Conduct an age analysis of the company workforce:
   ▶ Examine workforce structure by age to develop an age profile of the workforce.
   ▶ Examine workforce dynamics by age (e.g., hiring, placement, promotion, retirement).

(2) Review public policies and statutes:
   ▶ Age discrimination laws.
   ▶ Mandatory retirement and related benefit laws.
   ▶ Pension and Social Security regulations.

(3) Review hiring, promotion, and performance review policies and practices:
   ▶ Examine hiring standards and procedures.
   ▶ Study promotion patterns.
   ▶ Develop age-neutral performance review systems.

(4) Review training and career development opportunities:
   ▶ Get feedback from workers.
   ▶ Review counseling mechanisms.
   ▶ Examine training and development programs.

(5) Develop more flexible retirement and retention policies:
   ▶ Review retirement and pension policies.
   ▶ Explore alternative work arrangements such as part time, flextime, jobsharing, and phased retirement.

(6) Educate management on age factors:
   ▶ Executive management.
   ▶ Line supervisors and middle management.

Source: Adapted from "Aging and the Work Force: Human Resource Strategies," by Julia French, consultant to the Special Committee on Aging, U.S. Senate (1981).

There are a number of reasons why it makes good business sense to attract or retain older workers as part of a company's workforce. The extent to which future progress regarding the employment of older workers is made will depend on the degree to which corporations are better able to understand the changes making older workers an issue and to see how older workers can help them achieve corporate objectives.

Case Example: Retirees Fill Temporary Positions at Travelers Insurance

Travelers Insurance Companies usually need 120 to 150 temporary workers every week in the Hartford, Connecticut, home office. The company used to call temporary agencies automatically. Since 1981, however, supervisors first call Traveler's Retirees Job Bank. More than fifty percent of the time, Travelers retirees are prepared to fill the temporary positions.

The job bank is one element of the company's Older Americans Programs, which was instituted under Morrison Beach, chairman of Traveler's Executive Committee.

Case Example: Retiree Fills a New Management Position

Jerry Stanyer owns the Wedding Specialist, a bridal shop in Wichita, Kansas. Last year he wanted to open a new kind of store but he had trouble finding the right person to manage the business.

"I think we were looking in the wrong place," he says. "Newspaper ads didn't help; neither did the employment service."

So Stanyer called the Senior Employment Program, an employment effort now funded under the Job Training Partnership Act. Carolyn Brozek, the job placement specialist, knew just the right person for the job. Betty Lou Albright, who had been in retail sales with a major Wichita department store for years, was laid off when the store closed. She had looked everywhere for a job and had been repeatedly turned down because of her age. But her age and experience were just what Stanyer needed.

"I wanted someone really competent. I didn't want a rookie. It was a management job, and I didn't have time to train someone. The person had to be experienced."

Experience was imperative because Stanyer was branching out, opening a new kind of store—a bridal and formal fabrics shop. It was a new concept in the Wichita market, and Stanyer needed someone who could make it work.

Albright stepped into the job at full stride; going to trade markets, ordering fabrics, controlling inventory, maintaining sales, and everything else.

Business-Oriented Organizations that Address Older Worker Issues

American Management Association
135 W. 50th Street
New York, NY 10020
(212) 586-8100

National Alliance of Business
1015 15th Street, N.W.
Washington, DC 20005
(202) 457-0040

Business Roundtable
200 Park Avenue, Suite 222
New York, NY 10166
(212) 682-6370

Chamber of Commerce of the
United States
Employee Benefits and Policy Center
1615 H Street, N.W.
Washington, DC 20062

The Conference Board
845 Third Avenue
New York, NY 10022
(212) 759-0900

National Association of
Manufacturers
1776 F Street, N.W.
Washington, DC 20006
(202) 626-3700

International Society of Preretirement Planners
2400 South Downing Street
West Chester, IL 60153
(312) 531-9140

National Alliance of Business Clearinghouse Database

The National Alliance of Business is a clearinghouse and one of the best sources of information on this subject. The NAB Clearinghouse Database is an excellent source of information about the best programs, strategies, and reference materials that can help your company evaluate its need for older workers and structure its approach to this important issue.

For in-depth personalized research services on this or any other employment-related information, contact User Services, NAB Clearinghouse, 15th Street, N.W., Washington, DC 20005 (202) 289-2910.

Recruiting and/or Relocating the Dual-Career Couple

Another specific recruiting problem is the dual-career couple, which will make up another large segment of the workforce in the future.

The pressures on working couples have brought dramatic changes in the way they relate to their jobs, the way they run their homes and family life, and the demands they make on their employers. The emergence of the dual-career couple has also brought a dramatic change in the way companies treat employees, and in the policies and procedures used to manage them. Companies used to enforce nepotism policies (not hiring relatives to work in the same company). Now they need good people and are more likely to hire the dual-career couple.

Companies are starting to realize that they need to take a sensitive and flexible approach to helping the dual-career couple who frequently work in high level professional or managerial positions. They are adapting more flexible attitudes in managing couples, and in communicating with married employees who work in the same company.

Five Areas in Which You Can Prevent Potential Conflict in Recruiting Dual-Career Couples

- Do selective recruiting aimed at achieving a good fit for each person in each job. Try to match the people who want to stay put with stay-put jobs. Find out each person's strengths and weaknesses ahead of time in order to create the most effective job match.

- Be sure to give the employee and spouse a realistic job overview. Whether you are employing one or both people it is important to give them both a thorough overview of the company and its culture.

- If you are employing only one person, offer to help the spouse find work in the same city.

- If one employee will have increased travel responsibilities in the new job, be sure the spouse knows that and that you can work out any conflict the increased travel may create.

- Address issues surrounding promotion if the new job provides a promotion for one and not the other.

Transplacement: A New Employee Benefit

There are also important economic considerations in the relocation of dual-career couples. A new employee benefit offered by most large organizations today is called "Transplacement." In order to encourage an employee to relocate, the company offers job hunting benefits to a working spouse. Both employees in a dual career relocation receive the same benefits in most organizations, but this new benefit of transplacement is provided even to the spouse of an employee who may not be acutally working for the same company.

Economic Considerations in Dual-Career Relocations

Potential Advantages	*Potential Disadvantages*
Salary increase for the relocating employee.	Salary decrease for the relocating spouse.
Salary increase for the relocating spouse.	Loss of spouse's salary for X amount of time.
Lower cost of living in new area.	Higher cost of living in new area.
Lower cost of housing in new area.	Higher cost of housing in new area.
Better schools.	Benefits provided at increased cost to employee.

Benefits provided at no or lesser cost.	Fewer benefits provided.
Additional benefits, such as transplacement.	Loss of spouse's benefits coverage.
	Poorer schools for children, possible need for private schools.
	Cost of job-hunting for spouse where company does not provide transplacement benefit.

How to Handle the Employment of Related Persons

When you are hiring dual-career couples or other related persons you will experience a great deal of controversy unless you spell out your policies and procedures. A company can lose good people by not allowing spouses or relatives to work together, but the problems arise when policies are not articulated, and where spouses or relatives might report to each other.

The most workable situation seems to be where relatives are allowed to work in the same company but not to report to each other. Many companies go a step further and do not allow relatives to work in the same department. Following is a suggested policy for employment of related persons.

This is a hiring policy for persons related by residence, blood, or marriage that takes into account current national legal trends in human resource practices. It is suggested that you use this policy with necessary adaptations to make it reflect your company's specific management philosophy, organizational needs, and size. Because state laws vary and may affect legal requirements, it is also recommended that you become familiar with your state laws on this subject.

Sample Hiring Policy for Related Persons

The ABC Company will employ persons who are related by residence, blood, or marriage to an employee, provided the individual possesses the necessary qualifications. However, related employees will not be given work assignments that require one related member to direct, review, or process the work of another, or that permit one related member to have access to the personnel records of the other. If one employee marries another, both may retain their positions provided they do not work in the same department, are not under the supervision of each other, and neither occupies a position that has influence over the other's employment, promotion, salary, and other personnel decisions. The company may employ related persons for temporary positions provided a clear understanding exists that the employment relationship is temporary and will not necessarily lead to full-time employment.

For the purposes of this policy, a blood relative means: spouse, mother and father, mother- and father-in-law, sons and daughters, brothers and sisters, sons- and daughters-in-law, and aunts and uncles, nieces, and nephews.

Job Sharing: Making the Most of Two for the Price of One

Talk to almost any working woman with small children and you will hear, "I love my career, but I wish I could spend more time with the children and my husband." More and more women are doing just that today.

At Rocky Mountain Energy Company in Denver, two women share one computer programming job and both are happy with the arrangement. A husband and wife team of professors at William Gustavus Adolphus College in St. Peter, Minnesota divided a single position. She teaches one course and he teaches two in the religion department. Their salaries are prorated to reflect the difference in their teaching loads.

Job sharing implies a career orientation, a labor-force attachment, and a potential for upward mobility that in the past has not been associated with part-time work. It is a hot new trend away from the traditional forty-hour week. Employers like the idea, because they get two sets of talents or abilities for the price of one. At TRW in California, two people share one personnel recruiting position. There is a great deal of travel in the job and where one person got burned out in the past, two people now enjoy sharing the travel responsibilities. Companies also like the job continuity; if one person leaves, the second one can still do the job and train a new employee.

As with any new concept, however, there are pros and cons, and a good job-sharing program requires sound planning and good communications between the job sharers and the supervisor.

Positions where job sharing works best have one or more of the following characteristics.

- require a broad range of skills
- alternate periods of intense activity with slack periods
- require creativity
- are high-pressured enough to produce employee burnout
- require more than eight-hour-a-day coverage

Advantages and Disadvantages of Job Sharing

As in any innovative work concept, there are advantages and disadvantages. The Human Resource Manager needs to discuss both with the managers and supervisors in the departments where job sharing is a possibility.

Advantages

Job sharing can increase productivity in some instances.

Job sharing creates a wider pool of applicants.

Reduces costs in some instances.

Job sharing allows a mother to spend more time with her children, so she doesn't feel that she is abandoning them.

There is less job burnout.

Two people can sometimes come up with better ideas for doing the job than one person.

When one employee is on vacation, the other one can fill in.

Two people are trained on the job so if one leaves for good, the other one can do the whole job until a new person is hired and then train the new person.

Disadvantages

If the company provides benefits for part-time workers, it is necessary to provide two people with benefits instead of only one. Costs can increase.

It takes longer to learn a job if you only work part-time on it.

It's difficult to complete big jobs so one employee frequently has to leave work for the other, but workload overlap is usually understood in the job-sharing arrangement.

It can be more difficult to supervise two workers. It takes better communication skills, and specific methods are used to communicate between shifts.

Outside Temporary Help Agencies

One of the fastest growing personnel businesses today is the temporary help business. New companies are sprouting up all over the country; competition is fierce for large temporary help contracts.

Companies that downsized in the last three years are now using temporary help instead of hiring more permanent workers, and it doesn't look like the temporary help business is going to slow down any time soon.

The newest wrinkle in temporary help agencies are the older worker temporary businesses who are providing companies with experienced retired workers in specialized areas.

If you are hiring temporary or part-time employees and putting them on your company payroll, instead of using an outside temporary help agency there are some specific legal and administrative issues to consider.

Legal and Administrative Considerations of Using Temporary Help

Employers are not required to give any non-statutory benefits to part-time or temporary employees *except* enrollment in a company-offered qualified pension plan *if* the part-time or temporary employee works 1,000 or more hours per twelve-month period, according to the Employee Retirement Income Security Act of 1974.

There are certain administrative considerations of which you should be aware, however. Ask yourself these questions.

- How does the company define part-time or temporary?

- If benefits are granted, are the costs and coverages the same? Is coverage based on the number of hours worked?

- What are the procedures a part-time or temporary employee must follow to apply for a full-time position?

- If part-time or temporary employees become full-time, does prior company service count toward benefit eligibility?

- How can temporary employment status be extended when the duration of the assignment is exceeded?

Employee Leasing: Wave of the Future?

Some people say it is a revolutionary concept and that it will be a traditional business practice in the future. It is catching on, especially in blue collar and hourly worker jobs. There is a lot of misinformation and some skepticism about employee leasing. It may be a good idea, but it has to be closely administered and seems to work better for some businesses than others.

How Employee Leasing works: It works best for small business owners—probably 125 employees or less. By using an employee leasing firm, a small business person can eliminate the hassles of payroll, personnel administration, and labor relations.

Basically, a business person terminates employees en masse, then leases them back from a third party, which becomes responsible for all administrative and employee management tasks. The business owner retains the ultimate right to supervise the workforce on a daily basis and to hire and fire when desired. The company writes one check each pay period to cover payroll and benefits, plus the leasing fee. The leasing company then pays the employees, sometimes provides benefits, and handles hiring and firing at the direction of the business owner.

Most small companies cannot afford to provide medical or other benefits, but the leasing company, which usually has many companies and employees on its payroll, can negotiate with the HMO or an insurance company for group rates and can provide benefits at a much lower cost than the small businessperson can.

National media estimate that perhaps 75,000 employees work for 275 leasing firms nationwide, but there are no formal published statistics. Leasing firms have been around for years, but they didn't really take off until the Tax Equity and Fiscal Responsibility Act of 1982 was passed permitting employers to shift employee pension plans to qualified leasing companies and legally create a pension plan, as well as a personal tax shelter for the business owner.

The Employee Leasing Concept

Employee leasing takes the concept of contract labor one step further, and, according to Cormen Arno, private consultant in employee leasing, "Employee leasing is a service whose time has come . . . in the next 10 years 28 million employees will be leased."

What Worries Small Business?

Problems with workers and government are major concerns.

Finding competent help	74%
Federal tax forms and laws	71%
Motivating employees	69%
State/local tax forms and laws	68%
Workmen's compensation	57%
Competition from large firms	57%
Slow payments from others	55%
Federal health/safety laws	51%
Long-term interest rates	50%
Shoplifting and theft	45%
Money losses	43%
Short-term interest rates	43%

Personnel and paperwork rate highest on the list of small-business headaches, according to a national survey of 1,000 firms by the Heller/Roper Small Business Barometer. Most respondents said employees and tax forms pose more problems than actual business concerns such as competition, customer payments, and deliveries from suppliers.

Employee Leasing Services That Are Normally Offered

Administrative

Payroll Accounting:

- Calculating Wages and Overtime
- Issuing Paychecks

- Maintaining Payroll Records
- Time Records
- Federal, State, and City Tax Deposits

Required Deductions:

- Social Security
- Federal Withholding Taxes
- Federal Unemployment Insurance
- State Withholding Taxes
- State Unemployment Insurance
- Occupational Privilege Tax (City Head Tax)
- Any Health Benefits, etc. (Optional)

Tax Form Preparation and Record Keeping:

- W-2s
- W-3s
- W-4s
- 1099s
- 940s
- 941s
- 8109s

Additional Administrative Areas:

- Group Health Insurance
- Group Life Insurance
- Sick Leave Policies
- Vacation Policies
- Continuing Education Programs
- Personnel Policies
- Workmen's Compensation Claims
- Unemployment Claims

Companies that Use Employee Leasing

Bill Palmer is a property supervisor who oversees several apartment buildings in Denver. He supervises over fifty people and a yearly payroll of $600,000. Bill is a leased employee. So are the fifty people that work for him. They worked for the original property owner, but now work for a local leasing company. They still report to the original owner, but they have benefits and are paid by the leasing company.

John Doherty is the owner of ProSeal, Inc., a small company in New York City, who discharged all employees and leased them back from an outside leasing company.

Bartex Construction Company in Dallas terminated all of its construction workers at several locations and leased them back from Omnistaff, one of the country's largest leasing firms.

Pros and Cons of Employee Leasing

Some personnel people think leasing is a "cop out" for good personnel management. If employees are a company's most important asset, why would you let someone else manage them? Do employees feel alienated when they are terminated and picked up by another company? Here are just some of the pros and cons.

Pros

- No labor problems—the leasing company has to handle any labor problems.
- No recruiting and selection, or checking an employee out.
- The Tax Reform Act of 1986 (TRA '86) has changed some of the regulations regarding benefits for leased employees. TRA '86 provides the following guidelines for testing nondiscriminatory benefits coverage:

If leased employees are to be excluded from benefit coverage tests, the leasing organization must contribute 10% of pay, and cover all its employees who earn $1,000 or more in any one of the last four plan years.

- In addition, the company may not exclude leased employees if twenty percent or more of the non-highly compensated employees providing substantial services to the company are leased.
- Small companies can get decent health coverage that they couldn't afford on their own. They put themselves and their employees on the payroll of the leasing company and in most instances have some benefits.

Cons

- The leasing company has to recruit and hire all the people.
- The paperwork is significant for the leasing company.
- Cons for the client company are:

- It does make it more difficult to make personnel changes, and
- The leasing company is normally in another location so there is a delay in processing paperwork.

Renting Math Whizzes: A New Idea

Currently investment bankers hire "quants" or "rocket scientists" who are academics highly trained in mathematics and ask them to apply their quantitative skills to Wall Street deals. Now it seems that some banks that have quants on their full-time payroll are making them available for hire to outside companies.

At least one or two of these highly trained quants are thinking of opening their own independent "quant shops" and renting themselves out to organizations that need their specific quantitative abilities. If your organization needs highly trained scientists that command high salaries but are only used to full capacity at certain times of the year, consider quant consultants, or contact your local bank and ask if they have people on their staff that they could consider renting for specific jobs.

SUCCESSFUL INTERVIEWING TECHNIQUES

Just about anything that can be written or said about employment interviewing has been put into a book or taught in a management course. There are not a lot of new or creative ideas in the interviewing process. There are, however, ways that you can structure the interviewing process to make it more comfortable and productive for you personally. The key to success in interviewing is to develop your own style and to make that style comfortable for you and for the person being interviewed.

Interview Checklist: Twenty-one Pointers for Developing Your Own Style

As you gain experience, you will develop your own interviewing style. The following items should prove useful in this development stage.

1. Prepare the interview. Study the application form and any other information about the applicant before beginning the interview. In this way you can plan to explore those areas that require special attention and skip over questions already answered. This review helps structure the interview and saves valuable time.

2. Set the stage. It is important that the interview be conducted in quiet surroundings with a minimum of distractions. If possible, a private office should be used and interruptions avoided.

3. Establish rapport with the interviewee. Open with small talk that

eases tension and makes the applicant feel welcome and comfortable. Here is a word of caution, however. Some interviewers go beyond the bounds of rapport and become too friendly. Their objectivity is then biased by personal considerations. While it is all very well to discuss skiing, you don't want to let the fact that the person is a skier bias your thinking about the individual's job qualification.

4. Conduct the interview. A good interview progresses from non-threatening, job-related questions to more personal and what could be considered threatening interests, and education—all matters that the applicant expects, and progresses to more personality-oriented questions.

5. Encourage the candidate to talk. In the fact-finding stages of the interview, it is the applicant who has the facts—and the interviewer who wants the information. So, the candidate should be encouraged to talk—and the interviewer to listen, ideally seventy-five percent or more of the time.

6. Follow up the hunches or unusual statements. If an interviewee says, "Well, he was 'that kind' of guy and I just don't get along with 'that kind of guy'" ask more questions. You want to find out if his comment is just socialized hot air or a potential problem in attitude.

7. Learn how to play detective when you interview. Pursue an unusual comment and ask nonjudgmental questions.

8. Be ready to reveal aspects of yourself during the interview. Don't monopolize the interview talking about yourself, but when you share one or two things, you develop more rapport and warmth. If you can open up a bit, you will be more likely to open up the interviewee. There is a psychological side to one-on-one exchanges.

9. Show energy and ethusiasm. A job candidate looks at your enthusiasm and style and judges the company according to your attitude. A terse formal style will not make an applicant comfortable, and it will not illicit open responses.

10. Ask open-ended questions. You cannot illicit much information by asking questions that can be answered yes or no.

11. Watch body language. If a person tenses up on a question, that might indicate some hedging is included in the answer and you should pursue further questioning.

12. Take adequate time. It takes time to conduct a thorough interview. As much as one to two hours may be needed to review the background of a managerial prospect. An inexperienced clerical

applicant or a truck driver, on the other hand, might be interviewed in twenty minutes. The cardinal rule in all cases is to take whatever time is needed to get all the facts required for making a good decision.

13. Use a conversational approach. While the interview should follow a plan, specific questions should be phrased in a natural, conversational way. Sometimes, there are good reasons for varying the sequence of the interview. As applicants vary in knowledge and experience, it stands to reason that the interview approach will also vary to meet changing circumstances. The interviewer should, however, remain in control; it is dangerous to let an applicant "run away" with the interview and, much like the résumé, present only his or her story. Direct questions may be needed to pinpoint the specific reasons underlying such common generalities as "no opportunity for advancement," which is often given as the reason for leaving a previous place of employment.

14. Avoid leading questions. A leading question gives the respondent a cue to what the audience expects to hear. Questions should be asked in such a way that the applicant must provide a narrative answer.

15. Emphasize what is important. The employment interview should focus on work history in particular, and what the applicant has done in general, in order to predict successfully what the applicant is likely to do in the future. Past behavior is the best predictor of future performance. Most of the interview time should be devoted to experience and education.

16. Avoid moral judgments. An interviewer must suppress personal feelings about the behavior, morals, and standards of an applicant. Nor should the interviewer assume that he or she is a counselor whose role in life is "helping" applicants or criticizing their pattern of life. Instead, it is the purpose of the interviewer to find out what the applicant has done—and then, later, to decide whether or not the applicant meets the requirements of the position.

17. Take notes. It is necessary to take notes if the material collected by the interviewer is to be evaluated by someone else. But even if the interviewer is to make the employment decision, the information provided by the applicant should be recorded. Not only does this help the interviewer analyze the data after the applicant has gone, but it also helps the individual be thorough and systematic in covering all important aspects of the applicant's background. Few candidates will be disturbed by the notetaking process. Notetaking,

however, should be limited, with the interviewer maintaining as much eye contact as possible and listening closely to what is being said.

18. Obtain precise information. It is human nature for candidates to fill out the application blank in a way that makes them look "good." Likewise, the applicant will not call attention to periods of unemployment, involuntary terminations, and other negative information. For this reason, it is important that the interviewer find out what the applicant has done by accounting for all the time the applicant has worked. Reasons for leaving jobs must be probed carefully. Then, if contradictions between the application form and the interview are obtained, it is necessary to examine the reason for the inconsistency. It is unfortunate, but true, that a significant number of applicants will provide false information—much of which can be uncovered in a careful interview.

19. Listen with the third ear. The skillful interviewer listens to what is really being communicated, not just what is being said. It is estimated that a person can think seven times as fast as normal speech; an alert interviewer will use that time to analyze in depth what the interviewee is saying. Good listening is an active, not a passive, process. One can become very perceptive in the interview by listening to the undertones of the conversation.

20. Sell the job. As noted above, the interview is a two-way street. After the interviewer has the necessary information from the applicant, it is only fair to discuss the job and the organization. It is best to hold this discussion at the end of the employment interview, to avoid the applicant's slanting answers to meet the qualifications of the job. There is another reason as well: If the interviewer is convinced that an applicant is highly desirable, the interviewer should make every effort to interest the individual in joining the organization. If, on the other hand, the interviewer believes the applicant is not qualified or qualifiable for employment, then he or she should not try to "sell" the candidate. Never "oversell" applicants. After they get into the job they might be disappointed and leave.

21. Conclude the interview. After sufficient data have been exchanged between the interviewer and the applicant, and both are satisfied they have the information needed, the interviewer should then discuss the next step in the selection process. This step may be a meeting between the applicant and the prospective supervisor to determine the personal chemistry between them and to discuss the technical requirements of the job. If the applicant is not to receive

further consideration for employment, he or she should be notified—graciously and tactfully—as soon as you know you are not going to hire the person.

Questioning Techniques for Getting Useful Answers

To obtain the necessary answers from an applicant, you must use good questioning techniques.

Unstructured question.   Cannot be answered by a "yes" or "no"—will enable the applicant to speak openly and help the interviewer to better obtain the underlying reason for particular views on the part of the applicant. Questions beginning with Who, What, When, Where, Why, and How will elicit an unstructured answer.

Structured question.   Places the applicant in a position to answer either with a "yes" or "no." An elaborated answer is not necessarily given.

> Example: Q. Did you like your last job?
>   A. Yes.

Unstructured question combined with structured question.   A structured question may be followed by an unstructured question to help clarify the applicant's feelings, pinpoint a particular fact, or obtain additional information.

> Example: Q. Did you like your last job?
>   A. Yes.
>   Q. What in particular did you like?
>   A. Well, . . .

Use of silence.   A brief pause between questions allows the applicant more time to better elaborate on an answer if he or she desires.

Reflective feelings.   Interpretation by the interviewer of the applicant's statement as to content and feelings. Phrases beginning with: "It seems that . . ." or "It sounds like . . ." reflect feelings.

Active listening.   Repetition or restatement of what the applicant has said by the interviewer usually in the form of a question. Applicant is then aware of the interviewer's interest.

> Example: Q. What did you think of your previous employer?
>   A. He was all right, but a bit overbearing.
>   Q. Overbearing?
>   A. Well, he . . .

Assertions of understanding.   Neutral phrases that will place the applicant in a position to elaborate on his or her answer. These phrases might include: "I understand," "Uh-huh," or "Yes, I see."

Sample Interview Questions

1. One of the things we want to talk about today is your experience. Would you tell me about your present job?

2. What do you feel were your major responsibilities in your last job?

3. In your last job, what duties did you spend most of your time on?

4. What were some of the things about your job that you found difficult to do, and why do you feel this way about them?

5. How do you feel about the progress you have made with your present company?

6. In what ways do you feel your present/past job has developed you to take on even greater responsibilities?

7. What are some of the reasons you had for leaving your last job?

8. What were some of the things you particularly liked about your last job?

9. Most jobs have "pluses" and "minuses." What were some of the "minuses" in your last job?

10. Do you consider your progress on the job respresentative of your ability, and why?

11. What do you feel is a satisfactory attendance record?

12. In what areas do you feel your supervisor in your past job could have done a better job?

13. What are some of the things your boss did that you particularly liked or disliked?

14. How do you feel your supervisor rated your job performance?

15. What did your supervisor feel you did particularly well? What were major criticisms of your work? How do you feel about these criticisms?

16. With what kind of people do you like working? With what kind of people do you find it most difficult to work? How have you successfully worked with this type of person?

17. What are some of the things that are important to you in a job and why?

18. What are some of the things you would like to avoid in a job and why?

19. How do you feel your last company treated its employees?

20. How would you describe your supervisor? Present or past.

21. If you joined our organization, where do you think you could make your best contribution? Why?

22. Looking into the future, what changes and new developments do you anticipate in your particular field?

23. In general how do you describe yourself—your skills and personal abilities?

24. What do you regard as some of your shortcomings?

25. What traits or qualities do you most appreciate in a supervisor?

26. What do you think has contributed to your career success up to the present time?

27. What disappointments and setbacks have you had in your life?

28. What are your long-range career goals and objectives?

29. Are you currently active in any social or professional clubs and organizations? Any volunteer activities?

30. In what outside activities do you participate?

Inappropriate Questions to Ask Applicants

Questions seeking the following information are illegal and cannot be asked of an applicant before he or she is hired.

1. date of birth
2. maiden name
3. previous married name
4. marital status
5. name of spouse
6. spouse's occupation and length of time on the job
7. spouse's place of employment
8. number of children and their ages
9. arrest record
10. convictions may be asked, but you cannot refuse employment before they were convicted unless it is a bona fide job qualification
11. if child care has been arranged for the children
12. reasons that would prevent an applicant from maintaining employment
13. ancestry
14. national origin (color)
15. age
16. sex
17. religion

18. affiliations with: a) communist party, b) union
19. garnishment of wages

It should be kept in mind that much of the above is the type of information necessary for Personnel records and employee benefit programs once the individual is employed. However, the point that must be understood is that the information is obtained *after* employment and, therefore, can have no bearing on the employment decisions.

Inappropriate Questions to Ask Candidates for Promotion

Again, the same type of information I have indicated above is clearly illegal to seek from any candidate being considered for promotion and/or transfer within the company. As the employee has a work history with the company, discussions with the current supervisor, and review of the Personnel records as to work performance and potential, are far more valuable in evaluating an employee's qualifications than any of the above information. In other words, there is clearly no purpose served by seeking this information, and the interviewer should concentrate on relating the employee's qualifications, past performance, and potential ability to meet the job needs.

Errors Commonly Made by the Interviewer

1. asking leading questions
2. making decisions too early in the interview
3. following a stereotyped pattern of investigations, without recognition of individual differences
4. lacking knowledge of precise job requirements
5. letting pressure of duties shorten interview time
6. doing more talking than they should
7. failing to direct the interview and thereby wasting time
8. becoming overenthusiastic about a person during the initial interview
9. not knowing what to look for
10. tending to be overly influenced by individual factors, rather than considering the applicant as a whole
11. lacking skill in asking questions, in motivating the applicant, in probing, and in recording interview data

Other criticisms made of interviews and the mistakes that are frequently made in an interview include:

a. allowing one undesirable factor to influence their judgment
b. lack of preparation for the interview

c. under the pressure to fill a job, making up their minds before the facts are in, and then setting up interviews so that the candidate is selected

d. a tendency to become too routine, instead of adapting each interview to the individual

e. being interviewed by the candidate instead of doing the interviewing.

The following employment interviewing guide should assist you in the interview process.

Checklist for Use in Evaluating Interview Data

Consider the following personality traits of each applicant. Items preceded by a minus sign represent examples of unfavorable findings with respect to a given trait; those preceded by a plus sign represent examples of favorable traits. The column on the right is provided for your use in rating applicants.

	Applicant	
	+	−
PERSONAL FLEXIBILITY		
+ Has shown an ability to handle a number of job assignments simultaneously.	____	____
− Applicant's approach reflects a tendency to be structured— may be a perfectionist.	____	____
+ Seems to like jobs involving contact with many types of people and diverse job situations.	____	____
+ Appears to be flexible in personal approach.	____	____
PERSONAL MATURITY		
− Has tendency to rationalize failures.	____	____
+ Has learned to accept limitations.	____	____
− Displays chronic dissatisfaction with jobs, working conditions, peers, and superiors.	____	____
+ Has career goals and is optimistic about them.	____	____
+ Has mature outlook on life and work in general.	____	____
EMOTIONAL STABILITY		
+ Has shown an ability to maintain composure in face of adversity or frustration.	____	____
+ Has been able to maintain emotional balance in face of trying personal circumstances.	____	____
− Has had problems with bosses or teachers on more than one occasion.	____	____
− Is unable to deal with others' shortcomings.	____	____
− It appears the person allows emotions to rule business decisions.	____	____

ABILITY TO BE TACTFUL
+ The manner in which the person phrased remarks during
   interview reflects tact and consideration.   ———   ———
− In discussing relationships with subordinates, the person
   seems to reflect a lack of consideration and sensitivity.   ———   ———
+ The person is a good listener.   ———   ———
− Applicant "bad mouthed" previous employer.   ———   ———

IS A TEAM PLAYER
+ It appears the person has operated successfully as a
   member of a team.   ———   ———
− Is strongly motivated to be the "star."   ———   ———
+ Seems to place the accomplishments of the group ahead of
   personal ego.   ———   ———
− Displays poor interpersonal skills and shows tendency
   toward intolerance of others.   ———   ———

DISPLAYS FOLLOW-THROUGH
− Changed jobs too often.
+ Once the person starts a job, seems to hang in there.
− Interview indicates that the person starts more things than
   can logically be completed.   ———   ———
+ Has achieved one or more career goals.   ———   ———
+ Appears to follow through.   ———   ———

SHOWS INITIATIVE
+ Has demonstrated ability to operate successfully without
   close supervision.   ———   ———
+ Seems to have reached out for increasing responsibility.   ———   ———
+ Evidence indicates the person is a self-starter.   ———   ———
− Seems to dislike situations that are unstructured.   ———   ———
− When in a rut in a job, seems unable to leave a dead-end
   situation.   ———   ———

SHOWS ASSERTIVENESS
+ Seems willing to take a stand on what is right.   ———   ———
− Might not be sufficiently demanding of subordinates when
   the situation calls for it.   ———   ———
− Seems overly concerned with the feelings of others.   ———   ———
+ Has a positive assertive nature.   ———   ———

PERSONALITY TRAITS
+ Personality has considerable impact.   ———   ———
− Tends to be introverted.   ———   ———
+ Has an outgoing, personable style.   ———   ———
− Is ego-oriented.   ———   ———
+ Displays a great deal of empathy and sensitivity.   ———   ———

IS CONSCIENTIOUS
+ When necessary, would work overtime.   ——   ——
– Appears to be a clock-watcher.   ——   ——
– Shows a conscientious nature.   ——   ——

IS SELF-CONFIDENT
+ Reflects a realistic appraisal of abilities.   ——   ——
+ General manner and style reflect poise.   ——   ——
– Does not have sufficient confidence to discuss shortcomings.   ——   ——
– Appears overconfident and boastful.   ——   ——
– Lacks a sense of self-confidence in the interview process.   ——   ——

SHOWS HONESTY AND OPENNESS
+ Is willing to give credit when credit is due.   ——   ——
– Tends to exaggerate own accomplishments.   ——   ——
– Stories seem to be inconsistent in terms of other statements
   or findings.   ——   ——
– Bragged about "pulling a fast one."   ——   ——
+ Was willing to discusss unfavorable aspects of or experience
   in interview.   ——   ——

                                                          TOTAL   ——   ——

These twelve items are just a few elements that can be used effectively to assist in evaluating an applicant. Not all of them pertain to every applicant, but they will trigger ideas that will get you thinking about specific qualities you need for a particular job. You will come up with other questions and be able to make evaluations as you become more proficient at the interviewing process. *Remember:* Half of the interviewing is *listening*. When you listen to an applicant, you glean far more information than when you are *talking* to an applicant!

It is helpful to write a summary of your feelings immediately after the interview has taken place. Concern yourself with the most important findings in terms of the applicant's overall qualifications.

Interviewing is an art—as you get better at it, you can relax and enjoy the interaction and the personal give and take that makes the effort worthwhile. It is worthwhile when you find yourself hiring the best people for your job, and when your "batting average" improves over time.

PRE-EMPLOYMENT SCREENING AND TESTING OF APPLICANTS

By installing even the most basic screening procedures you can help cut company losses.

- Conduct reference checks with at least two previous employers concerning the accuracy of employment information supplied by the application and providing an evaluation of past performance. If past employers are reluctant to provide information try for "yes" or "no" answers to the question, "Would you rehire this person." Ask for the names of anyone else you might talk to that could give you more in-depth information.

- Verify current and past addresses.

- Thoroughly check educational qualifications and degrees claimed by the applicant.

- Carefully review the employment application in order to identify missing information, unexplained gaps in employment history, indications of transiency, unrealistic claims, reason for leaving each job, and other inconstancies.

- Conduct an in-depth interview to isolate factors with information that reflects dissatisfaction with a job, or a supervisor. Carefully probe into these areas in your conversation using open-ended questioning technique.

- Use a pre-employment honesty test if you have any questions or negative feelings about the applicant. One of the best is the Stanton Survey, mentioned later in this chapter.

Checking an Applicant's References

Experts say that ninety percent of all hiring mistakes can be prevented through proper reference-checking procedures. Yet reference checking seldom constitutes the one-third of the hiring process. The reason: Many employers don't make adequate reference checks because they are difficult.

Here are some major problems in reference checking.

1. Because of the possibility of litigation, many organizations have adopted strict policies against giving more than rudimentary reference data. So there is often a problem in obtaining any references at all from previous employers. Get written authorization from the candidate to contact his or her former (or present) employer. This can sometimes encourage that employer to talk more freely with you. Most applications now carry a statement authorizing a prospective employer to check.

2. Many of the references furnished by candidates themselves can be described as "setups" (someone who has been carefully "programmed" to respond the way the candidate wishes). Often, there is a personal relationship between the candidate and the person given as a reference, which makes for a built-in bias in the candidate's favor. Try to find out whether there is a family relationship, a

long-standing friendship, or an outside business relationship involved. If there is, discount the reference thoroughly.

3. An employee who does give a reference can be subject to an "I want
   to be a good guy" impulse. Here, perhaps, in its worst case, the
   person giving the reference may have terminated the candidate for
   outlandish behavior or lack of performance, but doesn't want to
   stand in his or her way. Telephone the person giving the reference,
   and get as many specifics as you can about how well the candidate has
   performed. Even the reference's tone of voice may indicate he or she
   is simply trying to "be a good guy."

Reference Checking: Some Horror Stories

Postal service employees and supervisors are calling on the post office to
tighten up its screening and reference checking procedures for new employees after the massacre of fourteen co-workers by an Oklahoma mail carrier.
Applicants with a tendency toward mental problems should be screened out
either in the interview or in the reference checking activity prior to hiring.

A member of the National Association of Postal Supervisors said that
eleven postmasters and postal supervisors have been killed by angry employees in recent years, not including two supervisors killed among those in the
1986 Oklahoma massacre. Since 1973, over fifty-four postal employees have
been murdered on the job. All but four of them were killed by fellow
employees.

Human resource managers must screen out mentally ill applicants, but
we also want to spot applicants who lie about their technical and academic
credentials before they are hired. An oil company in Denver hired a
technical/scientific type with a Ph.D., a requirement of the job. The company
failed to check the man's degree with the university he mentioned on his
résumé. Two years later his boss complained that the man couldn't do his job,
and the project the man was on was suffering. A quick check showed the man
had only a B.A. in geology, not a Ph.D., had not done well in college, and had
been dismissed from his previous job for poor performance. Human resource
people in the oil company were red-faced. The lack of credentials, ability, and
know-how cost the company a great deal of money in lost time on the project
and poor work product.

There are companies now that do nothing but reference checking for
other organizations. One such company in Framingham, Massachusetts, run
by Peter LeVine, is doing a lot of business with major corporations. Mr.
LeVine says there has been a twenty-percent increase in phony résumés since
1982.

Artel Communications Corp. hired Mr. LeVine's firm because they felt they had several applicants with inflated résumés. One such applicant claimed he headed international marketing at a company with sales of $35 million. Actually, the man had never headed international marketing, his company had sales of $2 million, and he had earned $250,000 less than he claimed.

At Presbyterian-University Hospital in Pittsburgh, officials failed to detect a phony résumé. They hired as an accounts payable supervisor a convicted forger who was living in a half-way house after being paroled from prison.

There are thousands of similar horror stories and most Human Resource Managers have at least one they can tell on themselves.

Reference Checking Guidelines: Making It Easier

These guidelines can be useful in culling out priority items you wish to check when talking to past employers.

- Did the person achieve the objectives of the past job?
- How were the candidate's working relationships?
- Can you confirm the achievements claimed by the candidate?
- For what kind of job would you recommend the candidate?
- Under what conditions can the candidate work best?
- Did the candidate have any problems?
- Would you rehire the candidate?
- Would you recommend the candidate for this job? (Describe the requirements of the job.)
- Can you give me the names of other people I could talk to about this applicant?

If the person is reluctant to discuss the applicant, go to questions that can be answered with "yes" or "no." You will get a better response. You might establish a network of human resource people from a wide range of organizations in your city and agree to exchange reference information on a strictly confidential basis.

Another idea is to take the human resource manager with whom you need to talk to lunch. People will sometimes answer questions about ex-employees face to face.

Polygraph Tests

The heaviest users of polygraphs are retailers and commercial banks, according to John A. Belt and Peter B. Holden of Wichita State University, who conducted a survey. Half of the companies studied in these categories use polygraphs, compared to twelve percent of industrial companies, twenty-five percent of transportation companies, four percent of life insurance companies, and twenty percent of all firms in the sample.

Companies using polygraphs cited three major purposes: verifying job applications (34.5 percent), with one in ten administering tests to all applicants; periodic checks of honesty (also 34.5 percent); and investigation of specific thefts and irregularities (89.5 percent).

Twenty-seven states have now outlawed lie detector tests as a condition of obtaining or continuing employment, and there is a great deal of controversy on this subject.

In Massachusetts, an employer that requires an employee or job applicant to take a lie detector test may be fined up to $200, and in the District of Columbia employers that violate a similar law may be civilly liable to the person who took the test. Employers in Virginia are barred from requiring prospective employees to answer polygraph questions about their sexual activities, unless such conduct has resulted in a conviction for the applicant.

Employers in Pennsylvania and California must obtain the written consent of an employee before administering psychological stress evaluators or voice stress examinations, respectively. Under a new Wisconsin law, employers are prohibited from using a polygraph, voice stress analysis, psychological stress evaluator, or similar devices to test an employee's honesty. However, the law does permit the use of an instrument or device to verify truthfulness or to detect deception, but only with the employee's written consent. Many companies have switched from polygraph exams to paper and pencil honesty tests to screen applicants.

Screening Applicants Who Are Potential Thieves

Employee theft is a crime that amounts to one percent of the gross national product each year—or $40 billion a year. It accounts for eighty percent of all crime against corporations. The first step in stopping employee theft is to reduce the number of potential employee-thieves through careful preemployment screening.

Experts on the subject say that one dishonest employee can steal as much as fifty shoplifters, and that employee-thieves can steal as much as $500 per day. Employees don't have to worry about fencing stolen articles, now they barter them—a VCR for credit in that amount at a gas station for example.

Preemployment screening is often confined to reviewing an application and conducting a brief employment interview. A kind of "once-over-lightly" approach can be dangerous for organizations that have products easily stolen, or where money is easily accessible, or where computer crime is a fairly simple matter.

Background checks of applicants are time-consuming and don't really turn up a great deal of information. A past employer may give an applicant a good recommendation just to keep from paying unemployment compensation. Polygraph tests are the most common way for companies to screen applicants, but they don't always work and they are expensive—up to $250 per person. The key to eliminating applicants who may be dishonest is improving overall hiring procedures.

Why Honesty Tests Are Becoming More Popular

Many companies are turning to paper and pencil honesty tests given at the time the applicant is interviewed. The idea behind written honesty tests is surprisingly straightforward. Ask people the right questions about their past behavior and current attitudes, and honest individuals will answer critical questions differently than those more likely to become behind-the-scenes thieves. Most honesty tests are inexpensive ($12 to $25) and easy to administer.

Examples of Employee Theft Highlight the Need for Improved Hiring Procedures

A large public utilities company in the West caught an employee who had stolen hundreds of thousands of dollars by setting up a dummy company in Oklahoma to which he shipped thousands of coils of copper tubing over a period of years. He was caught by chance when one of the shipments was returned to the utility by mistake and a shipping clerk checked with the accounting department who had no accounts receivable for the dummy company.

Theft in the high-tech industry was documented when court filings detailed an FBI and IBM sting operation. The operation was designed to stop high-tech theft in Silicon Valley and resulted in the arrests of eighteen Hitachi and Mitsubishi Electric employees and indictments against both companies for stealing IBM trade secrets.

Banks and insurance companies have discovered computer crimes where employees transferred small amounts of money to dummy accounts or to people outside the company over a period of time that amounted to huge losses.

Department stores, grocery stores, 7-Eleven outlets, and discount stores all experience significant employee theft, and most stores have loss prevention programs. It is a growing national problem and one with which Human Resource Managers should be concerned.

Several companies have perfected the paper and pencil honesty tests. The exams have been carefully compiled and each question has been tested at length and selected for its capability to distinguish honest and dishonest respondents.

The expanded use of honesty tests has raised some legal questions, however, in the area of privacy rights. The American Civil Liberties Union contends that the tests are an invasion of privacy and they are currently lobbying Congress for legislation to restrict their use. Even so, honesty tests are catching on and will be used more frequently in the future.

Most HR managers I have talked with who are using paper and pencil tests use The Stanton Survey. The Stanton Survey has been through rigorous validation studies and is currently being used by many of the Fortune 500 companies. How does it work?

Where to Get Tests

Information about tests can be obtained by calling or writing

- The Stanton Survey
  Mercantile Bank Bldg.
  1301 South Bowen Road
  Suite 430
  Arlington, TX 76013
  817-274-3632

Testing for Alcohol and Drugs

Experts estimate that business is losing approximately $16 billion a year to drug and alcohol abuse on the job. Employers say the only way to make inroads in the drug problem is to test workers. Job applicants in some companies, like American Airlines and Amoco, must have a urinalysis before they can be hired.

In 1982 only five percent of the Fortune 500 companies were screening employees for drugs, today over twenty-six percent have drug screening programs according to the Bureau of Business Practice. A few examples:

- Seattle-based Burlington Northern Railroad has tested applicants and employees since marijuana and alcohol were implicated in train accidents in Colorado and Wyoming that killed seven people.

- IBM, which employs almost a quarter of a million workers, has begun screening job applicants for drug use.

- The military spent $35 million to conduct three million drug tests in 1984.

- In Washington, DC, the Federal Aviation Administration ordered annual urinalysis tests to check the agency's 14,000 air traffic controllers for abuse of drugs and alcohol.

- In Houston, each of the 2,800 employees of the Metropolitan Transit

Authority can be tested for drugs or alcohol. Over several months, 18 drivers were fired after tests showed marijuana use.

Even though more companies are going to drug testing, there are concerns that tests could be mishandled and employees might be treated unfairly. There are also concerns that drug testing may be considered an invasion of privacy, but more companies are using them every day. Human Resource Managers must be careful in the administration of drug testing programs and should establish clearly defined policies and procedures and use qualified medical personnel.

In this regard, I have asked an expert on the subject, Carl E. Johnson, an attorney with Seyfarth, Shaw, Fairweather and Geraldson, Chicago, Illinois to provide the following overview on employee drug testing:

> Legally, employee drug testing is in its infancy. Employers need to be aware that the law is rapidly changing and that drug testing programs raise a host of legal issues. As of January, 1987, private sector employers without unions have broad rights to test applicants and employees for illegal drugs and to refuse to employ persons who test positive for such drugs. Public sector employers, however, should probably only test employees in safety-sensitive or law enforcement positions who are reasonably suspected of being under the influence of drugs while at work or in connection with annual physicals. Some cases also hold that such employees may be tested if reasonably suspected of off-the-job use of illegal drugs. Public sector employers should probably only test applicants for safety-sensitive and law enforcement positions.

> Both public and private employers with unions should bargain over testing programs, except where they are confident they can establish a union waiver of the right to bargain over changes in terms and conditions of employment. Employers should not blithely assume that arbitrators will regard positive test results as just cause for discharge.

> All employers should assume that testing programs will engender litigation. Testing programs, especially ones which are carelessly thought out or administered, are likely to lead to tort actions alleging defamation, invasion of privacy, assault and battery or infliction of emotional distress. Employers in most states and all employers who are federal contractors or who receive federal financial assistance should reasonably accommodate illegal drug abusers who attend work regularly and perform their jobs safely and acceptably.

Technical Issues: Test Selection and Design

There are a variety of commercially available tests and numerous testing laboratories, both large and small. The prudent employer will, after careful investigation, choose the best available lab and pay for the best available tests. The few dollars which can be saved by cutting corners will almost certainly be spent many times over defending additional litigation.

While some labs are equipped for blood testing, most current testing involves urine. There are important differences in blood and urine testing. Blood testing allows the toxicologist to draw some rough conclusions about when the drug was ingested and whether the subject was under-the-influence of, or impaired by the drug at the time of testing. On the other hand, urine testing, which is generally designed to pick up the presence of drug metabolites, not the actual psychoactive drugs, cannot determine whether the subject was impaired when tested or while at work. As the National Institute on Drug Abuse explained in March, 1986, "although urine screening technology is extremely effective in determining previous drug use, the positive results of a drug screen cannot be used to prove intoxicated or impaired performance."

With respect to time of ingestion, urine testing proves virtually nothing. Thus, a positive result for cocaine or heroin means only that the drug was probably ingested at some time during a 48–72 hour period prior to the time the urine specimen was given. This problem is particularly acute with marijuana whose metabolites are absorbed by and slowly released from fatty tissues. A positive result may mean that the subject ingested a single dose within the several days prior to testing or may mean that the subject is a chronic user who ingested one or more doses of strong marijuana sometime within an approximate two-month period prior to testing. See *Excretion Patterns of Cannabinoid Metabolites After Last Use In a Group of Chronic Users*, Ellis, *et al*, Clinical Pharmacology & Therapeutics, Vol. 38, No. 5, Nov., 1985.

There are at least four currently available urine screening techniques, all of which are probably acceptable as presumptive screens, but not accurate enough for an employer to use as the sole basis to fire someone. One technique is thin layer chromatography ("TLC"). When a urine specimen is dropped onto a special coated glass plate, the various chemicals in the specimen migrate to specific locations on the plate and show up as spots. Unfortunately, TLC is subjective, relies heavily on the skill and judgment of the technician, may have a high rate of false positives, and does not produce results which can be preserved easily for later use in a hearing.

Syva Laboratories sells what is probably the least expensive, easiest to use and widely used screening test. Its Enzyme Multiplied Immunoassay Technique ("EMIT") can test for a variety of drug groups. The test does not require as much technical skill as other methods, but is vulnerable to false positives produced by substances which are present in urine and whose molecules are similar to illegal drugs. Thus, a common pain reliever, Ibuprofen, can produce false positives for marijuana; certain cold and allergy medicines can produce positives for cocaine and amphetamines. For this reason, a number of courts and arbitrators have condemned testing programs which rely solely on EMIT tests. *See, e.g., Jones v. McKenzie*, 628 F.Supp. 1500, 1506 (D.D.C. 1986). On the other hand, there is a substantial body of research suggesting that EMIT testing is quite accurate.[1]

Hoffman-LaRoche markets a similar test, Radio-Immuno Assay ("RIA"), or Abuscreen, which uses radioactive tags instead of enzyme tags. The equipment needed, however, is more complex and expensive; technicians require extensive training and must be licensed. Recently, the Defense Department concluded that RIA screening is preferable because of its accuracy and suitability for high-volume testing programs. Finally, Abbot Laboratories has recently modified a technique used for years by hospitals for therapeutic drug monitoring for use in occupational drug testing. Apparently, Abbot's fluorescence polarization technology avoids many of the problems inherent in the use of enzymes.

Each of these four screening technologies have their advantages and disadvantages and should be explored. No employer, however, can safely rely upon any of these tests to decide whether or not to fire someone.[2] Rather, a confirmation test which is at least as sensitive and which depends upon a different methodology should always be run. *See Jones v. McKenzie, supra* at 1505–06. Only when both tests are positive should an employee be terminated. Positive screens which cannot be confirmed should not be acted upon and indeed, should not even be reported as positives.

While there are a number of available confirmation tests, Gas Chromatography/Mass Spectroscopy ("GC/MS") is the current state of the art. GC/MS testing, which can cost $100.00 or more, is highly accurate and gives precise information about very small quantitites of drug metabolites. The gas chromatograph is basically a gas-filled tube which separates the various chemicals in a urine specimen and measures the time it takes them to pass through the tube. The mass spectroscope then breaks the isolated chemicals down into fragments and compares the signature, or "fingerprint," of those fragments with a set of known chemical "fingerprints." For example, when the known "fingerprints" for marijuana match the "fingerprints" found in a sample, the technician can be virtually certain that a test subject had ingested marijuana. GC/MS confirmation is an essential component of a defensible employee testing program.

GC/MS tests, as well as certain screens, are so sensitive that they can pick up trace amounts of marijuana metabolites attributable to breathing smoke generated by someone else in a car or closed room. This is the so-called "passive inhalation" problem. If, however, the lab is instructed to

---

[1] Irving, Leeb, Foltz, *et al, Evaluation of Immunoassays For Cannabinoids In Urine*, 8 J. Anal. Toxicol. 192–96 (1984) (GC/MS confirmed 98% of EMIT positives); Frederick, Green & Fowler, *Comparison of Six Cannabinoids Metabolite Assays*, J. Anal. Toxicol. 116–20 (1985) (GC/MS confirmed 97% of EMIT positives).

[2] Presumably many pre-employment testing programs rely exclusively upon one of these screening techniques. While such reliance is technically questionable, there have been few, if any, court decisions condemning such a practice.

set the minimum reportable positive for marijuana at or above 100 parts per billion, virtually all passive-inhalers should test negative.

Not only should employers develop a sophisticated understanding of the available tests, they should also exercise extraordinary care in selecting a laboratory. Labs should be required to demonstrate that they adhere to rigorous quality control procedures, employ only thoroughly trained, highly-qualified technicians and can provide credible expert witnesses. Blind samples should be submitted as a quality check. Labs which are not state or Defense-Department certified, or which do not participate in the Interlaboratory Comparison Program of the College of American Pathologists perhaps should not be used. Finally, the lab should be required to document operator qualifications and its adherence to proper test procedures.

Similar care is necessary in designing a test procedure. At the outset, employers must decide whether or not employees will be required to urinate in the presence of observers. In the public sector, the courts have condemned the use of observers as unreasonably intrusive. Thus, in a decision which struck down the U.S. Customs Service program, a federal judge termed the use of observers a "gross invasion of privacy" which "constitutes a degrading procedure that so detracts from human dignity and self-respect that it shocks the conscience." *National Treasury Employees Union v. Von Raab*, U.S.D.C. E.D. La., Nos. 86-3522 and 86-4088, Nov. 12, 1986. *See also Capua v. Plainfield*, 643 F.Supp. 1507, 1514 (D.N.J. 1986). While the author is unaware of any similar private sector decisions, he believes the use of observers raises substantial employee relations and legal concerns. If observers are to be used, medical professionals and a medical setting are clearly preferable to company supervisors and the factory floor.

On the other hand, programs which do not use observers are vulnerable to tampering. Apparently, the addition of tap water, table salt, vinegar, enzymes and various other chemicals can disguise the presence of drugs in a urine sample. Moreover, samples can be switched and "clean" urine or fluids such as apple juice can be substituted. Reportedly, at least one Texas company is already in the business of selling "clean" urine. To detect sample switching, the urine's temperature should be measured promptly after it is voided; urine samples which are not close to 98.6°F should be rejected. The lab should also run tests for specific gravity, pH, sodium, potassium and creatinine levels to determine whether tampering may have occurred. Such tests should catch most doctored samples without exposing employers to the problems inherent in using observers.

Great care should also go into the design of specimen labeling, storage and shipment procedures. Specimen bottles should be sealed with tamper-proof evidence tape, numbered and initialed by the person providing the sample and a witness. Samples awaiting shipment should be kept in locked containers or freezers. When samples are shipped, evidence tape should again be used and a courier should be chosen who can provide a secure, documented chain of custody. Ideally, a paper trail should exist which documents the identity of every person possessing specimens, the date and time each transfer of possession occurs, and the unbroken condition of seals at every step.[3] Such procedures are essential to get test results admitted into evidence and to convince judges and juries that a testing program is reliable. Without such procedures, the employer's exposure to litigation will increase.

Legal Constraints on Testing

1. Statutory Constraints

As of January, 1987, San Francisco, California, is the only jurisdiction which, to the author's knowledge, directly regulates employee drug testing. Bills were introduced, but not enacted, in a number of states last year. In California, a bill was passed but vetoed by Governor Deukmejian on the grounds that it restricted testing too severely. In December, 1986, the New Jersey Assembly passed a bill which would allow random testing of persons in high-risk jobs, annual physical testing, testing in conjunction with employee assistance programs and reasonable suspicion testing. Governor Kean is reportedly opposed to certain of the bill's provisions. The New York State Legislature has recently completed hearings on a bill. Employers should expect and monitor continued legislative activity.

2. Constitutional Constraints

While private employers generally have broad rights to test applicants and employees, the rights of public sector employers to test governmental employees have been severely limited by recent court decisions. Most of this litigation has concerned the issue of whether testing programs are reasonable or unreasonable searches under the Fourth Amendment. Although a detailed discussion of these cases is beyond the scope of this chapter, certain rough generalizations are possible. First, persons whose jobs are safety-sensitive or who have law enforcement responsibilities may be tested where they are reasonably suspected of being under the influence of drugs while on the job. *Lovvorn v. City of Chattanooga*, I.E.R. Cases (BNA) 1041 (E.D. Tenn. 1986); *Allen v. City of Marietta*, 601 F.Supp. 482 (N.D. Ga. 1985). Reasonable suspicion has been defined as "specific objective facts and reasonable inferences drawn from those facts in light of experience," *McDonnell v. Hunter* (8th Cir. No. 85–1919, January 12, 1987). Persons with law enforcement responsibilities can probably be tested if they are reasonably suspected of off-the-job use of illegal drugs. *See McDonnell v. Hunter, supra* (24 hour rule); *City of Palm Bay v. Bauman*, 475 So.2d 1322, 1326 (Fla. Dist. Ct. of App. 1985). Public employers can perhaps test employees in

---

[3] After testing, specimens should be frozen and preserved by the lab for as long as practical. If a lawsuit or charge is filed, employers may wish to allow a retest of the original sample. Policies should clearly inform employees that they will have a certain number of days to arrange for a retest.

safety-sensitive or law enforcement positions in connection with annual physicals or upon their return to work after a long absence. *See Curry v. N.Y.C. Transit Authority*, 56 N.Y.2d 798, 437 N.E.2d 1158 (N.Y. Ct. of App. 1982). All but one court has condemned random testing. *See McDonnell v. Hunter*, 8th Cir. No. 85–1519, Jan. 12, 1987 (systematic random testing of prison guards permissible). Due process may require that confirmation tests be run and that public employees be allowed to arrange for retesting. *See Capua v. Plainfield*, 643 F.Supp. 1507 (D.N.J. 1986).

3. Handicap Discrimination

Federal contractors and recipients of federal financial assistance are required under the Rehabilitation Act not to discriminate against persons with handicaps unrelated to their ability to perform. The Act does not, however, protect persons whose current use of alcohol or drugs prevents them "from performing the duties of the job in question or whose employment . . . would constitute a direct threat to property or the safety of others." 29 U.S.C. § 706(7)(B). Most states have similar laws which would appear to protect functional drug users. The Rehabilitation Act and most state laws also protect former drug abusers and persons falsely perceived as abusers.

To determine their obligations under these handicap discrimination laws, employers must first divide drug users into three categories: recreational users, functional abusers, and abusers who cannot perform their jobs, attend work regularly or who represent demonstrable safety hazards.[4] Recreational users are not handicapped and thus, not protected. *McLeod v. City of Detroit*, 39 Fair Empl. Prac. Cas. (BNA) 225 (E.D. Mich. 1985). Abusers who cannot perform their job or attend work or who are demonstrable safety hazards may be disciplined or discharged for those job-related problems. Thus, in *Heron v. McGuire*, 42 Fair Empl. Prac. Cas. (BNA) 31 (2d Cir. 1985), the Second Circuit held that heroin addiction rendered a police officer unqualified to respond to emergencies or enforce the drug laws. *See also Biltz v. Northwest Airlines, Inc.*, 363 N.W. 2d 94 (Minn. Ct. App. 1985); *Coleman v. Illinois Bell Telephone Company*, 10 Ill. H.R.C. Rep. 2 (1983).

In the middle ground are those persons who are dependent on drugs but by and large, can perform their jobs acceptably. Employers probably must reasonably accommodate such illegal drug users. *See Hazlett v. Martin Chevrolet*, 25 Ohio St. 3d 279, 496 N.E.2d 478 (Ohio, 1986) (cocaine addict with acceptable job performance entitled to same leaves of absence as persons with other disabilities). While the law is largely undeveloped in this area, prudent employers will allow such employees at least one opportunity

---

[4] For practical and legal reasons, employers should not delegate the task of deciding whether drug users can continue to safely perform their jobs to physicians or Employee Assistance Program counselors. That decision should be made prior to referral to an EAP.

for rehabilitation, allow the use of any accrued paid time off, and perhaps allow such employees to take unpaid leaves of absence after their benefits are exhausted. Prudent employers will also ruthlessly document all performance and attendance problems. Applicants who test positive should probably be allowed to reapply later, perhaps upon a showing that they have completed a treatment program.

4. Defamation

Terminations for drug use are likely to engender lawsuits alleging defamation. *See Houston Belt & Terminal Railway Co. v. Wherry*, 548 S.W.2d 743 (Tex. Civ. App. 1976), *cert. denied*, 434 U.S. 962 (1977) former employee awarded $200,000 because of inaccurate test results). *Cf. O'Brien v. Papa Gino's*, 780 F.2d 1067 (1st Cir. 1986) (jury awards pizza parlor manager fired for drugs after polygraph test $448,200). To reduce their exposure to such claims, employers should *severely* limit internal and external disclosure of test results. Uninvolved co-workers and supervisors, family members, the media and unions cannot safely be told test results. Only persons with a real need-to-know should be told what they truly need to know. Second, the prudent employer will go to great lengths to design the most accurate and reliable test procedure possible. All indicia of malice or ill-will should be assiduously avoided and finally, reference checks should be handled with extreme care.

5. Invasion of Privacy

Employees may raise invasion of privacy claims in several drug testing contexts: they may allege that test results were wrongfully publicized, that their employer's investigation of drug use was overly intrusive or that their selection for testing itself constituted an invasion of their privacy. To reduce their exposure to such civil lawsuits, employers should be very cautious about random testing. *See I.B.E.W., Local 1900 v. Potomac Electric Power Co.*, No. 86–0717 (dictum) (D.D.C., March 18, 1986) (random testing is "unamerican," "hysterical" invasion of privacy). Second, employers should be hesitant to investigate or test an employee unless they can articulate a real and substantial business reason for doing so. *See Bratt v. I.B.M. Corp.* 392 Mass 508, 467 N.E.2d 127, 136 (Mass. 1984) (employer's business interests must be balanced against employee privacy interests); *O'Brien v. Papa Gino's*, 780 F.2d 1067 (1st Cir. 1986) (polygraph questions unrelated to job violated right to privacy). Third, test results should not be publicized. *See Satterfield v. Lockheed Missiles & Space Co.*, 617 F.Supp. 1359 (D.S.C. 1985) (limited internal dissemination is not actionable publicity). Fourth, consent forms should be used authorizing the limited disclosure of test results. Finally, employers must reduce employees' expectations of privacy by advance notice of the precise circumstances in which they will be tested, all drugs for which they will be tested, and the penalties for testing positive.

6. Other Legal Constraints

As mentioned in the introduction, most employers with unions should bargain over testing programs before implementing them. Not doing so may constitute an unfair labor practice, may jeopardize the employer's chances in arbitration (*see Gem City Chemicals*, 86 Lab. Arb, (BNA) 1023 (Kincaid, Arb., 1986) (employee cannot be discharged for refusal to take test where testing program implemented without bargaining), and may allow the union to obtain an injunction prohibiting testing pending an arbitration or bargaining (*see I.B.E.W., Local 1900 v. Potomac Electric Power Co.*, 634 F.Supp. 642 (D.D.C. 1986)). To reduce assault and battery claims, consent forms should always be executed prior to testing and physical force should never be used. To avoid intentional infliction of emotional distress claims, employers should avoid harassment, public disclosures of drug problems, ridicule, not involve the police without a good faith basis for doing so (*Norman v. General Motors Corp.*, 628 F.Supp, 702 (D. Nev. 1986), and select employees for testing pursuant to a rational policy (*Satterfield v. Lockheed Missiles & Space Co.*, 617 F.Supp. 1359 (D.S.C. (1985)). Finally, employers should be aware that testing programs may have a disparate impact on protected minorities and monitor their supervisors to ensure that minority group members are not disparately selected for testing.

Conclusion

Although this chapter has focused on the numerous potential sources of liability employers may face arising out of drug testing programs, employers should not forget that drug abusing employees are dangerous and unproductive or that tolerance of known employee drug abuse will expose an employer to great liability. Hundreds, if not thousands, of American employers have refused to employ drug users in recent years without triggering, or losing, very many lawsuits. Presumably, illegal drug users are reluctant to charge into court to enforce their "rights" to use dangerous and illegal drugs at and before work.

Genetic Testing: A Question of Privacy

Organizations that have concerns about hiring workers that have black lung or other similar diseases have used genetic testing to pinpoint possible problem areas. There, of course, are serious questions as to the use of this information. Researchers at California Biotechnology, Inc. have discovered a way to spot potential victims of heart disease. Applicants that are asked to have physical examinations could be subjected to genetic testing without their knowing it. Serious questions of business ethics will be raised if organizations pursue this course, and the whole subject is sure to heat up in the next couple of years.

Six EEOC Testing Guidelines to Help Establish Objective Standards

The EEOC has adopted six testing guidelines to help employers establish objective standards for selection, screening, and promotion of workers.

1. Job descriptions should be examined and their critical requirements established before tests are selected for screening applicants.

2. Tests used should be developed by reputable psychologists. Such tests should be administered by professionally qualified personnel who have had training in occupational testing in an industrial setting.

3. Rigidly inflexible minimum scores should be reexamined in light of the considerable research underway on differential selection.

4. Test scores must be considered as only one source of information and must be combined with other available information on performance, such as motivation, leadership, organizational experience, self-sufficiency, and dependability.

5. Tests should be validated within the setting where they will be used. Validation should be for as many separate groups as possible in preference to one large heterogeneous group.

6. It may be advisable for employers who deal with applicants from culturally deprived backgrounds to offer retests to candidates who are unsuccessful on their first test, these people are less familiar with the testing situation and may not do as well as they are able.

The Laws on Selection Procedures

Title VII of the Civil Rights Act of 1964, as amended by the 1972 Equal Employment Opportunity Act (EEOA), applies most directly to reference checking. The Age Discrimination Act of 1967 and the Rehabilitation Act of 1973 preclude discrimination based on age and disability. It is illegal to use applicant information if it has an adverse impact on groups of individuals protected by the law, unless it can be shown to be a business necessity, or unless there is no less-discriminatory selection procedure readily available. Although limitations apply, these restrictions do not prohibit the use of background investigations.

The uniform guidelines on employee selection, adopted in 1978 by the Equal Employment Opportunity Commission, the Civil Service Commission, and the Department of Labor, specify that no specific personnel selection procedure is prohibited, including reference checking, preemployment investigations, and tests, and any selection procedure must meet the requirements of all applicable laws. The procedure must be relevant to a specific position. Any selection procedure that discriminates against applicants on the basis of race, sex, religion, and so on, is prohibited. Employees can, however, seek information about applicants and interpret and use the information during the selection process.

MAKING THE RIGHT EMPLOYMENT DECISION: FIVE QUESTIONS TO CONSIDER

With regard to reference checking, the bottom line is making sure the criteria used in reaching employment decisions are pertinent but not discriminatory. Ask yourself these questions.

1. Are you being consistent? Are you sure job standards are applied evenly in all job classifications? If an item is grounds for denying a job to one applicant, it should be the same for any other applicant.

2. Do you use a telephone interview checklist? Using a standard format will keep you from digressing into areas not relevant to the job.

3. Are data relevant? Be sure information used for employment decisions is job-related. Eliminate unnecessary requirements, such as unusually tough physical or educational requirements.

4. Are you keeping written documentation? Be prepared to back up your hire or no-hire decision with written proof verifying that the decision was based on relevant information.

5. Are you using the Fair Credit Reporting Act? If an applicant is not hired because of information contained in a preemployment report, the applicant must be notified and the reporting agency must disclose the contents of its report to the applicant.

As you can see, recruiting and selection today are far different than they were even five years ago. New ideas, new policies and procedures, alternative work schedules, and a more open-minded approach to human resources management will be the key to success in recruiting and employment in the future.

Personnel Policies and Employee Communications: Handling New Issues in Today's Work Environment

CHAPTER 8

AN OUNCE OF PREVENTION—WHY PERSONNEL POLICIES ARE A MUST

The trend in personnel policies is to eliminate all of those policies that are not needed and beef up those that are important to the company. The policies that are needed today are the ones that guide supervisors in handling discipline and discharge, time off, harrassment, attendance, complaint procedures, rules, termination, and so forth. Costly litigation can be avoided by having policies in these areas, and by strictly enforcing them.

Case example:

An employee with personal business to attend to asked his supervisor for an afternoon off. The supervisor, rushed to make a deadline, hurriedly weighed the pros and cons of giving the employee an afternoon off. The employee's performance and attendance hadn't been the best, but he was caught up on his work so the absence would not be a hardship. The supervisor said, "Yes."

Midafternoon the department Vice-President came through the office looking for the employee to do a rush job for him. The supervisor had to tell the Vice-President he had given the employee the afternoon off. The Vice-President yelled, "Who gave you the authority to do that?"

Also, one of the employee's coworkers, who had a perfect record and was a good performer began to fume. She had asked for an afternoon off the week before to take care of personal business and her request had been denied.

THE PROBLEM—lack of a clear written policy.

If there had been a written policy that had been provided to supervisors and managers, the difficulties would have been avoided. The supervisor who received the tongue-lashing would have been spared the stress, and loss of self-esteem. The employee whose request was denied would have had more respect for her supervisor and the company.

The purpose of personnel policies is to provide guidelines for the fair and equitable management of employees in order to achieve corporate goals. A personnel policy creates the perception *and the reality* that you have made an attempt at fair play. It protects you from the frivolous charges of disgruntled employees.

As a human resources consultant, I write many personnel policy manuals and employee handbooks each year. I have my word processing people print out a generic policy manual with the most important policies plus a menu of policies any company could want. I then sit down with my client and review in depth what policies are needed for that client to be able to get the job done with a minimum of hassle to supervisors. I tailor the policy manual to my client's needs. I stay on top of current legislation, and court cases. A manual and handbook can be tailored using only two half days of the client's time and provide a finished product ready for the printer within ten days. It is well worth the time and effort.

Guidelines for Writing a Personnel Manual

- Prepare a list of all the policies you think your company needs. See the checklist that follows for ideas. Review the list with your management group and with supervisors who will be using these policies.

- Pull out all the policies you now have, and review them—bringing them up to date and discarding those that aren't needed.

- When writing policies be brief, eliminate trite and verbose language. Keep them short and to the point.

- Because some courts have ruled that employee handbooks and policy manuals can be considered employment contracts, it is *important* today to insert a clause that states the handbook or manual should not be considered an employment contract, and that employment is strictly an "at will" relationship. You may wish to obtain more specific language from your attorney.

- Keep the language simple. If it is too technical, people won't read it.

- Don't undercut your supervisors or managers' authority. You are paying them to manage, give them the opportunity to do so.

- Write policies that are realistic for your size and type of business.

- Avoid redundance—don't cover the same ground in two policies.

- Be sure your policies conform to local, state, and federal laws.

- Leave the lengthy details of benefit programs to a benefit handbook, don't include them in policies. Use the phrase, "This information is only a part of the plan, see the plan texts for details."

- Be careful not to sound "preachy," don't use condescending or patronizing language.

- Do not use sexist language. Instead of using the words "he" and "she" or "he/she" all the time, change the text so you can use "they" and "their." Avoid using qualifiers that reinforce racial, ethnic, or sex stereotypes.

Tips for Making Your Personnel Policies Easy to Read

Ask yourself these questions about the policies you write.

- Do they create a favorable impression?
- Would I be upset if I read these policies? Do they sound like they were written by a marine drill sergeant?
- Are they correct in every detail?
- Are they clear and complete?
- Do they promote goodwill?
- Are they necessary to avoid favoritism, discharge problems, and so forth? Will they help avoid litigation? Will they help management choose the best course of action and manage evenhandedly?
- Are they simple enough that people will use them?

Checklist of Personnel Policies

	Our Policy OK as Is	Current Policy Needs Updating	Don't Have a Policy— Need One
Absenteeism			
Accidents			
Affirmative Action			
Alcohol or Drug Use			
Benefits			
Bulletin Boards			
Company Rules			
Complaint Procedure (Employee)			
Confidentiality Agreement			
Demotion			
Disciplinary Action and Warning Notices			
Dress Codes			
Educational Assistance			
Employee Suggestion or Problem Outline			
Employment Procedures			
Equal Employment Opportunity			
Exit Interviews			
External Communication			

Falsification of Records	_____	_____	_____
Flexible Time Off	_____	_____	_____
Funeral Time Off	_____	_____	_____
Garnishments	_____	_____	_____
Grievance Procedure	_____	_____	_____
Holidays	_____	_____	_____
Jury Duty—Time Off	_____	_____	_____
Layoffs	_____	_____	_____
Maternity Leave of Absence	_____	_____	_____
Military Leave of Absence	_____	_____	_____
Organizational Bulletins and Bulletin Board Items	_____	_____	_____
Orientation—New Employee	_____	_____	_____
Overtime	_____	_____	_____
Ownership of Patents, Inventions, Royalties	_____	_____	_____
Pay Days	_____	_____	_____
Performance Appraisal	_____	_____	_____
Personal Leave of Absence (Without Pay)	_____	_____	_____
Personal Time Off	_____	_____	_____
Pre-Employment Physical Exam	_____	_____	_____
Professional Memberships	_____	_____	_____
Promotions	_____	_____	_____
References	_____	_____	_____
Relocation	_____	_____	_____
Safety	_____	_____	_____
Salary Administration	_____	_____	_____
Separation Pay	_____	_____	_____
Service Awards	_____	_____	_____
Sexual Harassment	_____	_____	_____
Smoking	_____	_____	_____
Solicitation	_____	_____	_____
Suggestions	_____	_____	_____
Support of Recreation Activities	_____	_____	_____
Telephone Use	_____	_____	_____
Temporary Part-Time Employees	_____	_____	_____
Terminations	_____	_____	_____
Testing	_____	_____	_____
Time Cards	_____	_____	_____
Training Programs	_____	_____	_____
Transfers	_____	_____	_____
Unemployment Compensation	_____	_____	_____
Vacation	_____	_____	_____
Visitors	_____	_____	_____

Voting	————	————	————
Warning System	————	————	————
Work Week	————	————	————
Worker's Compensation	————	————	————

SAMPLES OF THREE KEY PERSONNEL POLICIES

Three key policies that every company should have in order to avoid litigation are policies on Employee Complaints, Discipline, and Termination Procedures. Following are sample policies. Review their style and practicality for your needs and tailor them to your organization.

SAMPLE POLICY 1: EMPLOYEE COMPLAINT PROCEDURE

I. Policy

Good employee-employer relationships can exist only if employees believe they have been treated equitably and fairly within the management policies, procedures, and actions that influence this relationship. It is recognized that there are occasions when honest differences of opinion occur regarding the interpretation and application of policies and management actions.

The following procedure is established to provide an effective way for employees to bring problems and complaints to the attention of management, without fear of losing their jobs.

II. Procedure

Step 1   Employee discusses the complaint or problem with immediate supervisor. It is expected that every effort will be made to resolve the complaint in a fair and amiable manner at this level.

Step 2   If the employee is not satisfied with the first attempt to resolve the complaint and a response is not received within ten working days, the employee may discuss the matter with the department manager.

Step 3   If the problem still has not been resolved to the employee's satisfaction after the second step, a formal complaint may be directed to the director of human resources. A final determination is not made at this level. Within ten working days, the employee may take the complaint to the president of the company.

Step 4   The final decision on all employee complaints rests with the president.

III. Documentation and Procedure Control

A. It is understood that any employee who elects to utilize the Employee Complaint Procedure will be treated courteously and that the case will be handled confidentially at all times. An employee will not be subjected to discourteous treatment or reproach due to utilization of the Complaint Procedure.

B. Under no circumstance will a documentation file become part of an employee's permanent personnel file. However, Complaint Procedure documentation will be separately maintained by the human resource department.

C. Only those members of management with a need to know and who are in the employee's chain of command may have access to complaint procedure documentation.

The purpose of this policy is to encourage dialogue between the employee and management, in order to resolve the differences that may arise between two parties in an amiable, fair, and positive manner.

SAMPLE POLICY 2: DISCIPLINARY ACTION AND WARNING NOTICES

I. Policy

Open communication between management and employees, and the establishment of a friendly, cooperative work atmosphere go a long way toward eliminating serious disciplinary problems. If, however, disciplinary problems do arise, supervisors and managers should make every effort to ensure that employees have a thorough understanding of Company policies and an awareness of what is expected in the area of job performance.

The purpose of this policy is to provide for disciplinary action. *Application of these guidelines must be consistent and equitable, so that all employees receive like treatment for similar offenses.*

II. Procedure

The procedures described below are meant to assist supervisors and managers in determining a proper course of action when discipline is needed. They are guidelines, not a substitute for common sense. Documentation of all verbal and written warnings is important in order to avoid the situation of an employee being discharged for cause with no written proof of earlier warnings. In most cases, it is advisable to give an employee at least one documented verbal warning and one written warning before termination.

A. Warnings

Supervisors and managers should use their own judgment in determining the length of time between warnings. A minimum of three days and a maximum of sixty days is suggested as a guideline. The warning should be specific in describing what improvement is needed. Copies of the warning must be provided to the employee.

1. Verbal Warning: Before a written warning is issued, a verbal warning may be given to the employee. This verbal warning should be recorded.

2. Written Warning: If improvement is not made within the time period granted in earlier warnings, it will be necessary to issue a written warning. This may be done in the form of a memo. In such cases, signature of the employee acknowledges receipt of the written warning but may not indicate concurrence with the information contained in the warning. Copies of written warnings must be furnished to the Branch Manager and to the employee. If the employee fails to improve by the date given on the warning, other disciplinary action, including termination, may result.

3. Following the issuance of a written warning: There should be consultations with the employee to check on progress and improvement in the problem area. These consultations should be accurately documented as to the dates and outcome of the meetings.

III. Repeat Offenses

The procedures described above need not be followed if the employee repeats an offense for which warning has previously been given (preceding twelve months). In this case, the employee's supervisor should use discretion in determining the proper course of action.

Warnings and notifications that performance improvements are needed create communication between the employee and management in order to save a valuable employee and to make the person more productive. The intent is not to punish.

IV. Retention of Records

Records of verbal or written warnings will be removed from an employee's file and destroyed after the employee has improved behavior in the problem area to the satisfaction of the supervisor. Employees should not be unduly penalized in future years for past difficulties and problems.

SAMPLE POLICY 3: TERMINATIONS

I. Policy

When termination of an employee is indicated, it is the responsibility of the supervisor to follow the procedures set forth in this policy. The maintenance of accurate records and a thorough investigation of the reasons for termination are necessary to ensure fair compliance with Equal Employment Opportunity guidelines and to determine the employee's eligibility for Unemployment Compensation. All records of terminated employees should be sent to the Personnel Dept. as promptly as possible.

The rules and procedures for handling terminations vary according to the voluntary or involuntary nature of the termination, the length of the employee's service, and the general circumstances surrounding the termination. These rules do not apply to temporary employees, as they can be terminated without notice and are not eligible for the benefits afforded full-time employees until they have worked 1,000 hours. All terminations should be reviewed by the Human Resource Director.

II. General Rules

A. *Resignation Notice Period* will be two (2) weeks only, regardless of length of service. An extension of this two (2) week period will require department head approval.

B. *Failure to Report for Three (3) Consecutive Days* may be grounds for voluntary termination. Employees terminated in this manner are not eligible for rehire, unless there are extenuating circumstances, in which case the Department Vice President should be consulted.

C. *Termination for Cause* is an involuntary termination, and the employee is not eligible for rehire. A notice period is not required. Two examples of just cause for termination are insubordination and gross misconduct.

III. Termination Procedures

Supervisor collects all Company property, such as keys, credit cards, books, equipment, and so forth, as directed in the Company Administrative Manual. All terminating employees will receive a letter advising them of their insurance conversion rights.

IV. Timing

A. Voluntary Terminations
All forms associated with a voluntary termination must be received in

Accounting within twenty-four hours after the employee gives notice. The employee's final check will be provided on the next normal payday. (Depending on current State and Federal Law)

The final time card and proof of advance clearance must be transmitted to Accounting on the employee's final day. No checks will be issued prior to receiving this data. *Requests for paychecks sooner than these requirements are considered exceptions to policy and will require approval.*

B. Involuntary Terminations

If possible, all forms associated with an involuntary termination should be processed in advance so the employee can be given the last paycheck at the time of termination.

Two other personnel policies that have become more important in the past year are policies on smoking and on life-threatening illnesses such as AIDS. Following are discussions of these two issues and sample policies used by organizations such as Bank of America.

NO-SMOKING POLICIES—A SMOLDERING ISSUE

Smoking at work is an emotionally charged issue for both employees and the company. Most large employers have no smoking policies. Companies like Martin Marietta, IBM, U.S. West Direct, and hundreds of other organizations restrict smoking to specific areas.

Many states, like California, Oregon, North Dakota, Wisconsin, Florida, Alaska, Connecticut and New Jersey, currently have laws on smoking. In Colorado nine cities have no-smoking laws.

Some human resource executives say that it gets down to the bottom line. It has been said that it costs a company an additional $4,600 annually to have a smoker on the payroll. The average smoker spends about 34 minutes a day smoking instead of working. That amounts to 18.2 days a year, or almost four weeks of unproductive time. Additionally, smokers tend to get sick more often, which results in higher absenteeism and higher medical costs.

One human resource manager told me that his company had chosen to hire only nonsmokers and he feels that he is on safe ground because smokers are not a protected minority group. Even though some companies are taking this type of action, these actions are still rare. According to a nationwide survey conducted by the Tobacco Institute, of the 1,100 companies surveyed, only 2.5 percent of them have declared an outright ban on smoking on company property. Most companies restrict smoking to specific areas.

Guidelines for Smoking Policies

It is a good idea to address the issue as soon as you can before nonsmokers lobby for specific action. Being proactive rather than reactive gives the company the edge.

- In your policy manual, state the company's intention to accommodate both nonsmoking and smoking employees.

- Make sure employees understand that you are not trying to regulate personal habits, but only to ensure the comfort of all employees.

- Establish nonsmoking areas on the basis of actual usage in dining and recreational facilities. Make reasonable efforts to accommodate the rights and preferences of both smoking and nonsmoking employees.

- Make it understood that you hope employees will use common sense and courtesy to resolve any problems surrounding the smoking issue.

- If you can do it without creating more problems, try to assign nonsmokers to offices where other nonsmokers work and smokers to offices where smokers work.

- If you have workers who have medical problems and are especially susceptible to smoke, try to accommodate them by placing them in nonsmoking areas.

- Where possible, improve ventilation and monitor work areas for high concentrations of smoke.

- Communicate your smoking policy to all workers and implement a continuing communications program to ensure all employees know what is happening.

- Let workers have signs on their desks that say, "Please do not smoke." It is a polite way of letting smokers know the smoke bothers the employee and to please refrain from smoking in that area.

Many companies sponsor programs that help employees quit smoking. In addition, some companies give nonsmoking employees a reduced rate on life insurance premiums normally paid for by the employee. Some companies have also formed employee task forces appointing both smokers and non-smokers to the group, to help management resolve specific problems.

No-Smoking Policies

Some companies use no-smoking policies in their personnel policy manual, others just issue a memo setting out the details of a more informal policy. If you decide you want to formalize a personnel policy, following are a couple of samples. Remember to tailor them to your company—your particular environment—including the tone and choice of words.

SAMPLE POLICY 4: NO-SMOKING POLICY

Policy

As a result of the changing attitudes of employees at the XYZ Company, and the fact that a majority of current employees do not smoke, the company is taking action at this time to install a no-smoking policy. A variety of national reports, including one from the Surgeon General's office, verify the fact that smoking is a serious health hazard to smokers and to nonsmokers who work around smokers.

Effective January 1, smoking will not be permitted in any of our buildings except in private offices and in certain designated smoking areas. Designated areas are lunch room No. 2 and the small anteroom off the mailroom on the first floor. Smokers may also use the covered outside eating area on the east side of the building.

We wish to be considerate of both nonsmokers and smokers and to fairly address issues surrounding this no-smoking policy. Any employee who wishes to discuss the policy may do so at any time by contacting the human resource manager.

In order to help smokers who may wish to quit, we will pay a portion of any program that will assist employees in quitting smoking. This will be a one-time payment for each employee. Employees who quit for one year will be treated to a special lunch hosted by the president of the company, Mr. Fred Cummins, next January.

We are confident that implementation of this policy will go smoothly, and hope that we will all remain sensitive to the needs of both smokers and nonsmokers, in order to maintain a caring attitude toward one another.

SAMPLE POLICY 5: NO-SMOKING POLICY

Memo To: All Employees
From: The President   Date: Jan. 1st
In order to comply with legislation concerning control of smoking in places of employment, the following smoking policy is in effect:

Policy

- All outside areas within the fenced perimeter of the site are designated "NO SMOKING" areas.

- All laboratory, corridor, mechanical room, pilot plant, fabrication, library and shipping/receiving areas are designated "NO SMOKING."

- Each individual office will be a "SMOKING" or "NO SMOKING" area at the discretion of the occupant.

- Multiple office areas will be "SMOKING" or "NO SMOKING" at the discretion of the occupant at each desk.

- "NO SMOKING" areas will be designated in cafeteria #1 and the first floor conference room.

- "SMOKING" or "NO SMOKING" in all other conference rooms will be determined by the originator of the meeting after polling the attendees.

- The main lobby, restrooms, and locker rooms are designated "SMOKING" areas.

- Areas not specifically included in this policy shall be considered "NO SMOKING" areas.

- The following map shows designated smoking areas.

We emphasize the importance of this policy and remind you that failure to comply with these guidelines will result in appropriate disciplinary action. It is the company's intent to deal fairly with both smokers and nonsmokers and to provide a comfortable work environment for all employees. Specific problems regarding this no-smoking policy should be discussed with your supervisor, or the personnel manager.

POLICIES ON LIFE-THREATENING ILLNESSES SUCH AS AIDS

In the past year it has been estimated that there are approximately 2.5 million carriers of the AIDS virus in the United States. It is expected that this deadly disease will spread throughout the country and that the number of victims and carriers in the workplace will increase as well. Companies that take action against workers who have contracted AIDS could find themselves facing litigation under laws designed to protect the handicapped. Dismissed employees can also charge a company with defamation, invasion of privacy, or intentional infliction of emotional harm.

In 1983, The Bank of America was one of the few companies in the United States with a policy on AIDS for its employees. Under their policy the bank does not discriminate against workers who contract the fatal disease. It makes reasonable accommodations so that victims can continue their employment. It maintains employee benefits and workers are assured that their privacy will be protected. Following is a copy of the Life-Threatening Illness

Policy of the Bank of America.[1]

Policy:

Assisting Employees with Life-Threatening Illnesses

BankAmerica recognizes that employees with life-threatening illnesses including but not limited to cancer, heart disease, and AIDS may wish to continue to engage in as many of their normal pursuits as their condition allows, including work. As long as these employees are able to meet acceptable performance standards, and medical evidence indicates that their conditions are not a threat to themselves or others, managers should be sensitive to their conditions and ensure that they are treated consistently with other employees. At the same time, BankAmerica has an obligation to provide a safe work environment for all employees and customers. Every precaution should be taken to ensure that an employee's condition does not present a health and/or safety threat to other employees or customers.

Consistent with this concern for employees with life-threatening illnesses, BankAmerica offers the following range of resources available through Personnel Relations:

- Management and employee education and information on terminal illness and specific life-threatening illnesses.

- Referral to agencies and organizations which offer supportive services for life-threatening illnesses.

- Benefit consultation to assist employees in effectively managing health, leave, and other benefits.

Guidelines—When dealing with situations involving employees with life-threatening illnesses, managers should:

1) Remember that an employee's health condition is personal and confidential, and reasonable precautions should be taken to protect information regarding an employee's health condition.

2) Contact Personnel Relations if you believe that you or other employees need information about terminal illness, or a specific life-threatening illness, or if you need further guidance in managing a situation that involves an employee with a life-threatening illness.

3) Contact Personnel Relations if you have any concern about the possible contageous nature of an employee's illness.

4) Contact Personnel Relations to determine if a statement should be obtained from the employee's attending physician that continued presence at work will pose no threat to the employee,

---

[1] Reprinted with permission of Bank of America.

co-workers or customers. BankAmerica reserves the right to require an examination by a medical doctor appointed by the Company.

5) If warranted, make reasonable accommodation for employees with life-threatening illnesses consistent with the business needs of the division/unit.

6) Make a reasonable attempt to transfer employees with life-threatening illnesses who request a transfer and are experiencing undue emotional stress.

7) Be sensitive and responsive to co-workers' concerns, and emphasize employee education available through Personnel Relations.

8) No special consideration should be given beyond normal transfer requests for employees who feel threatened by a co-worker's life-threatening illness.

9) Be sensitive to the fact that continued employment for an employee with a life-threatening illness may sometimes be therapeutically important in the remission or recovery process, or may help to prolong that employee's life.

10) Employees should be encouraged to seek assistance from established community support groups for medical treatment and counseling services. Information on these can be requested through Personnel Relations or Corporate Health.

MANAGING ROMANCE AT WORK

You don't need a policy, but you do need some procedures that will be uniformly followed by all supervisors. Management has never been quite sure how to handle romance at work, but who has? Organizations are in a bind today as contemporary issues like romance on the job are forcing them into court and pressuring them for new guidelines that better fit the workforce.

Soon after Citibank began recruiting women managers, they found their men managers were marrying them, creating a problem with bank policy that said husband and wife can't work together. Citibank is a forward thinking organization. They developed a policy of not only employing husband and wife, but when they reach officer status and one is transferred to a job in another city, the bank will transfer both people, providing each of them with a job.

Denver-Based Law Firm Morrison & Foerster

Some firms are on the opposite side of this issue. A large law firm in Denver received front page coverage in *The Denver Post* when it fired four lawyers, two secretaries, and one legal assistant plus a top female lawyer in their Los Angeles office. The dilemma at Morrison & Foerster involved the managing partner of the Denver office and the head of its real estate department, a female partner in the Los Angeles office. When the female partner asked for a transfer to Denver to be near her fiancé, the request was denied.

Robert F. Hanley, nationally known trial lawyer with Morrison & Foerster, former chairman of the American Bar Association's Litigation Section, and the man who won a $1.8 billion verdict for MCI in an antitrust suit against AT&T, took up the cause of the two lawyers. Mr. Hanley said that with women making up fifty percent of the law schools now, marriage with a firm member is increasingly likely. He suggested a compromise—keep the married lawyers on until a problem develops and if it does, deal with it at that time. The Policy Committee of the law firm emphatically upheld their anti-nepotism policy. Morrison & Foerster were the losers—the entire group moved to another national law firm, Kirland and Ellis, with offices in Denver.

In the past, a single corporate edict effectively covered the subject of workplace romance: "Don't date your secretary." Today, with women working beside men in an increasing variety of jobs at all levels, and with society taking a more open and relaxed view of sex, the situation has become more complex to manage. Companies agree that more women entering the workplace has produced more romance. But that is where the agreement ends. Managers' attitudes about sex and romance range from accommodation to hostility. The most common response is to sweep it under the rug and hope it will disappear.

"I turn a blind eye," says the head of a small West Coast electronic firm. "I wouldn't know what to do if I did confront the issue. When it becomes a serious problem, I guess I'll have to talk to them . . . I may even have to fire one of them."

Officially, most organizations stress that they do not interfere in employees' personal lives unless problems involve sexual harassment or seriously impact job performance. Unofficially, many corporations take action against one or both employees.

Love Between Managers: Conflict of Interest?

Eliza G. C. Collins, an editor for *Harvard Business Review*, wrote an article entitled, "Managers and Lovers." Ms. Collins insists that love cannot be tolerated between executives in the same organization. She strongly favors managerial intervention as soon as it is apparent that an affair is underway and believes such situations should be treated as conflicts of interest. Collins says that objective decisions cannot be made in a climate where love is a factor and suggests that the couple seek outside help to give them perspective on the controversy that is likely to surround them. She also recommends that the person less essential to the firm be asked to leave and that the ousted executive be given full assistance in finding another job.

Her recommendations do not fit the needs of the contemporary worker. As in the case of Morrison & Foerster, companies could quickly lose all of their best people.

Practically speaking, managers and executives who encounter romance must understand that they are not dealing solely with the subject of romance. They are dealing with the problems of stress and emotional upheaval. Managers deal with stress daily with the problems of alcoholism, drugs, and conflict at work.

Look for the Real Issues Behind Office Romances

It is important to clarify and address the *real* issues. The key is not to keep trying to fit the business world into each employee's life, but to design work and policies that fit the lives and life styles of human beings. A severe shortage of workers is projected for the next decade. It will not be practical, or perhaps even possible, to fire one or both employees when they become romantically involved, or when they marry.

In the past, business has been legislated into being concerned about people and social issues. We now have laws on equal pay, affirmative action, pensions, safety, and so forth, because we didn't always do the right things as concerned business people. Termination because of romance or marriage could be a new area of legislation. Court precedents are already being set.

The projection that, by 1990, seventy-five percent of all women in America over age sixteen will be working outside the home gets our attention. As one woman commented, "What are you going to do? In this day and age, when over half the population is single or divorced, and everybody's working and looking, the workplace is the most logical setting for people to meet." Organizations that haven't already done so will have to adjust their policies to accommodate changing employee value systems and life styles, or run the risk of not having enough sharp, qualified people.

One executive put it this way: "We hire good, bright people. They are attractive and they pair up. The process of the world works that way. You can't legislate romance out of the workplace." Romance is here to stay, and it is becoming an integral part of the corporate culture.

The following checklist provides the format for you to complete a quick analysis of your current strategy to address the issue of romance at work.

Planning Checklist for Handling Romance on the Job

	Degree to Which Practiced		
	Yes	Sometimes	No

1. A clear cut personnel policy on employment of relatives exists.

2. The policy is communicated to all employees.

3. Supervisors have been advised how to handle the problems of romance that may arise on the job.

4. In cases where problems regarding romance occur between two employees in the same department, there is immediate counseling and a realistic discussion about work conduct.

5. Progressive *positive* discipline is taken if performance is adversely affected and counseling does not work.

6. There is even-handed application of *positive* discipline across the entire organization when it is called for.

7. Management does not interfere with an employee's personal time activities.

8. Sexual harassment is not tolerated, and when it is thought to be occurring, fast and direct action is taken to eliminate it.

9. When work romance affects productivity and interrupts the normal work process, quick but positive action is taken.

10. If a work romance is between two single people in different departments and does not adversely affect their work, no action is taken.

11. Employees are not allowed to give work assignments, direct, review, or process the work of a relative.

12. Romance on the job is not treated as a negative issue unless it becomes a performance problem.

Most companies don't stop to think about strategies for dealing with the problems that arise from work romances. They more frequently react to the problems of the moment. This in itself is a strategy and usually not a very effective one.

Following are some procedures that can serve as guidelines for handling romance problems when they arise.

Procedures for Handling Work Romances

- Treat the romance and any problems that arise from it as you would any other performance problem. Do not take action unless performance is affected.

- Deal with both parties—try to get them to understand the specific problems that are being caused by the romance and to correct their behavior if that is necessary.

- Take immediate action when the morale of the staff is being adversely affected. By action, I mean call the two people in and discuss the problem with them. Try to be open and honest in your dealings with both the staff and the two people involved. Just make it understood what you expect in terms of performance and behavior on the job. Let the couple know that their on-the-job relationship is creating problems and tell them what you expect of them in the way of change. You cannot invade their privacy off the job. Neither can you fire one of them unless you are prepared for a sticky court battle, but you can manage their performance on the job. Within the next ten years, romance at work will be such a common occurrence that discussion of it will seem trite.

- If the couple marries and you have a nepotism policy, you can enforce it. However, the best policy is to ask one of the people (if they work together in the same department) to take a transfer. Let the couple decide which one will transfer. Nepotism policies are falling by the wayside today. Companies are learning to better manage the problems surrounding the employment of relatives.

Emphasize that the company does not want to interfere in employees personal lives—that you must, however, manage problems that adversely effect the functioning of the department and the productivity and morale of your other employees.

A survey of 100 executives asked how they would handle the situation if one of their male managers was dating a female in the same department. Their primary concern was the impact on work performance and company reputation. "If they are both competent, and good performers and their relationship isn't disrupting the department, I don't feel it's necessary to do anything" was the common response. In many similar situations the fact is, however, that one or both parties have been fired.

In Michigan, a waiter at the Gandy Dancer, an Ann Arbor restaurant, was told he could quit, be transferred, or be fired if he married his fiancée, a waitress at the same restaurant. The waiter quit, married his fiancée and sued `his employer, C. A. Muer Corporation, for discrimination. The court decision awarded him reinstatement and back wages.

Training is the answer to making people more aware of romance as an issue in the workplace today. The following case study can be used in a workshop setting as an awareness exercise.

Romance Awareness Training Workshop

The workshop can accommodate a group of twenty five-thirty people. Break into smaller groups of five. Hand out case study.

Ask groups to work on the problem for thirty minutes. Ask one person in each group to act as recorder for the group.

Case Example: Romance on the Job

Jane Smith is a marketing representative for a large electronics firm on the west coast. Rick Allen is the marketing vice president with the same firm. Jane and Rick have been dating secretly for over a year. Even though they have been careful not to be seen together in or near the office, their coworkers are aware that there is something going on between them. Rick's boss is also aware of their romance. The company has a policy against nepotism; however, the couple has no plans to marry as yet. Rick's boss has told him to break off the relationship or he will fire Jane.

- What action, if any, should Rick take?
- What should Rick tell Jane?
- What should Rick tell his boss?
- Is the company policy legal?
- What action should Jane take?
- Will Jane sue the company if she is fired?
- If she does, will she win?

At the end of thirty minutes, ask the recorder for each group to give you their answers.

Compile the answers into one list. Pick the best answers from the list and summarize what actions the group feels should be taken and why.

Ask the group if these actions are the ones they think would have been taken three years ago, five years ago. Discuss wrongful discharge and what part it might play in this case.

To enliven the group, you can use actual case studies you know about instead of the one provided here. Just don't use an actual case of someone that will be in the workshop!

Tip: It's a good idea to treat the issue of romance at work as you do any management issue. If it becomes a performance problem, treat it as you would any performance problem.

Don't inflate the issue and don't always fire the woman if you decide to take action. If you have a nepotism policy, allow one of the married employees to take a transfer to another department or work site. Look closely at any nepotism policy. Today twenty-two states have laws against firing an employee for nepotism.

SEXUAL HARASSMENT: TRAINING IS THE KEY TO ELIMINATING IT AT WORK

The Court has said that workers who have been sexually harassed by their supervisors may sue their employers on grounds that such behavior creates a hostile environment, even if the loss of a job or a promotion isn't directly involved. The Court has further ruled that a company may be held liable in sexual harassment suits even if management isn't aware of the problem.

The problem human resource directors run into in trying to make supervisory staff aware of the problems of sexual harassment is that what is kidding to one person, may be stressful and threatening harassment to another. The only way to ensure that everyone in your company understands what sexual harassment is is to provide training programs that address the issue head-on.

Training programs make people at all levels of the organization more aware of the seriousness of this issue. Many times management isn't aware that there is a problem of sexual harassment. Awareness is the key word here.

Once there is an awareness on the part of management that there may be a sexual harassment problem, it is a good idea to let executives know what sexual harassment unchecked can cost the company in terms of morale, corporate credibility, and dollar impact.

The stakes can range from the $5,000 from the Minnesota Supreme Court awarded a harassed Continental Can Company employee to the $100,000 judgment against Denver-based Johns Manville Company, and awards are growing. The Ford Motor Company has to pay $140,000 in compensation for a supervisor's verbal sexual harassment of a female employee. In the latest and most significant sexual harassment case, the court ruled that managerial ignorance is no excuse.

In the case Vinson v. Taylor, according to plaintiff Mechele Vinson, an employee of Maryland-based Capital City Federal Savings & Loan, a supervisor at the bank, Sidney Taylor, asked her to go to bed with him saying that she "owed him." What then followed, according to one labor attorney, was a "pattern of fornication," of 40 or 50 occurrences over the next two years. Vinson said that she was forced to submit to Taylor's advances during and after business hours.

As in all sexual harassment cases, there were many questions. Why didn't she complain sooner? According to her attorney, Vinson didn't tell anyone because she was afraid of physical retribution. According to Vinson's attorney, the bank knew that this supervisor had a history of making passes at employees. The bank, however, denied that its officers had any idea sexual harassment was going on.

The Supreme Court noted the EEOC guidelines which define "sexual harassment" to include "unwelcomed sexual advances, requests for sexual favors, and other verbal or physical conduct of a sexual nature." EEOC guidelines and the decision of the Supreme Court both note that sexual misconduct constitutes harassment whether or not it is directly linked to the grant or denial of an economic benefit. For a "hostile environment" harassment claim to be the basis for a lawsuit, the Court said, the harassment "must be sufficiently severe and pervasive 'to alter the conditions of [the victim's] employment and create an abusive working environment.' "

The Supreme Court also addressed the issue raised by the bank that the sex-related conduct was "voluntary" because the Plaintiff was not forced to participate against her will. The Supreme Court rejected this claim. It stated: "The correct inquiry is whether respondent by her conduct indicated that the alleged sexual advances were unwelcome, not whether her actual participation in sexual intercourse was voluntary."

The importance of the Vinson case is more than a mere presentation of the facts. In rendering its decision in favor of Vinson the U.S. Court of Appeals for the District of Columbia decided that it doesn't matter whether an employer knows there is a problem with sexual harassment on the premises . . . the very fact that a supervisor sexually harasses an employee is enough to make the firm responsible.

In recent years the law has been clearly headed in the direction of greater responsibility of employers for the acts of its employees; and when the Supreme Court held in favor of Vinson in this sexual harassment case, it accelerated this trend.

There are basically four tests of policy and process that courts seem to apply to sexual harassment cases.

1. Has the employer made an unequivocal statement, which has reached every employee, that it is not company policy to condone sexual harassment?

2. Does the employer conduct diligent reviews of supervisory decisions to hire, fire, and promote employees, so that the employer can be expected to become aware of incidents of supervisory misconduct?

3. Has the harassed employee notified someone in higher management of the harassment incident?

4. Is there a mechanism for the employee to use to notify management that there is a problem?

5. Once made aware of the existence of a problem, has the employer made a prompt and adequate effort to investigate and resolve the issue?

What Organizations Are Doing to Stop Sexual Harassment

Organizations are responding to this challenge in a number of ways. At Minneapolis-based Dayton-Hudson Corporation, employees were made aware of the organization's stand on harassment through publication of a policy statement in an internal employee newsletter. Most corporations today include reference to sexual harassment in their personnel policies and also post notices on bulletin boards that say sexual harassment is not condoned.

One of the most proactive organizations in the area of eliminating sexual harassment in the workplace is the DuPont Company. They have several programs. One program is designed to teach women employees how to avert sexual harassment, rape, and other safety risks in and out of the workplace. DuPont has invested $500,000 in their program. This large outlay of funds reflects the growing concern among many employers nationally about sexual harassment. In the DuPont program women are taught assertiveness and other skills that help them cope with harassers. DuPont also threatens harassers with disciplinary action, including discharge, and their policy is enforced.

Another company that has adopted a firm sexual harassment policy and training program is Merck & Co. They have an extensive training program for employees that incorporates video dramatization and questionnaires as well as group exercises and discussion sessions. Over 5,000 of the company's 17,000 employees have been through the two three-hour programs.

Workshops are an important training vehicle and there are many good films to use in sexual harassment programs. One film is published by the Bureau of National Affairs and is entitled "Preventing Sexual Harassment."

When it gets down to conducting actual training on the subject, the effectiveness of what you say will largely depend on how you say it. Early in the actual session, it is important to get the snickering out and deal with the anger—this issue does make a lot of people angry. One way to do that is to go right at the tort law issue. Once they see the similarity to regular assault and battery, and that they have personal liability, they get the idea of how serious harassment really is.

Training programs to show managers how to avoid charges of sexual harassment should be offered at least once a year and all supervisors and managers should attend at least one training session.

TRAINING MANAGERS TO OVERCOME THEIR HOMOPHOBIA— THE FEAR OF HOMOSEXUALS

Managers are today addressing many new issues. Some of these issues are uncomfortable to deal with because they fall outside of regular everyday frames of reference. One such issue is managing a variety of people, people of color, of different religions, and different sexual preference. Today, there is a large and growing body of judicial and statutory law concerning the legal status of homosexuals. As this body of law grows and as homosexuality becomes more visible, managers will require new guidelines and training programs for managing the homosexual employee.

We used to see a proliferation of fliers about workshops on how to manage woman on the job. Perhaps the next wave of training brochures will target homosexuals. I have never felt you have to use a different set of management skills to supervise women, minorities, or homosexuals. You need a certain set of skills to manage human beings. What many people lack is an ability to see people without seeing color, sex, or sexual preference.

Regardless of our management skills and abilities, we do experience a certain amount of fear of the unknown. When people talk or act differently than people we live with or are used to dealing with, there is a fear of outcomes, a fear of making a mistake; and managers may need to acquire some added skills.

Effective HRD managers should be proactive. If we are proactive, we can anticipate problem areas, and design programs to address emerging issues. Homophobia is an emerging issue and awareness programs are needed to assist managers and homosexuals (some who are also managers) in dealing with this issue.

A new book entitled "Sexual Orientation and the Law" by Roberta Achtenberg provides practical problem-solving coverage of the unique legal questions related to sexual orientation. Write Clark Boardman Company, Ltd., 435 Hudson Street, New York, NY 11014 for information on the book.

How to Deal with AIDS in the Workplace

The issue of AIDS presents human resource managers with a formidable problem. One that we could not even have imagined a few years ago. Employees that contract AIDS run up huge medical expenses (one guess is approximately $147,000 per case), and fellow workers experience tremendous stress and fear about contracting the disease. Employees who have the disease are frequently banished by the company, and experience a form of discrimination that is almost as bad as the illness. Human resource managers are caught in the middle. Between companies who don't want to incur the high medical costs, or deal with fellow workers who refuse to work with AIDS victims, and employees who deserve to be treated with compassion and decency.

Most companies have dealt with AIDS on an ad hoc basis. IBM has a straightforward policy: Treat AIDS victims as you treat other sick employees. When the employee is medically fit, he is allowed to remain on the job. When necessary, he and his coworkers are provided with counseling. Companies that adopt this approach will not have trouble conforming either to the law or to common decency.

Employees afraid of working with an AIDS victim may have some legal protection under two federal statutes. The Occupational Safety and Health Administration requires that workplaces be free of recognized hazards, and the National Labor Relations Act says that employees cannot be penalized for refusing to work out of legitimate fear for their safety. As far as I know, the NLRA provision has not been tested, but the OSHA regulation has been. Nurses in a San Francisco hospital wanted to wear gloves and masks that supervisors found unacceptable. The State OSHA board decided against the nurses.

Some employees have lost their jobs when they refused to work with fellow employees who had AIDS. At one major bank, two pregnant women refused to work near an employee with AIDS and were told that if they didn't return to their jobs their absence would be regarded as a voluntary resignation. They never went back. It is generally felt that failure to take a strong position could put a company at risk for a successful charge of employment discrimination.

The costs of medical care are going to become burdensome as the number of employees with AIDS grows. The Public Health Service has said that the cost of caring for AIDS patients could reach $16 billion by 1991. That is nearly 2.4 percent of total expected personal health care expenditures in the United States, which is $650 billion. Much of the burden of health care costs falls on corporations as 70 percent of United States workers have health insurance that is provided by employers who typically pay about 80 percent of the cost.

Supreme Court Extends Handicap Law to AIDS Victims

On March 3, 1987 the Supreme Court ruled that people with contagious diseases are protected by The Rehabilitation Act of 1973. The Court in a 7 to 2 vote said businesses and government entities receiving federal aid are barred from discriminating in employment or otherwise against people with contagious diseases.

Although the ruling didn't specifically mention AIDS, it is considered to be a contagious disease, and lawyers on both sides (plaintiff/management) feel that AIDS-based discrimination is illegal.

Human resource attorneys and consultants have varying views. Some say all companies should have personnel policies and procedures for handling AIDS, others say that a policy is risky. A policy that seems right one year may not be sensible two years later, and adjusting your personnel policies to changing circumstances may be less awkward if there is no written policy. On the other hand, when there is no policy you run the risk of managers handling sick employees in a variety of ways that invite claims of discrimination. With or without a personnel policy, human resource managers should be preparing for problems with AIDS. Gregory J. Brandes, Attorney with Cotter & Company in Chicago, Illinois provides the following overview and policy for dealing with legal issues of AIDS.

POLICY AND LEGAL ISSUES FOR THE HUMAN RESOURCES MANAGER

Acquired Immune Deficiency Syndrome (AIDS) has stricken nearly 30,000 Americans, most of them employed adults between the ages of 20 and 49. Caused by a virus that attacks the immune system's "T" helper cells, it has been fatal in over 56% of the cases reported as of January 1, 1987.

Employers face a dilemma when a worker has AIDS. State handicap laws protect most AIDS sufferers from disease-related discrimination, but other employees sometimes object to working with or near an AIDS sufferer. Discharging the afflicted employee without cause has usually resulted in costly litigation and adverse verdicts. Thus, employers must find ways to accommodate both the afflicted employee and any of his co-workers who may be afraid of being exposed.

- Educate Employees about the disease and the methods of transmission that have been identified. Medical information helps dispel fear of the afflicted worker.

- Formulate and implement a Company policy that provides specific guidance on the key issues of accommodation, benefits, attendance, work performance and confidentiality.

- Train managers and supervisors how to apply the policy consistently and fairly and what to do when the employee's performance suffers because of the disease.

- Document all actions taken under the policy. Should litigation result from some application of the policy, this documentation will be vital evidence of the Company's efforts to accommodate the employee.

- Protect employee privacy at all times. Much of the litigation which has arisen over AIDS is attributable to management's failure to ensure confidentiality or to defamatory statements made by supervisors and other employees.

Do not "wait-and-see." Nearly 1% of Americans have been exposed to the virus and could develop the syndrome within the next decade. Employers should act now to develop procedures to deal with a case if one ever arises among their employees. The best approach is a policy of reasonable accommodation of the interests of both the afflicted employee and his coworkers.

AIDS AT WORK

The Problem—When an employee has AIDS he can be expected to miss work, spend time in the hospital and experience some emotional trauma. The employer should expect these changes to be noticed by other employees. The employer should also expect that some employees will object to working with the AIDS victim, perhaps vehemently. The employer is thus faced with inconsistent obligations; he must treat the AIDS victim fairly but must also protect the other workers and address their concerns where legitimate.

The Solution—Employers should formulate a plan for dealing with AIDS in their workplace before any cases occur. This plan should be embodied in a corporate policy and promulgated, implemented and applied consistently throughout the company, with support from the highest levels of management.

The policy should provide for the reasonable accommodation of both the suffering employee and his coworkers, to the extent possible under all the facts and circumstances. Federal handicap discrimination laws require such accommodation and AIDS is fast becoming recognized as a handicap in many states and jurisdictions.

Since the policy provides guidance to front line supervision and protects the employer in litigation, it should be carefully written and reviewed by counsel before implementation. Remember that it will be used to make day-to-day decisions, so it should be clear and complete, with specific procedures detailed.

POLICY GUIDELINES

Like all corporate policies, an AIDS policy should include the usual language indicating the purposes of the policy, the employees it applies to and who is responsible for its application and implementation. In addition, however, it should include:

1. A promise that the employer will attempt to "reasonably accommodate" the needs of both the afflicted employee and his coworkers. This is the same standard that applies to handicapped

employees under the federal Rehabilitation Act. It requires only that effort be made to make it possible for the afflicted employee to continue to work; it does not require that the employer change his entire operation.

2. Specific, clear procedures for protecting the afflicted employee's privacy. Information should be available only to those with a "need to know" and disseminated only with written consent from the employee.

3. Directions for front line supervisors on how to report AIDS cases and handle and document the afflicted employee's absences, performance deterioration, attitude and relations with coworkers.

4. Details of the employee education program.

5. A case management committee composed of representatives of the personnel, medical, insurance and legal departments. This committee, in most cases, will be the only ones who have access to confidential employee information and will decide all issues relative to the cases which arise.

6. Lists of outside agencies or organizations that supervisors and managers can contact for help. It should include the company Employee Assistance Program, if available, as a primary resource, but may also include support groups, mental health professionals and other community resources.

The policy should be promulgated in the usual fashion, with group meetings to explain it once, the same way, to all employees, follow-up meeting held by individual supervisors with small groups and individual employees and documentation of all implementation steps.

Finally, the policy should stress that management must require adequate productivity from all employees at all times in order to stay in business. While the afflicted employee will be dealt with fairly, the employment relationship will have to be terminated eventually.

Education—AIDS is a frightening, deadly disease and a very emotional issue for many employees. Before undertaking any kind of policy regarding AIDS, the workforce should first be educated about the disease and the methods of transmission that have been identified. Education will both prevent some problems from arising and permit easier resolution when a conflict does arise.

The education program should include medical information about the disease, hygiene recommendations that can help prevent its spread and the message that the AIDS policy is supported by upper management. The education program will help employees accept the policy as well as the prospect of working with an afflicted employee.

Training—All managers should participate in the education program to gain a full understanding of the disease and to show their support for the rest of the policy. They should also be trained in every detail of the plan and given specific instruction on how to deal with circumstances that are likely to arise in the interpretation and application of the policy. A procedure manual should also be made available for future reference when questions arise that cannot be easily decided from the policy.

The training should take place before the policy becomes effective. Since supervisors are vital to the implementation of any corporate policy, and will perform the necessary training of employees, they need complete information so that they can properly answer employee questions.

Health Care—Employers and their insurers have paid the bill for AIDS medical care in the United States. Since the average AIDS patient incurs medical care costs of $147,000, employers have begun searching for ways to reduce the risk of hiring someone who has the disease and reduce the cost of cases that arise among current employees. Some of the options currently in use or under consideration include better case management by a representative of the employer or his insurer, periodic medical examinations to aid in early detection of the diseases which comprise the syndrome, and treatment at home or in a hospice instead of hospitalization.

AIDS Testing—The human body produces natural antibodies to fight the AIDS virus. Several tests are available which can detect these antibodies in blood samples taken from those at risk. Proper testing method requires, however, that a sequence of tests be run over a period of several months and this sequence costs several hundred dollars. It is thus not practical to test employees or applicants for the disease.

Workplace Hygiene—Though the AIDS virus is hardy, it is not invincible. It will not survive most common methods of sterilization and is destroyed by common household bleach used in a 10:1 dilution. It is much easier to destroy than the virus which causes Hepatitis B, and the Center for Disease Control, which monitors AIDS and provides guidance on dealing with the disease, recommends that the same procedures be used to sterilize for both viruses. Those recommendations, and others, are contained in the Department of Health and Human Services report entitled, "Guidelines For Preventing Transmission of AIDS in the Workplace," published in the November 15, 1985 issue of the Federal Centers For Disease Control Morbidity and Mortality Weekly Report. The report has been supplemented to provide recommendations specific to food and beverage and personal service workers and health care personnel. Summaries are available in most law libraries.

AIDS AND THE LAW

Common Law—Employees with AIDS retain the same rights as all other employees with respect to the recent developments in wrongful discharge law. In jurisdictions where the courts have recognized a cause of action for violation of implied contract of employment, the employer will still have to analyze whether he has just cause to discharge an employee with AIDS. Similarly, some states may find a violation of public policy where an employer discharges an employee solely because he has AIDS.

Every employment decision which takes into account the fact that the employee affected has AIDS, should be carefully reviewed by counsel, since it is likely to result in litigation. Even where the victim is an employee at will, such a decision could cause adverse public and employee relations problems within the community and the workplace.

Aids Legislation—The federal government has thus far failed to enact any significant legislation concerning AIDS. Some AIDS-related legislation has been proposed, but Congress has enacted only bills directing the use of AIDS research funds.

The Justice Department ruled in June, 1986, however, that an employer does not commit actionable discrimination when it makes an adverse employment decision based on the reasonable perception that an employee who has AIDS could transmit it to other employees. The Equal Employment Opportunity Commission has disputed the ruling and employers should not rely on it.

Thirty-three states and the District of Columbia have declared AIDS a protected handicap either by legislation, court decision or opinions of the state equal employment opportunity agency. California, Florida and Wisconsin have banned the use of the AIDS blood screening test in the making of employment and/or insurance decisions and several cities, including Los Angeles, Denver and San Francisco have enacted ordinances prohibiting various forms of discrimination against persons having or suspected of having AIDS.

Since local law will govern any litigation which may arise when any action is taken by the employer of a person who has been diagnosed as having AIDS, management should consult local counsel in the applicable jurisdiction to review the action prior to implementation. It is also advisable to have local counsel provide general guidance on the law prior to the drafting of the corporate AIDS policy, so that it can be tailored to comply with the law of each jurisdiction in which it will be effective.

AIDS Litigation—In Arlene v. School Board of Nassau County, the U.S. Supreme Court will decide whether a teacher who lost her job when she tested positive three times for tuberculosis is "handicapped" within the meaning of the federal Rehabilitation Act of 1973. The Act describes a handicap as some "impairment" which affects a "major life activity" of the individual in a significant way. Since AIDS, like tuberculosis, is a communicable disease, the case is expected to provide an answer to whether AIDS falls within the proper definition of "handicapped" under the federal law. Oral arguments were heard in the case on December 3, 1986; a decision is expected in early 1987.

In state court litigation the AIDS cases which have been decided have centered on three key issues:

—whether the employer could discharge an employee with AIDS based solely on the fear that it could be communicated to other employees;

—whether children and teachers who have AIDS can be permitted to attend school; and

—whether the discharge of an afflicted employee satisfied the just cause standard in a union context.

Case law is limited since many AIDS litigants die before their cases can come to court. In the published decisions, however, courts and arbitrators have thus far uniformly found that AIDS is a protected handicap and that the fear of transmission by casual contact is unfounded. At the present time there appears to be no type of employment decision that can be made based solely on the fact that an employee has AIDS. The best approach, then, to avoid litigation, is one which stresses cooperation and which balances the needs of the afflicted employee with those of his coworkers and the employer. Such cooperation is the only approach that seems to be sanctioned by the current federal and state regulations pertaining to AIDS.

Guidelines for Managing Employees with AIDS

- Manage the employee in a compassionate manner. A person with AIDS is going through a very traumatic experience. Losing a job and being ostracized by fellow employees will put an added burden on the employee.

- AIDS should be handled no differently from any other major illness.

- So far, no one has caught AIDS from working with someone who had it, unless they had sexual contact. Educate other employees. Hire a trained consultant to come in and talk to your workers to quiet their fears.

- An employee with AIDS has the same right to privacy as any employee, so handle medical information in a confidential manner.

- Do not fire the employee. Some companies ask that the employee with AIDS get a doctor's certificate saying the person is well enough to work.

- If the employee is too ill to work, let him stay at home but continue medical coverage; and if you can, continue at least some portion of the person's salary.

- If you can, provide counseling, either through your Employee Assistance Program, if you have one, or through an outside consultant trained to handle such cases.

- Conduct workshops or group counseling for coworkers who have experienced AIDS-related stress.

- Consider having a written policy on AIDS.

- In most cases, doctors advice that AIDS victims need not be restricted from working if they are well enough.

If you think an employee might have AIDS, but you are not sure, you shouldn't push the issue. You cannot legally insist an employee take an AIDS antibody test.

Many companies continue medical coverage and the employee's salary but do not allow the employee known to have AIDS to continue to come to work. Every company has to arrive at its own procedures for dealing with the problem. Many companies have not had an AIDS situation come up, but with AIDS continuing to spread throughout the country, most organizations will have to deal with it at some point in time.

If you have a problem, it is a good idea to contact an expert on the subject. There are groups in nearly every city that can provide educational materials. The Washington Business Group on Health in Washington, DC, a corporate policy group, distributes information. Associations like the American Management Association and the American Society for Personnel Administration also have information and educational materials. Education of your workforce is the most important step you can take.

The government has issued the following guidelines on AIDS in the workplace, saying in effect that where you work is not where you contract the disease. They give employers two main guidelines.

First, routine screening to see who may be infected with the virus is a waste of time.

Second, employers should not place restrictions on workers known to be infected.

Where to Find Reference and Educational Materials on AIDS

The AIDS Foundation in San Francisco has produced a videotape and booklet called *AIDS Education in the Workplace*. The project was funded by seven major corporations. The Foundation sells the videotape and booklets for $398 and uses the proceeds to support education. Write to 333 Valencia Street, San Francisco, CA 94103. The New York Business Group on Health sells the transcript of an AIDS Seminar they sponsored called *AIDS and the Workplace* for $25 to members and $50 to nonmembers. Write to the Group at 622 Third Avenue, New York, NY 10017.

There is also a newsletter published by the Bureau of National Affairs,

Inc. 2445 M Street, NW Suite 275, Washington, DC 20037 entitled *AIDS Policy & Law*, that would keep you up to date on current policy and practice.

A LOOK AT WHAT'S NEW IN EMPLOYEE COMMUNICATIONS

There is no way to effectively deal with human resources today without a sophisticated program for employee communication that utilizes all types of media. Here's a sample of some innovative communications programs:

Installing an Employee Hotline

If you have an employee problem you sense is heating up and you are not sure what it is, install a short-term hotline.

Have a telephone company install a telephone and hook up an answering machine. Put it in an office or file room that is kept locked. Publicize your hotline in your employee newsletter, by word of mouth, posting fliers on bulletin boards, and so forth.

Tell employees to call in on the hotline any time of the day or evening with questions or concerns. If they leave their names, guarantee them a personal answer within twenty-four hours. If they don't want to leave their names, tell them you will answer any work-related questions in the following issue of the company newsletter. In serious situations, start a special weekly newsletter and answer all calls for information quickly.

Follow through on your commitment—don't slip up, or your hotline will not do the job you wanted it to do.

The Company Newsletter

Newsletters are one of the best ways to communicate with employees. Newsletters provide a means for communication both up and down in an organization. One way to do that is to have employee/reporters throughout the company so that input spans the organization. The newsletter should not be written by one person who makes all the decisions as to what will be included. If it is written from one voice and one viewpoint, it will be boring and won't be read.

Use contests, word puzzles (that relate to your business), and lots of pictures of employees. Interview key management people to explain policies and practices. Have a "feedback" section that answers questions from employees—and from your hotline if you have one.

Have both employees and management critique your newsletter from time to time to ensure it is doing the communications job that you need done.

Companies that have a news service, telex equipment, or television available on the premises can implement a new type of daily newsletter—utilizing the computers or other printing methods.

Current news, printed out in a daily newsletter or bulletin format can be made available to employees in the cafeteria or in their work areas. It can include late breaking news and the current company information. Add unusual items to "spice it up."

Hottest Tool in Employee Communications—The Corporate Video Newscast

Many corporations are putting together their own corporate video newscasts, giving employees the latest information about the company. Employees always complain they don't know what is going on in the company. Corporate newscasts communicate anything from new products to employee benefits.

American Express has a TV Newscast that goes out to 37,000 employees in the United States, Canada, and Britain in a videotape. Sears weekly videotape news is called *Intercom*. Illinois Bell Telephone has a monthly videocast called *NewsScope*. It's an eleven-minute color presentation. With a map of Illinois behind her, an anchor woman from the community relations department opens the program by giving the top headlines and interesting company news.

Most big users of videotape company news broadcasts find that they are popular with employees. Some companies run surveys of their employees from time to time to find out what they want to see—what questions they want answered.

The Kellogg Company reported on its weekly newscast, *TV Network*, that one production department had set a record for packaging the most small boxes of cornflakes. The following day the department broke that productivity record, and surpassed production each succeeding day for three more days.

If employees can quickly grasp the employer's side of a controversial issue through in-house television, they are more likely to accept the company position and pass the information along to other employees.

Employee Communications Programs Can Take Many Forms

In order to keep communications flowing up as well as down in an organization, companies are utilizing lots of new and innovative programs.

Banc One Corporation of Columbus, Ohio does teleconferences for all workers. Quaker Oats, Fairchild Industries, and Hershey use videos, TRW uses "skip-level sensing" so workers can mix with managers two levels above them. At Giant Food, Inc., employees send suggestion letters directly to the chairman.

Case Example: Offbeat Lectures Stimulate Employee Communication at Bell Labs

Every month or so Bell Labs schedules a lecture on some offbeat subject like "learning to fly," or the "mystery of bird navigation" or "amorous whales and acoustics." Mostly they are topics that would make a good *Scientific American* article. Bell employs a lot of workers from diverse disciplines—astrophysicists, linguists, computer gurus, and so forth. The lectures are designed to get these employees out of their narrow disciplines and get them thinking about other issues, to get them to do problem solving in new areas. Bell Labs is as concerned with long-range creativity as with everyday efficiency.

These lectures cost about $750 each and Bell uses closed circuit television hookups to send the lectures to outlying locations. Employees hope that all the restructuring at Bell will not eliminate this good program.

Case Example: U.S. Home's Unusual Communication Program

On Wednesday evenings in Houston, Texas, about a dozen men and women gather to discuss business books. This isn't a college seminar, it is a new management development program at U.S. Home Corp. From a list of fifty top management books, fast-trackers choose what they will read and discuss each week. It is an innovative way of developing management people.

Many forward-thinking organizations have implemented innovative development programs to meet the needs of today's workers. Effective human resource managers should be on the leading edge of creative employee communications.

Tying Employee Communications to the Corporate Culture

Because employees are so much more sophisticated about the media today than they were even five years ago, the style of all communication aimed at employees has to be savvy, honest, and to the point. How do we design communications programs that meet those objectives? Look first at employee attitudes.

WHAT EMPLOYEES EXPECT FROM THEIR JOBS: INSIGHTS FROM A REVEALING SURVEY

There are some revealing statistics on employee attitudes in Hay Management Consultants' strategic report, entitled, "Linking Employee Attitudes and Corporate Culture to Corporate Growth and Profitability."* The following

---

* Reprinted with permission of Hay Management Consultants, Philadelphia, PA.

information is excerpted from that report and provides valuable insights into what most employees expect from their jobs.

We asked employees whether they are treated with *respect* by their organizations. Their answers reflect egalitarian attitudes in fast-growth organizations, especially among managers, professionals, and clericals. About 60 percent of the employees surveyed in faster-growth organizations responded favorably. Employees in slower-growth organizations were more inclined to report their managers are being out of touch with their employees. Only 30 percent of the professionals surveyed in this sector felt they were treated with respect. Overall, less than 50 percent of the managers, professionals, clerical and hourly employees felt they were treated with respect.

The next part of the survey concerned what employees *value*. The following table shows the results:

Faster Growth	Common	Slower Growth
Challenge Learning	Pay/Benefits Respect Supervision Advancement	Authority Security

Note, in the center, the values common to employees: pay and benefits, respect, supervision, and advancement. But note also that, in faster-growth organizations, what employees uniquely value are *challenge* and *learning*. In contrast, what employees in slower-growth organizations uniquely value are *authority* and *security*. These are the key levers for managing human resources!

The data on values becomes even more relevant and powerful to managing human resources when broken down by job level:

Employees' Values	Faster Growth	Common	Slower Growth
Middle Management	Challenge Advancement	Pay/Benefits Accomplishments	Decision making Supervision
Professionals	Challenge	Pay/Benefits	Respect
Clerical/Hourly	Advancement	Pay/Benefits Respect Supervision	Security

Managers in faster-growth organizations value *challenge* and *growth*; in contrast, managers in slower-growth organizations value *power* and *control*.

Professionals in faster-growth organizations also value *challenge*, but those in slower-growth organizations value *respect*—the very thing they report as not getting!

Clericals and hourly employees have much the same values; in faster-growth organizations they want a *chance to get ahead* and grow in the organizations, while those in slower-growth organizations are *security seekers*. So, at all levels the values shared by those in faster-growth organizations are values geared to growth and the changes that accompany it. Therefore, when communicating with employees who have these values we must gear our messages to growth, change, challenge and respect in order to be heard.

Information from surveys like this Hay Management survey is valuable to human resource professionals because it allows us to validate what we are experiencing in the workplace on a daily basis. The tremendous number of changes we are seeing in the workplace itself, and in the new worker, have created a need for us to be more flexible in our approaches to the overall management function. We also need to be more flexible and more creative in the way we write and manage personnel policies and in our employee communications.

Special Concerns Facing HR Managers: Terrorism, Theft of Trade Secrets, Alcoholism, and Drug Abuse

CHAPTER 9

HUMAN RESOURCE DIRECTORS ARE UNPREPARED FOR TERRORISM

The full impact of terrorist activity has not hit most United States organizations, but experts say it will in the next few years. Threats come from many quarters that terrorism will be brought across our borders and many United States based companies and their human resource departments have not prepared for this eventuality.

Most large multinational companies have experienced, well-equipped security departments. They use both their own people and outside companies that furnish training and sophisticated equipment. The security industry can provide a variety of services. They can provide guards to protect homes and offices of potential targets; they can offer bodyguards to ward off terrorists. They can furnish hidden cameras; sensors; electronic surveillance systems; bulletproof, bombproof cars; radios; and infrared goggles that allow the wearer to see in total darkness. Almost any type of equipment that a company needs is available today, and growing in sophistication.

The American Society for Industrial Security (ASIS) publishes an excellent magazine that keeps the security industry current on specific developments in training and on the newest security equipment. If you are a multinational organization with executives in hot spots of the world, you can easily purchase an executive office equipped with closed-circuit television monitors, cameras, and audible signals. And, if you are an HR Director with responsibility for international travel planning, you might want to contact the World Status Map Company, 301-564-8473 for current information on the "hot spots" for international travel.

Four Ways to Deal with Employee Protection

If this all sounds too much like a James Bond movie, you have only to read the newspapers and watch nightly television news reports of American kidnap victims around the world to understand how really "close to home" terrorism is moving. According to experts, the key to all of this is a nonemotional approach to protection of employees, and there are four general considerations.

1. Have a constant awareness of what is going on around you.

2. Train employees to have a cool but generally serious attitude about security.

3. Provide a perimeter of security around all facilities that is not "fear" based, but that couples a solid business attitude about the need for security with equipment such as lights, locks, sensors, and closed circuit television. Overseas locations may need guards and more sophisticated equipment.

4. Provide specific training for CEOs and top level executives traveling outside the United States that includes personal self-defense, defensive driving techniques, and the basics of survival if kidnapped.

The Bureau of National Affairs has a great deal of information on kidnapping and terrorist activity in multinational organizations. A company called Risks International sells information from its computerized data base on terrorist activities. The company is located in Alexandria, Virginia. Large multinational organizations pay over $1,000 per year for this data.

The Insurance Company of North America, and the American International Group, Inc., a holding company whose insurance subsidiaries cover many companies with multinational operations, advertise in national newspapers to sell kidnap insurance. Your chances of being kidnapped are greater than your chances of being killed in a plane crash, according to an article in *The Wall Street Journal.*

Ransom demands have gone from $1 million in the 1970s to from $5 to $10 million in the 1980s. Lloyds of London, the company that underwrites most of the international kidnap insurance, claims that the gross annual income from kidnapping is approximately $70 million.

HELPING CORPORATE EXECUTIVES AVOID THE TERRORIST THREAT WHEN TRAVELING ABROAD

The week following the American raid on Libya, almost two million Americans changed their plans to travel abroad. Most of those people were vacationers, but thousands of them were corporate travelers who decided to be safe rather than sorry, and delay business trips until the bombing incident was not so fresh in the minds of would-be terrorists.

Human resource executives are well aware there is a risk of American business people traveling abroad being singled out by terrorists. The government is working to tighten security for American travelers, but it is still primarily up to the individual traveler to take precautions when traveling abroad. Jan Stevens, Vice President of Marketing for TeleLink, M Inc., travels to Europe twice a year. Her company provides orientation and training on overseas travel, and personal self-defense programs for employees who must travel abroad in the course of their work. The company will also pay the cost of language courses. We helped Jan's company put together an orientation program that includes some of the following overseas travel tips.

- If possible (depending on length of stay) use only carry-on luggage so that you are not standing in unguarded open areas waiting for your suitcases. Limit the amount of carry-on luggage to one or two pieces to minimize the time spent in security check areas. Do not carry expensive looking luggage with American names or logos. Don't carry business papers in your luggage.

- Don't wear your corporate business clothes to travel in. Wear jeans, older slacks, jackets, sweaters, or shirts. Don't wear obvious brands of American shoes or accessories. Don't wear expensive, flashy, religious, or company logo jewelry. Don't carry business cards that identify your company or your position.

- Pick hotels that are not known to be frequented by Americans, but are known to be safe. Pick a room high enough to put you above street attack or bombing but not so high you couldn't be rescued in case of fire.

- Do not go to bars or street cafes known to be American hangouts and don't sit outside in any street cafe.

- Learn to speak at least a few words and phrases in each language of any country you plan to visit. It not only helps in doing business, it could help you in a hostage situation.

- When you arrive in a foreign airport, try to get through customs or ticketing and behind security checkpoints as quickly as possible. Find a place to stand even in a secure area where you can observe what is going on. Pick direct flights whenever possible to minimize enroute stops. Have tickets issued in your name not your company name and don't have the company name on any of your belongings, including suitcases.

- If you must use business papers in your work, try to mail them ahead to your hotel. Don't carry briefcases or papers that identify you with your organization, especially if they happen to be government papers.

- Don't take a car or cab to which someone in a foreign airport tries to direct you. Stick to vehicles you recognize and pick yourself. Vary your type of commercial transportation if you stay several days in one city. Don't use expensive looking limousines.

There are many more things of which you should be aware, but these tips are some of the most important ones. The main thing to remember when traveling anywhere is to keep your eyes and ears open. Be aware of what is going on around you. Observe the landscape and look for unusual looking people, vehicles, or packages. Don't put yourself in a position to be a target.

WHO IS LIABLE WHEN AN EMPLOYEE IS KIDNAPPED?

Litigation takes place in about ninety percent of all employee kidnappings. It has become a commonplace liability of all multinational organizations. One reason is because it is always possible to criticize the way a corporation handled negotiations for an employee's release.

Most experts in the field of employee security advise that the corporation can best protect itself against litigation from victims or their families by providing employees with control over their own security and advising them in advance of the potential dangers of their assignments—also, by providing a reasonable budget to the employee for training and equipping themselves and their facilities. This was affirmed by the federal court in New York in the 1980 case of Gustavo G. Curtis and Vera Curtis versus Beatrice Foods Company.

Case Example: Industries Gran Colombia, S.A.

Curtis, the CEO of Industries Gran Colombia S.A., wholly owned Colombian subsidiary of Beatrice Foods, was kidnapped on a highway in Bogota in September 1976 and held for $5 million ransom, a sum that neither he nor his local company could pay. After seven months of captivity, Beatrice Foods secured his release with a ransom payment of $30,000. Mr. Curtis sued Beatrice Foods for $200 million in damages, claiming the company had been negligent in handling the kidnapping. The case was dismissed and appeal was denied.

In his ruling, the judge observed that Mr. Curtis failed to assure his own safety by means of tightened security despite having "the authority to take whatever actions he thought necessary. . . . Moreover, Curtis had prior training in how to deal with such situations." In fact, Curtis had been warned by the United States Embassy in early 1976 that he was a potential target, and in 1975 he had attended a security conference arranged and paid for by Beatrice Foods.

This case points up the need for human resource directors to quickly become attuned to current security issues that might impact their organizations, and to be prepared to handle the majority of incidents that could occur in the United States and abroad.

HELPING EMPLOYEES COPE WITH VIOLENCE

Whether the violence is personally or secondarily experienced, whether it is coping with death like the Oklahoma postal murders, or terrorism, or kidnapping, violence of any kind is a highly debilitating experience. Dealing with the aftermath of the crisis, and continuing to work when you are in shock or grieving is not easy. Kenneth J. Fisher, ACSW, a Denver psychotherapist, provides the following ideas:

Most organizations today provide expert counseling services for employees who have experienced some type of violence. Workshops on post-trauma counseling were a major topic at the North American Congress on Employee Assistance Programs in Toronto, Canada in 1986, and are increasingly common on association meeting agendas in the United States. How should an organization respond to violence that occurs on the job? Here are some ideas.

1. Immediately contact an expert in post-trauma counseling. Find one in advance of needing one so that you have the information at your fingertips in an emergency.

2. Gather information on the incident. What happened? How did employees feel? What action was taken? Did help arrive quickly? What could have been done to prevent the incident?

3. Were physical facilities safe and secure? If not, why not? What can be done in the future to make them more secure?

4. Appoint a task force to review the incident and what occurred afterward to ensure as much as possible that it won't happen again.

5. Have small group meetings to let employees talk about the incident and get their feelings out in the open.

You need experts to help you deal with violence and to get feelings out in the open quickly. Let employees know that you will do everything you can to prevent another similar occurence.

THEFT OF TRADE SECRETS: CORPORATE SECURITY GOES UNDERCOVER

All companies, regardless of their size or the complexity of their products, have valuable trade secrets. Some companies' trade secrets are naturally more valuable than others. The company's survival might even depend on the confidential retention of trade secrets. Patents and copyrights don't cover customer lists, financial projections, or test results that competitors might pay dearly to possess.

In his book *The Trade Secrets Handbook**, Dennis Unkovic identifys five categories of trade secrets:

1. Inventions, industrial processes, and key technical information
2. Technical information and materials
3. Marketing, purchasing, procurement, and customer and corporate planning information
4. Financial, accounting legal, and securities-related information
5. Other corporate data

A trade secret program should be established for most companies. The program doesn't have to be long and involved. Mr. Unkovic states in his book that there are at least eight major elements that appear in most comprehensive corporate trade secret protection programs.

1. The need for physical isolation of trade secrets within designated areas.
2. Accountability and tracking custody of trade secrets.
3. The requirement of uniform trade secret marking procedures.
4. The role of mechanical security procedures.
5. Dealing with your employees at every stage of the relationship.
6. Limiting risks when revealing trade secrets to third parties.
7. The need to deal with unsolicited submissions of proprietary information and employee developments.
8. The requirement of periodic updates of corporate trade secret information.

Another area that human resource directors have to be concerned with is the area of employee suggestions. What do you do if an employee submits an idea that is a trade secret—and turns out to be quite valuable to the company? Most courts support claims of an employer to inventions developed by an employee during the term of employment and while at the place of employment. There are serious questions of who owns trade secrets brought up in court all the time.

Some Actual Examples of Employee Trade Secret Theft

The CEO of a high tech manufacturing operation in Denver called in the personnel director. "Hire the best private investigator you can find; we have an employee stealing trade secrets and I want him found." The director hired

---

* Reprinted with permission of Dennis Unkovic from his book *The Trade Secrets Handbook*, Prentice-Hall, Inc. 1985.

Ray Pezolt, president of Pezolt Investigations. He planted his janitor "operative" in the company. The operative acted stupid, but in fact he was a sharp former captain with the Army's OSI branch and held a Ph.D. in criminology.

The operative circulated throughout the company, gathering valuable information from desk tops and trash containers. He listened to conversations regarding highly sensitive equipment new to the high tech industry. Then he overheard a conversation about an agreement being made by a terminating supervisor to give the competition an off-hours company tour, and caught the employee.

In another case, the theft of computer products from a software firm in California took place when an employee decoded trade secrets, passed them to a black market broker, who in turn sold them to a Soviet agent in Mexico City. (The movie *The Falcon and The Snowman* is based on this case.)

Probably the most notorious trade secret theft case was Hitachi's undercover purchase of trade secrets stolen from IBM. The FBI and IBM staged a "sting" operation and caught Hitachi employees in the act.

A comprehensive trade secrets program will normally bring the theft to light and the culprits to trial before serious damage occurs.

Soviet Spies—FBI Director Says Your Firm Could Be the Next Target

Over 3,000 officials from Communist countries, about 35 percent of them spies, work out of 180 offices in the United States, according to FBI counterintelligence sources. FBI Director William Webster said on television, "I do not think there's been another time in our history when our country has been under such a sophisticated espionage assault."

Soviet spies in the United States have targeted the 12,000 or more companies working on defense contracts, and the thousands of smaller defense subcontractors whose high technology products could be put to military use.

Case Example: Lockheed Corp.

Nation's Business magazine reported the case of a group of Soviet specialists in aeronautics being taken on a State Department sponsored tour of three major defense contractors. The Russians visited plants operated by Lockheed, Boeing, and McDonnell-Douglas.

One company, Lockheed, was manufacturing the L-1011 commercial wide-body plane. The Russians were kept far away from sensitive defense facilities at the plant; however, there seemed no harm in showing them how a civilian aircraft was made.

The Soviet visitors were interested in the L-1011 because it was a big, lightweight plane that could carry large numbers of people at high speeds. The Russians had not figured out how to make such a plane.

The specialists visiting the Lockheed plant were wearing shoes with adhesive soles. Metal parts picked up by their soles at the plant (and at the other two plants as well) were later analyzed in a Moscow laboratory. From that analysis, the Soviets learned enough about jumbo-jet metallurgy to build bigger and faster troop- and cargo-carrying aircraft.

An Eastern European spy revealed that bit of Soviet trickery in 1981, after defecting to the West.

EMPLOYEE LOOSE TALK SPILLS TRADE SECRETS

The cloak-and-dagger theft of trade secrets using operatives and spies is only one security problem. The most common situation that occurs in the theft of trade secrets is simple employee "loosetalk" and situations that occur in the human resource area where new employee interviews are conducted.

This is the so-called legal use of intelligence gathering techniques. Some of it is acknowledged by companies as just good business—competitor surveillance is necessary in order to stay on top of the latest developments in the production and marketing of products. Most business people believe that competition has intensified and become global and that competitive intelligence is a necessary ingredient in strategic planning.

Consultants now offer books and seminars on competitor surveillance. Companies like FIND/SVP in New York City will monitor clients' competitors for a fee. One book, *Competitive Strategy*, by Harvard Business School Professor Michael Porter, offers advice on how to gather corporate information. In addition, there are now some 2,000 computer databases available to the public. Control Data Corporation has one called Economic Information Systems. Another company, Business Research Corporation in Brighton, Massachusetts, provides subscribers with the full text of research reports on companies by security analysts and investment bankers.

When Congress passed the Freedom of Information Act in 1966, lawmakers and journalists hoped the legislation would help the public learn about government secrets. Today less than ten percent of the requests for documents, tapes, and photographs come from reporters, laymen, or scholars. The bulk of the requests are from businesses and business consultants. The government is leaking trade secrets. The people who make the requests for information are not required to tell the agency on whose behalf they are filing the request, why they want the information, or how they plan to use it. Many executives think that these loopholes facilitate corporate spying.

Employees Are the Greatest Threat to Trade Secrets

Companies with valuable trade secrets require employees who will have access to them to sign a contract obligating the person to maintain the confidential nature of the trade secrets. The agreement is frequently a part of an employment contract, but because many employers do not use employment contracts, a separate trade secret agreement should be used. The following example of an employee secrecy agreement is taken from Dennis Unkovic's book *The Trade Secrets Handbook*, Prentice-Hall, Inc., 1985. Dennis is an attorney and a partner in the firm of Meyer, Unkovic, and Scott located in Pittsburgh, Pennsylvania.

EMPLOYEE SECRECY AGREEMENT

I, _____, am an employee of _____ Company. As part of my duties, I have access to trade secrets of my employer such as _____. All knowledge and information I gain from those trade secrets and the trade secrets themselves, including all unpatented inventions, designs, know-how, trade secrets, technical information and data, specifications, blueprints, transparencies, test data and additions, modifications, and improvements thereon which are revealed to me shall for all time and for all purposes be regarded by me as strictly confidential and held in trust by me. I will not reveal or disclose the trade secrets to any other person, firm, corporation, company, or entity now or at any time in the future unless my employer instructs me to do so in writing. This secrecy protection will continue even if I no longer am employed by _____. I understand that if I reveal the trade secrets to unauthorized persons I personally may be subject to penalties and lawsuits for injunctive relief and money damages as well as possible criminal charges by my employer.

I acknowledge that I have read and understood the contents of this Agreement and freely sign it with the intent to be legally bound hereby.

WITNESS

_____   _____
                                                  (NAME)

_____   _____
(PLACE SIGNED)   (DATE)

From a legal standpoint, it is important that the secrecy agreement be signed before the employee starts to work. Courts are more likely to enforce a secrecy restriction if it is agreed that the employee would not have been hired unless he agreed to the secrecy provisions. An employee who is asked to sign a secrecy agreement after commencing employment may later assert he never voluntarily agreed to the restrictive conditions.

CORPORATE TECHNIQUES FOR GAINING INFORMATION ABOUT COMPETITORS

An experienced interviewer for a high tech company in California interviewed a university student who had been employed by a competitive computer company for the summer. The interviewer proceeded to skillfully question the student about his summer job. The questioning went on until the student had evaluated all of the commercially available software packages capable of performing a certain function. The student, eager to prove his competence, provided in-depth information on the competitor's products.

Many companies have highly trained teams of interviewers who not only interview competitor's employees who are looking for new jobs, but also attend conferences and discuss at length valuable proprietary information and then carefully sort out the most competent people to target for hiring. This practice isn't considered unethical and it goes on all the time.

Monitoring Competitive Information in Help Wanted Ads

One aggressively competitive organization on the East Coast keeps tabs on competitors through help wanted ads that provide a great deal of information on what jobs are available, when and where new facilities will be opened, and what types of skills are needed. The human resource director in each of the company's locations is charged with this surveillance activity. The CEO says, "There certainly isn't anything unethical about monitoring help wanted ads. It's just good business. But there is a fine line between monitoring ads and interviewing for trade secrets."

Executive Search Firms Can Be Sources of Competitor Information

Some executive search firms will search out and hire away top executives or key technical people from companies who are not their clients. They readily admit that if you are a client company, they will contact the best people from your competitors and recruit them. Some less reputable search firms will also gather as much proprietary information as they can when they interview those employees. One search firm interviewed people they knew were not viable candidates for a position, but who worked in sensitive jobs and passed the information obtained in the interviews on to their client company. This is obviously not an ethical practice, but it is very common today.

How One Personnel Director Tracked Down a Corporate Scam

The personnel director in charge of security for a California real estate company was called in by his boss, who was thinking of investing a great deal of money in a large real estate deal. The boss was suspicious of the deal but couldn't put his finger on the exact reason. He instructed his personnel director to hire the best private investigator he could find to check out the other real estate developer.

The personnel director was referred to a private investigator by a human resource manager in another corporation because they had used the man very successfully in a similar situation. He met with the investigator the following week.

The investigator surreptitiously took photographs of the real estate man and his luncheon companions, checked his license plate numbers, and those of his companions, and learned that the man associated with people believed to be underworld figures. He also learned that these men, although never convicted, were suspected of laundering money from drug deals.

The human resource manager reported the findings to his boss who backed out of the deal.

TIPS ON PROTECTING COMPUTER SECURITY

Computer crimes are usually discovered by accident. There still seems to be no specific foolproof way of avoiding them. There is an old but true story told in computer circles about several teenage boys on the East Coast who devised a way to cheat the Pepsi-Cola Company. They decided to try and tap into Pepsi's computer and direct it to send them free cases of Pepsi.

The boys used school computers. They asked their fathers, who used computers at work, how to access the computers and the unsuspecting fathers provided critical information such as phone numbers, passwords, and so forth. The kids experimented until they cracked a Canadian time-sharing facility with twenty-two commercial users and nearly achieved their goal.

New software is continually being developed that can protect the on-line portion of the computer, and most companies closely audit their computer function. But every company needs some basic security procedures.

Secure, Inc., experts on computer crime, provide some general advice.

- Never trust your computer systems to just one person. There may be too much temptation. No single person should ever have absolute control of your computer.

- Have a specific policy on computer crime and always follow through with it. If someone is caught stealing information, he or she should be terminated immediately.

- Use passwords. Change passwords when an employee in the computer area leaves. Don't use shared passwords.
- Always store a second set of critical programs and file off-site. Have a plan in case of disaster.
- Restrict the number of people who work with data and restrict user read, write, and execute permissions. Maintain input and output user controls. Verify reentered data.
- Audit all logs, reporting of errors, unauthorized transactions and system interruptions, or system use.
- Restrict terminal use, locate terminal in secure area. Have people log in and out. Review override procedures that let people bypass internal controls.
- If you suspect abuse or theft, hire an outside computer security consultant to thoroughly test and check your procedures.

Guidelines for Implementing a Basic Security Program

If you don't have a full-time security expert on staff, it is a good idea to hire a security consultant to assist in establishing your total security program. Here are some guidelines, however, for taking basic security precautions.

- Screen job applicants for potential security risks and for past criminal convictions. Be especially careful in checking applicants for jobs as security personnel. The New York State Commission of Investigation recently revealed that 20,000 of the 30,000 individuals hired as security guards in the state in 1982 had criminal records and that all of the 20,000 had been working as guards before their records were uncovered.
- Implement a policy on theft that states employees caught stealing will be terminated and carry out the policy without exception.
- Establish security procedures that include outside lighting, secure areas, locks, alarms, sensors, and so forth. Be sure procedures include what employees are to do in case of disaster, fire and bombing.
- Mark company equipment for theft prevention and recovery.
- If your company has trade secrets, and government contracts or subcontracts, use employee identification badges and special passes in restricted areas. Require employees to sign secrecy agreements *before* they are hired.
- Use card keys on all doors except one door designated for public use.

Provide employees with card keys. Take extra precautions at the public entrance. Have a panic buzzer installed for receptionists to use in case of emergency.

- Have a formal, well-communicated evacuation plan in case of fire or other disaster.

- Set up a log and monitor all people who come into the facility. Record who the person has come to see and time in, time out.

- If you are a manufacturing facility, retailer, or have valuable small equipment that can be carried out in lunch boxes, handbags, and so forth, conduct spot checks and ask employees to open handbags, boxes, and sacks.

- Use honesty tests in hiring and with current employees when you suspect you might have a thief on the payroll.

Security Staffing

In large organizations there are security guards and usually a security director that is a Certified Protection Professional, licensed by the American Society for Industrial Security. In most mid-size and small companies the people in charge of security have no training or background in the function. Their training usually comes from attending seminars. Most organizations, when they implement a security function, hire a security consultant to help them set up their procedures and purchase their basic security equipment. The term "security" now encompasses many diverse areas, and human resource managers who have the security function reporting to them should acquire some expertise in each of the areas.

COMPANY ACTIONS IN CASES OF EMPLOYEE THEFT

Most companies enforce a policy that employees will be fired if they are caught stealing, either from the company or from fellow employees. Some organizations employ other sanctions or handle the situations on a case-by-case basis. The following chart is from surveys conducted by the American Society for Personnel Administration and Bureau of National Affairs.

WHERE THE SECURITY FUNCTION REPORTS IN MOST ORGANIZATIONS

In most organizations, the security function reports to a Security Director, who in turn reports to the Director or Vice President of Human Resources or Personnel. The number of levels naturally depends on company size. The following chart shows the Administration of Company Security Programs in a

Table 9-1—Company Actions in Cases of Employee Theft

	Percent of Companies						
	All Companies	By Industry			By Size of Workforce		
		Mfg.	Nonmfg.	Nonbus.	Under 250	250–999	1,000 or more
	(587)	(300)	(197)	(89)	(204)	(247)	(121)
Circumstances under which company would take legal action for employee theft—							
Under all circumstances	32%	28%	39%	27%	35%	30%	29%
Theft of merchandise/equipment totals a specific dollar amount	35	40	28	35	34	37	35
Handled on a case-by-case basis	20	18	21	25	16	18	30
Employee is a two-time offender	5	6	4	6	7	5	3
Company would not take legal action	10	12	8	8	10	11	7
Circumstances under which an employee would be fired for stealing company property—							
Under all circumstances	76	78	77	64	73	78	75
Theft of merchandise/equipment totals a specific dollar amount	13	12	13	17	16	13	8
Handled on a case-by-case basis	9	9	8	12	6	8	17
Employee is a two-time offender	5	4	6	7	7	5	3
Company asks employees suspected of theft to submit to a polygraph test							
Never	69	73	60	79	80	66	58
Sometimes	24	23	28	16	15	26	34
Usually	6	3	10	5	2	8	8

Percent of Companies

	All Companies	By Industry			By Size of Workforce		
		Mfg.	Nonmfg.	Nonbus.	Under 250	250–999	1,000 or more
	(587)	(300)	(197)	(89)	(204)	(247)	(121)
Individual responsible for company security—							
Security director	33%	21%	46%	47%	14%	32%	67%
Personnel director	27	40	17	7	28	32	17
Facilities/plant manager	8	9	5	11	12	8	3
Management not elsewhere specified	8	8	6	11	14	6	4
Administrative staff official	7	5	12	7	9	8	4
Risk manager	3	2	3	6	3	4	2
Financial officer	2	2	2	—	2	1	2
Other	3	4	2	3	3	4	2
No individual in charge	5	5	6	5	9	5	—
Department responsible for company security—							
Personnel	34	49	23	8	30	39	32
General administration	29	20	39	38	37	26	21
Maintenance/housekeeping	9	10	6	14	12	9	7
Plant engineering	8	10	4	14	7	10	7
Security/safety	6	3	6	17	2	4	18
Operations	4	4	6	1	6	4	3
Finance	2	1	4	1	2	2	3
Other	4	2	8	3	4	3	7
Head of security has CPP license	6	5	8	2	1	5	15
Training/background of security staff—							
Attended seminars/workshops	45	37	53	52	29	43	71
Previous job experience	39	35	46	39	24	39	68
On-the-job training (current job)	11	10	10	17	4	11	21
Formal education program	8	4	6	21	3	5	21
Law enforcement background	8	6	11	9	4	6	17
Other	1	2	1	1	1	*	3
No training or experience	27	34	19	21	44	23	9

Note: Percentages may add to more than 100 because of multiple responses.
*Less than 0.5 percent.

373

survey of 587 companies conducted jointly by the American Society for Personnel Administration and Bureau of National Affairs.

These charts were taken from an excellent report on Company Security. For a copy of the entire report, contact the American Society for Personnel Administration, 606 North Washington Street, Alexandria, VA 22314.

FIGHTING ALCOHOLISM AND DRUG ABUSE IN BUSINESSES

Alcoholism on the job has been a serious corporate problem in the United States for years. *U.S. News and World Report* reported that there are over ten million American alcoholic workers. Employers, unions, and insurance firms are all attempting to do something about problem drinkers at work and help them get treatment. *Dun's Business Month* magazine reported in 1982 that employee assistance programs have grown from 400 to over 5000. Most companies today either have their own on-staff personnel to run an employee assistance program or they hire outside consultants. The Department of Health and Human Services estimates that more than $50 billion is spent annually on alcohol and substance abuse programs.

The alcoholic or drug abuser worker is no longer a blue or white collar worker. Today's alcohol or drug user is just as likely to be a female or male executive.

Who Abuses Drugs?

The executive drug addict may be a man or a woman. They are both abusing cocaine, prescription drugs, and alcohol. The government reports that over twenty-five million people have tried cocaine. Four to five million people in the United States use cocaine monthly. Fifty billion dollars is spent on cocaine in the United States every year. Forty-five percent of the people on cocaine today are women.

The Profile: The average person is 29 years old, a college graduate, and makes over $25,000 per year. An executive of a California electronics firm, himself a recovered cocaine addict, says that at least sixty percent of the sixty employees he supervises use cocaine regularly.

Sixty-five percent of the people on cocaine have some type of job impairment. Corporate absenteeism has been climbing—experts say that in most cases as much as fifty percent of absenteeism and on-the-job accidents are related to drugs and alcohol.

One psychologist who has treated more than 250 Silicon Valley employees in the past five years says that twenty-five percent of her patients work in quality control areas, many of them on jobs related to national defense.

Many young Wall Street brokers and investment bankers are hooked on cocaine. "When you make a half million a year," said one twenty-nine-year-old investment banker, "you can afford a cocaine life style."

A forklift operator at a small Long Island business smokes a joint in the parking lot at lunch time, assures the boss he's fine, and then runs his forklift into a door. A Denver construction worker snorts cocaine and later falls through a newly constructed elevator shaft, a Houston pharmaceutical company has to throw out a batch of contaminated products because the quality control inspector was stoned. The Nuclear Regulatory Commission announces that twenty-one guards at the San Onofre nuclear facility in California have been suspended for suspected drug use.

A Burlington Northern train runs off the track in Denver, several people are killed—drug use is confirmed. A nurse in a Boston hospital says "I had a syringe with 100 milligrams of Demerol and a patient who only needed fifty milligrams." She had a headache and sneaked into a bathroom, injected the Demerol into her hip and within minutes the headache was gone. That was the start of a drug abuse problem for the nurse.

A petrochemical plant in Louisiana exploded some years ago, killing four men and causing millions of dollars in damage. According to a toxicologist and drug consultant who worked with the company, the men had been taking amphetamines when the emergency alarm went off—they did nothing but laugh.

One executive, the CEO of a large high tech firm in California, not only uses cocaine himself, but buys it from his employees. A Denver stock broker throws a party for hundreds of his clients and friends where silver bowls of cocaine are passed around by white gloved waiters. The abuse of drugs by executives has become a serious problem nationwide. The demand for facilities that can treat addicted executives has grown dramatically.

Drug addiction may induce employees or an executive to steal from the company to help support the habit. Drugs can also impair the judgment of an executive in crucial times. One stock broker said that he and his colleagues were using cocaine every day when they were committing more than $5 million of the company's trading capital. It may be easier for executives—they have more money, more time, and more privacy for taking drugs.

National Car Rental's personnel director, in their in-house magazine said, "I think it's the biggest problem in industry today. Nothing else even compares to it."

How to Help Stop Drug Abuse in Your Company

Get professional help for a person you suspect of using drugs. Do not confront the person one-on-one. Together with a counselor, let the employee know that you are aware of his or her drug use and that you want to help the person get assistance.

The greatest fear most people have is that they might lose their jobs. Assure employees they won't lose their jobs if they get into treatment and get off drugs. Often the only person who can push an employee into treatment is his boss by the threat of job loss.

Implement an employee assistance program (EAP) either by using an EAP consultant or by hiring a trained professional to be on staff. If you suspect anyone of using drugs, insist they talk to the EAP counselor. It's best that the supervisor not confront a drug user until there is a professional counselor available.

What to Do with Suspected Pushers on the Payroll

Many companies have discovered they have pushers on their payrolls. If you even suspect you have someone selling drugs in your company, investigate and take action immediately.

A year ago Justine Control Systems, Inc. CEO, John Justine, had suspicions. Productivity was down, profits were down, and he had heard rumors that he had a drug problem in the plant. He called in the personnel manager and told him to find an experienced private investigator. The investigation took nearly seven months but the investigator found two people making sales; nearly thirty employees were implicated. The investigator used five "plants" working two shifts. The "plants" made buys and talked to employees who were on drugs.

The personnel manager and the investigator called in the police who staged a drug bust in the parking lot during the shift change. Drug sniffing dogs were brought into the plant and lockers were searched. The ringleader was a shift supervisor who had been with the company for fifteen years. He was forced to open the trunk of his car, and police found marijuana, cocaine, and various other drugs.

Within three weeks after the drug bust, when the employees who were known users and pushers were fired and arrested, the plant's productivity increased by nearly twenty percent. Employee turnover gradually decreased and monthly profits began to rise. Experts say chances are good that if you have drug users on the payroll, you also have a pusher.

Clues to Suspected Drug Use or Sale

- increase in absenteeism
- workers frequently going to cars or lockers during breaks
- small groups of employees who scatter when you approach
- physical evidence such as bent spoons, metal bottle caps with burn

marks, medicine droppers, crude hand-rolled cigarette butts, and syringes

- employees using two or three times the sick leave and filing more medical claims

- workers making a lot of secretive phone calls

- employees going to the washroom often and staying for long periods

Experts in the field can provide some information. When you are looking for security experts be sure to check them out before contracting with them. Ask for references. CAUTION: Don't accuse anyone of drug abuse unless you have the facts.

A Hot Issue—The Right to Search for Drugs at Work

The worker has no legal protection from search while on an employer's premises. Lockers and desks can be searched unless the employee happens to have an employment contract that specifically addresses this issue.

In addition, if you have a union there are avenues for appeal and for filing a grievance. If you let employees know that you intend to search lockers or desks for drugs, you are putting them on notice that if drugs are found they will be terminated. You should post the policy and strictly enforce it.

If you do not enforce your no drugs policy, you could have another problem. In California an arbitrator took the side of twenty-five fired Lockheed workers who were let go after a police drug bust at the plant. Lockheed had to reinstate the workers with back pay. Lockheed had not enforced their search and fire policy in the past and the arbitrator thought the workers deserved a reminder that the boss really meant what he said.

As the termination-at-will doctrine erodes, a company's ability to fire employees will be increasingly questioned and the procedures used in searching for drugs and in termination could be impeded.

Testing Applicants or Employees for Drugs

More and more companies are using preemployment urinalysis tests before hiring people. They are also requiring the same tests for people on the payroll whom they suspect of using drugs. Some employees have sued, but most companies feel testing is necessary.

More than twenty-five percent of the Fortune 500 companies now do routine urinalysis tests on employees and job applicants. Many of the companies require a preemployment physical examination and routinely use the tests given in the examination to screen for drugs. If they find drugs, they don't hire the person but they don't usually give drugs as a reason.

If you give the tests, they had better be correct, however. Don't label someone a drug user unless you know you are right. In fact, you had better be able to prove it in court because there could be heavy legal damages. Most companies give at least three different tests to an employee before accusing the person of being on drugs and following with termination.

As concerned human resource managers, we need to know as much as possible about alcohol and drug abuse and how to handle it. If we are to administer employee assistance programs, we should know as much or more than the counselors in order to effectively impact the company in this area.

GENETIC SCREENING OF APPLICANTS

Some companies are going a step further and doing genetic screening. A company called Omnimax, Inc. of Philadelphia claims it is developing a reliable test to determine an individual's general susceptibility to illness at work. There is both a positive and a negative side to the issue of genetic testing.

Companies would like to know before they assign someone to a specific job that they are not assigning an employee who, for example, might have a propensity to black lung disease to a job in an underground coal mine. Companies are concerned that they might be held liable if they fail to conduct such tests and assign genetically unsuitable employees to high risk jobs. On the other hand, genetic testing will certainly be tested in the courts and is considered by many groups to be an invasion of privacy.

HOW TO START AN EMPLOYEE ASSISTANCE PROGRAM FOR DRUG AND ALCOHOL ABUSE

Employee assistance programs are a popular new benefit offered by many organizations. Saving employees from alcohol and drug abuse or from the stress of serious emotional problems is just good business. The objective of an employee assistance program is to offer a method by which supervisors and managers can effectively and constructively deal with the problems of their employees, and employees can seek help for personal difficulties without jeopardizing their job status or promotional opportunities.

How Drug and Alcohol EAPs Work

The employee's immediate supervisor is the key to a successful Employee Assistance Program (EAP). There are five main elements of an EAP.

Observation
Documentation
Confrontation

Referral
Follow-up

Observation   Monitoring job performance is the supervisor's responsibility. There are certain warning signs, which—if they form a pattern, or become habitual—may indicate that job performance deterioration is due to a personal problem. These fall under three main categories.

1. *Absenteeism*

    - excessive use of sick leave or unauthorized leave
    - repeated Monday and Friday absences
    - tardiness—either in coming to work or returning from lunch or breaks
    - leaving work early
    - excessive absences from the job location—to make phone calls, visit the water fountain, or rest rooms
    - peculiar and increasingly improbable excuses for these absences

2. *Lowered Job Efficiency*

    - making mistakes and having to redo jobs
    - wasting materials
    - production slowdown
    - missing deadlines
    - poor judgment and decision-making
    - spasmodic work performance
    - poor safety consciousness
    - customer complaints
    - coworker complaints

3. *Habits and Attitudes*

    - change in physical appearance, dress, and/or general behavior
    - overreaction to real or imagined criticism
    - intolerance, angry outbursts, unreasonable resentments
    - withdrawal—avoidance of contact with supervisor and/or coworkers
    - confusion, inability to concentrate
    - loss of memory
    - strong mood swings

Any one or a combination of these "symptoms" can and do show up with anyone—briefly and occasionally. However, with an employee seriously troubled by personal problems, they will *become excessive* and begin to *form a noticeable pattern* over time.

Documentation It is important for effective use of the EAP that the performance deterioration pattern be documented, otherwise it is hard to prove that such a pattern exists.

Documentation should be:

- consistent—so that the pattern becomes obvious
- specific—leaving no room for argument; generalizations can easily be denied, specific facts cannot
- in writing—leaving no doubt in either the supervisor's or the employee's mind about specific facts

Confrontation Confrontation need not be the difficult, emotionally destructive experience it is often considered to be—if it is *objectively based on job performance.*

Some guidelines on how to stay objective are:

- Don't generalize—be specific. Again, documented facts are hard to deny.
- Don't get personal or judgmental—stick to the facts.
- Don't get tangled up in listening to excuses or explanations of underlying problems—keep coming back to the facts and point out that problems may be dealt with through the EAP.
- Don't leave the employee with only negative feedback—offer the option of constructive action by contacting the EAP.

Referral The employee cannot be forced to use the EAP. However, the employee can be told that disciplinary action will be temporarily suspended when the EAP is utilized. The decision to accept help and undergo treatment is the responsibility of the employee. The employee shall be expected to gain control over personal problems within a reasonable length of time, and improve performance to an acceptable level.

If the employee refuses help, disciplinary action should be followed through.

If the employee accepts help, the supervisor should:

1. advise the EAP counselor that the employee will be making an appointment and the reason(s) for the referral
2. assure the employee that confidentiality will be respected and that

   - the supervisor will not discuss this matter with other employees

- the EAP counselor will only inform the supervisor (1) whether or not the employee has contacted a counselor and (2) whether or not the employee is cooperating in the EAP.

- set guidelines for what is reasonable and acceptable in terms of time and expected job improvement.

Follow-up   Keep in touch with the EAP counselor, especially if there appears to be further "slippage" in work performance. Provide support, but do not "carry" the employee. Deal with slips in performance immediately. Remain consistent in evaluating reasonable and acceptable performance.

The EAP counselor stresses the following points.

- Referral to the EMPLOYEE ASSISTANCE PROGRAM is an *option* that the supervisor may take. This does not constitute a waiver of management's right to invoke disciplinary measures in those situations where it is deemed appropriate.

- The criterion for continued employment is *always* satisfactory job performance.

- For maximum utilization of the Employee Assistance Program, the employee should be referred to the EAP counselor while there is still time to get the employee back on track, *before* there is no other choice but termination.

EAPs also utilize twenty-four-hour hotlines. The program is usually communicated to the employees through company newsletters, the employee handbook, company meetings, and so forth.

Employee Assistance Program Policy No. 1

If you are getting ready to implement an EAP program, here is a sample policy.

The management of XYZ Company believes that it is in the best interests of the employees and the company to have an employee self-help program, to be utilized by employees or their dependents when personal problems are adversely affecting their job performance.

We recognize that a wide-range of human problems that are not directly associated with job function can affect an employee's work performance. These problems include physical illness, mental or emotional upset, alcoholism, and drug abuse, to name a few. In addition to the medical program, the company has initiated an *Employee Assistance Program* (EAP) with the intent of identifying these problems at the earliest possible time and recommending appropriate treatment on an individual and confidential basis.

There is no intention on the part of the company to pass judgment on an employee who may be suffering through a personal problem. However, as these problems affect an employee's health and job performance, resolution of the problem is in the best interests of both the employee and the company.

The Company has established this policy out of concern for the well-being of its employees as well as the need to accomplish its business goals.

Policy

A. All full-time and part-time employees and their dependents are eligible to participate in the Employee Assistance Program.

Note: part-time employees must work at least twenty hours each week.

B. The confidentiality of all communications with reference to the employees and participation in the EAP will be considered privileged medical information, and treated in the same manner as any other medical record or information.

C. No employee's job security or promotion opportunities will be jeopardized by a request for counseling or referral assistance.

D. The employee, on the other hand, shall be expected to gain control over his or her personal problem in a reasonable length of time, and improve his or her performance acceptability as a condition of continued employment. During this time, so long as the person is making a genuine effort to correct the problem, the supervisor shall defer disciplinary action making it clear, however, that the employee can *either accept help and follow through with the Plan Program or risk discipline up to and including the possibility of discharge.*

E. Employee Assistance Program services provided by the program administrators will be offered at no cost to employees. Such services include short-term counseling, assessment, planning, and referral. If treatment is required, the cost may be partially covered by the company group medical plan. Treatment costs not covered by the group medical plan will be the responsibility of the employee. Claims can be filed, using the present procedures.

F. Only employees who recognize they have a problem and agree to cooperate through rehabilitation will be permitted to participate in the company's approved EAP program. Nonparticipants, or participants who repeatedly fail to respond to treatment through lack of cooperation on their part, and whose work continues to be unsatisfactory, will be held responsible for work performance; and normal personnel procedures will apply.

G. For the purpose of this policy, a "troubled" employee is defined as that employee evidencing declining job performance that appears to be caused by behavioral problems, or induced by the use of alcohol or drugs. Employees experiencing emotional, marital, financial, or legal difficulties to the degree that job performance is impaired are also considered "troubled" employees and are included in the program.

H.   The Employee Self-Help Program does not constitute any waiver of management's right to invoke disciplinary measures in misconduct situations where it is deemed appropriate. The performance standards are not being changed. The only change is the offer of a new service, one which hopes to help employees get back to standard and thus save valued people and jobs. Work performed up to standard is still the basis for continued employment.

How an Employee Gets into the Program

- *Self-Referral*
  Employees who are experiencing personal problems are encouraged to take it upon themselves to seek assistance from the EAP. All communications and information received by the administrators of the program through such self-referral will be kept strictly confidential. No one other than the individual and the administrator will know if or how the program is being used by that individual.

- *Referral by Others*
  Anyone may suggest that an employee or a member of the employee's family seek help through the program. The program administrators can provide assistance to persons who are concerned about someone else's problem, but unsure what to do.

- *Supervisor Referral*
  When a supervisor becomes aware of a developing pattern of unsatisfactory job performance that cannot be corrected through the company's standard policies and procedures or the employee's own efforts, the supervisor may suggest or recommend to the employee that he or she seek the support and assistance of the program. In this case, also, the program will remain strictly confidential.

  It is recognized that it is not the role of any supervisor or manager to attempt to diagnose or resolve the employee's personal problems. However, it is the responsibility of the supervisor to be clear about his expectations regarding the employee's job performance, to document these expectations, and to take appropriate disciplinary action in the event the employee's job performance consistently fails to meet acceptable standards.

- *Documentation and Procedure Control*

  All documentation in the personnel records of employees will relate solely to job performance and will include no reference to the employee's suspected personal problems or participation in the Employee Assistance Program.

  The company assures that there will be absolutely no discrimination against any employee in terms of job security or promotional opportunities based in any part on his voluntary use of the program. Neither will use of the program alter, in any way, the standard administrative practices applicable to job performance requirements.

- *Implementation*

  Development and implementation of the Employee Assistance Program is the responsibility of the human resource director.

It is a good idea to write a special letter of introduction to employees when you implement your EAP. Following is a sample announcement letter.

Sample EAP Announcement Letter

A MESSAGE TO ALL EMPLOYEES AND THEIR FAMILIES:

The XYZ Company is pleased to announce that an Employee Assistance Program (EAP) is being made available to all employees and their dependents. This service has proven successful in many business locations and is being offered because it can benefit both the employees and the company.

All of us at one time or another are troubled by personal problems. Happily we can solve most of these problems by ourselves; however, there are some who cannot, some whose problems are so serious that they affect their jobs and even their lives. We are referring to problems resulting from marital stress, financial difficulties, alcohol or drug abuse, or extreme emotional problems.

We believe that employee's personal problems are private—unless they are causing the employee's job performance to deteriorate. When that happens the problems become a matter of concern to the company—not only because of poor job performance but, more importantly, because a fellow employee is in trouble.

The objective of the EAP is to offer a method by which the company can take *constructive* action in dealing with the employees who have personal problems that make life difficult and impair performance. The goal is to help an employee find professional assistance when it is needed because the employee is unable to cope with the problems alone. The program is available to all employees, as well as their family members, spouses, children, parents, siblings—anyone who is a significant other in the life of an employee.

The EAP program seeks to remedy and not to punish. Its sole purpose is to help the employee to regain self-confidence so that personal pride and job productivity are not lost.

XYZ Company job performance standards are not being changed. The only change is the offer of this new service—which hopes to help employees get back to standard and thus save valued people and jobs. Work performed up to standard (or brought back to an acceptable standard) is still the basis for continued employment. It should be understood that the EAP does not constitute any waiver of management's right to use disciplinary measures in situations where they are deemed appropriate.

Everything about this program is confidential. The names of persons using the EAP will be known only to the administrator of the program (and to those immediately concerned, such as the supervisor *if* referral comes by that method). No records will be open to management. No records of problems discussed with the administrator will ever appear in an employee's personnel file. Neither the employee's job security nor chances for promotion will be jeopardized by use of this Employee Support Program.

The EAP may be utilized in one of three ways:

1. by self-referral,
2. by referral through one's own supervisor, if you and he or she discussed the matter in the course of reviewing job performance, or
3. by referral from a peer.

It is our sincere hope that you or any member of your family who is experiencing problems that you are unable to handle on your own will avail yourselves of this fine program.

Sincerely,

John Doe, President
XYZ Company

Employee Assistance Program Policy No. 2

As an employer, XYZ Company is committed to maintaining and strengthening our most important resources—our employees. In support of that tradition, XYZ has initiated an employee support program dedicated to serving the needs of our employees. The program has been planned in recognition of the tremendous losses possible when employees' problems go unresolved—both human losses and the resultant loss of service to the people within the company.

Many personal problems, such as family or marital strife, financial or legal difficulties, alcoholism and drug abuse, health or medical, can seriously hinder or diminish an individual's job performance. Not only are there losses in personal effectiveness, but absenteeism, low productivity, and other cost consequences are associated with such problems. The following reflect the company's concern for the well-being of employees as well as the dedication to efficient accomplishment of its business goals.

1. XYZ Company recognizes that employees or members of their families may have personal problems that adversely affect the employee's job performance.

2. It is not the intention of the company to pass moral judgment on an employee who may be suffering through a personal problem. However, as these problems affect not only the employee's health and happiness but also job performance, the XYZ Company believes that their resolution is in the best interests of both the employee and the company.

3. XYZ Company encourages any employees who are experiencing personal problems to take it upon themselves to seek assistance from the Employee Assistance Program. All communications and information received by the administrators and counselors of the program through such a self-referral will be kept strictly confidential. No one other than the individual and the counselor will know if or how the program is being used by that individual.

4. The confidentiality of all communications with reference to the employee and these illnesses will be preserved as privileged medical information, and treated in the same manner as any other medical record or information.

5. Employees will not have their job security or promotion opportunities jeopardized by their request for counseling or referral assistance.

6. When a supervisor becomes aware of a developing pattern of unsatisfactory job performance which cannot be corrected through XYZ's standard policies and procedures, or the employee's own efforts, the supervisor may suggest or recommend to the employee that he seek the support and assistance of the program. In this case also, the program will remain strictly confidential. It is recognized that it is not the role of any supervisor or manager to attempt to diagnose or resolve the employee's personal problems. However, it is the responsibility of the supervisor to be clear about his job performance expectations of the employees, to document specifically and accurately any deviations from these expectations, and to take appropriate disciplinary action in the event the employee's job performance consistently fails to meet acceptable standards.

7. All documentation in the personnel records of company employees

will relate solely to job performance and will include no reference to the employee's suspected personal problems or his participation in the program. The company assures that there will be absolutely no discrimination against any employee in terms of job security or promotional opportunities based in any part on his voluntary use of the services. Neither will use of the program alter, in any way, the standard administrative practices applicable to job performance requirements.

Success Rates of EAPs

Experts feel that the success rates of EAPs are excellent. Most companies that implement an EAP also implement procedures for tracking success and drop out ratios. Employees who are referred usually stay in the program until they have gotten the help they need to alleviate their problems. Because they want to keep their jobs, some drop out and then reenter the program when performance again is at issue. The highest rate of success of EAPs is with self-referrals to the program.

There is general agreement among human resource managers I have talked with that whether you have an in-house EAP or use outside consultants, the EAP overall is beneficial. It provides a framework for dealing with costly and personal problems at work. Before we had EAPs, human resource managers had to handle much of the counseling of troubled employees themselves. But most human resource professionals are not trained counselors. The serious drug and alcohol problems most companies are experiencing today make an employee assistance program a business necessity.

How the Internationalization of Business Impacts HRM

CHAPTER 10

KEY ISSUES FACING MULTINATIONAL OPERATIONS

American companies are putting more emphasis than ever before on understanding foreign markets, on globalization, and on the internationalization of their operations, including concern for human resource management in the current tenuous international climate.

United States-based international companies are the third largest economic block in the world, surpassing the gross national product of every country except the United States and the Soviet Union.

Over 474 of the Fortune 500 firms have significant international operations. Three hundred and one firms do from ten to fifty percent of their business overseas according to the Conference Board. Of the Fortune 100 companies, fifty-six report that more than half their corporate revenues come from overseas operations; and the United States Department of Commerce estimates more than 3,500 American companies have some involvement in overseas trade.

There are several reasons for the rapid expansion into overseas markets. Some companies are attempting to expand their sales and some want to take advantage of lower wages and so develop production facilities in countries where they have markets.

Only the largest companies have full-time human resource professionals on staff, devoted exclusively to multinational problems, but it is important to understand the key issues in multinational operations.

Internationalization: The Trend Toward Hiring Foreign Managers

Hiring foreign managers is becoming more popular with larger American corporations. Non-Americans now hold more than one-third of the top management positions in eighty-five companies recently surveyed by The Conference Board. The internationalization of top level positions in American companies will continue as expansion into new markets creates the need for expertise in unfamiliar customs, markets, labor pools, distribution systems, and cultures. Also, the high priority American and European companies place on having their foreign operations managed by local managers with a faculty for English as well as other languages will produce a growing number of skilled and talented managers whose ultimate career objective might be a job in corporate headquarters. We should stay current on these trends in order to participate in organizational development and succession planning.

Another important issue is the growing need for language fluency. Most executives of United States firms speak the language of the countries in which they work, even though few United States companies formally require language fluency. In European firms, managers are often required to speak the local language, and many European managers are expected to speak English, which is considered the international communications language throughout Europe. Language fluency and cross-cultural expertise will be a big need in human resource training and development programs in the future.

Globalization: Increasing Market Share by Standardizing Products Worldwide

The idea of globalization is catching on in many firms. Basically, most companies today seek to increase market share by standardizing products worldwide. They can then lower costs and siphon business from companies that customize products for individual markets. It is important to understand the process of globalization in order to handle administration of human resource issues on an international scale.

Theodore Levitt of Howard Business School is high on globalization. In his book, *The Marketing Imagination*, he points out mass communications and high technology are creating similar patterns of consumption in diverse cultures, the emergence of global markets allows corporations to standardize manufacturing and distribution of products as diverse as cosmetics and television sets. Global companies make concessions to cultural differences. Automakers like Toyota, for example, produce cars with steering columns on the right or left side, depending on the destination of the cars. But that requires only a minor modification. Most other features of the product are the same.

In addition, multinational companies have to understand complex compensation issues and the often complex and conflicting benefits laws of various countries. For example, here are seven complex provisions of the social security regulations in just one country: Colombia, South America.

- Employees of firms doing business in Colombia are eligible for a social security retirement benefit at age 60 (55 for females). It amounts to 45 percent of the final three years' average earnings, plus 1.2 percent of final average earnings for each year of service after the first 500 weeks, plus 14 percent of the minimum wage for the wife and 7 percent for each child.

- The maximum social security benefit is twenty-two times the minimal legal wage, up to ninety percent of the worker's final average earnings.

- Labor code pension (payable by the employer) applies to workers with twenty years of service, ten of which must have been before 1967. It amounts to seventy-five percent of the final year's earnings up to twenty-two times the minimum wage. It is payable at age fifty-five (fifty for women).

- The employee is eligible for a "penalty pension" if he or she has between fifteen and twenty years of service and is retired or terminated without cause after age fifty.

- A penalty pension also is payable if the employee has ten to fifteen years of service and is retired or dismissed without cause at age sixty or later.

- A worker terminated without cause after ten or more years of service is entitled to a benefit payment of forty-five days pay for the first year on the job, plus an amount for each additional year. Employees terminated for cause are entitled to a "cesantia" or termination indemnity of one month's pay for each year of service since 1963.

- Survivors of employees who die from non-work-related causes receive a benefit equal to a year's salary. If the employee had made fewer than 500 weeks worth of contributions to the social security system, a survivor's pension equal to the social security old age pension also is paid.

Costs to employers for these and other mandated benefits can add up to as much as forty-five to fifty-five percent of covered salaries.

Companies doing business overseas should get good advice before making decisions about compensation and benefits for overseas workers.

What Globalization Means for Businesses

Globalization impacts companies in several areas.

- Recruiting and selection take on new dimensions. You may be recruiting more nationals in the foreign countries than American workers. Recruiting overseas is far different than recruiting in the United States. Each country has its own unique set of problems.

- Compensation and benefits must be reviewed in light of local regulations and pay practice if you plan to hire both United States workers and local nationals.

- Policies and procedures for managing the many details of transfer, relocation, and settlement of expatriates must be agreed on, implemented, and communicated to management and employees who will be affected.

- Tax considerations must be reviewed for each country in order to establish a policy for tax treatment of expatriates.

HOW TO CHOOSE THE RIGHT EMPLOYEES FOR OVERSEAS ASSIGNMENTS

One of the most significant problems organizations have in their overseas operations is in picking the right people for an assignment. The "wash out" rate in all organizations is very high. Because of the high rate of turnover of expatriates, most companies today are putting a new emphasis on selection.

How effective is your program of selecting personnel who are most likely to succeed in overseas assignments? How well do you prepare them for the specific cultural demands of the country in which they will be living and working? Do you include their wives and teenage children? They, too, represent your company in the community—and are the most frequent cause of the premature return of families.

Some companies have added in-house experts to help them in employee selection, others utilize outside consultants to help in selection of expatriates. One such consultant is Virginia M. Berg, Ph.D., of Athens, Georgia.

Dr. Berg specializes in helping companies identify the criteria used in the decision-making process. An outside consultant can

- Help identify the kinds of problems people face in different areas.
- Suggest red flags in selecting personnel for assignments in different parts of the world.
- Provide guidelines, lists of resources, and specifics to help you plan (or revise) your selection, orientation and training programs.
- Show how pertinent divisions of your organization can keep up with changes in the countries where you operate.

Dr. Berg provides the following information to help Human Resource Managers set selection criteria for expatriate employees.*

What to Look for When Selecting Job Qualifications

Those involved in the decision-making process of selecting an employee for an overseas position face the challenge of finding the person who seems at least risk of experiencing difficulty in an unfamiliar culture, and one who will

---

* Adapted from "Selection Criteria and Objectives for Expatriate Employees," by Virginia M. Berg, Ph.D., Athens, GA.

most effectively represent the company in the foreign environment. Most personnel decisions have been based primarily on the technical competence of the candidate because of both the ease in identifying and measuring such qualities and the lack of certainty about the importance of other characteristics.

Before making such decisions, it is necessary for those involved in the selection process to have a clear and comprehensive understanding of the objectives of the company in staffing the position, the primary reasons for expatriate failure, and the personal characteristics and qualities that have been found to enhance the ability of employees to perform effectively overseas.

The results of a poor decision can be costly, not only in terms of actual costs, which are estimated to range between $55,000 and $85,000 per expatriate failure, but also in terms of corporate relations, efficient operations, and the personal losses of reputation and self-concept of the employee. Recent research indicates a current expatriate failure rate of between twenty-six percent and forty percent. Because cost of failure is so high, there is a need for improved selection and training methods.

Key Reasons Why Some Expatriates Fail

A survey of eighty United States international corporations indicates that, in their opinion, the most important reasons for an expatriate's failure to function effectively in a foreign environment, in descending order were:

1. the inability of the manager's spouse to adjust to a different physical or cultural environment
2. the manager's inability to adapt to a different physical or cultural environment
3. other family related problems
4. the manager's personality or emotional immaturity
5. the manager's inability to cope with the responsibilities posed by the overseas work
6. the manager's lack of technical competence
7. the manager's lack of motivation to work overseas

The first consideration in the selection process should be to formulate an adequate job description based on the factors critical for success in the specific position. This should include an analysis of the type of position, the motive for sending the employee overseas, and the general demands of the host country. These demands can include the need to conform to religious restrictions, the geographical and physical demands of climate, the amount of personal freedom, and the availability or lack of such comforts as reliable transportation, familiar food and entertainment, and schools.

In addition, more specifically job-oriented considerations include the amount of contact with nationals, socially, politically, and at the work site; the amount of personal supervision of those whose concepts of work and custom may differ; and the level of decision-making that must take place with no consultation available from other experts.

HOW TO PREPARE A SELECTION MODEL FOR RATING APPLICANTS FOR MULTINATIONAL ASSIGNMENTS

Figure 10-1 is a selection model that can help you formulate a basis for objective selection. One of the advantages of thorough prescreening and setting of objectives is the ability to use these same objectives when evaluating the success of each placement, with the additional benefit of refining the company's screening and selection process for future placements. Once the objectives are set in a written format, not only is the decision-making process simplified, but these same objectives can be used as a basis for the interview during the formal selection process on an ongoing basis.

You could classify overseas job assignments into four major categories.

1. Chief executive officer—whose responsibility is to oversee and direct the entire operation

2. Functional head—whose job is to establish functional departments in a foreign affiliate

3. Trouble-shooters—professionals whose function is to analyze and solve specific operational problems

4. Rank and file employees

Generally, job assignments in the first two categories involve more extensive personal contact with the host nationals and a longer stay in the foreign country, and thus should require a heavier weighting in the area of personal relations abilities.

The selection model should be specifically designed to accommodate the needs of each company, and the needs of individual placements within the operation. A minimum standard for each category should be set, below which an applicant's rejection should be predetermined. A five- to seven-point system allows adequate flexibility for decision-making.

The model development and the selection process should both be based on input from several people involved in the decision process. Suggested as part of the selection team are a personnel professional, a psychologist, the candidate's immediate supervisor, other people familiar with the candidate's work, and a host national or returnee familiar with the locale.

Four Task Related Areas to Consider

In developing the framework for the model, task requirements and the potential problem areas, which are more easily defined, should be listed first, without regard to specific solutions. A variety of sources, such as information from host country nationals, estimates of reasons for previous failures (both of this company and of other multi-national companies), and suggestions from the available literature should be considered.

It may help to group items in this first column under the general headings of technical, environmental, personal, and family considerations. Then each group can be subdivided so as to specifically relate to individual needs.

Once these task-related categories have been listed and defined, objectives should be determined and listed in a second column. The second column, listing specific objectives for each category, may be included here, or determined at this point and included in a separate report to keep the selection model format from being too lengthy.

A third column should be devised, this time listing requirements that relate to such variables as personality traits, interpersonal abilities, or personal and family characteristics.

In the fourth column, some appraisal method should be used for each candidate. A value scale with relative numerical weights would be easiest to use, although room for comments should be left in this column. An odd number totaling either five or seven is suggested. As each category is considered, the candidate's estimated potential for satisfying the position requirements should be noted. Scores may be connected for a profile in each category.

Considerations under each category will vary with the situation, as will the requirements considered necessary, but in each case the requirements should reflect the needs and objectives of the position. Some of the qualities to be considered under technical considerations are the amount of confidence of the applicant in his or her ability to fulfill the requirements of the job, the ability to produce results with little or no supervision, and the amount of skill in motivating others.

Environmental considerations may well include the ability to analyze the local situation and act accordingly, to be tolerant of differences of culture and custom, to respect the values of others, and to handle political and economic differences with diplomacy.

Selection Model Figure 10-1

Considerations	Objectives	Requirements	Evaluation	Comments
I. Technical				
Lack of technical expertise available at site.		Need person with good technical background and skills in training others	Rating 1 2 3 (4) 5	
Little contact with home office and peers		Candidate should be able to make independent decisions without advice and support from others	Rating 1 2 3 4 (5)	
Local employees have poor understanding of U.S. management techniques-paternalistic		Requires person with managerial and leadership skills	Rating 1 2 (3) 4 5	
			Score I 12	
II. Environmental				
Desert climate, isolated, little variation in temperature		Should be in good mental and physical health	Rating 1 2 3 4 (5)	
Difficult political and religious restrictions		Requires diplomatic person, tolerant of local customs	Rating 1 2 (3) 4 5	
Requires strong language skills		Knowledge of local language. Skill in learning new languages	Rating 1 2 (3) 4 5	
			Score II 11	

III. <u>Personal</u>

Highly stressful situation-political instability, terroristic threats

Candidate should be able to handle stress well without resort to drug and alcohol misuse

Rating 1 2 3 ④ 5

Great deal of personal contact with host country nationals—varied social obligations

Need flexible person who adapts well to change

Rating 1 2 3 4 ⑤

Score III 9

IV. <u>Family</u>

Little contact with other Americans. No employment available for wife

Requires stable marital relationship, wife with flexible attitude and interest in other cultures

Rating 1 2 3 4 ⑤

Lack of activities. No U.S. sports, music, schools, etc.

Needs cooperation and support of family members, children willing to adapt to changes

Rating 1 2 3 ④ 5

Score IV 9

Total score 41

Other Important Factors

Some factors that influence the family are (1) the strength of ties to others who must be left behind; (2) the importance of religious and community ties, the breaking of which may cause significant stress; and (3) the attitudes of spouses and children towards change.

Test results are important, but the interview is the most effective and informative selection technique and should be used once the screening instruments have determined the potential candidates.

It is advisable to incorporate as much of the orientation into the selection process as possible. If the candidate is exposed to films, audio/visual presentations, literature, or discussions with others about the overseas position before the interview, the trained interviewer will be able to ascertain a great deal about positive or negative attitudes towards the unfamiliar situation. Critical or demeaning attitudes, lack of tolerance, or enthusiasm and curiosity about the new culture will be evident.

Be sure to include the spouse and, if possible, the children at some time during the interview stage. The degree of family cohesiveness, and the supportiveness of individual family members, may be obvious during this period. A rigid, inflexible attitude, the importance of certain items not available overseas, or the potential for resistance by teenage children are better brought to the surface before the final decision is made. A positive and flexible attitude toward change, the patience and desire to learn about a new culture and the awareness of future hardships are all necessary qualities. The interview period is the time to allow the candidate and his or her family the opportunity to realistically assess both the advantages and disadvantages.

Once the interview stage has been completed, the candidate and spouse should be given an opportunity to experience the new situation first-hand, with a visit to the site. There, they should be given a realistic picture of actual living conditions and be allowed to talk with other expatriates already there, so they can assess for themselves the reality of conditions in the new post. When they return, they will be more realistically able to assess their ability to be successful in the new culture. Despite the cost of this visit, the cost of a premature return will be much greater, not only for the company, but in terms of stress upon the candidate's career, health, and family situation.

Sample Expatriate Policy for Overseas Employees

Most companies provide an expatriate policy and guidelines for employees to follow when they are considering an overseas assignment. Here is a sample expatriate policy.

EXPATRIATE POLICY

I. Compensation

Purpose

To assist in the administration of compensation policies for employees assigned to locations outside their home country. The objective of this policy is to provide equitable compensation practices in order to:

1. attract and retain personnel

2. provide sufficient financial incentive for the employee to want to live and work overseas

3. enable expatriates to retain the level of purchasing power they had in the United States

4. provide a program that will be fair and competitive and will keep the expatriates (salary-wise and salary-range-wise) in line with United States counterparts.

Scope

This policy applies to expatriate employees in executive or managerial positions who are transferred from their home country to executive or managerial positions in a foreign location. Wherever possible, non-executive or non-managerial positions should be filled with local workers. Exceptions to this provision must be approved on an individual basis by the corporate office. The provisions of this policy are subject to review for those expatriate employees who remain at a foreign location for a period of time in excess of three years.

Practice

Our company uses a Balance Sheet Approach. The compensation balance sheet separates allowances, adjustments, and differentials from base pay and offsets differences between United States and foreign costs and other economic factors.

1. *Base Pay*—Equivalent of salary paid for a comparable position in the domestic organization. Base salary for an expatriate employee shall be determined by the application of the company's position evaluation program and duties and responsibilities of the position to which assigned.

2. *Expatriate Premium*—Fifteen percent is added to base pay as a

tax-free incentive designed to compensate for separation from familiar working and living conditions, separation from friends, relatives and business associates, and from the normal channels of advancement in the domestic organization.

3. *Hardship Allowance*—Has no relationship to the level of job or living costs. Hardship allowance is a percent added to base pay and is determined by the following:
   a. geographic isolation
   b. inadequate housing
   c. lack of cultural and recreation facilities
   d. inadequate transportation
   e. lack of food and consumer services
   f. unfavorable climate
   g. conditions dangerous to life or physical well being
   h. exposure to disease and unsanitary conditions
   i. inadequate medical facilities and health control
      Hardship allowance is determined by weighing these factors to arrive at a tax-free percent of base pay.

4. *Living Allowance*—An offset to assure "no-gain-no-loss" approach to expatriates as a result of cost differences in the United States from the foreign post.
   a. *Housing differential for non-company furnished housing*—To offset any excess housing costs, i.e. those that are over and above what an employee might reasonably expect to pay for housing and utilities in the United States. Where foreign housing costs are less than housing costs at home, the employee would not get a credit. The employer will pay actual shelter costs at the foreign location that exceed the assumed United States monthly shelter costs based on the employee's marital status and income.
   b. *Cost of Living Differential*—An offset for any differences between costs of goods and services (excluding housing) at the foreign post and those in the United States. Cost of living percentage differentials are applied to the percent of income the employee spends at the foreign post. Living cost differentials will be reviewed periodically, but not more than quarterly for significant changes at the expatriate's post of assignment.

5. *Hypothetical Tax*—An offset designated to ensure the employee income tax on Company-earned income is equal to but does not exceed what he would have been paid on base salary only, had the employee remained in the United States. With the use of the hypothetical United States tax, the Company assumes all the foreign tax of the employee to prevent double tax. For the

purposes of determining United States Federal equivalent tax liability, deductions will be made on base pay only, at the tax rates currently applicable in the United States. In the calculation under this policy, personal income generated outside of Company sources is not included.

6. *Adjustments for Foreign Government Requirement Payments*—An offset reimbursing the employee for amounts that must be paid toforeign programs—such as social security *or* reimbursing the Company for amounts it must pay the employees for legally required programs such as profit sharing, bonus plans, and so forth.

Educational Allowances

To provide financial assistance to expatriate employees working abroad and accompanied by school age children, who are faced with above normal school expense due to the locale to which they are assigned.

1. *Amount*—The Company will reimburse the difference in cost of tuition, books, and necessary fees between the cost in the United States and the additional cost incurred abroad.

2. *Eligible children*—To qualify for educational allowances children must be dependent wards of the expatriate employee.

3. *Expatriate's children* attending college in the country of origin, or elsewhere, are entitled to one round trip economy class air fare per year, or its equivalent, if attending college outside of the country of origin, to visit their parents at the foreign post.

Shipment of Household Effects

The Company will pay all reasonable costs for shipping the expatriate's household furnishings between the country of origin and the foreign post. For short-term assignments, storage of a portion of the expatriate's household furnishings may be provided.

Included in moving costs are:

1. packing and crating
2. customs duty and tariffs
3. temporary storage in country of origin and at foreign post
4. overland transportation in country of origin and in the foreign country
5. insurance in transit
6. unpacking and/or crating

7. conversion or alterations of appliances and installation of necessary fixtures, electrical outlets, and so forth.

Moving costs of expatriates from one foreign post to another or for repatriation will be covered in accordance with this policy.

Benefits Plans

While expatriates are on foreign assignment, Company benefits will continue without interruption. Company benefits such as group medical insurance, life insurance, and pension will be computed on United States base pay only.

General Letter of Agreement— Employees in agreement with an offer made by the Company will be provided with a letter of agreement outlining pertinent details regarding the foreign assignment. Such details will include date and place of assignment, anticipated length of assign ment, move and travel allowances, provisions for home leave, and repatriation. Accompanying the letter of agreement will be a compensation summary.

Orientation— A special orientation program will be held for each employee that is being considered for a foreign assignment. A detailed check list including all phases of his assignment, compensation, benefits, and so forth will be discussed. The employee should feel that he has a direct line of communication with the domestic Company and should be provided with the names of people that he may contact in the Company in case of emergency or personal problems.

Point of Origin— To provide an equitable base for the administration of expatriate policies, the Company has designated _____ as the point of origin for all expatriate employees.

II. Home Leave

Purpose

It is the policy of the Company to enable and encourage each expatriate employee to take home leave annually. It is intended that such home leave be spent in the employee's home country. However, as an option, employees may be permitted to take their home leave outside their home country. Employees electing the home leave option will be reimbursed for actual travel expenses so long as they do not exceed the travel expenses that would be incurred if the employee and authorized family members were returning to their point of origin.

Expatriate employees will qualify for home leave as set forth in the Vacation Policy with the following exceptions.

- Employees accepting a permanent foreign assignment must take all earned vacation before the foreign assignment commences.

- Expatriate employees must complete one year of foreign service before being eligible for home leave.

- New employees on permanent foreign assignment must complete one year of service before being eligible for vacation.

- In addition to normal vacation time, an extra two weeks of home leave is provided for each year. An expatriate will be eligible for the two additional weeks after completing one year of foreign service. Thereafter, the extra two weeks of home leave will be on a calendar year basis.

Travel time will not be considered as part of vacation time. There will be a stopover allowance as defined in the Procedure portion of this policy. This stopover time is based on the normal travel time via the most direct route from the country of foreign assignment to the United States.

Scope

This policy applies to expatriate employees, assigned on a permanent basis.

Practice

An expatriate employee will schedule home leave after completing one year of continuous service in a foreign location. To qualify for home leave, an employee must leave the country of assignment for a minimum period of fourteen days; however, it is not necessary to return to the home country. Employees choosing not to return to their home country will be reimbursed for actual travel expenses that would be incurred if the employee and authorized family members were returning to their point of origin. Home leave expenses will be reimbursed for only *one* trip per year.

Stopovers will be permitted according to the following schedule.

Location   Stopover Allowance

_____   _____

_____   _____

_____   _____

_____   _____

The Company will provide overnight accommodations and meals for expatriates on stopovers in the amount that is receipted up to _____ per day for the employee, _____ per day for spouse, and _____ per day for each dependent. Travel and stopover time will not be considered part of vacation time.

Excess baggage allowance will be provided up to a maximum of 100 pounds including the allowance provided by the transportation used by the expatriate in returning to his place of assignment. First class air transportation under current policy provides for 66 pounds per traveler. The Company will pay the amount equal to excess baggage costs on the difference between 66 and 100 pounds. Should the expatriate choose to fly tourist class, the Company will pay for 34 pounds of excess baggage in addition to the allowance provided for tourist class air travel. This allowance applies to each family member requiring an air fare.

Should air freight or surface transportation be used to ship these commodities to the expatriate's place of assignment, the reimbursement for these shipping costs will not exceed the excess baggage allowance as stated above.

III. Automobiles

Purpose

To provide expatriate employees assistance in securing adequate transportation for business and personal use in countries where the cost of a privately owned automobile is substantially greater than the cost of a similar vehicle in the United States.

Scope

This policy applies to expatriate employees that will be assigned to a foreign location in excess of seventeen months.

Procedure

The Company will provide a basic car at each foreign location. This car is to be determined by the foreign manager with approval of the Departmental Vice President. This basic car will be priced in the United States with the price being established as the cost of the vehicle to the employee. If the basic car cannot be priced in the United States, the cost to the employee will be established on the price of an intermediate class vehicle in the United States. The Company will cover the difference between the United States price and the actual cost of the automobile in the foreign location. At this point, a fixed percentage ratio of ownership is established between the employee and the Company.

It will be the responsibility of the employee to secure and maintain liability and collision insurance, with the Company named as the insured. Insurance, taxes, and normally assessed fees will be shared at the same ratio as ownership in the vehicle.

This vehicle so purchased by the employee will be for personal use. Any business use of this car will be reimbursed at the current rate per mile established in the United States.

On reassignment from the foreign location, the expatriate will have responsibility for obtaining an equitable sale price for the vehicle. On sale of the vehicle, the Company will share in the selling price at the same ratio as established when the vehicle was purchased. A similar reimbursement will be made for an insurance settlement in the event the vehicle is destroyed by casualty or collision.

The need for drivers will be surveyed on a location-by-location basis.

IV. Automobile (Expatriate Temporarily Assigned to Foreign Location)

Purpose

The purpose of this policy is to provide temporary expatriates with adequate means of transportation while on assignment in foreign countries.

Scope

This policy applies to expatriates who will be assigned to foreign duty for a period of more than sixty days but less than eighteen months.

Procedure

When it is planned for an employee to be assigned to a foreign location for a period in excess of sixty days, but less than eighteen months, the Company will provide local transportation for the expatriate employee. This car may be purchased by the Company or provided on a lease basis depending on the recommendation of the location Vice President.

The expatriate will be responsible for the operating cost of the vehicle, including minor maintenance (gasoline, oil, tires, etc.). Significant repairs will be the responsibility of the Company.

The Company will provide the necessary insurance coverage as required by the location.

Disposal of the vehicle will be at the discretion of the Company.

Vehicles will not necessarily be provided for temporary expatriates, but will be based on an as-needed basis and the availability of alternate means of transportation.

Should an expatriate's assignment be changed from temporary to permanent, the normal expatriate automobile policy will automatically apply.

V. Physical Examinations

Purpose

To determine the physical fitness of an expatriate employee and family for the service and location for which the employee is being considered.

Scope

This policy applies to expatriate employees and their families. It is designed as a safeguard to employees to assure that the expatriate and the family are in good health and are capable of living in the place of assignment without undue hardship.

General

Expatriate employees and family members who will be living in the foreign location will be required to have complete and thorough physicals before undertaking a foreign assignment. The Company will pay the cost of these physicals for the employee and his family. Subsequent physicals will be required during home leave on a yearly basis.

COMPENSATING OVERSEAS EMPLOYEES: THIRTEEN MAJOR ITEMS TO CONSIDER

The most important items to consider in overseas compensation procedures are:

- *The General Method of Payment*—You may need to consider a variety of compensation arrangements when you install the mechanics of the program in each country.

- *Base Pay*—In most organizations, the base pay of expatriates is the same as it is in the United States. Most companies use a balance sheet philosophy. This philosophy basically means that it is the intent of the company that the employee should neither gain nor lose financially because of an overseas assignment.

- *Overseas Premiums*—Most organizations pay an overseas premium in addition to the base pay of an employee based overseas. This premium compensates for those unique functional responsibilities placed on the employee in a foreign assignment.

- *Amount of Income Paid in United States Dollars*—There are a combination of factors that come into play when an employee is paid overseas.

The key ones are the local exchange regulations and controls, the local management salary structure, local income tax regulations, and the preferences of the expatriate and management involved. Some companies encourage expatriates to receive part of their compensation in the local currency, about the same amount a local national would receive in salary, and then to accept the balance in United States currency and bank it in the United States. This is done to downplay what might be considered a conspicuous life style in the host country.

- *Housing Allowance*—Most organizations pay a housing allowance. There is a wide variety of methods used by companies to figure what an expatriate's housing allowance should be. One method is to pay total housing costs less estimated United States housing costs with the company paying eighty-five percent and the expatriate paying fifteen percent of the remainder. In many companies, the local manager who understands the housing situation sets the housing allowance.

- *Entertainment Allowance and Club Memberships*—Most companies reimburse expatriates for legitimate business-related expenses. The amount of the allowance or type of club membership may depend on the level of the employee. In some instances the employee must pay a portion of the cost of a club membership.

- *Educational and Language Training Allowances*—Nearly all organizations who have expatriates offer paid educational and language training. The language training may also include the spouse and children.

- *Cost-of-Living Allowance*—Most organizations provide a cost-of-living allowance to all expatriates, and many companies use the State Department C-O-L indices in calculating the allowances. Another Company, Organizational Resource Company also provides information of C-O-L. The larger accounting firms also provide information to their clients who reimburse expatriates for cost of living.

- *Tax Equalization*—Most multinationals provide a tax equalization provision in their compensation package for expatriates. Generally the policy and procedure is to deduct hypothetical United States and state taxes and assume all United States and foreign taxes that result from company compensation. Some corporations pay foreign excess tax only on salary and bonus and not on total compensation.

- *Transfer Costs*—All multinational corporations that we are aware of pay the total cost of transferring the employee abroad. Some companies put a ceiling on what and how much an employee can take abroad. Companies also have specific auto policies. In many cases the expatriate must pay the cost of shipping an automobile. Many companies furnish cars at the location for use of expatriates.

- *Dollar Devaluation Adjustments*—Most organizations make adjustments in overseas compensation every time the United States dollar is devalued in relation to local currency. This helps the expatriate maintain a relatively normal standard of living for the location.

- *Bonus and Stock Plans*—Many companies have extra bonus and stock plans for overseas executives to help compensate for dangerous or uncomfortable conditions.

- *Employment Contract*—Many corporations now require that an executive or professional employee being chosen for overseas assignment sign an employment contract, or a letter of understanding. The contract states that the expatriate agrees to stay a certain period of time and sets out all the conditions of the transfer and what happens if the employee does not stay through the period agreed on.

TIPS ON CONTROLLING EXPATRIATE COSTS

Because the costs of transferring and maintaining executives abroad has accelerated so significantly, organizations are now looking for opportunities to control expatriate staff expense. A rule of thumb on cost can be three or four (maybe even more) times base salary. A checklist of items to review and ways to control expatriate costs will help you focus on budget considerations and specific areas for review.

Expatriate Cost Checklist

	Yes	No
Plan an audit or broad review of expatriate staffing policies. Are people being sent overseas that aren't needed?	——	——
Specific objectives are established for each expatriate job.	——	——
The length of each expatriate assignment is established in advance of transfer.	——	——
Short-term, part-time, and rotational assignments of workers are utilized where possible to avoid relocation of the family.	——	——
Whenever possible, the organization encourages single employees to take overseas assignments rather than families.	——	——
Conduct a review of expatriate assignments to see if years can be cut off the tour. Each year cut relates to significant dollars saved.	——	——

Be proactive in understanding foreign tax regulations in order to take advantage of all credits, timing of payments, and so forth.　　——　——

Review the cost benefit analysis of shipping all household goods to the foreign country as opposed to renting both the house and household goods.　　——　——

Do you use shipping companies that are knowledgeable in foreign shipping in order to use maximum amounts for shipment by weight and volume?　　——　——

Do you consider car or van pooling of expatriates instead of furnishing each person with a car?　　——　——

Have you considered cutting the entertainment allowance and club membership? Entertainment allowances tend to grow very fast. If there is not a specific need for club membership, perhaps that could be eliminated.　　——　——

There are other ways to cut expatriate costs, but these are a few of the more obvious ones. It is not wise to be too frugal or cut expenses to the point that expatriates and their families are uncomfortable and want to return prematurely.

CULTURE SHOCK AND HOW TO OVERCOME IT

Cultural insensitivity can result in missed opportunities, lost business, and ruffled feelings on both sides. A thorough cultural orientation for expatriates and their families is a good investment in their future success. It is also a worthwhile investment in terms of public relations and goodwill for the company. Employees are the company to customers and business associates and their sensitivity or lack of sensitivity to cultural issues is viewed as a company responsibility.

Case Example: PHI International's Success Has Been Built on Cross-Cultural Savvy

PHI International, Inc. of Miami is owned by Pedro Hernandez who came to the United States twenty years ago from Cuba. Pedro understands that cultural differences are the key to doing business successfully in other countries. Pedro's company exports $6 million per year in building materials to countries in the Caribbean and South America.

You have to put yourself in the shoes of your customers—accommodate them, provide your products and your services when the customer wants them, and be prepared to wait patiently when the customer is preoccupied or just wants to sit for hours and sip a cup of coffee. If I am going to be successful, I have to accommodate my customers, not try to change them.

Pedro says the people he deals with are procrastinators one minute, then in a rush to get things done the next. He has trained his sales staff to understand the cultures they deal with and to understand that, whatever the customer's timing is, it is all right. Not an easy idea to get across to salespeople who are trained to sell and deliver as fast as possible.

Most companies that have expatriate employees train them in the culture of the country they are being assigned to long before the transfer actually occurs.

Tips for Maintaining Cultural Sensitivity

Having a degree of sensitivity to the opportunities and problems of the people around you is just as important in the United States as it is overseas, but it is more difficult in a foreign country because normally you do not speak the language. It then becomes more critical to watch the body language and the nonverbal signs people give when they communicate. Here are some tips for becoming more sensitive to a new culture.

- Watch body language. If you don't understand body language, read one of the many books written about it. Spend some time watching people in your new country. Body language provides different signals in a foreign country.

- Learn some of the key words of the country. You should learn the language if you plan much time there. Take a Berlitz course and at least learn some key phrases before you go. A language course will also provide tips on how people communicate in that country.

- It is very important to learn about the customs of your new country. An American businessman lost a huge corporate account with the Saudis because as he was about to wind up after a several-hour marketing meeting, he leaned back in his chair and put his feet up on the table facing his clients. A custom well-known to most people doing business in the Middle East is that you do not show the soles of your shoes. The American lost the account and was recalled by his company as a result of his lack of sensitivity.

- Learn what you can about timing. It is everything when it comes to communicating or getting a job done in a foreign country. People in Europe and South America, for example, move much slower than Americans. You must take time to get things done. In Japan, you must pay more attention to age-old customs and be sensitive to tradition. Most Americans have to learn to slow down.

Case Example: Getty Oil Company's Three-Day Cross-Cultural Orientation

Before any Getty Oil Company employee sets foot on foreign soil, there is a three-day cross-cultural orientation seminar to attend. When their expatriates land in their new country, they "hit the ground running." In a foreign country every aspect of living can be different: food, housing, climate, work habits, work hours, social and cultural habits, language, taboos, and so forth. At first they just seem strange, but after awhile, they become more difficult to deal with on a daily basis—culture shock sets in.

You are usually the one that provides the orientation programs, interfaces with the expatriates and their families, and gives ongoing communication and support after the employee has been relocated. If you are setting up a new program and have no previous experience with cross-cultural training, it is a good idea to contact a director in another company who has had more experience.

Companies That Have Cross-Cultural Training and Orientation Programs

Getty Oil Company

Sperry Corporation

Hewlett-Packard

Westinghouse

3M Company

IBM

Also, nearly all large banks with overseas branch banks have expatriate programs.

For more information on training programs, contact The Society for Intercultural Education, Training and Research, 1414 22nd Street, N.W., Washington, DC 20037. Phone 202-862-1990.

EMPLOYERS FACE NEW CHALLENGES UNDER THE IMMIGRATION REFORM AND CONTROL ACT OF 1986

On October 18, 1986, Congress passed The Immigration Reform and Control Act of 1986. The Act became effective November 6, 1986. With this new Act, Congress made it unlawful for employers to employ illegal aliens. *This law affects all employers, and ignorance of the law will be no excuse or defense to a violation.* Following is a succinct review of this new Immigration Act presented by Robert G. Heiserman, a Denver attorney engaged in private practice with a concentration on immigration, nationality, citizenship, and naturalization law.

Mr. Heiserman is a member of the Board of Governors of the American Immigration Lawyers Association.

It is too early to fully assess the impact of this new legislation. As of this writing, the federal agencies charged with its implementation have yet to publish proposed rule-making. Even so, it is possible to summarize the key points.

The most important aspect of the provisions of the new law is that it will now be unlawful for any person or other entity to hire, recruit or refer for a fee for employment in the United States any alien, knowing that the alien is not authorized to be employed in the United States. Even if the alien is authorized to work, the employer must follow verification procedures. An unauthorized alien under this provision is defined as an alien who is not a lawful permanent resident of the United States or authorized by the Attorney General to work in the United States. In addition, the continued employment of any alien in the U.S. who the U.S. employer knows is an unauthorized alien, or who becomes an unauthorized alien after the date of the enactment of the law can trigger sanctions against the U.S. employer. The bill does contain a savings clause. The sanction provisions do not apply to any unauthorized alien who is hired, recruited, or referred for employment prior to the enactment of this bill. Continued employment of these unauthorized aliens is also exempted from the sanction requirement of the bill. IRCA sanctions apply to the employment agencies, unions, and contract laborers as well as U.S. employers. It may be that unauthorized aliens who are referred through the State Job Service facilities may be exempt from the implementation of this provision. However, regulations will have to be drafted to clarify this point.

How U.S. Employers Can Reduce the Risk of Sanctions

Any U.S. employer who demonstrates good faith compliance with the Employment Verification System (EVS) has an affirmative defense to any charge under the employer sanctions provisions of this law. The EVS requires a sworn statement by the employer that the employer has verified by review of appropriate documentation that reasonably appears on its face to be genuine, that the alien is authorized to be employed in the U.S. The prospective employer is required to sign a notarized statement of compliance with the provisions of the immigration law. Acceptable documentation that can be used to comply with the EVS to establish employment authorization and identity includes the following: a U.S. passport; certificate of citizenship; certificate of naturalization; an unexpired foreign passport that has an employment authorization notation that is still valid and has been entered into the passport by the Immigration and Naturalization Service; an alien registration receipt card Form I-151, or I-551 (green card) or other "alien card" including any photo or other I.D. that the Attorney General specifies in the regulations that will be drafted under this provision. Other types of documentation of employment authorization that may also be accepted include a Social Security card without employment restriction, a U.S. birth certificate or evidence of U.S. nationality by birth abroad, or any other documents that the Attorney General may deem appropriate by regulation. Additional documentation of identity can also include a driver's license, or state I.D. card with a photo, or whatever other documentation the Attorney General may designate by regulation. Copies of the documentation reviewed by the employer for prospective employees must be retained for review by the Immigration and Naturalization Service (INS) and Department of Labor, as well as copies of the verification form that will be created by the government for use in enforcing this legislation. The verification documentation and forms must be retained by the employer for three years, if the individual was recruited or referred to the employer, but not hired. If hired, the documentation must be kept for the same period, or one year after termination of employment, whichever is later. Employers attempting to comply with the EVS system are exempt from the prohibitions against copying certain documentation such as naturalization certificates. However, the copies of these documents cannot be used for any other purpose. The privacy and security of any information provided under this law is assured. The law specifically provides that there will be no national identity card. Specific procedures will need to be formulated by regulation to implement this directive. In summary, the only acceptable basis for denying employment to an individual under this law is that the alien lacks the proper authorization to work in the United States.

Enforcement Procedures

The Attorney General will establish by regulation a procedure for the filing of written, signed complaints against potential violators and for investigation procedures. There will also be created within the INS a unit with the primary duty of prosecuting U.S. employers who are in violation of the employer sanctions provision. The INS and the Administrative Law Judges (ALJ) who will be designated to preside over hearings in these proceedings will have reasonable access to all records in the possession of the INS and the U.S. employer under investigation. The ALJ will also have the authority to subpoena witnesses and evidence at any designated place for a hearing. Once a complaint has been filed under the employer sanctions provisions the employer can request a formal hearing before penalties can be imposed. However, a hearing is not required unless requested by the employer. There must be a 30 day notice prior to the scheduling of any hearing on this matter. The hearings themselves will be conducted in accordance with the Administrative Procedure Act. They will be held at the nearest place to where the employer resides or where the violation occurred. If the employer doesn't request a hearing, the Attorney General's order of sanctions will become the final unappealable administrative decision. The order must include findings of fact and imposition of sanctions for it to be valid.

Penalty Provisions

IRCA includes two types of penalty provisions: civil and criminal. The civil penalties can include a cease and desist order at the discretion of the ALJ and civil fines as follows:

- For the first order, the fine will range from $250–$2,000 per unauthorized alien

- The second order under the sanction provisions will result in a fine of $2,000–$5,000 per unauthorized alien

- In the case of any person or entity previously subject to more than one order, fines range from $3,000–$10,000 per unauthorized alien

The ALJ also has authority to order the employer's compliance with the immigration law under the supervision of the INS for a three year period and such other remedies as are deemed appropriate. If a violation occurs by a separate subdivision of the employer entity, then each division of that employer in violation is subject to the above referenced penalties.

For paperwork violations the civil penalty is a fine not less than $100 nor more than a $1,000 fine per each individual with respect to whom such violation occurred. Paperwork violations under the immigration law occur when a U.S. employer fails to retain the documentation required for the period of time required.

There will be no provision for administrative appellate review for orders issued under the employer sanctions provision of this new law. The ALJ's decision becomes the final administrative decision unless the Attorney General modifies the decision or vacates the order within 30 days. Once the administrative decision becomes final, there is a provision for limited judicial review. Within 45 days of the final order, the U.S. employer can file an action in the U.S. Court of Appeals for a review of the administrative determination. If a U.S. employer who has a final administrative order issued against him fails to comply with that order the Attorney General can file suit in the appropriate U.S. District Court to seek compliance with the order. However, the U.S. employer cannot use this type of a court action to collaterally attack the final order in the administrative proceeding.

The second type of penalty provision under employer sanctions is criminal. The primary provision is as follows: Any U.S. employer who is found guilty of a pattern or practice of violation of the verification procedures under the immigration law. The offending employer shall be subject to a fine of up to $3,000 per unauthorized alien, imprisonment of up to six months, or both.

In addition, the Attorney General can file a civil action in U.S. District Court requesting a permanent or temporary injunction or restraining order, as appropriate, against any U.S. employer who continues to violate the immigration law in respect to a pattern or practice of violation of the employer sanctions provisions.

The U.S. employer cannot require an alien to post a bond or security, or to pay or agree to pay, any amount of money to guarantee, or indemnify the employer against any potential liability if the alien is or may become an unauthorized alien under the new law. If a U.S. employer is found guilty of violating this provision, the employer entity is subject to a fine of $1,000 per violation and the requirement of restitution to the employee, or to the general fund of the Treasury if the employer cannot be located.

Implementation of the New Law

The first six months beginning on December 1, 1986, after enactment of the Immigration Reform and Control Act of 1986 will be a public information period. There will be no enforcement against U.S. employers of unauthorized aliens during this period and there will be an emphasis on public education of the provisions for employer sanctions under the new law. Beginning on June 1, 1987, for a 12 month period any U.S. employer found in violation of the employer sanctions provision will be issued citations which will merely be warning notices of violations without the imposition of any penalties against the employer.

The Immigration and Reform and Control Act of 1986 specifically provides for yearly reports by the General Accounting Office for the first three years of implementation of the new immigration law to document the impact of the law, especially concerning any discrimination against U.S. workers. If the Task Force created to review the GAO reports determines that the new immigration law has resulted in a pattern of discrimination in employment against other than unauthorized aliens on the basis of national origin and Congress agrees then employer sanctions may be terminated within 30 days of the last report. There are also specific guidelines to guard against unfair employment practices which may occur when U.S. employers attempt to comply with the provisions of the employer sanctions under this law. Theoretically, the law prohibits discrimination in hiring, referring, or firing any employee because of national origin or citizenship status, unless that employee qualifies as an unauthorized alien under the immigration law.

There are exceptions to this general provision. If a U.S. employer has three or fewer employees, then the anti-discrimination provisions do not apply to that employer. Also, if discrimination claims can be made under Section 703 of the Civil Rights Act of 1964, then there is no basis to make a claim for discrimination under this immigration law. Also exempt from the employer sanctions is discrimination based on a requirement of U.S.

citizenship if it is required by state or federal regulations. For example, national security may require U.S. citizen workers in certain areas of the military and other security settings. However, the bill does provide that an employer can prefer a U.S. citizen over an alien worker, even a lawful permanent resident, if the two workers are equally qualified. The U.S. employer offered this choice will not be subject to sanctions under the unfair employment practices section of this law.

Any person or INS officer who feels that a U.S. employer has violated the unfair employment practices of this law can file a formal complaint. This complaint will be filed with a Special Counsel appointed by the President to investigate and issue complaints and prosecute those complaints before an ALJ. Any identified discriminatory activities that occur under the auspices of compliance with the immigration law can be the basis for such a complaint. If the complaint is deemed valid, the ALJ can issue a cease and desist order and impose a civil penalty of $1,000 per individual discriminated against, or if the employer was previously subject to a similar order, $2,000 per individual. It is also possible for the ALJ to order reinstatement or hiring of the affected individual with or without a back pay remedy, but it cannot be imposed for an occurrence more than 2 years prior to the filing of the complaint with the Special Counsel. In any complaint concerning unfair immigration-related employment practices, the ALJ may allow a prevailing party, other than the U.S., a reasonable award of attorney's fees if the losing parties argument is without reasonable foundation.

This is an overview of the various provisions of the Immigration Reform and Control Act of 1986 that most directly affect U.S. employers. There are also specific additional provisions concerning agricultural employers and workers which have not been discussed, but the provisions in this article will apply to that group as well. Until the Attorney General promulgates regulations outlining particular procedures, the actual implementation of the new law will not be clearly defined. However, this summary should provide some guidance for employers and their legal advisors.

Following are lists and charts setting out employer sanctions, and penalties, enforcement time periods, employment verification systems, and a summary of eligibility for legalization programs under the new Act.

Employer Sanctions Penalties
Civil

PAPER WORK VIOLATIONS: (Failure to maintain required
verification documentation)
Fine of not less than $100 nor more than $1,000 per individual
required to be documented.
SURETY VIOLATION: (Requiring prospective employee to be bonded or pay
money to indemnify employer if em-
ployee is or becomes unauthorized alien)
Fine of $1,000 per violation and possible restitution to individual affected.
EMPLOYMENT, RECRUITMENT OR REFERRAL OF
UNAUTHORIZED ALIEN: (Cease and Desist Order plus fine)
First Violation Order
— Fine of $250–$2,000 per unauthorized alien
Second Violation Order
— Fine of $2,000–$5,000 per unauthorized alien
Previously Subject to More Than One Violation Order
— Fine of $3,000–$10,000 per unauthorized alien

Criminal

For person or employer entity engaging in a pattern or practice of
violation of employment, recruitment, referral, or employment
documentation provision.
Fine of not more than $3,000 per unauthorized alien, or
imprisonment for not more than six months, or both.
Government may also seek a permanent or temporary injunction,
restraining order, or other federal court order against offender.

Employment Verification System (EVS)
Employer's Affirmative Defense to Charge of Violation of Employer Sanctions Provisions

Employer must verify *identity* and *employment authorization* for each individual employed, recruited, or referred for employment.

Documentation of Identity and Employment Authorization	*Documentation of Employment Authorization*	*Documentation of Identity*
1. U.S. passport	1. Social Security Card without employment restriction	1. Driver's license
2. Certificate of U.S. Citizenship	2. U.S. birth certificate	2. State I.D. card with photo
3. Certificate of U.S. Naturalization	3. Evidence of U.S. nationality by birth abroad	3. Other documentation as designated by U.S. Attorney General
4. Unexpired foreign passport with valid employment authorization from INS	4. Other documents designated by U.S. Attorney General	
5. Alien Registration Receipt Card Form I-151, or I-551 (Green Card)		
6. Other "alien card" including any photo I.D. approved by U.S. Attorney General		

Above information must be copied and verification form completed for each individual employed, recruited or referred for employment.

Documentation must be retained for 3 years if individual recruited or referred, but not hired. If hired, documentation must be retained for 3 years or 1 year after termination, whichever is later.

Enforcement Time Periods for Employer Sanctions Under IRCA

NON-AGRICULTURAL EMPLOYERS

11/6/86	12/1/86	6/1/87	6/1/88	12/1/89
Date of Enactment of IRCA	Public Information Period (Sanctions not enforced)	First citation period. Government will issue warnings	Sanctions fully enforced	Sanctions may be terminated by Comptroller General if determined that sanctions cause widespread discrimination. Congress must agree.
Employees on this date are exempt from sanctions				

SAWS (Seasonal Agricultural Workers) EMPLOYERS

11/6/86	12/1/86	6/1/87	12/1/88	12/1/89
Date of Enactment of IRCA	Public Information Period (Sanction not enforced)	First citation period—Government will issue warnings only (No penalties issued)	Sanctions fully enforced	Sanctions may be terminated by Comptroller General if determined that sanctions cause widespread discrimination. Congress must agree.
Employees on this date are exempt from sanctions				

Summary of Eligibility for Legalization Programs
Under the Immigration Reform and Control Act of 1986 (IRCA)

Temporary Resident Status— Non-Agricultural

1. Authorized to work and reside in U.S. temporarily and travel.
2. In U.S. in unlawful status on 1/1/82.
3. Resided continuously in U.S. since before 1/1/82 in unlawful status.
4. Brief, casual and innocent absences will not break continuous residence.
5. Residing in U.S. on 11/6/86.
6. Can only apply in U.S. during established 12 month period, 30 day period if processed for deportation.
7. Must be admissible as immigrant.
8. Must apply to adjust to permanent resident within designated one year period by demonstrating basic citizenship skills and admissibility as immigrant.
9. No numerical limitation on adjustment to permanent status of qualified applicants.
10. Must process temporary and permanent applications through Attorney General designated qualified voluntary, State, local and community organizations and persons.
11. Application confidential.
12. Granted employment authorization and permission to stay in U.S. during application processing.
13. Certain public welfare unavailable for 5 years from grant of temporary resident status.

Temporary Resident Status—Special Agricultural Workers (SAWS)

1. Authorized to work and reside in U.S. temporarily and travel.
2. Not required to be in U.S. on 11/6/86.
3. Resided (not required to be continuously) in U.S. and performed seasonal agricultural services (SAS) in U.S. for at least 90 man-days during 12-month period ending 5/1/86.
4. Can apply in U.S. or at U.S. Consular posts outside U.S. during established 18-month period, 30-day period if processed for deportation.
5. Must be admissible as immigrant.
6. If qualify as temporary resident and performed SAS for at least 90 man-days during each 12 month period ending, 5/1/84, 5/1/85, and 5/1/86 *shall* qualify for permanent resident status within 1 year of grant of temporary resident status or day after end of 18 month application period, whichever is later. Otherwise *shall* be adjusted 2 years after grant of temporary resident status or day after 18 month application period, whichever is later.
7. Numerical limitation for SAW adjusting to permanent status in one year is first 350,000 persons who apply. Others must wait two years.
8. Must process temporary and permanent applications through A.G. designated qualified voluntary, State, local and community organizations, *farm labor organizations, associations of agricultural employers* and persons.
9. Application confidential.
10. Granted employment authorization and permission to stay in U.S. during application processing.
11. Aid to families with dependent children not available for 5 years from grant to temporary resident status.

Labor Relations: A New Era

CHAPTER 11

WHERE LABOR RELATIONS ARE HEADING IN THE 1990s

This new era in labor relations may mean greater worker satisfaction, higher productivity, and a stronger position for America in the changing world marketplace. Labor-management confrontation will not work in today's environment, where whole job classifications are disappearing and where companies are reorganizing and moving to eliminate the need for unions. Workshops and films on remaining union-free are proliferating and unions are regrouping and targeting new areas to organize.

These huge job losses have had a sobering effect on unions and on bargaining strategies. Strike activity has been at a thirty-eight-year low, and there has been an upturn in economic activity. But there are still over eight million unemployed people.

Eighty-five percent of the private workforce is still non-union, and the fastest-growing job areas, service workers, restaurants, hospitals, retail stores, and so forth, are still paid minimum wage or only a dollar or two more. There are roughly ten million workers at minimum wage ($3.35 per hour) and another twenty million at $4 to $5 per hour.

All of this organizational change and trends like downsizing, (layoffs) and outsourcing (moving jobs outside the country) have changed the desire of workers to join unions or strike for more pay and benefits to bargaining for job security.

Wage Increase Patterns

The United States has experienced a sharp deceleration in wage increases. For example, 1981 and 1982 were recession years. Unemployment rose while inflation declined. Average pay increases decreased from nine percent to six percent. Then, surprisingly, as the economy began to recover, pay increases fell again, down to five percent in 1983 and four percent in 1984.

Union employees surprisingly have fared the worst in the area of pay increases. Wage hikes in new contracts have fallen to record low percentages in the last two years; and for the first time since 1969, union wage gains fell behind those of non-union workers. The main reason for this drop is the continuation of concession bargaining and union givebacks of raises and benefits.

Two-Tier Labor Contracts and How They Work

Unions don't like two-tier wage contracts but they were forced to accept them in lieu of wage cuts for workers already employed by companies who needed financial relief in poor economic times. Most two-tier contracts were negotiated in 1983 and 1984. The two major two-tier labor agreements negotiated in 1985 were Pan American World Airways flight attendants and a pact reached with Teamsters truck drivers.

Under a two-tier structure, newly hired employees are paid less than employees already on the payroll. Wages are often substantially less than the last union contract. Two-tier contracts are destructive to union solidarity. They are a plan for unequal pay for equal work and that reverses years of labors' achievements in reaching equal pay levels in all job classifications.

The new contracts have saved employers hundreds of thousands of dollars. American Airlines saves $100 million a year with its two-tier contract. The contracts have not caused any work slowdowns or wildcat strikes, but there is an uneasy truce between labor and management, and Human Resource Managers are in the tenuous position of having to jockey back and forth between labor and management in implementing these programs and keeping them running smoothly.

There are basically two types of contracts. One type is permanent and the other temporary. In a permanent system, employees placed in the lower tier never do achieve parity with the other workers in the same job. In a temporary system, employees hired at less than employees currently in the same job can advance by one or possibly several steps to wage parity.

Case Example: American Airlines Likes Multiple Tiers

At American Airlines, for example, a DC-10 pilot with top seniority can make $127,900 a year. The new two-tier system, however, is designed so that newly hired pilots will earn only about half as much flying the same plane no matter how many years they fly. The lower-paid pilots will naturally resent the difference in pay over a period of years. The same type of program is in place for American Airlines mechanics. There is a twelve-year progression to the top rate of $17.89. Under the old contract, they reached the maximum rate in two years.

Another company, Lockheed Aircraft, said that employees hired after October 1, 1983, in all but the most skilled unionized jobs, have to work over two or more years, maybe even as long as four years, to attain the minimum starting rate paid employees hired before the cutoff date. Lockheed unions, including the machinists at the Marietta, Georgia installation where Lockheed is building a new military cargo plane, are not happy about the two-tier plan. But the two-tier wage plan has saved Lockheed an enormous amount of money. Lockheed has hired 2,800 workers on the lower tier in Georgia and over 1,200 in California at their Sunnyvale facility.

Case Example: Two-Tier Wage Plan in Supermarkets

Two-tier wage plans have hit the supermarket industry in a big way. The Giant Food Chain introduced two-tier wage plans in Baltimore, persuading their union to accept a new category of worker called a "service clerk" to do new and unconventional jobs.

Safeway Stores have gone to multiple-tier plans in some areas. These plans generate large savings but they also create poor morale in an industry that already has high turnover. Turnover of thirty to forty percent is common. Resentment may take time to build but it does build—and it destroys the old idea of promoting teamwork, eliminating conflict, and increasing productivity.

When a union dominates a market area, it can get rid of a two-tier wage system. Unions will use the dissatisfaction of the multiple-tier wage programs to organize companies. In 1979, Local 584 of the Teamsters won a bitter strike over the two-tier system. There was disparity of as much as $125 per week. Two-tier systems were incorporated into contracts concerning over 200,000 workers in 1985 and no one knows how many people are working under the system in non-union companies.

You will need to stay on top of this issue because there will be a great deal of controversy in the next few years.

Why Salaried Plants Are Becoming Popular

What do Dow Chemical, TRW, Eaton Corporation, Dana Corporation, and Rockwell International have in common? They have all instituted a shift from an hourly wage rate to a salaried pay program. The trend today is away from the dominating management style, the "do it my way or nothing" attitude of management.

TRW now has twenty domestic plants on a salary basis compared with only three a decade ago. According to a survey conducted by the Conference Board, salaried compensation systems ranked ahead of other benefits in employee preference. Flextime, payment-for-knowledge plans, autonomous work teams, and productivity bonuses were among the items that ran behind the salaried wage plans in popularity.

There is a lot to be said for these new plans—basically blue collar workers are no longer forced to punch in and out, they are paid sick days and have personal time off the job. Work rules and job classifications are either liberalized or eliminated. Blue collar workers are treated more like professionals, and, by all reports, these salaried programs have increased productivity and morale in companies where they have been implemented.

You need to realize there are problems in the implementation of a salaried pay program, especially where a plant has been operating for some time, and where there is a union. Success in implementation depends on several things: geographic location, the regional labor relations climate, the strength of the union if there is one, and so forth. If the company is implementing the program in a new plant in an area that has not historically been organized by unions, the start up should be fairly simple.

TRW started its Lawrence, Kansas cable plant as a salaried plant and hired most of its workforce right out of high school. As most of the people hired had not worked before, they easily accepted the salaried work environment.

Dow Chemical has made a more gradual shift to salaried plants. Because Dow has had a long history of union representation, it was more difficult to switch. Union decertification was necessary and that is a lengthy process. Union representation in Dow's domestic facilities has now dropped from 100 percent to less than 50 percent.

Setting Compensation Levels: Three Variables to Consider

If you decide to move to a salaried program, there are basically three variables to look at in establishing compensation levels.

1. the financial health of the plant
2. prevailing wage scale in similar companies
3. prevailing wage scale in the same geographic region

If you are thinking of going to an all-salaried program it is a good idea to contact a knowledgeable consultant or a company that has already gone through the process and ask if they are willing to share information on the conversion. There are many things to consider before making such a move.

Case Example: Why MADTEX Manufacturing, Inc. Moved to a Salaried Plant

Bill Madden owns MADTEX Manufacturing, Inc. with a large facility in Phoenix, Arizona. Because of rapid growth during the past three years, he felt it was time to take a look at his entire organization. Bill had heard about another company's move to a salaried plant concept and decided he wanted to try the more participative style of management in his plant. Bill's plant was not unionized.

Bill reorganized his workforce into twenty work groups, each made up of from five to fifteen people. He appointed one of his best supervisors as a group facilitator to help groups work through problems and to promote the team spirit he thought it would take to make the project work.

With the help of supervisors and the group facilitator, work groups set work standards, reviewed productivity levels that would meet projected profits, decided who would be hired, how many people were needed to achieve their goals, and how quickly people would move through the ranks, by establishing progressively more difficult skill levels in job classifications. Employees are paid for what they know and how well they perform the job. Management has to ensure that challenging jobs are available and viable economic objects are communicated.

A human resource consultant, experienced in the problems of shifting workers from hourly to salaried compensation programs, helped Bill through the initial start-up of the salaried plan. The whole change was a major shift in thinking and in the culture of the organization.

The key to the success of the changeover in Bill Madden's mind was the extra time and effort put into communicating the whole program thoroughly from the top to the bottom of the organization. Supervisors and managers were given preinstallation training in how to communicate the new program and how to make it work. There were training programs in team building, conflict resolution, communication, and motivation. A special newsletter was instituted to concentrate on all aspects of the change and an employee hotline was installed to answer workers' questions. If an employee called in and gave a name, the question was answered by getting back to that employee within twenty-four hours. If the employee called and did not give a name, the question was answered in the next weekly newsletter.

After five years, Bill Madden's plant has experienced a thirty-percent increase in productivity and corresponding increases in profits. Morale is higher and turnover has dropped significantly. Salaried plants could just be the most popular method of compensating workers in the future.

With the increase in automation of plants there is a greater emphasis on salaried programs. Also, when a company moves to a smaller facility and installs more automated equipment, fewer supervisors are needed and that promotes a more participative style of management.

A superficial salaried program with a few symbols—a common parking lot, the President eating in the cafeteria, but no serious participative programs and poor communication won't work. Communication is important. If only twenty percent of your workforce understands the program and believes in it, the other eighty percent of your workforce will be against it, and sabotage your efforts.

Labor's Biggest Push—A Job for Life

Unions that traditionally went for more money in bargaining have now set their sights on job security instead. To push for more money could mean companies would outsource and jobs would be lost. So bargaining now is focusing on job security.

Case Example: The General Motors Contract

The trend-setting agreement between General Motors and the United Auto Workers in 1984 has set the pattern for labor negotiations for years to come. In that settlement, the United Auto Workers received the most comprehensive job-protection arrangement ever negotiated in a major industry.

Under the new contract, for six years General Motors will not lay off a worker with at least one year's seniority who is displaced by new technology, consolidation of parts plants, productivity gains, or the transfer of work to other facilities. If any of these situations occur, workers will be placed in a "job bank." Workers placed in job banks will enter training programs, transfer to other plants, perform nontraditional jobs (could be volunteer/charitable work) or fill in for regular workers on leave. While in the job bank, they will earn their regular pay. The company funds this program on a pay-as-you-go basis, subject to a $1 billion cap by 1990.

General Motors will also invest up to $100 million in projects to create new jobs. The job bank program will be aided by a business development committee that will make suggestions for creating jobs in old or underutilized GM plants. They might also suggest new ventures in communities that have been severely affected by layoffs in the auto industry. The main criteria for the new venture is that it be practical, affordable, profitable, and that it produce a significant number of jobs.

Non-union companies are also making serious attempts to avoid layoffs. The Hewlett-Packard plant in Colorado gave employees the opportunity to take time off without pay in order to avoid a major layoff.

IBM has had no layoffs in more than forty years, although it went through economic problems twice between 1972 and 1975. Rather than reduce their workforce, the company gave new assignments to 17,000 employees and completely retrained 7,000 of them.

Both labor and management understand workers' desire for job security programs.

DOES EVERY COMPANY NEED A UNION?

Unions did a great deal for employees years ago when the "hit 'em over the head" type of management prevailed. Years ago, smokestack industries, the early automobile industry, and the manufacturing and garment industries all needed unions to force companies to treat their workers fairly. Today companies are smarter and there is a desire on the part of most management people to treat employees right without union involvement.

A company's first consideration in whether a union will be successful in organizing their workers should be the way their first-line supervisors and managers treat employees. Most organizing campaigns are won or lost based on how supervisors and managers handle the day-to-day problems of their workers and the grievance/arbitration process is a major factor.

Fourteen Common Issues in the Grievance Arbitration Process

The grievance/arbitration process is a concern to labor and management, as it is expensive and disrupts normal work operations. It is, however, a very important process for both sides. As important as it is, the process still remains something of a mystery to many people, including the human resource generalist who isn't responsible for labor relations, but on a day-to-day basis must interface at some point in the process.

Here are fourteen grievance topics that seem to come up over and over in most companies.

SENIORITY—Organizations that are unionized usually have strong seniority systems. Almost all disputes on seniority are over a management bypass of the system. Workers with seniority may have not been given consideration in overtime, transfers, promotions, training, or work scheduling.

TRANSFERS—Transfer denial based on performance issues like absenteeism or the ability to perform a job.

SUSPENSIONS—Grievances over suspensions are among the most common. Suspensions most often occur over absenteeism, avoidable accidents, insubordination, or job performance.

DISCIPLINARY ACTION—Grievances over written warnings on topics such as absenteeism, tardiness, insubordination, and performance.

VACATIONS—Grievances arise when a employee isn't allowed to take a vacation at the specific time requested.

GRIEVANCE PROCESS—Problems arise when the union accuses the company of not meeting or bargaining in "good faith."

SAFETY—A grievance usually occurs in this area when the union charges that a work procedure, condition, or area is unsafe.

DISCRIMINATION—An employee may charge that he or she is not being treated equally or that there is favoritism.

PERFORMANCE APPRAISALS—These disputes usually result from an employee charge that an evaluation was not done, or if done, did not accurately reflect his or her performance.

DENIAL OF SICK BENEFITS—This grievance usually occurs when sick benefits are denied.

EXCUSED TIME—A dispute may arise when management refuses to grant leave without pay.

WORK OUT OF CLASSIFICATION—A grievance may be the result of management's request that an employee perform work not contained in his or her job description.

TRAINING—Some disputes arise when management either refuses to train employees, or an employee feels there is discrimination in choosing workers for training.

TERMINATIONS—Discharges for absenteeism, poor performance, avoidable accidents, and insubordination are the most common types of termination.

It is important for you to provide specific guidelines to managers on how to handle labor relations issues as they arise. Following is a sample labor relations handbook. It should be customized to your particular organizational circumstances.

Training supervisors and managers to enforce policies and procedures evenhandedly and to eliminate discrimination and favoritism will go a long way towards avoiding the need for lengthy grievance/arbitration proceedings.

Warren L. Tomlinson, Labor Attorney with the law firm of Holland and Hart in Denver, Colorado, provides the following brief overview of the national labor scene.

Labor Overview

We are seeing a decline in the percentage of unionized workers, today, and a "new era" of bargaining dealing with wage concessions and two-tier wage agreements, and substantial legislative and court activity involving worker privacy and individual rights issues.

Several factors are setting the stage and tone for union-management relations and activities. The weak economy and the poor financial condition of many large companies has resulted in reorganizations under the bankruptcy laws and numerous corporate acquisitions and mergers. These actions often changed the balance of power between particular unions and particular employers and also frequently resulted in different individuals with new attitudes and objectives representing employers in dealing with their unions. As some companies were able to reject union contracts in bankruptcy proceedings and others were able to escape an unfavorable union contract when the operation was sold, economic concessions were often obtained from unions. This in turn applied pressure on competing companies in the same industries to obtain concessions from their unions to remain competitive.

An extremely modest increase in the cost-of-living index has also provided a climate which makes large pay increases difficult for unions to achieve. The declining number of union members has reduced the funds available to unions for organizing activities and financing strikes. In addition, employers were becoming increasingly sophisticated in using their legal right to resist union organizing activities and to permanently replace economic strikers.

Today we are seeing a retrenchment and consolidation rather than large pay increases and improved working conditions. Perhaps partially as a result of these factors, many of the employment battles are not being fought at the bargaining table but waged in Congress, the state legislatures and in the courts. The issues which reach those forums usually center around workers' rights and workers' privacy.

Decline in the Percentage of Unionized Workers

The clear trend in recent years in the United States has been a decline in the percentage of unionized workers. In 1956, union members constituted 33.4% of the civilian work force. By 1980, that percentage had dipped to 23.0%.[1] In 1984, approximately 17.3 million out of 92.2 million workers, or 18.8%, were unionized. Current figures available show a decline. There are over 17 million people out of a work force of 94.5 million, or 18.0%, now unionized.[2] There has been a drop both in the percentage of the work force which is unionized and the total number of union members.

Unions are acutely aware of their membership declines and resulting losses of revenue and power. They have attempted to increase their organizing effectiveness in a number of ways. They have recently targeted certain industries for specific organizing efforts. For instance, a coalition of unions, environmentalists and community activists has been formed to attempt to organize the nearly two million workers in the high technology industry, nearly all of whom are non-union. The coalition indicates that it will stress health and safety and job security issues in its organizing activities.[3] Blue Cross/Blue Shield plan employers have also been targeted for increased organizing activity by a coalition of eight unions.[4] Organizing

---

[1] U.S. Bureau of Labor Statistics, 1980 report.
[2] 59 *White Collar Report* 146 (1986).
[3] 59 *White Collar Report* 285 (1986).
[4] 59 *White Collar Report* 517 (1986).

efforts also are being concentrated on hospital workers, college faculty members and numerous categories of public employees.

The AFL-CIO has recently decided to take aggressive and unorthodox action to bolster organizing. It announced the creation of a new office to teach its affiliate unions how to attempt to win recognition from recalcitrant employers by the use of "corporate campaigns." Such campaigns are designed to persuade those close to the employer, such as its banks, creditors, customers and stockholders, that they should convince the employer not to resist union organizing activity.[5] For instance, a bank that a particular employer uses might be told that union funds will be withdrawn from the bank unless the bank either persuades the employer to stop resisting the organizing activity or stops making its loans to the employer.

Apparently these activities will be directed primarily against large employers. The planned AFL-CIO activities appear to be patterned after those undertaken by a couple of highly publicized labor consultants during the past two years. Such campaigns have been conducted by the consultants against employers in the meat packing and the nursing home industries. The AFL-CIO announced that Blue Cross-Blue Shield plan employers would be among the first employers targeted for its corporate campaigns. Time will tell whether this organizing tactic will be successful, but it should be anticipated that there will be an increase in corporate campaigns for at least the next year or two.

Negotiated Pay Increases

The concession bargaining which started in the early 1980s continues. Contracts containing wage concessions are being achieved by some employers in nearly all industries.[6] Two additional wage structure devices which have gained popularity in recent years continued to be used. Two-tier wage plans, under which new employees receive lower wages than existing employees, continued to be achieved in a substantial number of contracts. One survey found that 17% of union contracts now contain a two-tier wage system. In about 40% of these contracts, rates for new hires catch up with those of existing employees over time; under the remainder of the contracts the rates remain lower permanently.[7] In another survey, one-third of the unionized companies surveyed stated that they intended to seek two-tier wage scales in future negotiations.[8]

In the face of this increased desire by employers for two-tier wage plans, union resistance to such plans continues and is probably increasing.

---

[5] 59 *White Collar Report* 310 (1986).

[6] Brookings Papers on Economic Activity, Vol. II (1985).

[7] 59 *White Collar Report* 503–04 (1986).

[8] *Business Week*, p. 37 (Dec. 29, 1986).

In addition, some employers have misgivings about the viability of continuing two-tier wage plans on an indefinite basis.

The second wage device, which has increased in popularity recently, is the granting of a one-time or "signing" bonus to employees at contract ratification time. From the standpoint of management, such bonuses have the advantage of making additional money available to employees at a critical time without increasing on a more or less permanent basis the overall wage rates, and the cost of those benefits which are tied to the wage rates. A number of top union leaders have voiced their displeasure with such bonuses and their intention to oppose the granting of bonuses in the future.[9]

Fringe Benefits and Working Conditions

Consistent with the other bargaining trends, fringe benefit improvements are usually achieved by unions at the bargaining table, but much of the fringe benefits bargaining activity now revolves around a continuing escalation in the cost of providing medical care, and the efforts of employers to at least slow down their cost increases and in some instances reduce their cost of providing medical benefits. According to a report from the Health Care Financing Administration of the U.S. Department of Health and Human Services, the expenditure for health care has multiplied tenfold nationwide in the last 20 years.[10]

The Bureau of Labor Statistics reports that 29% of all employees having major medical coverage are under a plan requiring employees to pay the first $150 or more of expenses before reimbursement by the insurance plan. This figure is up from 21% in 1984 and 12% in 1983.[11] It is quite likely that this cost-sharing trend will continue. Also, it is likely that the increase in the number of health maintenance organizations (HMO's) and preferred provider organizations (PPO's), which has been going on for several years, will continue. In addition, union contract provisions are appearing with increasing frequency which require second opinions before surgery, require that certain surgical procedures be conducted on an out-patient basis, provide financial rewards to employees who find overcharges in their hospital bills, and place limits on the duration of hospital stays for specified types of surgery.

Many of the other bargaining table disputes now center around efforts by unions to protect employees from the effects of corporate acquisitions and mergers and from layoffs caused by loss of work by the employer. With increasing frequency, unions were demanding strong successorship clauses, namely, clauses which provide that in the event of a sale or other disposition of an operation, the seller will require the

---

[9] 59 *White Collar Report* 180 (1986).
[10] 60 *White Collar Report* 187 (1986).
[11] 59 *White Collar Report* 428 (1986).

purchaser to assume and agree to be bound by the seller's union contract. Such a clause prevents a purchaser from attempting to negotiate a "better deal" with the seller's union, or even avoid union recognition if the purchaser does not hire a majority of its work force from the seller's employees. In certain industries in prior years unions did not appear to bargain hard for such successorship clauses, apparently reasoning that their strength in the industry made such clauses unnecessary. However, the current trend appears to be that more unions in more industries are making vigorous demands for a strong successorship clause.

Layoff protection issues are also prominent at the bargaining table. Unions frequently propose more restrictions on the employers's right to subcontract work, often proposing a requirement of notice to the union and an opportunity to consult or negotiate when an employer is considering the introduction of new technology. Sometimes proposed contract clauses require company-paid retraining programs for laid off employees, and often seek improved early retirement pension benefits. If it is your intent to maintain a union-free environment the following handbook may, with modifications, fit your needs.

MANAGER'S GUIDE TO EMPLOYEE RELATIONS—A LABOR RELATIONS HANDBOOK

INTRODUCTION

As a manager you are "The Company" to the people you manage. You have the closest, most direct, and most frequent contact with them. What you do and what you say, your actions and your words establish the Company's reputation for your employees. Your actions determine whether or not our company is judged to be a good place to work. The Company's programs and policies succeed or fail depending on how you carry them out. It then follows that your "people skills" are a major factor in determining the success of our Company and your own career progress.

The guidelines in this handbook were developed to help you in human resource management. They are, however, not a substitute for good judgment in dealing with the problems and concerns of the individuals whom you supervise.

Employee Relations Problems—Common Causes

Day-to-day employee relations problems are most frequently caused by:

- inconsistency in the application of personnel policies and procedures
- favoritism
- lack of fair but firm discipline

- failure to listen and to follow through
- failure to keep employees informed, particularly about changes that are going to affect them
- changes in procedures that appear to be arbitrary

Sometimes it seems employees are imagining that a problem exists. Whether real or imaginary, however, it is your responsibility to recognize the situation and to deal with it effectively. Failure to accept the fact that a problem exists can result in a more serious situation. Continued denial of the existence of a problem can result in employees turning to alternate sources of leadership, either within their own group or outside the Company.

From time to time, any supervisor will need assistance in solving particularly difficult employee relations problems. There are several sources of help available to you, including your own manager, Vice President, or Human Resource Director.

Recognizing Problems

Employees who complain may help you in identifying problem areas. However, not all employees feel comfortable discussing a problem, thinking that you either cannot or will not resolve the situation to their satisfaction. In such cases, employees may indicate the existence of problems to you through changes in attitude, behavior, or job performance.

In extreme cases, employees may act in concert to present complaints or effect work stoppages. Finally, if the situation becomes even more critical, there may be signs of unauthorized literature, strangers on the premises, or loitering outside; new patterns of communications and/or increasing questions about benefits and company policies relating to salaries and overtime pay.

Look for these signs—

- a drop in productivity
- change in employee attitudes
- change in the way people work
- increasing absenteeism
- increasing turnover
- more complaints
- refusal to work overtime
- resistance to following new instructions
- destruction of work or equipment
- unusual grouping of employees at breaks or meals

- management not included in conversations
- unauthorized literature
- increasing number of questions about pay and benefits
- strangers on the premises

Handling Problems

Once a problem is identified, events tend to move quickly. The following will act as a guideline for the effective handling of a problem.

Complaints from a Single Employee

- Discussions should be held in a private office away from the work area. Listen carefully and attempt to isolate the real problem.
- If you are unable to resolve the problem yourself, or if you need further authorization or clarification, end the interview, promise a prompt reply, and follow through.
- If a problem cannot be resolved to the employee's satisfaction, discuss the problem with your manager, Vice President, or Human Resource Director. If further action is required, follow the steps outlined in the *Problem Review Procedure.*

In all of the following situations, contact your manager or the Human Resource Director. If they are unavailable, have a fellow manager present as you follow the prescribed outline.

Complaints from a Group

- Under no conditions should you deal with a group (two or more people) or committee or anyone purporting to represent a group.
- Instead, try to talk to members of the group individually. Make clear that you are talking only about an employee's individual problem.
- If the group is too large or too cohesive to be separated into individuals, do not attempt to deal with them but rather call on your Human Resource Director for guidance.
- In talking to an individual, follow the same procedures for "Complaints from a Single Employee." If an employee refuses to talk to you, direct the employee to return to work and continue with another member of the group.
- If the employee refuses to return to work, advise the individual that continued refusal may result in disciplinary action.
- If the employee continues to refuse, direct the employee to resume normal activities or leave the premises.

- If the employee refuses, advise the employee to leave the premises immediately and that he or she is subject to disciplinary action up to and including discharge.
- Report the incident to the Human Resource Director.

Note: It is very important to avoid dealing with a group, or even giving the appearance of dealing with a group. It is conceivable that the National Labor Relations Board might view such direct dealing as recognition of the group as a collective bargaining agent. You could then in effect be dealing with a third party. The determination as to whether you bargained with the group depends on what actually happens and what is said, but you should never put yourself in the position of being unable to prove what you said to a group. Your own testimony may not stand up against the group whose testimony differs from yours.

A Group Request for a Meeting

- There may be an occasion when an employee group requests a meeting with management to discuss their complaints. Let the group know that you cannot meet with them, but would gladly arrange meetings with an individual employee who wishes to discuss a problem.
- Invite the employee into your office or other private area and attempt to determine the nature of the problem.
- If you cannot resolve the problem or need further assistance, authorization, or clarification, promise a prompt reply and follow through.
- Report the incident immediately to the Human Resource Director.

A Petition or List of Complaints

- Do not discuss a petition or list of grievances with any employee group. If you have knowledge of the existence of such a petition or list, notify the Human Resource Director immediately.
- Offer to discuss specific complaints with individual employees.
- If, during the interview, the employee is not satisfied, refer him or her to the Human Resource Director.
- Forward the document to the Human Resource Director.

An Unauthorized Work Stoppage

A work stoppage occurs when two or more employees, acting together, refuse to perform assigned work or refuse to abide by established rules, regulations, or management directives. Some examples of work stoppages are:

- walking off the job without permission.
- refusing to leave the work area at the end of scheduled work time.
- refusing to perform work as directed.
- refusing to work overtime.

Note: It may difficult to determine if a refusal to work overtime is an unauthorized work stoppage as defined above. The determination relates to whether the refusal results from concerted group activity. You must therefore ask each employee individually to work the overtime and note in writing the reasons for each refusal.

Action to Be Taken

- If possible, have a management witness present.
- Do not deal with a spokesman or committee purporting to represent the employees.
- Specifically instruct each employee to resume normal duties.
- It the employee refuses, provide a warning that continued refusal may result in the employee being permanently replaced.
- If the employee continues to refuse, direct the employee to resume normal work or leave the premises.
- If the employee continues to refuse, advise the employee to leave the premises immediately and that he or she is subject to disciplinary action up to and including discharge for refusal to do so.
- Report the incident to the Human Resource Director.

The Human Resource Director Should:

- advise and assist supervisors and managers in carrying out this procedure.
- obtain all relevant facts, such as time, place, number of employees involved, and their names.
- consult with management to determine the final course of action.

Work Slowdowns

If you determine that a work slowdown is taking place, direct each employee to cease the unauthorized act, and proceed as you would for a work stoppage.

Unidentified/Unauthorized Visitors

You have the responsibility to make certain strangers who come into the work area are properly identified and that they are on authorized business. If you are not satisfied on either point, escort the stranger to the nearest exit.

Policy on Third Party Representation

Management firmly believes that the interests of our employees can be served without the presence of a third party. To that end, management commits its efforts to the maintenance of an environment that renders unnecessary the intervention of a third party.

Further, it is our policy that only the Human Resource Director has the authority to recognize a bargaining representative or group of employees.

Organizing Drive

A third party may publicize intent to organize our employees. The following situations may occur should our employees be the target of an organizing drive.

- Distribution of leaflets, pledge cards, and/or solicitation of employees by non-employees.
  (1) If any unauthorized visitor is distributing leaflets to or soliciting employees on company property, direct the person to leave immediately.
  (2) If the person refuses, remove the individual from premises.
  (3) Remove all loose literature and cards from premises and forward them to the Human Resource Director.
  (4) Report all instances to the Human Resource Director.

A Third Party's Demand for Recognition

- If he or she appears in person:
  (1) Immediately call witnesses equal to or greater than the number of individuals accompanying the third party.
  (2) If the third party demands verbal recognition, tell him or her that you do not have the authority to discuss this matter. Refer the third party to the Human Resource Director.
  (3) If a third party presents cards and asks you to verify employee's signatures or names, refuse to accept or look at the cards or any other material offered. Acceptance or verification of such material under these circumstances has been interpreted by the National Labor Relations Board as recognition of a third party for the purpose of collective bargaining. Refer the third party to the Human Resource Director.
  (4) Make a record of the conversation.
  (5) Do not argue or discuss the matter. Close the conversation

quickly. Ask the third party to leave; and if necessary, escort the person to the nearest exit.

- If the person telephones:
  (1) Refuse any request or demand for third party recognition.
  (2) Refuse to meet with the person.
  (3) Refer the person to the Human Resource Director.
  (4) Report all information to the Human Resource Director.
- If the person sends a letter or telegram:
  (1) Refer the letter unopened to the Human Resource Director.

In situations of this kind where there is the possibility of third party involvement, you should make a note of all pertinent facts and report the matter to the Human Resource Director. In no case should you discuss these matters with any other individual or group. If you do not have a Human Resource Director on staff, contact a labor relations consultant or labor attorney.

Picketing Situations

The presence of a picket line presents both a practical and a legal question. From the practical point of view, it is an obstacle to maintaining normal operations. Consequently, you and the Human Resource Director should:

- direct employees who are not picketing to go about their normal duties without regard to the picket line activity.
- inform employees that their failure to cross the picket line puts them in the position of strikers and they may be permanently replaced.
- keep an accurate count of employees at work each day.

Picket lines frequently give rise to complicated legal problems. You can help to avoid these if you:

- do not speak to any member of the picket line except when directed to do so by proper authorities.
- avoid any arguments or contact with pickets.
- direct other employees to avoid the picket line whenever possible.

The Human Resource Director or attorney should:

- advise and assist managers.
- obtain all relevant facts: course of action, time, place, number of employees involved, etc.

- assist line management in determining impact of picketing on operations.

- assist line management in making whatever changes in operations are necessary to lessen impact of picketing.

- assist line management in implementing contingency plans subject to final approval by the Human Resource Director or appropriate Vice President.

- consult with appropriate management representative to determine final course of action.

The Director's Role in a Third Party Organizing Campaign

During an organizing drive, there are many things to consider aside from picketing. Primarily, the question of what may or may not be said to employees is most important. The National Labor Relations Board has held that managers are spokesmen for the Company and, therefore, what they say can be attributed to the Company.

Companies do not, however, win organizational campaigns by remaining silent. Therefore, an understanding of what to say or what not to say is important. Generally you may legally say anything you choose so long as it does not violate one of three general rules.

- Don't threaten an employee with reprisals.

- Don't interrogate an employee(s) about activities.

- Don't promise an employee any economic benefit.

Here's a more specific listing of the do's and don'ts that must be observed during an organization drive.

You may tell your employees the following.

1. We do not believe representation by a third party is either necessary or desirable.

2. We believe the best interests of our employees will be served by continuing their direct relationship with the Company and our management rather than through a third party.

3. The Company has and will continue to treat its employees equally and fairly, paying salaries and benefits equal to or better than the industry for comparable work.

4. The management of the Company is always willing to discuss any subject of interest to employees.

5. It is important to understand that a third party has its own interests

aside from the interests of its members. In case of conflict, the third party's interests come first.

6. The *Problem Review Procedure* permits employees to voice their thoughts or complaints to management thereby assuring them of personal consideration.

7. Employees do not have to talk to third parties.

8. Employees do not have to give their names and addresses to third parties.

9. Employees do not have to attend any meeting called by a third party.

10. Employees do not have to sign cards distributed by a third party and should not do so unless they want to lose their individual rights.

11. A third party cannot guarantee anyone's job—only his own work efforts protect his job.

12. We believe that employees should not pay dues, initiation fees, assessments, and fines for the things they are getting and will continue to get without representation by a third party.

13. We sincerely believe that our employees will not benefit from being represented by a third party.

You may not:

1. threaten or otherwise intimidate employees directly or indirectly.

2. threaten to discharge or discipline employees or lay off employees.

3. interrogate employees regarding their feelings.

4. promise employees special favors or treatment to vote against third party representation.

5. ask employees how they intend to vote or how they believe others will vote.

6. ask employees whether they have signed or intend to sign a card.

7. visit the homes of employees for the purpose of urging them to reject a third party.

8. make statements to employees that they will be discharged or disciplined if they are active on behalf of a third party.

9. spy on meetings.

Conclusion

This *Managers Guide to Employee Relations* may help you identify and handle employee relations problems and to let you know where you can go for help.

Many of the things you see or hear may have little meaning by themselves. However, put together with reports of other managers, your experience may reveal a pattern that will enable management to anticipate employee relations problems. That is why it is important that you report to your manager or Vice President and Human Resource Director all occurrences of unauthorized visitors, solicitation, group complaints or requests for meetings, and so forth. Of course, picketing and actual demands from a third party should be referred immediately to the appropriate management.

You may find this guide useful in carrying out your day-to-day responsibilities as a manager. The prompt and equitable review of employee problems and the resolution of such problems at the lowest possible organizational level is vitally important to the employee relations environment of the Company. An employee problem exists whenever an employee feels that there is a job-related problem (real or imaginary) that has not been resolved to his or her satisfaction. In such instances, the employee should be encouraged to use the *Problem Review Procedure*, and the supervisor is responsible for ensuring that the problem is promptly and fully processed until the employee is satisfied with the decision made or until the procedure is exhausted.

Problem Review Procedure

Step 1   The employee should discuss the problem with the immediate supervisor and if the employee is not satisfied with the results of this discussion, a meeting should be arranged with the next level of management.

Step 2   If the problem has not been resolved to the satisfaction of the employee, the employee may make a formal written complaint to the Department Manager. Forms for the complaint may be obtained from the Human Resource Office. The Human Resource Director will also be available for guidance and assistance.

Step 3   If the employee is still dissatisfied after discussing the problem with the Department Manager, a meeting should be arranged with the Vice President. This appointment may be made by the employee directly or through the department manager or the Human Resource Director.

Step 4   If, after Step 3, the situation is still unresolved, the employee may submit the written statement to the President of the Company. The final decision will be made at this level.

The employee may drop the complaint at any step of the procedure. It is recommended that there be no more than a ten-day time period between each step.

Note: If you don't have a full-time Labor Relations or Human Resource Director, it is important to find an experienced labor consultant or labor attorney at the first sign of union organizing activity.

PREVENTIVE LABOR RELATIONS: A CASE STUDY

Employee relations at Tektronix, Inc. includes a "preventive" labor policy—but one that is communicated in positive terms. In a conversation with John Heilman, Personnel Relations Manager, at Tektronix, Inc., I found a company and a Personnel Director concerned with the welfare of their employees. Tektronix, Inc., is a high-tech company headquartered in Beaverton, Oregon. Tektronix ranks 252 on the *Fortune 500* (1985 sales of 1.5 billion). Most of Tektronix' 20,000 employees work in the Portland metropolitan area, although the company has operations throughout the country and around the world. All the company's facilities are non-union (except where mandated by law, such as the Netherlands).

John Heilman stresses that the environment at Tektronix is positive and management works to keep it that way. Even the company's policy on labor unions—which is communicated to employees in the employee handbook—is stated in positive terms.

"It is our intent to provide a work environment," Mr. Heilman says, "where our employees wouldn't even consider unionization as an alternative."

Compensation includes a strong incentive factor: thirty-five percent of pre-tax earnings are set aside every year for profit-sharing, and distributed to employees according to their base pay.

At a time when most companies are experiencing growing legal challenges to discharges—or fear they may be hit with increasing lawsuits—Tektronix has avoided many problems through a very strong Review Process (internal grievance procedure) that often takes a case to the President of the company. Involuntary terminations are all approved by the President for employees with five or more years of service.

I interviewed Mr. Heilman in order to learn more about the company's labor relations philosophy and their work climate.

Ms. Cook: As the economy improves, a number of labor unions are talking about some stepping up union organizing activity. Do you, at Tektronix, have a stated policy on labor unions?—One that you communicate to your employees?

Mr. Heilman: Yes, we do. The electronics industry, of course, is only lightly organized. And our own operations—both here in Portland and around the country—are entirely non-union.

We in the industry think a major reason for that is "enlightened management." Electronics is a relatively new industry, and we have the benefit of other employers' experience over the years—the things they did right, the things they did wrong. We've tried to learn from those experiences and shape a work environment for our employees that is conducive to getting out a quality product to meet customer needs—and doing it efficiently.

On the issue of unions as such, we don't tell our employees that it is the company's intent to "avoid" or "prevent" unionization. Rather, throughout our environment, we try to emphasize the positive. And on the subject of unions, we prefer a positive statement. We prefer to say that it is our intent to provide the kind of work environment where unions aren't needed in the first place—a work environment, in other words, where our employees wouldn't even consider unionization as an alternative.

Ms. Cook: Do you have a statement to that effect in your employee handbook?

Mr. Heilman: Yes, we do. Let me give it to you. The following statement in the handbook discusses unions:

TEK EMPLOYEE HANDBOOK

Unions

Historically, Tektronix has offered good working conditions, wages, and benefits, and worked to provide a good quality of work life for all of us. These, combined with the established Review Process and an open-door environment, are simply appropriate, common-sense practices.

Through open communications, we believe that managers stay aware of the needs and concerns of their fellow employees. It is expected that all people will be treated with dignity and respect. We believe, therefore, that employees should have no need for unions or other outside representation.

Tek is managed so that most employees feel they have a personal stake in the Company's success, and in the decisionmaking that affects job conditions. All of us have a stake in the Company through profit sharing, and many of us have taken advantage of the opportunity to buy Tek stock at reduced rates.

Tek recognizes that unions have been helpful for some people in different circumstances. However, we also believe that Tek people, working together at all levels of the Company, can continue to maintain fair employment practices and a good working environment without intervention of outside organizations.

Ms. Cook: Do your supervisors and managers have instructions on how they are to respond to possible labor activity?

Mr. Heilman: We did not have a written statement in the past, partly because the industry is so lightly organized—and partly because we had not always been as big as we are now. Tektronix was formed in 1946; and today we have some 20,000 employees worldwide.

With the company getting so large and spreading out both geographically and organizationally, it is a growing concern that we inform our managers of their responsibilities—and so a statement has been included in our Policy Manual. It embodies the point of view we have asked our managers to take through the years.

TEK POLICY

UNIONS AND OTHER OUTSIDE INVOLVEMENT

Intent   Tektronix policies and practices encourage understanding and fairness among all employees. It is expected that all people will be treated with dignity and respected as individuals. We therefore believe that employees should have no need for unions or other outside representation.

Policy   Managers are responsible for providing leadership that addresses the needs of employees. Employees should not feel the need to organize together for purposes of collective bargaining, or to seek outside involvement (union, government, other otherwise) to resolve problems.

Even in the best of circumstances, however, some discontent may arise among employees. Managers observing any indicators related to organizing activity or outside union intervention must communicate them immediately to the Human Resource Manager and the Corporate Development and Personnel Relations Director.

Reference   Corporate Development and Personnel Relations Director, Human Resource Department

Additionally, Human Resources personnel have been trained and conduct a one-day supervisory/ manager training session to help ensure they understand their roles and responsibilities. The objectives of this "Excellence in Employee Relations" program are:

- Increase awareness of the basic legal requirements relating to U.S. labor law.

- Increase understanding of the importance of effective people management.

- Define and relate the manager's role to effective people management.

- Provide a framework for basic evaluation of the work environment.

Ms. Cook: Does every employee get an annual performance review?

Mr. Heilman: All our employees get an annual performance review, and we intend that those who are classified non-exempt get a semi-annual review. Each pay grade has a salary range and we have a pay for performance policy.

Ms. Cook: On the subject of benefits generally, what key benefits do you have?

Mr. Heilman: The cash and deferral options under a very generous profit-sharing plan (35 percent of pre-tax earnings allocated for distribution to employees according to their base pay) are offered under the provisions of Section 401(k). Under normal conditions, profit-sharing substantially increases our employees' income.

We have just implemented a new flexible benefits program for all employees. The program has a very small core of common benefits for everyone and many alternatives for medical, dental, life, accident, etc., insurance. The plan also includes spending accounts to cover unique or uncovered expenses in other areas, e.g. day care, eye, hearing, deductible, etc.

One hundred percent reimbursement is provided for job-related training and education, while 50 percent for all non-job-related education is reimbursed. Extensive on-the-job and after hours training and education are utilized to help people stay current and acquire new skills and knowledge in our dynamic industry.

Ms. Cook: How do your wages stay competitive in your industry?

Mr. Heilman: We participate in numerous salary surveys—a few for the local area and region and several general surveys. Additionally, we thoroughly evaluate electronic industry and international surveys to ensure our salary structure is on target.

Ms. Cook: How do you see Tektronix recruiting the technical and engineering people you will need during the 1990s?—Most of your jobs are in the Portland, Oregon metropolitan area, are they not?

Mr. Heilman: They are—and that has been an on-going problem that we've had to come to grips with. The Portland area is becoming a rapidly growing high technology center. Among other things, we are providing several million dollars for use by the area's colleges and universities, with particular focus on attracting and retaining high caliber teaching staffs.

We recruit professional employees nationally, of course, and we consider ourselves well-known both for our products in the market and for our desirable working and living conditions. Both of those factors are strong pluses in any national recruiting program.

Ms. Cook: Finally, what about the legal programs surrounding discharges that are a growing problem for most companies today? Do you have many lawsuits arising from terminations?

Mr. Heilman: No, we don't. Of course, as the economy flattened out and job security became a growing concern, we saw more and more employees turn to the EEOC, or to state agencies, seeking assistance, in some cases, seeking assistance perhaps as a means of "feeling better" about a termination.

But setting aside considerations involving the economy—we require at Tektronix an internal review prior to any involuntary termination, and that process has probably headed off many of the legal questions that might otherwise have arisen. All managers are required to "recommend" termination as the first step in this process. Even when the necessity for termination seems clear, our intent here is to stop the manager from actually implementing his or her decision to discharge until the decision can be reviewed.

In some cases, where immediate action is appropriate, the manager can, in effect, suspend the employee—but the paperwork on the eventual termination is not completed until the approval process is completed. The process usually includes an interview with the employee; and if an employee has been with us five years or more, the President of the company reviews the termination before it is actually implemented.

CRITICAL ISSUES FACING LABOR IN THE 1990s

Human Resource Directors have to stay current on labor relations issues. Labor issues can be expensive to resolve, especially if the company ends up with a union or in litigation. Here are some critical issues that both labor and management will face in the next three to five years in the United States.

- the continuation of concession bargaining that started in 1982 and 1983 when companies were having serious economic difficulties and the problems of concessions in one company create pressures on competitive companies for the same concessions—so concessions will continue to be a thorn in unions' negotiating plans.

- the need for companies to offset any wage increases with corresponding productivity increases.

- the need of companies to limit the number of high-wage, high-seniority core workers.

- there may be increased bargaining for one-time lump sum raises that don't increase base pay. Experts say that the high tech industries will not create as many jobs as are being lost in the shrinking smokestack industries that were once organized labor's power base. High tech workers are resisting the idea they need unions.

- the desire of organizations to eliminate agreements that grant automatic wage hikes or costs of living increases (COLAS).

- job security is becoming a problem. More companies are turning to overseas production and to lower cost domestic firms—they call it outsourcing.

- if labor is to survive, there is a need to organize whole new segments of industry—office workers, high tech workers, professionals, and so forth.

- the growth of the so-called cottage industry is going to heavily impact unions. Some experts predict that as a result of the explosion in electronics and computers, up to twenty percent of all American workers will be working out of their homes by 1990.

- the number of new plants being started in the United States by other countries, including Japan, is increasing and these outside employers do not want unions and employ management techniques to avoid them. Less then twenty-five percent of Japan's United States plants are unionized.

- the perception of a "mob" influence in unions does not enhance their ability to attract new-age workers. A president's commission on organized crime reported four big unions are controlled by organized crime.

- the Court has given employers carte blanche in firing unions. In the case of the National Labor Relations Board versus Bildisco and Bildisco, the court in effect repealed the provision of the 1935 National Labor Relations Act that forbids either party to repudiate a freely negotiated labor-management agreement before its expiration. The result gave employers carte blanche to tear up union contracts merely by filing a bankruptcy petition without waiting for a court hearing. Management can now slash wages, fire employees at will, cancel group health insurance, and eliminate pensions and work rules.

  Continental Airlines voided its collective bargaining agreements through Chapter 11 Bankruptcy filing and the filing was upheld in court.

- an NLRB ruling on moving union jobs to nonunion plants was upheld on appeal. In an unanimous decision a three-judge panel upheld the NLRB decision in a case involving employees at the Milwaukee Spring Division of Illinois Coil Spring Company. The NLRB decision said there wasn't any pertinent provision in the division's labor agreement that prohibited the company from moving work during the life of the pact. The NLRB held that an employer may, after satisfying any obligation it might have to bargain about the decision, move work from one plant to another to escape the higher labor costs of the union-organized plant.

- cuts in employee benefits are going to have to go deeper, and employees will have to pick up more of the costs of benefits because of the constantly rising cost of medical benefits.

- increased automation has reduced the threat and the effectiveness of walkouts as a bargaining tactic. The nationwide strike against American Telephone and Telegraph highlighted the degree to which high technology is reducing the effectiveness of walkouts. Increased automation was the main reason the system's 150 million phones operated without major disruptions and state-of-the-art equipment allowed AT&T management to keep up with the bulk of calls—those that are dialed direct.

- training and retraining are key issues with workers. They are demanding that as technology eliminates jobs, retraining programs prepare them for career changes.

- two-tier labor contracts are taking hold in a big way and unions have been forced to accept them in lieu of wage cuts for already employed workers. This seems to be an ongoing trend.

- salaried plants are also catching on. They are part of a trend in the employee-involvement movement, quality circles, profit sharing, and so forth. Companies like TRW, Dow Chemical, Dana Corporation, and Rockwell International today regard the concept as an alternative to traditional management compensation methods. Organized labor says they are just another way to try to decertify unions.

- companies are hiring consultants to help them retain a non-union environment, or to help them decertify a union. Anti-union films help companies fend off organizing efforts. Before they watched "Working Without Unions," twenty percent of 108 business students at two Baltimore colleges said they were pro-union; afterwards only six percent felt the same way. The sixty-eight percent who called themselves anti-union before seeing the film increased to eighty-five percent afterwards.

- robots will replace thousands of workers in the next five years. The United States Department of Transportation has estimated that 400,000 of the 900,000 auto workers will face permanent displacement after car manufacturers complete automation plans by the end of this decade. It has also been estimated that robots may create several thousand new jobs.

General Motors estimates that by 1990, 14,000 robots will replace 28,000 workers in their auto plants. GM plans to retrain at least half of the displaced workers for higher-skilled, higher-paid jobs.

MANAGEMENT'S CRITICAL ISSUES FOR THE 1990s

- Keeping a wage spiral from reoccurring after five years of concession bargaining that has kept wages lower than they would otherwise have been. Companies that are rebounding economically will have to address the issue as good technical and professional people become more difficult to attract and to retrain.

- Job security is a big issue with workers, and management will have to make concessions in this area.

- It will be necessary for managers to learn how to manage the cottage industry—the worker who works at home. New policies and programs will be needed to motivate, compensate, and communicate with this class of worker.

- Supervisors and managers will need to become bilingual and cross-cultural as United States companies open more plants overseas and as more foreign companies open plants in the United States, as the Japanese have.

- Now that many companies have taken Chapter 11 bankruptcy to eliminate unions and have cut wages and benefits of workers, they must treat workers right, using participative management styles, flexible benefits, and communications programs that work in order to retain the current union-free culture.

- We are moving toward mega corporations, with mergers and acquisitions a common occurrence. Management of these mega corporations will have to be different if they are to be successful. People feel lost in the huge corporation. They are very low-touch and tend to get "out-of-touch" with their human resources. Because so much of their success depends on their human resources, new programs will be needed to communicate up and down throughout the organization.

- As more companies merge and downsize, hundreds of thousands of workers, supervisors and managers are being laid off—terminated. These workers may never work again in their field. If organizations don't take action to help retrain this workforce, these workers will eventually join the welfare ranks or be part of the homeless and chronically unemployed. This is a growing and serious issue and should be a concern of American industry. On the positive side of unemployment, many unemployed are becoming entrepreneurs and creating small businesses that are competing for business in new growth areas.

- Management will be forced to rethink its prejudices about hiring or retaining older workers because they will be badly needed in the next decade.

- Management will have to deal with issues they have ignored in the past. One such issue is dealing with romance on the job. As women continue to enter the workforce in huge numbers, romance will become more prevalent. Companies currently handle the subject very poorly, but as management finds it needs all the good people it can attract, it will begin dealing with the subject in a more open and positive manner.

- There is still a condescending attitude in most organizations toward women in management and towards the promotion of women into top management. There is a visible ceiling in most organizations for women at management levels. As the need for talented, high-performance individuals increases, this attitude and practice will have to change.

OTHER IMPORTANT LABOR RELATIONS ISSUES AND TRENDS OF THE FUTURE

The Quest for Equal Opportunity for Women in the Workforce

Possibly some of the toughest issues management will face in the next decade are the issues of equal pay, comparable worth, and equal opportunity in promotions for women above manager level in all organizations.

The biggest single employment trend in the last decade was the trend of women entering the workforce. It has been projected that by 1990 over seventy-five percent of all women in the United States over age sixteen will be working outside the home. That figure has already reached sixty percent.

The Women's Labor Project, a group of women lawyers, law students, and legal workers who do legal and educational support work for women workers, believes that unionization of women's jobs and active participation by women in unions will help them achieve workplace equality.

The Women's Labor Project currently assists in organization efforts in largely female workplaces, doing workshops on legal and collective bargaining issues affecting women. This group is part of the National Lawyers Guild and has labor committees and labor projects in most major cities across the country, including a National Labor Law Center in Washington, DC.

The fact that more women are organizing to press for equal opportunity in wages and in promotional opportunities reflects a mood that pervades an ever-increasing segment of the workforce and should not be overlooked in corporate strategic planning.

Increased Use of Industrial Robots

General Motors has 5,000 robots on the job and plans to have 14,000 by 1990. Those 14,000 robots will replace 28,000 assembly line workers.

The growth of robots is taking place now for two primary reasons:

1. the development of the microprocessor, a computer small enough to use as the "brains" of a robot

2. wage inflation

Two decades ago, a typical assembly-line robot cost about $4.20 an hour (averaged over its lifetime), just slightly higher than the average factory worker's wages and benefits. Today, the robot can still be operated for less than $5 an hour, while most employees in the auto industry make between $15 and $20 an hour.

One of the earliest countries to realize the economic benefits of robotics was Japan. Although most of the original research and development on robotic technology occurred in the United States, Japan currently has about 13,000 of the world's 17,500 robots. The United States has about 2,500 robots, and West Germany, Sweden, Italy, Poland, Norway, France, Britain, and Finland have the rest.

Both labor and management are taking steps to soften the impact of increasing numbers of industrial robots by providing resources for:

*   retraining of displaced workers
*   maintaining current salary levels for workers placed into lower-rated jobs

The Rise of Part-time Workers

Their rising numbers are creating labor conflicts and keeping a huge segment of workers in low-pay, no-benefits jobs. There is rising dissatisfaction among the six million Americans who are part-time workers but who want the pay and benefits of a full-time position. On average, part-time workers make $4.50 per hour compared with $7.80 average pay for full-time workers. At this level, part-timers who are lucky enough to work a full 2,000 hours a year are still only at the Federal poverty level. This is an issue that will lead to increased labor-management conflict.

An Improvement in the Image of Unions

Unions have hired the Madison Avenue public relations establishment to help them improve a tarnished image. They have also hired television stars to do pro-union commercials and are spotlighting such issues as sexual harassment, unfair firing, comparable worth, and so forth.

Organized labor is campaigning full-bore to sign up white collar and service workers. Also, the growing number of health-maintenance organizations and big medical-care corporations is prompting more unionization among American medical workers, including physicians and other high-paid professionals. The reason is doctors who are working for salaries rather than for themselves are losing income and power to corporate managers. Even so, unions face an uphill struggle in signing up physicians. Only about 10,000 of the nation's 460,000 doctors now belong to unions.

Unions are also getting more sophisticated in their ability to "read" their members and the public. The United Auto Workers commissioned a poll designed to measure public attitudes on issues such as compensation from foreign auto makers. They also poll union members more frequently in order to identify key issues.

Management Will Continue to Fight to Keep Unions Out

Corporations are hiring high-paid consultants to help them retain a union-free environment. White collar workers, professionals, and high tech workers are resisting union organization attempts. Among workers in high-technology industries, for example, unions have managed to gain few footholds. According to the American Electronics Association, only 90 union contracts were found among 1,900 member companies in a 1982 survey. Moreover, unions won only 7 of 44 representation elections in the electronics industry from 1977 to 1982—compared with 14 wins in 56 elections during the previous 6 years.

Even though they don't always agree, labor and management are trying harder to get along. All in all, there does seem to be an effort on the part of both labor and management to "get along." Companies in manufacturing, mining, and transportation are seeking their unions' help in surviving. Unions are now acting jointly with management in developing new products and production technology, deciding on plant location and layout, and organizing employee buyouts of failing companies and plants. The involvement of union leaders in business decision-making is a major change that has potential for improving the competitive edge of those companies.

Following the GM and Ford models, unions are likely to demand decision-making roles or stock ownership in return for wage cuts, and this may call for changes in union and management philosophy. The United

Steelworkers, for example, has reversed its longtime opposition to employee ownership and is formulating strategies to help members buy total or partial ownership in plants that otherwise would be closed. These trends are all major shifts from policies of the last decade and are forerunners of things to come in this new era of labor relations.

SAFETY—A RENEWED CONCERN FOR BOTH GOVERNMENT AND INDUSTRY

The number of work-related injuries and illnesses in private industry rose 11.7 percent in 1985. The Labor Department reported that this very significant increase is of deep concern and that it will step up its efforts to assure that the American workplace is as safe as it can be. Also, several serious chemical explosions injured thousands of people in the United States and abroad in 1985.

In the United States there were eight incidents of injury or illness reported for every 100 full-time workers in 1985. This was the largest single-year increase in the history of OSHA, dating back to 1973.

Shortly after the announcement of the tremendous increase in illness and injuries on the job, there was another announcement by the Occupational Safety and Health Administration, and by the Secretary of Labor, that it will toughen its workplace safety inspection policy by making spot checks of companies that generally are exempt from full-scale inspections.

OSHA will target its inspection efforts on high-hazard manufacturing and chemical companies. All companies with operations that have reported high levels of illness or injury should beef up their own inspection capability to avoid corporate losses as well as the loss of time on the job and the unnecessary stress and illness put on valuable employees.

Health and Safety—Growing Issues with American Workers

American workers are becoming more vocal and more active and concerned about their work environment. Three Mile Island and the Karen Silkwood case have made employees more aware of health hazards in the workplace. In the past, some companies told workers they were working in a safe environment when they were not. Take the case of the hundreds of lawsuits against the Manville Corporation for asbestos poisoning, and the thousands of black lung cases around the country filed by employees who worked for years in the underground coal mines.

Today workers have more savvy—they do not just take a supervisor's word for their safety; they find out for themselves. More employers are beginning to feel an ethical responsibility for the health and safety of workers.

If they do not, there will be more deferal regulation, and renewed efforts on the part of OSHA to ensure safe working conditions.

New state laws have begun to protect the whistleblower and more cases are coming to light both in the press and in the courts with regard to unsafe working conditions, chemical dumping, and so forth. Human resource directors who have responsibility for safety must take that responsibility seriously.

Since the inception of the Occupational Safety and Health Act there have been problems. OSHA's effectiveness in improving safety and health in the workplace has been questioned by the companies it regulates as well as workers, and other regulatory agencies that must interface with the agency.

Human Resource Managers all have their own theories about the emphasis that should be put on safety and on OSHA in their particular companies and work environments. The one issue that will not go away, however, is the issue that all Human Resource Managers have a responsibility to ensure workers have a safe place to work and that accidents are reported and there is follow-through to eliminate hazards. No matter what management thinks of OSHA, it is still the law.

NEW DIRECTIONS IN EMPLOYEE RIGHTS

Beyond OSHA, beyond EEO, beyond Unions, there is a revolution in employee rights in the making in America. If a company makes a change in a pension plan, issues a no-smoking policy, installs a computer monitoring program, listens to employee telephone conversations, or openly fires an employee thought to have AIDS, it could be invading the privacy and ignoring the rights of employees.

Some organizations feel that many workplace rules are unfair and greatly increase the potential for stress-related illnesses. Employee rights may well be the next regulated area of employment.

INDEX

A

Absenteeism, 156
Abuse, drugs, 60
Abuse, of medical records, 87
Abuse, substance, 163
Acquired immune deficiency syndrome (AIDS), 75, 88, 89, 332, 343, 344, 345, 346, 347, 348, 350, 351, 458
Acquisitions, 23
Administrative procedures, 61
Administrative system, 7
Adoption benefit, 157
Advertising, 271
Affirmative action plans, 95,97
Age discrimination in employment, 113
Alcoholism, 359
American Association of Retired Persons (AARP), 192
American Airlines, 30,236,426
American Can Company, 170
American Civil Liberties Union, 308
American Express, 159
American Federation of State, County and Municipal Employees (AFSCME), 159
American Graduate School of International Management, 231
American Management Association (AMA), 351
American Society for Industrial Security (ASIS), 359
American Society for Personnel Administration (ASPA), 22,351
American Society for Training & Development (ASTD), 221
Arbitration, 431
Arrest record, 78
Asset reversion, 127
Assessment, 8
Assessing an organization, 3
Assessment center methods, 236
Athletic events, 76
Atlantic Richfield Company, 20
Audio cassettes, 76
Audiographic, 229

B

Bank of America, 38,217
Base period payroll, 200

Bendix Corporation, 236
Benefit, adoption, 157
Benefit calculation, 201
Benefit communications, 204
Benefit consultant, 203
Benefit cost control, 61
Benefit letter, 206
Benefit, nanny, 157
Benefits, new, 116
Benefit plans, 401(k), 172
Benefit programs, 109–207
Benefit provisions in Tax Reform Act, 117
Benefits test, 136
Benefits valuation, 137
Benefits video, 205
Big brother in the workplace, 83,89
Bilingual, 230,231
Bilingual education, 106
Birthing centers, 160
Black owned businesses, 94
Blue Cross, 198
Boise Cascade Corporation, 236
Boycotts, 94,95
Booze Allen Hamilton, 256
Bureau of Business Practice, 308
Bureau of National Affairs, 351
Business Clearinghouse, 283
Business-Oriented, 282
Business Round Table, 283

C

Cable legislation, 101,102
Cafeteria plans, 139,140
Calculating the cost of benefits, 109–202
Career fields, 105
Carnegie Foundation, 211
Cash incentives. 43,44
Caterpiller Company, 193
CBS, Inc, 111,190
CEO compensation, 37
Chamber of commerce, 283
Change agents, 4
Changing, the new worker, 74
Charging health care, 159
Chase Manhattan Bank, 84
Checklist of personnel policies, 323
Child care, 146,150,151

Child care benefit, 150
Child care costs, 147,151,155
Chrysler corporation, 104
Civil Rights Act, 77,89
Civil Rights Commission, 77
Civilian labor force, 280
Citicorp, 104
COBRA letters, 142–145
Communication, 24
Communication, employee, 354
Communicating employee benefits, 203
Company stretch, 11
Compa ratio, 59
Comparable worth, 30,96,99,100
Compensating expatriates, 408,409
Compensation committee, 41
Compensation consultant, 40
Compensation, executive, 40,41
Compensation levels, 428
Compensation programs, 29,56,57
Competitive pressures, 68
Competitor surveillence, 368
Complaints, handling, 438
Computer Based Training (CBT), 211,257
Computer literacy, 104,224,256
Computer monitoring of employees, 89,251
Computer security, 369
Computer training, 257,258
Computerized personnel records, 261
Conflict of interest, 335
Conflict resolution, 11
Confrontation meetings, 8
Connecticut general, 172
Consolidated Omnibus Budget Reconciliation
        Act (COBRA), 109,113,141,142
Consultant, 256
Consumer price index, 121
Contemporary compensation issues, 33
Contemporary organizations, 12
Contemporary worker, 113
Contribution limits, 54
Contributory plans, 125
Controlling expatriate costs, 410,411
Controlling overseas expenses, 64
Cook, Mary & Associates, 236
Coors, Adolph Company, 94
Coors, boycott, 94
Coping with violence, 363
Corporate communication program, 74,75,76
Corporate culture, 3,9,10
Corporate fast trackers, 21
Corporate social responsibility, 102
Cost analysis, 212
Cost benefit analysis, 212
Cost containment, 109

Cost control, 61,180
Cost-of-living increases, 38,57,60,121
Cottage industry, 453
Critical issues, 3
Critical labor issues, 450,454
Critical management issues, 453
Cross cultural, 230,231
Cross cultural training, 413
Culture shock, 411,412

D

DanRiver Mills, 261
Dana Corporation, 30
Data Base, 20
Day care, 148,155
Day Care Consortium, 148,155
Decentralized pay system, 37
Defined benefit plan, 120,179,183
Deduction for dividends, 132
Deferred compensation, 30,49
Defined contribution plans, 179,180,181
Demands of the worker, 72
Demotion, 83
Demographics of the workforce, 112
Diagnostically Related Groups (DRGs), 110
Disabled, 275
Discounted nonqualified options, 47
Disciplinary action, 326,431
Disciplinary procedures, 82
Discussion groups, 75
Discipline and discharge, 82,83
Discrimination tests, 135
Documentation, 326
Downsizing, 287
Drug tests, 308,309
Dual career couple, 73,92,283,384
Dual career relocation, 93

E

Economic benefit, 52
EDP pay, 32
Eligibility tests, 135,136
Employee Assistance Program (EAP),
        113,163,164,378–384
Employee benefits, 193
Employee benefit communications, 204
Employee benefit letter, 206
Employee communications, 352
Employee complaint procedure, 82, 325
Employee handbook, 82,447
Employee hotline, 352
Employee leasing, 129,288–291
Employee newsletter, 75,352
Employee privacy, 83,84,85
Employee relations, 436

Employee Retirement Income Security Act
   (ERISA), 77,176,178,188
Employee rights, 71,72,72,77
Employee secrecy agreement, 367
Employee Stock Ownership Plans (ESOPS),
   112,113,117,131,133,173,174,182
Employee with AIDS, 350
Employment-at-will, 78
Employment decisions, 318
Employment of related persons, 285
Employment relationship, 72
Employment Training Panel (ETP), 217
Equal Pay Act, 77
Equitable Life Insurance Company, 37
ERISA and Rabbi Trusts, 52,54,55
Estate tax, 133
Ethics, 105,188
Evaluation in Organizational Development (OD),
   8
Evaluation process, 97
Evaluating interview data, 300
Excise Tax on Asset Reversion, 131
Executive:
   compensation, 40
   incentives, 42
   pay, 37,39,41
   stock programs, 45
Expatriate:
   compensation, 408
   costs, 66,410,411
   employees, 395
   incentives, 67
   policies, 66,400–408
   selection, 396
EXXON, 19,173

F

Fair Credit Reporting Act, 318
Fair information practices, 86
Fair Labor Standards Act, 77
Fairness of recordkeeping, 85
Family patterns, 114
Fast trackers, 21
Fast track managers, 14
Favoritism, 436
FCC, 101
Federal Bureau of Investigation, 307
Federal contractors, 314
Federal Mine Safety Act, 78
Federal Privacy Act, 78
Federal Reserve Bank, 84
Ferraro, Geraldine, 96
FICA, FUTA, 120,140
FMC Corporation, 104
Final average pay, 183

Financial Accounting Standards Board, (FASB),
   46,113,179
Financial incentives, 67
Fired, 81
Fixed formulas, 44,45
Flat dollar plans, 183
Flexible benefits, 109,110,113,167,168,170
Flexibility, workforce, 278
Foreign service taxes, 66
Fringe benefits, 435
Future trends, 105
Futuristic facilities, 106

G

General Dynamics, 37
General Electric, 104,219
General Motors, 34,37
General Tire & Rubber Company, 84
Genetic testing, 316
Giant Food Stores, 33
Globalization, 392
Goal setting, 8
Goodrich, B.F., 37
Grace & Co., W. R., 110
Grievance process, 431
Gunther decision, 97,98
Gunther guidelines, 97

H

Handicapped applicants, 275
Handicap discrimination, 314
Handicap law, 344
Handicap litigation, 275
Hardship Withdrawal 401(1) Plan, 127
Hard to fill jobs, 274
Harvard Business Review, 335
Hay Management Consultants,
   9,31,99,354,355,356
Health Care Coalitions (HCCs), 197,198
Health care costs, 112,159
Health Maintenance Organizations (HMOs),
   110,194,195
Health plan rules, 137
Health and safety, 457
Hearing examiner, 83
Hewlett Packard, 225,232,233
High tech industry, 30
Highly compensated employees, 135,138
Hispanic businesses, 95
Hoffman LaRoche, 311
Home-based employees, 260
Home exchange program, 67
Home health care, 160
Homophobia, 343
Homosexual, 89,91,343

Honeywell, 37,67
Honesty tests, 307
Hotline, 75,352
Human resources:
   consultants, 4,236
   costs, 62
   development, 11,211,212
   information systems, 250
   management, 106
   planning, 22
Human Resources Planning Society, 22
Human rights, 78
Husband and wife teams, employment, 271

I

Iacocca, Lee, 37
IBM, 84,307,329
Immigration Reform and Control Act, 78,413–422
Implied contract, 81
Implied good faith, 81
Implementation of Organizational Development (OD), 8
Inappropriate questions, interview, 298
Incentive plans, 35
Incentives, executive, 42
Incentive levels, 44
Incentive opportunity, 43
Incentives for overseas assignment, 409
Incentive stock options, 45,47
Income deferral, 49
Income replacement, 185
Independent appraisals, 132
Individual award determination, 43
Individual development plans, 15,17,18
Individual practice association, 110
Industrial robots, 455
Innovation, 103
Integrated plans, 183
Integration, 11
Integration rules, 120
Interactive training, 225,227
Interest assumption, 54
Interest exclusion, 133
Intentional discrimination, 97
Internal ranking of jobs, 97
Internal Revenue Service, 177
Internationalization of business, 391
International Society of PreRetirement Planners, 283
Interviewing techniques, 292
Interview questions, 298
Interviewing errors, 299
IRAs, 117

Invasion of privacy, 84,315
Investment risk, 182
Issues management, 9,10,11,12,103,104,105

J

Job description, 39,58
Job evaluation, 39,58
Job-for-life, 430
Job sharing, 286
Justice department, U. S., 101

K

Key position back-up summary, 16
Kidnapped, executive, 362
Knight-Ridder Newspapers, 271

L

Labor and management, 71
Labor department, 35
Labor overview, 432
Labor relations, 425
Labor relations handbook, 436
Language training, 230
Lawsuits, privacy, 260
Laws on selection procedures,
Layoff, 217,218,436
Leasing employees, 129,288,289
Legal constraints of testing, 313
Legal services, 104,158
Leveraged buyout, 174
Liability, when kidnapped, 362
Life threatening illness policy, 332
Linking employee attitudes and corporate culture, 10
Litigation, avoiding, 81,82,83
Limits on contributions, 132
Line of business rule, 138
Lockheed Corporation, 34,365
Lump sum pay increase, 30,35,36

M

Maintaining employees overseas, 65
Management:
   by objective, 8,39
   climate studies, 10
   incentive pool, 46
   decision laboratory, 231
   development, 211–216
   succession planning, 15,17,236
Managerial ladder, 19
Manager's guide to employee relations, 436
Manager's evaluation, 16
Managing homosexuality, 89
Managing romance at work, 334
Mandatory retirement, 78

Martin Marietta Company, 329
Massachusetts Mutual Insurance Company, 172
Matrix management, 12,13
Maternity leave, 102
McDonalds, 163
Measuring human resources costs, 62
Measuring performance, 39
Mesa Petroleum, 37
Measuring human resources development, 216
Medical costs, 193–199
Medical examinations, 86
Medical Information Bureau, 88
Mental fitness, 163
Merger:
   and acquisition, 23,24,453
   and the human resources information system,
     250
   mania, 22
   successful, 23
Mile High Cable, 101
Minority discrimination, 94
Minimum wage, 34
Minnesota Mutual Insurance 37
Mitsubishi, 104
Monsanto, 231
Morale, employee, 156
Multinational corporations, 65,228
Multinational employees, 64
Multinational operations, 391
Multiple compensation strategies, 29,31
Multiple tier labor contracts, 426
Multiple policy lines, compensation, 29
Mutual interest bargaining, 71

N

NAACP, 94
Nanny care, 157
National Alliance of Business, 283
National Association of Manufacturers, 283
National Association of Postal Supervisors, 304
National Audio Visual Association, 223
National Instutite of Alcohol Abuse, 163
National Labor Law Center, 454
National Labor Relations Board (NLRB),
   78,451,452
NCR, 193
Negotiated pay increases, 434
Nepotism, 275
New beginning program at CBS, 191
New collar class, 265
New worker, 72,73,74,265,266,271
Newsletter, 352
Nondiscrimination tests, 135
Nongrandfathered distributions, 126

Northrup Corporation, 84
Nuclear Regulatory Commission, 375

O

Objectives, human resource development, 215
Occupational Safety and Health Administration
   (OSHA), 77,78,457,458
OD interventions, 8
Office automation, 104,240
Office romance, 336
Off the cuff, reason, 81
OD interventions, 8
Oil Chemical and Atomic Workers Union, 35
Older workers, 105,277
Omnibus Budget Reconciliation Act of 1986, 78
Organizational Development (OD), 3
Organizational development checklist, 5
Organizational objectives, 6
Organizational overview, 76
Organizational problems, 12
Outpatient costs, 199
Overt conflict, 11
Overtime pay, 30
Overcoming culture shock, 411
Overseas assignment, 68,394
Overseas operations, 64

P

Page layout, script, 221
Paid sabbaticals, 163
Parental leave, 157
Past discrimination, 98
Part-time workers, 288,455
Pay:
   for performance, 30,37
   level, 31,32
   related plans, 183
   strategies, 31
Pan American World Airways, 33
Pension asset reversion, 112,188
Pension benefits, 172–193
Pension fund, 179
Pension security, 188
Performance:
   appraisal, 60,82
   bonus, 38
   criteria, 39
   share plans, 47
Personal computers, 212, 224, 225
Personal records, 83
Personnel files, 83,84
Personnel manual, 322
Personnel policies, 321
Physical Fitness Programs (PFPs), 161,163
Pickens, T. Boone, 37

Plan description, 177
Planning in OD, 8
Plant shutdowns, 78
Polaroid, 250
Policies, 59
Polygraph, 78,305
Pool incentive, 43
Preemployment screening and testing, 302
Preferred provider audit, 194,196,435
Preferred Provider Organizations (PPOs), 110
Pregnancy Disability Act, 113
Prepaid legal services, 158
Preretirement counseling, 189
Preretirement educational Program, 190
Preretirement planners, 283
Problems, 439
Problem review procedure, 445
Productivity and personal fulfillment, 71,156
Productivity standards, 38
Profit sharing, 181
Profit sharing carryover, 122
Profitability, 8
Project management, 13
Promotion and raises, 81
Promotional opportunities, 8
Privacy, 83,84,85,260
    Act of 1974, 84
    of computer, 257
    protection study commission, 86,88
Public sector employees, 91
Publicity, 271,274
Pushers on the payroll, 376
Put options, 132
Pyramiding of pay premiums, 66

Q

Qualified Domestic Relations Order (QDRO),
    125,130
Qualified retirement programs, 179
Questioning techniques, 296
"Quickie" seminars, 235

R

Rabbi Trust, 50–53
Recordkeeping practices, 85
Records retention, 327
Recruiting, 156, 283
Recruiting ideas, 274
Recruiting, the new worker, 265–269
Reference checking, 302
Rehabilitation Act, 344
Related persons, employment of, 284
Reliance Electric Company, 193
Relocation, 284
Renting math whizzes, 292

Reshaping human resources development, 212
Restricted stock grants, 47
Retirement counseling, 111,188
Retirement planners, 283
Retraining, 278
Retraining programs, 217
Right-to-know laws, 78
Robots, 254,256,455
Rockwell International, 30
Rollovers, 133
ROLM, 163
Romance at work, 334–339

S

Sabbatical, 114,163
Safety, 457
Salaried plants, 34,427,428
Salary database, 32
Salary increases, 35
Salary planning, 61
Salary structure, 59
Salary reduction section 401(k) Plans, 117,181
Same-sex partners, benefits, 91
Sample interview questions, 298
Sample personnel policies, 325
Sanctions under Immigration Reform Act, 419
Savings, thrift plans, 181
Screening applicants, 302,306
Screen in, 276,277
Script, video, 221
Sears, 104
Secrecy agreement, 367
Security clearance, 90
Security staffing, 371
Selection:
    employees for overseas assignment, 394
    expatriates, 396
    of management employees, 236
    procedures, 317
Service awards, 76
Severance pay, 78
Sex:
    -based wage discrimination, 96
    segregated jobs, 97
    and salary, 96
Sexual harrassment, 340,341,342
Sexual orientation and the law, 343
Sexual preference case, 90
Single pay structure, 32
Simulation, wage cost, 252
Small Business Administration, 71
Smoking policies, 329–332
Smith Kline, 84
Social responsibility, 102

Social system, 7
Social Security Administration, 177
Social Security benefits, 183,185
Social Security taxes, 54
Society for Intercultural Education, 231
Southland Corporation, 21
Spencer, Charles D. Associates, 117
Stablizing the workforce, 279
Stanton Survey, honesty testing, 308
Stock appreciation rights, 48
Stock-based incentives, 45
Stock Options:
   incentive, 47
   discounted, 47
   nonqualified, 46
Strategic system, 7
Subminimum wage, 34
Submarket pay, 32
Substance abuse, 163
Successful merger, 23
Succession planning, 15,17,236
Succession plan back-up summary, 16
Supplemental Retirement Programs (SERPs),
   50,184
Survivor benefit requirements, 130
Suspension, 431
Systems approach to OD, 7

T

Tandem computers, 163
Tax-free rollovers, 133
Tax Reform Act of 1986 (TEFRA), 78,109,113
Taxing benefits, 113
Teachers salaries, 35
Teamsters union, 33
Team building, 8,13
Technical/scientific ladder, 19
Technical system, 7
Teleconferencing, 225
Temporary help, 129,287,288
Termination, 82,83,328
Termination-at-will, 80,82,181
Terrorism in HRM, 359,360,361
Testing, 302
Testing for drugs, 308
Testing guidelines, 317
Test selection and design, 309
Theft of trade secrets, 363,364
Thin Layer Chromatography (TLC), 310
Third-party interventions, 8,441
Time of deferral action, 53
Top down approach, 215
Top-heavy accrual rule, 120
Trade secrets, 364,366

Training:
   by phone, 225
   computer, 257,258
   cross-cultural, 413
   and development, 211
   games, 233,234
   needs, 214
   trends, 235
Training & Development Journal, 235
Transplacement, 93,284
Transferring, 93,94
Traveling abroad, 360,361
Treasury department, 110
TRW, 30
Two-tier labor contracts, 426,427
Two-tier pay contracts, 31,33,34

U

Umbrella plans, 48
Unauthorized work stoppage, 439
Unions, 33,87,88,96,430,433,448
Union Pacific, 231
Union, Oil Chemical and Atomic Workers, 35,86
United Auto Workers, 104,158
United States Defense Department, 220
United States Department of Labor, 106,178
United States Department of Health and Hospitals, 156
United States Supreme Court, 96,101
U.S. West, 41
Utilization review, 198

V

Value of employee benefits, 137,204
Verbal warning, 82
Vesting, 182
Vesting schedules, 180
Videocassettes, 76
Videodisc, 1,218,219
Video newscast, 353
Video scripting, 221
Video training, 221,229
Video writer, 221
Vinson vs. Taylor, 340
Violence, in HRM, 363

W

Wage hikes, 33
Wage increase patterns, 425
Warning notices, 326,327
Washington business group on health, 351
Welfare benefit provisions, 117,134,175
Whistleblowers, 78,81
Whiz, math, 292

Williams Pipe Line Company case, 86
Working:
  at home, 105,453
  conditions, 435
  women, 105
Women's employment issues, 454
Women's labor project, 454
Wrongful discharge, 90
Withdrawals 401(k) plans, 124

X
Xerox, employee information systems, 247

Y
Younger workforce, 279

Z
Zimmerman, Honora, 4